AF

SI

# The
# Protection and Management
# of our
# Natural Resources, Wildlife and Habitat

**W. Jack Grosse**
*Professor of Law*
*Chase College of Law*
*Northern Kentucky University*

1992 OCEANA PUBLICATIONS, INC. DOBBS FERRY, NEW YORK

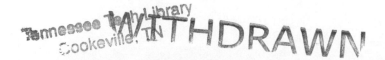

Library of Congress Cataloging-in-Publication Data

Environmental law: protection and management of natural resources

W. Jack Grosse

1. Environmental law--United States. 2. Conservation of natural resources--Law and legislation--United States. I. Environmental law: protection and management of natural resources

KF3775.G76      1992

344.73'046--dc20

347.30446

ISBN: 0-379-20215-8

Manufactured in the United States of America.

THIS BOOK IS DEDICATED TO NORMA, DOUG, LISA AND TOM

# TABLE OF CONTENTS

# Acknowledgments

Several people have made significant contributions to the completion of this book. Without their efforts this project would have been delayed beyond the three years already devoted to its creation.

I would like to acknowledge the research and writing skills of Grenda Sanders in the preparation of Chapter II, The State Ownership Doctrine, and of Michael Murray in the preparation of the Chapter VI section on the dolphins. Also, I would like to acknowledge the assistance of Scott Porter in the research and writing of the Chapter VI section on eagles, burros and horses.

The final organization of the manuscript and its mechanical production were accomplished with the substantial input of Alice Phirman, faculty secretary. She was able to manage the computer and orchestrate its output with masterful skill.

In addition, I would like to acknowledge the support and encouragement of the administration of Chase College of Law, in particular that of Dean Henry L. Stephens.

# The Delight Song of Tsoai-Talee

I am a feather on the bright sky
I am the blue horse that runs in the plain
I am the fish that rolls, shining, in the water
I am the shadow that follows a child
I am the evening light, the lustre of meadows
I am an eagle playing with the wind
I am a cluster of bright beads

I am the farthest star
I am the cold of the dawn
I am the roaring of the rain
I am the glitter on the crust of the snow
I am the long track of the moon in a lake
I am a flame of four colors
I am a deer standing away in the dusk
I am a field of sumac and the pomme blanche
I am an angle of geese in the winter sky
I am the hunger of a young wolf
I am the whole dream of these things

You see, I am alive, I am alive
I stand in good relation to the earth
I stand in good relation to the gods
I stand in good relation to all that is beautiful
I stand in good relation to the daughter of Tsen-tainte
You see, I am alive, I am alive

N. Scott Momaday,
from Carriers of the Dream Wheel,
Harper & Row

*THE*
*PROTECTION AND MANAGEMENT*
*OF OUR*
*NATURAL RESOURCES, WILDLIFE AND HABITAT*

# CHAPTER ONE

# HISTORY AND INTRODUCTION

In passing the National Environmental Policy Act of 1969 Congress declared as its purpose "a national policy which will encourage productive and enjoyable harmony between man and his environment; to promote efforts which will prevent or eliminate damage to the environment and biosphere and stimulate the health and welfare of man; to reach the understanding of the ecological systems and natural resources important to the nation; . . ."[1]

In carrying out the purposes of the passages of the National Environmental Protection Act, Congress declared a national policy as follows "the Congress recognizing the profound impact of man's activity on the interrelations of all components of the natural environment, particularly the profound influence of population growth, high density urbanization, industrial expansion, resource exploitation, and new and expanding technological advances and recognizing further the critical importance of restoring and maintaining environmental quality to the overall welfare and development of man, declares that it is the continuing policy of the federal government, in cooperation with state and local governments, and other concerned private and public organizations, to use all practical means and measures including financial and technical assistance, in a manner calculated to foster and promote the general welfare, to create and maintain conditions under which man and nature can exist in productive harmony, and to fulfill the social, economic, and other requirements of present and future generations of America."[2]

In order to carry out the policy set forth by Congress and the Act, it mandated that the federal government assumed the responsibility to use all practical means to "improve and coordinate federal plans, functions, programs, and resources to the end that the nation may: (1) fulfill the responsibilities of each generation as trustee of the environment for succeeding generations; (2) assure for all Americans a safe, healthful, productive, and aesthetically and culturally pleasing surroundings; (3) obtain the widest range of beneficial uses of the environment without degradation, risk to health or safety, or other undesirable and unintended consequences; (4) preserve important historic, cultural, and natural aspects of our national heritage, and maintain, wherever possible, environment which supports diversity and variety of individual choice; (5) achieve a balance between population and resource use which will permit high standards of living and a wide sharing of life's amenities; and (6) enhance the quality of renewable resources and approach the maximum obtainable recycling of depletable resources.[3]

---

[1]  42 U.S.C.A. § 4321.
[2]  42 U.S.C.A. § 4331(a)

1

# WILDLIFE AND HABITAT

In the process of discussing the background and need for the National Environmental Protection Act at the time it was being considered, the New York Times in an editorial on May 3, 1969 stated "by land, sea, and air the enemies of man's survival relentlessly pressed their attack. The most dangerous of all these enemies is man's own undirected technology. The radioactive poisons from nuclear tests, the runoff into rivers of nitrogen fertilizers, the smog from automobiles, pesticides from the food chains, and the destruction of top soil by strip mining are examples of failure to proceed and control the untoward consequences of modern technology."

Dr. David M. Gates, Director of the Missouri Botanical Gardens and Chairman of the Board of Advisors to the Ad Hoc Committee on the Environment, spoke at the congressional hearings on the National Environmental Act and had this to say, "the complexity of the earth's ecosystem and its component parts of individual ecosystems makes understanding it and the management of it a massive challenge . . . .

Today we are implementing a extremely complex system: The ecosystems the earth, the units of the landscape, and we do not know the consequences of our actions until it is too late. We need to study ecosystems in advance and work out the strategies of living with the landscape."[4]

The sentiments expressed in NEPA are reflected in the various pieces of legislation enacted by the federal government to manage and administer the natural resources of the country. Forests, rivers, wilderness areas, refuge systems, oceans, and animals, are part of the nation's natural resources which are needed to be protected and managed in order to assure that the American people of present and future generations may benefit from their continued existence.

There are many facets involved in the protection of the environment. Of primary importance, of course, is the protection of mankind itself from the ravages of air and water pollution caused by heavy concentrations of industrialization. These matters directly involve the concepts of public health and safety, and are extremely important in the concept of environment protection. However, there are other important aspects to the protection of the environment. Congress in the Wild and Scenic Rivers Act declared as its policy that "certain selected rivers of the nation which with their immediate environments, possess outstanding and remarkable scenic, recreational, geologic, fish and wildlife, historic, cultural, or other similar value . . ."[5] These values as expressed in the Wild and Scenic Rivers Act relate to man's psychological and emotional

---

3   42 U.S.C.A. § 4331(b).
4   1969 U.S. Code Congressional and Administrative News, page 2755-56.
5   16 U.S.C.A. § 1271.

well being which could be construed as an indirect type of human health and safety.

One important category of the nation's natural resources is wildlife.

Historically man has viewed animals as objects which exist for his use. This view has caused mankind to focus more on the modern industrial and scientific uses to which animals can be put rather than on any concern for animals or their needs. The explosion of scientific research especially in the life sciences has created an almost insensible demand for research animals. In addition, we focus on animals as suitable for purposes of food or sport. Therefore by concentrating on the needs of mankind solely and ignoring the needs of animals, we have abused them in subtle ways including habitat destruction and pollution.

In earlier times, dealing with animals reflected a lack of concern, affording animals almost no protection from man. However, some recent events have changed our attitudes. The effects of environmental degradation has taught us something about our interdependence with all of the elements of nature including animals and their habitat. This new look has led many to look on animals as worthy of consideration in a different context. This new context involves the consideration of human animals and non-human animals and their habitats as a part of an integrated whole.

Early concepts of animals can be found in early Judaeo-Christian writings, Greek philosophically reasoning, and Roman theory and practices. In a passage from the Holy Bible, it is provided:

> So God created Man in his own image . . . and God said to them, "Be fruitful and multiply, and fill the earth and subdue it; and have domain over the fish of the sea, and over the birds of the air, and over everything that moves above the earth."[6]

This passage has been frequently interpreted to mean that man is superior to all animals and has complete power over them even extending to the power to destroy. Early Greek philosophers supported this view by creating a hierarchy in which plants occupied the lowest rung, animals followed, and man was at the apex. This classification was based primarily on the kind of soul that each of the units possessed. Only man possessed a rational soul, and therefore he was superior to both plants and animals which possessed non-reasoning souls.

When the Roman Empire came into being, the superiority of man over animals was carried to a much more active stage of consideration. The

---

6    Genesis, Ch. 1, verses 27-28.

# WILDLIFE AND HABITAT

Roman Emperors accumulated vast collections of animals from conquered lands to establish what later would become zoos and circuses in modern times. Of course, history is replete with accounts of the sport of animal combat where animals were pitted against animals and humans.

Following the fall of the Roman Empire and up to the advent of Darwin's work on the evolution of the species, mankind's attitude about animals did not undergo significant change. The Christian church after the fall of the Roman Empire did encourage kindness toward animals but primarily for the reason that such kindness might encourage man to exercise kindness toward each other. It is true that this attitude of kindness toward animals was the foundation for much of the anti-cruelty legislation which was to follow hundreds of years later, but even this attitude was not focused on any right the animal might have, but rather on the effect that such treatment might have on man's treatment of man.

Darwin's view of nature as a dynamic, changing, interdependent web of creation, was a challenge to the Greek hierarchy model and a repetition of the Christian attitude that man was superior to the other animals occupying the same world space. Darwin's concept was that man and animal differ only in degree and not in kind. Unfortunately, Darwin's work had no real effect on moral and legal concepts about animals. As a result only the moral foundation laid by the early philosophers and the Christian church that it was morally right to be kind to animals continued to prevail.

From earlier times both statutory and common law have contained rules which concern animals. Earlier Athenian law forbade the killing of game because it might cause Athenians to concentrate their efforts on the chase rather than on the pursuit of art. Later Roman law classified things into public and common property and the latter embraced animals ferae naturae. The consequence of classification as common property meant that things in this classification belonged in common to all citizens of the state. Ownership of such animals was vested in those who took them. Thus ownership was established by those who first possessed wild animals.

The Romans did not seem to place any restriction on the power of an individual to possess game, although the Institute of Justinian recognize the right of an owner of land to forbid another from killing game on his property. This restriction, however, was more of a recognition of the right of ownership of land than an exercise by the state of its authority to control the taking and use of common things.

In feudal Europe the right to acquire animals ferae naturae by possession was recognized as being subject to government authority and power. This civil law restriction was positioned directly opposite the concept that the pure law of nature gave to everyone the right to capture animals which prior to possession had been part of the common good. While many doubted if the sovereigns of medieval Europe had the right to reserve hunting to themselves and forbid it to their subjects, nevertheless, the king justified his authority on the ground that such civil laws were nothing but restrictions on those things which the natural law would otherwise permit. Perhaps Blackstone put it best when he stated, referring especially to the common ownership of game:

> After all there are some few things which notwithstanding that general introduction in continuance of property must still unavoidably remain in common being such wherein nothing but a usufructuary property is capable of being had; and therefore they still belong to the first occupant during the time he holds possession of them and no longer. Such (among others) are the elements of light, air and water, which a man may occupy by means of his windows, his gardens, his mills, and other conveniences; such also are the generality of those animals which are said to be of ferae naturae or of a wild and untameable disposition which any man may seize upon and keep for his own use or pleasure.[7]

A man may, lastly, have a qualified property in animals ferae naturae, propter privilegium, that is, he may have the privilege of hunting, taking, and killing them in exclusion of other persons. Here he has a transient property in those animals usually called game so long as they continue in his liberty and he may restrain any stranger from taking them; but the instant they have departed to another liberty, this qualified property ceases

> . . . a man can have no absolute permanent property in these as he may in the earth and land; since these are of a vague and fugitive nature and therefore can admit only of a precarious and qualified ownership, which lasts so long as they are in an actual occupation but no longer.[8]

As to the royal prerogative Blackstone says:

> There still remains another species of prerogative property, founded upon a very different principle from any that has been mentioned before; the property of such animals ferae naturae, as are shown by the denomination of game, with the right of pursuing, taking, and destroying them; which is vested in the King alone and from him derived to those of his subjects as has re-

---

[7]   2 Bl. Com. § 14.
[8]   2 Bl. Com. § 394.

ceived the grants of a chase, a park, a free warren, or free fishery. In the first place then, we have already shown in a deed that it cannot be denied that by a law of nature every man from the prince to the peasant has an equal right of pursuing and taking to his own use all such creatures as our ferae naturae, and therefore the property of nobody, but liable to be seen by the first occupant, and so it held by the imperial law even so late as Justinian's time . . . but it follows from the very end and constitutes a society that this natural right as well as many others belonging to a man as an individual may be restrained by positive laws and enacted for reasons of state on the proposed benefit of the community.[9]

This practice of the government of England from its earliest times has put on the authority to control and regulate the taking of game or ferae naturae. This common law of England was undoubtedly vested in the colonial government and most certainly passed to the states with the separation from the mother country.

The concept that animals were insensate property and were meant to exist solely for the purposes of mankind was a prevailing colonial view. It is true that the Puritans of the Massachusetts Bay Colony enacted a statute designed to prevent cruelty toward animals in the 1600s. But other than that one vain attempt, any animal right interest was submerged into the needs and desires of entrepreneurs and market and recreational hunters.

Without question, wildlife assumed an extremely important role in the economy of the early American colonies. Wildlife such as deer, turkeys, and birds not only provided a ready supply of fresh meat but also became an important source of income in the form of furs, hides, down and plumes. Eventually, of course, the colonist would develop a domestication systems for flocks and herds, but until that time animals could not expect nor receive any form of protection.

The post-Revolutionary period did not mark any substantial change in mankind's attitude toward wildlife in the United States. Some states passed legislation in the attempt to control the taking of wildlife, but of course this was done only for the purpose of guaranteeing the continued existence of wildlife for the purposes of food or trade. These various attempts were only of a limited success because enforcement capabilities and the vastness of the American Frontier prevented any effective curtailment of the exploitation of wildlife.

---

9   2 Bl. Com. § 410.

# HISTORY AND INTRODUCTION

The various bounty laws enacted by the states were examples of the disregard for any attempt to protect animals. From the 1700s forward states offered money in return for dead animals. Bounties were offered for lions, wolves, bears, wildcats, and various other species with the result that several species were driven close to extinction toward the end of the 19th Century. By 1900 almost every species of larger mammals in the continental United States had been eliminated from its original living range.[10] In 1874 an act of Congress was passed to prevent the use of slaughters of the buffalo in the territories of the United States.[11] This bill was pocket-vetoed by President Grant based on the belief that the continued elimination of the buffalo would enable the government to better control the Indians who relied upon the buffalo for food and clothing.

In short, the plentiful wildlife existing in America at the time that the first European settlers came, began to disappear. With the onset of migrating humanity, field and forest suffered from plowed prairies and overgrazed deserts, and market hunting cut heavily into wildlife and its habitat.

With the advent of the 20th Century, wildlife was in dire circumstance and it was faced with further deterioration. Several groups such as the New York Sportsman Club (formed in 1844), the American Society for Prevention to Cruelty to Animals, the American Ornithologist Union, the Audubon Club, the Sierra Club, and others formed a nucleus for the first crude conservation movement in the United States. While the attempts of these groups were laudable, they were very feeble. Nevertheless, the collective efforts of these groups were successful in getting the first federal wildlife statute, the Lacey Act of 1990, passed. This act made it a federal offense to transport wildlife across state lines if the animals were taken in violation of state law. As a result of the efforts of many of the conservation groups, state wildlife laws were passed in several states.

Early 20th Century statutes which had an impact on wildlife included the Migratory Bird Treaty with Great Britain (1916), the Migratory Bird Treaty Act (1918), and the Migratory Bird Conservation Act (1929).[12]

The 1930's in America proved almost disastrous to the wildlife in America. Not only was there economic depression, but the weather patterns which produced dust storms and drought resulted in the wildlife and habitat destruction almost unparalleled in the history of the country. Game provided necessary free food and people who were

---

10  J. Tefethen, An American Crusade for Wildlife, 29 (1975).
11  H.R. 921, 43rd Cong. 1st Sess., 1874, Cong. Rec. 5413 (1874).
12  39 Stat. 1707, 16 U.S.C.A. § 703 et seg., and 16 U.S.C.A. § 715 et seq.

hungry used this inexpensive method of food provision to satisfy their needs.

In addition to the reduction in the wildlife population because of food necessities, the drought seriously effected the habitat and had an adverse effect on the breeding seasons of water fowl.

In response to this serious impact on wildlife, the conservation leaders and others pushed forward and were able to enact the Duck Stamp and Fish and Wildlife Coordination Act of 1934 and the Federal Aid and Wildlife Restoration Program of 1937.[13]

Most of the efforts to improve the condition of wildlife focused on the wildlife itself. The central reasons underlying these approaches to wildlife conservation related to the preservation of the wildlife with a view toward improving conditions for the benefit of the species itself. A slightly different approach was taken in the early 1960s when the country's tiny community environmental promoters had to discuss wildlife and its habitat from an environmental perspective. The very earliest of theories propounded by this group was to devise programs whereby American industry would be stopped from ruining the public health and from poisoning land, air and water.

By the end of the decade there was increased public concern with what had been termed as an "environmental crisis." In 1969 fifty people met in the foothills of Virginia's Shenandoah Mountains to discuss various legal approaches that might be tried to defend the environment. Various approaches to improving the protection of the environmental were discussed including government action under the "Public Trust Doctrine," common law court developed law which protected property from injury under various common law decisions and opinions, use of the Constitution to establish a healthy environment, and federal legislation. Shortly thereafter President Nixon signed into law the National Environmental Policy Act. Following closely on the heels of the NEPA, 43 USCA § 4321 et seq., other federal laws were passed including the Clean Air Act, the Clean Water Act, and the Endangered Species Act.[14]

These new laws coupled with the advent of various environmental protection agencies ushered in a new era of environmental awareness and protection.

Beginning with the 1960s the focus shifted from the protection of individual wildlife toward a much broader view - wildlife and habitat as part of the environment.

---

13  16 U.S.C.A. § 718 et seq., 16 U.S.C.A. § 661 et seq., and U.S.C.A. § 669 et seq.
14  42 U.S.C.A. § 7401 et seq., 33 U.S.C.A. §1251 et seg., and 16 U.S.C.A. § 1531 et seq.

# HISTORY AND INTRODUCTION

Following these activities of the 1960s which resulted in federal involvement in the environment through various statutes, numerous other federal statutes were passed. Although they concentrated on particulars of wildlife or animal species, nevertheless they did so on the theory that all of wildlife and its habitat was a part of the broader concept of the environment.[15]

The result of all of these activities, both statutory and legal, can be summed up in former Secretary of the Interior, Stewart Udall's observation: "Today, environmental law is part of the warp and woof of American life. It impacts on policy making in all levels of government. Environmental law organizations exert a powerful influence on law making in Washington - and guide the enforcement and implementation of the nation's environmental laws."[16]

---

[15] See, The Marine Mammal Protection Act of 1972 (16 U.S.C.A. §1361 et seq., Antarctic Marine Living Resources Act of 1984, 16 U.S.C.A. §2431 et seq.) and the Fishery Conservation and Management Act of 1976 (Magnuson Act - 16 U.S.C.A. §971 et seq.
[16] Trends: The Legal Eagles, The Amicus Journal, Winter 1988.

# CHAPTER TWO

## THE STATE OWNERSHIP DOCTRINE

Man's idea of himself, of society, his relationship to wilderness and wildlife, have necessarily undergone tremendous changes through history. Wilderness holds a variety of culturally inbred meanings.[1] The biblical origins of western society portray the wilderness as desolate, wild, dangerous, and uninhabited land. Wilderness, in its desolation and cruelty, manifested God's paternal wrath against disobedient man.[2]

However, Christians also portrayed wilderness as a place to need God, to feel serene, to bast and become one with the creating Father.[3] Such contrasting ideas of the same phenomenon created an ambivalence to wilderness and wildlife that still exists and prevails.

Early pre-historic man, by necessity, saw wilderness and the creatures within it, as a threat to his existence. It was necessary for man to alter his environment to survive.

Today, wilderness, wildlife, how much of it survives, and where it survives, are dependent on the value modern society places upon it. This value is reflected in the passage and enforcement of laws mandated to perpetuate that survival. Man's capability to totally destroy wilderness is his capacity to destroy himself. The destruction of the wilderness, and the diversity of life forms it supports, is the destruction of the delicate ecosystem which is the umbilical cord of man's existence.

As early as the Roman Empire, animals *ferae naturae* were considered to be like the air and oceans in that they were the property of no one. Yet unlike the oceans and the air, wild animals could become the property of anyone who captured or killed them. Apparently the only restriction in Rome on the right to acquire property in wild animals was that a private land owner had the exclusive right to reduce to possession the wild life on his property. This restriction was more "a recognition of the right of ownership in land than an exercise of the state of its authority to control the use and taking of that which belonged to no one in particular but was common to all."[4]

Governmental regulation of the right to take wildlife soon became evident in feudal Europe. The lords and barons of Europe desired to keep

---

1   Stankey, Beyond the Campfire's Light: Historical Roots of Wilderness Concept, Nat. Resources J. 9.
2   *Id.* at 12.
3   Britton, Battling Satan in the Wilderness: Antagonism, Spirituality, and Wild Nature in the Four Gospels, Proc. National Wilderness Research Conference: Current Research 406 (1986).
4   Geer v. Connecticut, 161 U.S. 519, 523 (1986).

weapons out of the hands of those whom they had conquered. Nothing could do this more effectively than a prohibition of hunting and sporting. It was the policy of the conqueror to reserve this right to himself and those whom he chose. The general common population was forbidden, by law, not only from carrying arms, but from use of nets, snarls, or other means of destroying the game.[5]

Restrictions on hunting and fishing were very early imposed in England for similar reasons. Land was parcelled out to nobility with the Saxon invasion. That land not parcelled out became known as "royal forests" in which the king alone had the right to hunt. The Norman Conquest in 1066 brought about a great expansion of the royal forests and an elaborate system of royal forest laws, courts, and officials to administer them.[6]

The King's claimed exclusive right to hunt also expanded beyond the royal forest. The king soon claimed the sole right to pursue game or to take fish anywhere in the kingdom. By means of various royal franchises, he frequently allowed favored nobility to hunt or fish. The franchise of "park" granted the holder of the right thereof to kill "superior" animals such as deer, fox, and marten on his own land. A "chase" allowed the holder to hunt those animals on the land of others. A franchise of "free-warren" authorized its holder to kill "inferior" creatures such as fowl and hares in a particular area so long as he has not prevented others from doing so. There were similar franchises on the right to fish.[7]

By the thirteenth century, so many fishery franchises had been granted that navigability of England's rivers was substantially impeded by the number of private weirs placed in them. The problem was so great that in 1215 the Magna Charta directed their removal throughout England. This directive was later expanded to forbid the king from granting private fisheries in tidal waters.[8]

As Royal authority over wildlife was gradually taken over by Parliament, "qualification statutes" became the method of control. These statutes prohibited the taking of game by anyone not "qualified" by having the requisite amount of wealth or land prescribed in the statute. Thus, the system of class discrimination and the practice of keeping weapons out of the hands of commoners was promulgated.[9]

---

5   3 W. Blackstone, Commentaries 413.
6   Lund, British Wildlife Law before the American Revolution: Lessons from the Past, 74
    Mich. L. Rev. 49, 60-61 (1975).
7   Bean, The Evolution of American Wildlife Law 11 (1983).
8   MacGrady, The Navigability Concept in the Civil and Common Law: Historical
    Development, Current Importance, and Some Doctrines That Don't Hold Water, 3 Fla.
    St. U.L. Rev. 513, 555 (1975).
9   Lund, *supra* note 6, at 52-60.

# STATE OWNERSHIP

## The State Ownership Doctrine

The American Colonials, rebelling against class-based privilege, transformed the concept of fish and game ownership by the sovereign king to ownership by the sovereign people.[10]

The earliest game laws in North America are thought to have been the grant of hunting privileges to New Netherlands colonists in 1629, the Massachusetts Bay Colonial Ordinance of 1647, and the New Jersey Concessions Agreement of 1678.[11] By the time of the American Revolution, all colonies except Georgia had closed seasons on some species.[12] It is clear that the sovereign power to regulate was not actively asserted in the nineteenth century and that the result was unparalleled slaughtering of Wildlife populations, of which the wholesale killing of buffalo and passenger pigeons are but the better-known instances.[13]

*Martin v. Waddell* was the first case to come before the United States Supreme Court concerning the relationships of government and citizen with respect to wildlife.[14]  An issue was the right of a riparian landowner to exclude all others from taking oysters from certain mudcats in New Jersey's Raritan River.  The landowner claimed to own both the riparian and submerged lands of the river.  He traced his title to a grant in 1664 from King Charles II to the Duke of York which purported to convert "all the lands, islands, soils, rivers, harbors, mines, minerals, quarries, woods, marshes, waters, lakes, fishing, hawking, huntings, and fowlings" within certain described metes and bounds.

Chief Justice Roger Taney believed the legal question was more than the interpretation of a deed of title.  In his view, the original deed from the King to the Duke "was an instrument upon which was to be founded the institutions of a great political community".  He felt it necessary to consider first "the character of the right claimed by the British Crown[15] and second whether the character changed when title to the lands passed from the King to the Duke and ultimately to the plaintiff. Taney declared that "dominion and property in the lands under them were held by the King as a public trust" and that "it must be regarded as settled in England against the right of the king since Magna Carta" to make a private grant of such lands and waters.[16]  That is, by virtue of his public trust responsibilities, the King was without power to abridge "the public common of piscary.[17]

---

10 J. Trefethen, An American Crusade for Wildlife 69-75 (1975).
11 Coggins & Hensley, Constitutional Limits on Federal Power to Protect and Manage Wildlife:  Is the Endangered Species Act Endangered?, 61 Iowa L. Rev. 1108 (1976).
12 P. Matthiessen, Wildlife in America (1959).
13 Etling, Who owns the Wildlife?, 3 Envtl. L. Rev. 23 (1973).
14 41 U.S. (16 Pet.) 367 (1842).
15 *Id.* at 409.
16 *Id.*
17 *Id.* at 412.

Also if the public trust charter of navigable waters and their submerged lands survived a grant by the King of his proprietary interest in them, did it also survive the American Revolution? Justice Taney declared that it did.

"When the people of New Jersey took possession of the regions of government . . . the powers of sovereignty became immediately and rightfully rested in the state.[18]

Thus, the public trust doctrine was done. Although this declaration greatly expanded the Magna Carta's limited prohibition against the creation of private fishing rights into a much broader prohibition against the creation of any sort of private rights in the submerged lands of navigable waters, it is now well established in American law.[19]

In 1984, in *Lawton v. Steele*,[20] a New York statute for the appointment of fish and game protectors was challenged on constitutional grounds. The Supreme Court confirmed that the police power of the state includes the right to contain the "unrestrained exercise" of the destruction of wildlife. "It is within the authority of the legislature to impose restriction and limitation upon the time and manner of taking fish and game . . . The power to exact such laws has long been exercised, and so beneficially for the public that it ought not now to be called into question."[21]

The development of the doctrine of state ownership of wildlife continued, largely ignoring Justice Taney's qualifier that the powers assumed by the states were subject to the rights since surrendered by the Constitution to the general government.[22]

In *Smith v. Maryland*, the Supreme Court considered the validity of a Maryland law that prohibited the taking of oysters from the state's waters by means of scoop or drag.[23] The shipowner was licensed by the United States to engage in the coasting trade. The Supreme Court rejected his argument that the state law interfered with the exclusive federal power to regulate interstate commerce[24] and held that the state's ownership of the soil conferred upon it the authority to regulate the taking of oysters from that soil.[25] The Court left many questions unanswered in *Smith v. Maryland*, which it emphasized in its opinion:

18   *Id*. at 416.
19   Sax, The Public Trust Doctrine in Natural Resource Law: Effective Judicial
      Intervention, 68 Mich. L. Rev. 471 (1970).
20   152 U.S. 133 (1894).
21   *Id*. at 139.
22   Bean, *supra* note 7, at 14.
23   59 U.S. (18 How.) 71 (1885).
24   U.S. Const. art. I, § 88, cl. 2.
25   59 U.S. at 75.

The law in question does not touch the subject of the common liberty of taking oysters, save for the purpose of guarding it from injury, to whomsoever it may belong, and by whomsoever it may be enjoyed. Whether this liberty belongs exclusively to the citizens of the State of Maryland, or may lawfully be enjoyed in common by all citizens of the United States; whether this public use may be restricted by the States to its own citizens, or a portion of them, or by force of the Constitution must remain common to all citizens of the United States; whether the national government, by a treaty or act of Congress, can grant to foreigners the right to participate therein; or what, in general, are the limits of the trust upon which the State holds this soil, or its power to define and control that trust, are matters wholly without the scope of this case, and upon which we give no opinion.[26]

*McCready v. Virginia*[27] gave the court an opportunity to answer one of the unanswered questions posed in *Smith*. In *McCready*, the Court upheld a Virginia Statute prohibiting citizens of the other states from planting oysters in Virginia's tidewaters. By declaring that the state owned not only the tidewaters but the fish within them, so far as they are capable of ownership by which ruling,[28] it substantially expanded the holdings of *Martin v. Waddell* and *Smith v. Maryland*. Thus, Virginia could regulate not only the taking and planting of oysters in those tidewaters but could exclude citizens of other states altogether because such a regulation "is in effect nothing more than a regulation of the use by the people of their common property".

In 1891 in *Manchester v. Massachusetts*,[29] the Court upheld a statute prohibiting the use of purse seines for the taking of menhaden in Buzzard's Bay. The Court's opinion stated that because the Bay was a body of navigable water within the state's territorial jurisdiction, the authority of regulation of the fish within it belonged to the State. "The subject is one which the state may well be permitted to regulate within its territory, in the absence of any regulation by the United States."[30] The Court did not place that authority on the States' ownership of the fish. The Court pointed out that the regulation in question served a valid public purpose, the preservation of menhaden which served as a food source to other fish which were a food source for humans, and therefore for the common benefit.[31] The opinion reflects a fundamental nineteenth-

---

26  *Id.*
27  94 U.S. 391 (1876).
28  *Id.* at 394.
29  139 U.S. 24 (1891).
30  *Id.* at 265.
31  *Id.*

century conception of the purpose of wildlife law, the preservation of a food supply.[32]

In *Geer v. Connecticut*, the defendant appealed his conviction under state law for possessing game birds with the intent to ship them out of state. The birds had been lawfully killed there; only Geer's intent to ship them outside the state was unlawful.

Under common law, wildlife belonged to the person who reduced it to possession. The legal question was the same as that presented in *Smith*, whether the statute improperly interfered with the power of Congress to regulate interstate commerce.[33]

In his opinion, writing for the majority, Justice Edward White thoroughly examined "the nature of the property in game and the authority which the State had a right lawfully to exercise in relation thereto." Tracing the history of government control over the taking of wildlife from Greek and Roman law through the civil law of the European continent and the common law of England, White concluded that the states had the right "to control and regulate the common property in game," which right was to be exercised "as a trust for the benefit of the people." [34] Those conditions the state could affix on the game incident to this right of control could remain with the game even after being killed.

The Supreme Court in *Geer* refused to analyze the effect of state regulation of wildlife on interstate commerce because the states, as sovereigns and as representatives of their citizens, "owned" the wildlife within their borders.[35] The Court found that this "ownership imported the right to keep the property, of the sovereign so close, always within its jurisdiction for every purpose".[36] Thus, the Court concluded that how a state regulated wildlife within its borders was "completely internal commerce . . . [and might] be considered as reserved for the State itself."[37]

Addressing the narrow legal question of whether conditions affixed by Connecticut improperly impeded interstate commerce, White offered three alternative grounds on which to uphold the state law. First, without deciding the question, he asserted that in view of the "peculiar nature" of the state's ownership of game, "it may well be doubted whether commerce is created by the killing and subsequent sale of such game." Second, even if it did constitute commerce, it was at most only intrastate commerce.[38] Finally, even if interstate commerce were impeded,

---

32   Bean, *supra* note 7, at 16.
33   *Id.*
34   161 U.S. 519, 528-29.
35   Hughes v. Oklahoma, 441 U.S. 322, 327 (1979).
36   161 U.S. at 530.
37   *Id.* at 531 (quoting Gibbons v. Ogden, 22 U.S. (9 Wheat) 1, 8 (1824).
38   Bean, *supra* note 7, at 17.

the "duty of the State to preserve for its people a valuable food supply" authorized the exercise of the state's police power to that end so long as interstate commerce was only "remotely and indirectly affected."[39]

However, the court stated that the power found in the states could continue to exist only "in so far as its exercise may not be incompatible with, or restrained by, the rights conveyed to the Federal Government by the Constitution."[40] Nevertheless, by intermixing questions of State authority to regulate the taking and disposition of wildlife with such technical property concepts as "ownership;" *Geer* sparked a long and continuing debate about the respective powers of the state and federal government over wildlife.[41]

### Authority for Federal Wildlife Regulation

Four years after the opinion in *Geer* was handed down, Congress passed the Lacy Act of 1900.[42] Ruling on the grant of power by the Constitution to the Congress to regulate Commerce between the states,[43] "The Congress shall have the power . . . to regulate Commerce with foreign Nations, and among the several States, and with the Indian Tribes . . ." The Act prohibited the interstate transportation of "any wild animals or birds" killed in violation of State law.[44] The purpose of the Act was to enlist the aid of the federal government, through its powers over interstate commerce, in the enforcement of state game laws.[45]

The Lacy Act further strengthened the State's regulatory authority over wildlife by including a provision taken almost verbatim from legislation designed to permit "dry" states to prohibit the importation of alcohol. It stated that whenever any dead wildlife were imported into a state, they were subject to its laws as if they were killed there.[46] The Lacy Act sanctioned a state's prohibition of the game lawfully killed in other states, whereas *Geer* upheld the authority of a state to prohibit exportation of game legally killed within the state. In view of some courts, the Act was an abdication of federal powers affirmatively to regulate interstate commerce.[47]

*Geer v. Connecticut* shielded state programs regulating wildlife from scrutiny under the commerce clause of the Constitution for nearly a century.[48]

---

39  161 U.S. at 528.
40  *Id.*
41  Bean, *supra* note 7, at 17.
42  Ch. 553, 31 Stat 187 (current version at 16 U.S.C. § 701), and 18 U.S.C. § 42 (1976 & Supp. V 1981).
43  U.S. Const. art. I, § 38, cl. 2.
44  Ch. 553, 31 Sta. 188 (1990) (current version at 16 U.S.C. § 3372(a) (1976 & Supp. V 1981)).
45  Bean, *supra* note 7, at 18.
46  Ch. 553, 31 Stat. 188 (1900) (repealed 1981).
47  Bean, *supra* note 7, at 18.

# WILDLIFE AND HABITAT

In 1979 the Supreme Court in *Hughes v. Oklahoma*[49] overruled *Geer* and struck down as repugnant to the Commerce Clause an Oklahoma statute.[50] The statute prohibited only "naturally" seined minnows from being removed from the state; it did not restrict removal of commercially grown minnows.[51]

In isolated cases over the next several decades, the Supreme Court further retracted its earlier language according to ownership priority to the states, but never in a definitive enough context.[52] *LaCosta v. Department*[53] carried over the qualification that states could regulate *ferae naturae* only "so far as [the animals were] capable of ownership," and the 1928 *Foster Fountain* case distinguished *Geer* in striking down a state law regulating the processing of shrimp.[54]

In another shrimp case in 1947, *Toomer v. Witsell*[55] the Court went further by stating that: The whole ownership theory, in fact, is now generally regarded as but a fiction expressive in legal shorthand of the importance to its people that a State have power to preserve and regulate the exploitation of an important resource.[56]

In *Hughes v. Oklahoma*, Hughes was licensed by Texas to operate a commercial minnows business. Hughes was arrested by an Oklahoma game ranger after purchasing a load of natural minnows from an Oklahoma dealer & transporting them to Wichita Falls, Texas.[57] Hughes contended at trial and on appeal that the Oklahoma statute was violative of the Commerce Clause.[58]

In overruling *Geer*, the Court noted that the state "ownership" theory had never been extended to resources other than wildlife.[59] The Court noted that just fifteen years after *Geer*, the Court in *West v. Kansas Natural Gas Co.*[60] had implicitly rejected the theory that states "owned" natural resources such as gas within their borders. The Court in West presupposed a rejection of the state ownership theory.[61] The *West* Court stated that the statute of Oklahoma which recognized gas to be subject of intrastate commerce but sought to prohibit it from being transported in interstate commerce with the purpose of conservation of

---

48   U.S. Const. art. I § 58, cl. 3.
49   441 U.S. 322.
50   Okla. Stat. tit. 29, § 4-115(B) (Supp. 1980).
51   441 U.S. at 325.
52   Coggins & Hensley, Constitutional Limits on Federal Wildlife: Is The Endangered
     Species Act Endangered?, 61 Iowa L. Rev. 1111 (1976).
53   263 U.S. 545, 549 (1924).
54   *Foster Fountain Packing Co. v. Haydel*, 278 U.S. 1, 11-12 (1920).
55   334 U.S. 385 (1948).
56   *Id.* at 402.
57   441 U.S. at 324.
58   Hughes v. State, 572 P.2d 573.
59   441 U.S. at 329.
60   221 U.S. 229 (1911).
61   441 U.S. at 329-30.

a natural state resource was an unconstitutional prohibition of free trade and interstate commerce.

The Court stated,

> If the States have such power a singular situation might result. Pennsylvania might keep its coal, the Northwest its timber, the mining States their minerals . . . to what consequences does such power tend? If one State has it, all States have it; embargo may be retaliated by embargo, and commerce will be halted at State lines.[62]

The Court in *Hughes* cited *Foster-Fountain Packing Co. v. Haydel*[63] in which a Louisiana statute forbade transporting shrimp out of state before their heads and shells had been removed.[64] The statute was struck down as "economic protectionism abhorrent to the commerce clause" because the statute attempted to retain the economic benefits of processing shrimp within the state without sacrificing the economic benefits of a national market.[65] The Court noted that even where wildlife was concerned, not all state restrictions were immune from Commerce Clause analysis.[66] The *Hughes* Court noted that those statutes imposing the most extreme burdens on interstate commerce (complete embargo) were most immune from Commerce Clause challenge because of the state "title" to its resources.[67] The Court noted that the reasoning in *Foster Fountain* was similar to that in the natural gas cases. In those cases, the *West* analysis had prevailed: whenever a state statute had displayed "the evils of protectionism" it had been struck down.[68] The natural gas cases ignored the "title" theory and concentrated instead on the purpose and effects of the statute.[69] In *Hughes*, the Court expressly rejected the *Geer* theory of state ownership of wildlife,[70] and held the "purpose and effects approach applies to other natural resources" [71] The "affecting commerce" test was first adopted in *NLRB v. Laughlin Steel Corp.*[72] In *Laughlin*, the Court held that the National Labor Relations Act, which regulated labor practices "affecting commerce," was within the federal commerce power. It did not matter that the practices regulated were not themselves in the "flow of commerce," so long as the practices affected commerce.[73]

---

62  221 U.S. at 255.
63  278 U.S. 1 (1928).
64  *Id*. at 332.
65  441 U.S. at 333.
66  441 U.S. at 330-31.
67  441 U.S. at 335.
68  441 U.S. at 330-31.
69  *Id*. at 333.
70  *Id*.at 335 (citing Douglas Seacoast Prods., Inc., 431 U.S. 265 (1977) and Baldwin v. Montana Fish and Game Comm'n, 436 U.S. 371 (1978)).
71  *Id*.
72  301 U.S. 1 (1937).
73  Axline, Constitutional Law - The End of a Wildlife Era: Hughes v. Oklahoma, 60 Or.

# WILDLIFE AND HABITAT

## The Pike Test

Having rejected the title theory, the Court applied the three part test, first articulated clearly in *Pike v. Bruce Church, Inc.*[74] to determine whether state regulatory schemes violate the Commerce Clause.[75] The test is first, does the challenged statute regulate even-handedly, with only incidental effects on interstate commerce, or does it discriminate against interstate commerce, either on its face or in effect? Second, if the statute discriminates against interstate commerce, does it serve a legitimate local purpose? Third, are alternative means available that would serve this legitimate local purpose without imposing as great a burden on interstate commerce?[76]

Not every statute that is facially discriminatory will be held to be invalid if the other two tests are met.[77] The *Hughes* Court stated, however, that facial discrimination invades the strictest scrutiny of any purported legitimate local purpose and of the absence of non-discriminatory alternatives.[78] Strict scrutiny, with few exceptions, is the death knell for the challenged statute.[79]

The Court found that the challenged statute in *Hughes* discriminated on its face against interstate commerce because it "overly blocked the flow of interstate commerce at the state's borders.[80]

Although the Court recognized a legitimate interest in conservation and protection of animals, the method the state used to further this interest was impermissible in the absence of a showing that less discriminatory means were unavailable.[81] The Court states that once discrimination is demonstrated, "the burden falls on the State to justify it both in terms of the local benefits flowing from the statute and the unavailability of the non-discriminatory alternative adequate to preserve the local interests at stake".[82] Oklahoma was unable to do so in *Hughes.*

---

L. Rev. 416, n.32 (1981).
74  397 U.S. 137 (1970).
75  441 U.S. at 336.
76  *Id.* at 336.
77  Broude & Du Mars, State Taxation of Natural Resource Extraction and the Commerce Clause, Federalism'court has Modern Frontier, 60 Or. L. Rev. 7, 29 (1981). In no case in which the Court has found discrimination against interstate commerce has it upheld the discrimintory regulations. This may be due to an unarticulated premise that if a state chooses the least discriminatory alternative for furthering a local interest, it is not discriminating at all.
78  441 U.S. at 337.
79  Broude & Du Mars, *supra* note 77, at 29.
80  441 U.S. at 336-37 (quoting Philadelphia v. New Jersey, 437 U.S. 617, 624 (1978).
81  *Id.* at 337-38.
82  *Id.* at 336 (quoting Hunt v. Washington State Apple Advertising Comm'n, 432 U.S. 333, 353 (1977)).

Until *Hughes*, the Court had adopted a two-tiered definition of Commerce, distinguishing between articles that were "in the flow of commerce" and articles that either had not yet entered the flow of commerce or had arrived at their distinctions and left the flow.[83] The Court later abandoned the two-tiered definition of commerce because it obstructed effective federal regulation of commerce.[84] However, state regulation of articles or activities before they entered the flow of commerce was not subject to Commerce Clause attack.

The Hughes Court, in a footnote, stated "The definition of "commerce" is the same when relied on to strike down or restrict state legislation as when relied on to support some exertion of federal control or regulation."[85] This holding struck down the rule that the State may confine the consumption of natural resources like fish, game and streams-resources which have not yet been reduced to private possession and ownership to consumption occurring wholly within the state's borders.[86]

Even if a challenged regulation is discriminatory on its face, or in effect, the first element looks to whether the challenged regulation deals evenhandedly, with only incidental effects on interstate commerce.[87] Although western states facially discriminate against interest commerce, because they require non-residents to pay higher fees than residents in order to hunt in the state, they do not necessarily violate the Commerce Clause.

In *Baldwin v. Montana Fish* and *Game Commission*[88] the state passed a discriminatory licensing scheme in which non-residents were charged substantially higher fees for hunting elk than that imposed on residents. The law was challenged as violating the privileges and immunities clause of article IV (2) or the Equal Protection clause of the Fourteenth amendment to the Constitution.

The plaintiffs charged that the case was controlled by *Toomer v. Witsell*, [89] a 1948 case in which a group of Georgia citizens brought suit challenging several South Carolina statutes governing commercial fishing in the three-mile zone off its coast. Among the statutes challenged was a provision imposing upon non-resident commercial shrimp harvesters a license fee of $2,500, which was 100 times greater than the fee charged residents. The Court in *Toomer* found this differential fee to be "so great

---

83    Broude & Du Mars, *supra* note 77, at 18-22.
84    Hammer v. Dagenhart, 247 U.S. 251 (1918) (child labor practices not subject to federal commerce power); United States v. E.L. Knight Co., 156 U.S. 1 (1985) (sugar monolopy not subject to federal commerce power).
85    441 U.S. at 326, n.2.
86    L. Tribe, American Constitutional Law 335.
87    441 U.S. at 336.
88    436 U.S. 371 (1978).
89    334 U.S. at 421.

that its principal effect is virtually exclusionary," and in violation of the guarantees of the privileges and immunities clause.[90] The Court in *Baldwin* distinguished *Toomer* on the basis that it involved the licensing of an activity for a "commercial livelihood." Since recreational sport hunting was not a "fundamental" right, it was not protected by the Privileges and Immunities Clause. [91] Because the Court did not regard sport hunting as a fundamental right, they considered *Geer* and other early cases considering state ownership of natural resources.[92]

The Chief Justice in his separate concurring opinion recognized that the special interest Montana citizens have in their elk allowed the State to charge non-resident hunters higher license fees for a non-fundamental right to hunt those elk without offending the Privileges and Immunities Clause.

In the opinion of the three dissenting justices, the consideration of whether sport hunting is fundamental or not is irrelevant. The question to be answered is whether the State has proper justification for discriminating against citizens of other states.[93] The Supreme Court, less than a year later, concluded "that time has revealed the error" of *Geer* and expressly overruled it in *Hughes v. Oklahoma*.[94]

The facts in *Hughes* were very similar to *Geer*. The defendant *Hughes* was a Texas minnow dealer who was arrested for violating an Oklahoma statute prohibiting shipment of minnows seined in the State's waters for purpose of sale out of State. He had purchased them from a licensed Oklahoma dealer and transported them for sale across state lines.

While recognizing "the legitimate state concerns for conservation and protection of wild animals underlying the 19th Century legal fiction of State ownership,"[95] the Court concluded that "challenges under the Commerce Clause to state regulations of wild animals should be considered according to the same general rule applied to state regulations of their natural resources".[96]

The question posed by *Hughes* as concerns the *Baldwin* decision is whether *Baldwin* may have been decided differently if the challenge had been based on the Commerce Clause rather than the Privileges and Immunities Clause.[97] Although *Baldwin* held sport hunting is not a funda-

---

90   *Id*. at 396-97.
91   436 U.S. at 386-88.
92   436 U.S. at 386-87.
93   *Id*. at 392.
94   441 U.S. 322 (1979).
95   *Id*. at 336.
96   *Id*. at 335.
97   Coggins, Wildlife and the Constitution: The Walls Come Tumbling Down, 55 Wash. L. Rev. 295, 318 (1980).

mental right, it could certainly be viewed as affecting commerce. Mr. Baldwin was an outfitter and licensed hunting guide whose livelihood depended substantially on out-of-state big game hunters.[98]

If the *Pike* test[99] would have been applied, the Court would have had to examine whether the degree of burden placed upon interstate commerce was justified by a legitimate local public interest and whether that interest could be promoted with a lesser impact on interstate activities.

The public trust doctrine and doctrine of State ownership at Common law were used by the States to regulate more than the management of wildlife within a state. It was the common law means by which a state could recover monetary damages. [100]

Most states now have statutes which impose strict liability for "all costs of cleanup or other damage" resulting from chemical or other spills.[101] Such general legislation frequently fails to be specific enough regarding the sort of "property" for which damage recovery is authorized, or how its value is to be measured, leaving open the questions most important in the common law actions. One of the first cases brought before the Supreme Court on this issue was *Commonwealth v. Agway, Inc.*[102] In that case, the state of Pennsylvania brought an action against Agway, Inc. for its negligent pollution of a stream in which 72,000 fish were killed as a result. The state sought to recover from the polluter the commercial value of the fish. The question was whether the state's property interest in the fish was sufficient to support an action for monetary damages. The Court held that because the state lacked "possession" of the fish and drew a distinction between the state power as a sovereign and as an "owner" of wildlife, citing *Missouri v. Holland* and *Toomer v. Witsell*. The Court held possession was a prerequisite of ownership. Because the state lacked ownership, it could not maintain the action for damages.[103]

The Court in *Maryland v. Amerada Hess Corp.*[104] and *Maine v. M/V Tamano*[105] recognized the state's public trust responsibilities and gave them "technical ownership."[106] The Maryland Court declared that "if the State is deemed to be the trustee of the waters, then, as trustee, the State

---

98  *Id*. at 331.
99  441 U.S. at 336.
100  *See* Halter & Thomas, Recovery of Damages by State for Fish and Wildlife Losses Caused by Pollution, 10 Ecology L.Q. 5 (1982).
101  *See generally id*.
102  210 Pa. Super. 150, 232 A.2d 69 (1967).
103  *Id*.
104  350 F. Supp. 1060 (D. Md. 1972), motion for relief denied, 356 F. Supp. 975 (D. Md. 1973).
105  357 F. Supp. 1097 (D. Me. 1973).
106  334 U.S. at 421.

must be empowered to bring suit to protect the corpus of the trust, i.e., the waters- for the beneficiaries of the trust - i.e., the public".[107]

The cases were settled out of court so the issue of damages and measurement of damages was not answered.

In *State v. Jersey Central Power & Light Co.*[108] the state brought an action as *parens patriae* for the death of about 500,000 menhaden resulting from the operation of a nuclear power plant. The plant utilized water from a nearby river for cooling purposes. The warmed water was discharged back into the river. This warmed water caused the menhaden, who usually migrate to warm water in winter, to remain in the river during the winter. When the plant was forced to shut down in midwinter, the river water froze and caused a massive fish kill.

The trial court held that "the State has not only the right but also the affirmative fiduciary obligation to ensure that the rights of the public to a viable marine environment are protected and to seek compensation for any diminution in that trust corpus".[109] The court, however, awarded only $935, the market value of the fish killed. Although the court admitted there was environmental damage, it did not speculate on the monetary damage.

The defendant sought a rehearing on the basis that there had been no proof of negligence. The trial court upheld its judgment on the basis that the defendant was strictly liable for creating "an ultra-hazardous situation." The Appellate Division agreed with the trial court that the state had an affirmative duty to seek recovery and affirmed the lower court's decision. However, it rejected strict liability as a basis of recovery. It looked at the act of pumping warm water into a stream as not being ultra-hazardous, but rather that the defendant should have known the sharp reduction of water temperature would have an adverse impact on aquatic life.[110]

The New Jersey Supreme Court reversed the judgment on the ground the defendants' actions had not caused the death of the fish.[111] It declared the discontinued pumping of warm water merely accelerated the temperature drop, and that the operation of the power plant was a lawful activity.[112]

---

107  350 F. Supp. at 1067.
108  69 N.J. 102, 351 A.2d 337 (1976).
109  125 N.J. Super. 103, 308 A.2d 671, 674 (1973).
110  133 N.J. Super 375, 389, 336 A.2d 750, 757 (1975).
111  69 N.J. 102, 351 A.2d 337 (1976).
112  69 N.J. at 111, 351 A.2d at 342.

Whether the states have the right to recover damages at common law for injury to wildlife under state ownership is questionable since the *Hughes* decision.[113]

*In re Stewart Transportation Co.*,[114] in which an oil spill killed migratory waterfowl, the defendant challenged whether the state or federal government could recover for damages on the grounds that neither "owned" the birds.[115] The Court concluded that both governments have a "sovereign interest in preserving wildlife resources" and that therefore they could seek damages under either *parens patrial* or public trust doctrines. According to the Court, these doctrines constitute separate theories of the same cause of action:

> under the public trust doctrine, the State of Virginia and the United States have the right and the duty to protect and preserve the public's interest in natural wildlife resources...Likewise, under the doctrine of *parens patrial* the state acts to protect a quasi-sovereign interest where no individual cause of action would lie.[116]

However, where laws have been passed regarding wildlife, the state common law and statutory law are preempted. [117]

At the federal level, a number of statutes have authorized suits to recover injury to natural resources.[118]

Most significant is the Comprehensive Environmental Response, Compensation and Liability Act of 1980,[119] also known as the "Superfund" legislation, authorizing the President or authorized representative of any state, to recover from anyone who causes the release of any of a broad range of hazardous substances such sums as are necessary to restore, rehabilitate, or acquire the equivalent of, damaged natural resources.[120] The Superfund expressly preserves the right of the states to

---

113 Bean, *supra* note 7, at 44.
114 495 F. Supp. 38 (E.D. Va. 1980).
115 *Id.* at 38.
116 *Id.* at 40.
117 City of Milwaukee v. llinois, 451 U.S. 304 (1981) holding that enactment of the Federal Waters Pollution Control Act amendments of 1972 displaced the federal common law of nuisance as a basis for state actions against neighboring states on their citizens.
118 The Clean Water Act Amendments of 1977, 33 U.S.C. § 1321(f)(4) expanding the scope of recovery against one who causes a spill of oil or other hadardous substance in navigable waters to include not only the costs of removal, but the cost to the state or federal governments of restoring or replacing the natural resources damaged by such a spill. U.S.C. § 1813 (a)(2) and (d) (supp. IV 1980), the Outer Continental Shell Lands Act Amendments of 1978, recovery for injury resulting from an oil spill. Bean, *supra* note 7, at 45, nn.179, 180.
119 42 U.S.C. §§ 9601-9657 (Supp. IV 1980).
120 Bean, *supra* note 7, at 45.

impose additional liability or requirements on persons releasing hazardous substances within the state.[121]

The issue of monetary damages was addressed extensively in com of *Puerto Rico* in Zoe Colocotomi. The defendants in that case spilled oil which contaminated approximately two acres of costal mangrove forest in a sparsely populated area of Puerto Rico. Puerto Rico argued that to limit recovery to the diminution of market value of the affected lands would frustrate the intent of the Puerto Rican statute to preserve natural areas, and that the area had considerable ecological value, even though it had little commercial value.[122]

The district court calculated the damages using the "replacement cost " of individual organism as a basis. The court allowed biological damages in excess of 5 million dollars. The appellate court taking its guidance from the various federal statutes mentioned, reasoned that the cost of replacement was appropriate or when such replacement was appropriate only when such replacement was part of a larger restoration program.

The federal attitude during the 19th century toward wildlife was generally one of unconcern.[123] The federal government made some inroads during the latter part of the century. Yellowstone and Yosemite National Parks were established, followed by passage of an act in 1894 providing for protection of wildlife within the park boundaries.[124] A Federal Commission of Fish and Fisheries was organize in 1871, and the Division of Economic Ornithology and Mammology, begun in 1886, was the precursor of the Biological Survey.[125] In 1874, Congress enacted a law to prevent further indiscriminate slaughter of bison in the territories. However, it was pocket-vetoed by President Grant.[126] Further, in 1886, Congress enacted legislation forbidding the passing of game protection laws by territorial legislatures. The few legislative actions which were taken seemed premised on the assumption that congressional powers to regulate wildlife did exist insofar as territories were concerned. [127]

Pressure from such groups as the Audöbon Society and anti-cruelty leagues, brought on by the near extinction of the buffalo and other species, and the decline of some bird populations for the use of their feathers to decorate hats, brought about congressional enactment of the Lacy Act in 1900.[128] In passing the Lacy Act,[129] Congress relied on the consti-

---

121  42 U.S.C. § 9614(a).
122  628 F.2d at 673.
123  Coggins & Hensley, *supra* note 11, at 1109.
124  Act of May 7, 1894, Ch. 72, 28 Stat. 73 (53d Cong., 2d Sess. 1894).
125  P. Matthiessen, *supra* note 12, at 282, n.61.
126  *Id.* at 282.
127  Coggins & Hensley, *supra* note 11, at 1110.
128  *Id.* at 1111 (citing Burr, Toward Legal Rights for Animals, 4 Envt'l Affairs 207 (1975).

tutional grant of power to regulate commerce between the states.[130] They prohibited the interstate transportation of "any wild animals or birds" killed in violation of law.[131]

The statute forbade transportation or sale in interstate commerce of animals illegally in the state of origin. The Act enlisted the federal government's powers over interstate commerce to aid enforcement of state game laws.[132]

One provision prohibited the importation of certain named animals; and those animals that the Secretary of Agriculture may...declare injurious to the interests of agriculture or horticulture.[133] This source of exercise of federal authority, the congressional power over foreign commerce, has never been challenged.[134]

In response to the decimation of the passenger pigeon and the depletion of a number of other birds, the Lacy Act authorized the Secretary of Agriculture to adopt all measures necessary "for the preservation, distribution, introduction, and restoration of game birds and other wild birds", subject to the laws of the various states and territories. [135]

Twelve years later, the scope of the statute was challenged in *The Abby Dodge*,[136] when the United States brought suit against a vessel for violation of a federal statute prohibiting the taking of sponges from the Gulf of Mexico or the Straits of Florida by means of a driving apparatus.[137] The vessel owner claimed the sponges were taken in Florida's territorial water, and that if the federal statute pertained to such waters it was unconstitutional because the taking of sponges there was a matter exclusively within the authority of the states. Chief Justice White, author of the *Geer* opinion, agreed. He did not invalidate the statute, however, but construed it to apply only beyond Florida's territorial waters.[138] Justice White's *Abby Dodge* decision was the first (and last) statement by the Supreme Court that the state ownership doctrine precluded federal wildlife regulation.[139]

On the heels of the Lacy Act, the first wildlife refuge thereafter established was at Pelican Island, Florida, in 1903, and President Roosevelt's National Conservation Commission was set up under Gifford Pinchot

---

129 Ch. 553, 31 Stat. 187 (current version at 16 U.S.C. § 701, and 18 U.S.C. § 42 (1976 & Supp. V 1981).
130 U.S. Const. art I, § 8, cl. 2.
131 Ch. 553, 31 Stat. 188 (1900) (current version at 16 U.S.C. § 3372(a)).
132 Bean, *supra* note 7, at 18.
133 Ch. 553, § 2, 31 Stat. 188 (1900) (current version at 18 U.S.C. § 42 (1976).
134 U.S. Const. art. I, § 8, cl. 3.
135 Bean, *supra* note 7, at 18.
136 223 U.S. 166 (1912).
137 Act of June 20, 1906, ch 3442, 34 Stat. 313 (repealed 1914).
138 223 U.S. at 175.
139 Bean, *supra* note 7, at 19.

in 1908. Sea otters were federally protected in Alaska in 1910.[140] The Fur Deal Treaty, between Great Britain and the United States relating to Fur Seals in the Bering Sea, was entered into in 1911.[141]

In 1913, Congress passed the Migratory Bird Act as a part of the Appropriations Act for the Department of Agriculture. The Act declared all migratory game and insectivorous birds "to be within the custody and protection of the government of the United States" and prohibited their hunting except pursuant to federal regulations.[142] This legislation was struck down in *United States v. Shauver*.[143] The government attempted to support its law on the basis that the migratory character of the birds made them subject to its power to regulate interstate commerce. The Courts looked to *Geer* as precedent for rejecting this arguments. The Goverment argument that the law was supported by the property clause [144] was likewise rejected on the basis that *Geer* had placed "property" in wildlife in the States, and the statute was beyond delegated federal power.[145]

While the *Shauver* case was before the Supreme Court on appeal before the Supreme Court, the United States concluded the Migratory Bird Treaty Act[146] on August 16, 1916, with Great Britain, on behalf of Canada, for the protection of migratory birds. The Supreme Court dismissed the government's appeal in *Shauver* after the passage of implementing legislation in 1918. The constitutionality of the 1913 Act was never decided.[147]

The question of constitutionality of the 1918 Act was brought before the Court in *Missouri v. Holland* in 1920. In this case, the state of Missouri filed a bill in equity seeking to restrain Ray Holland, a United States Game Warden, from enforcing the Act within the state. The Court held that the Treaty and its implementing legislation took precedence over state law by virtue of the Constitution's Supremacy Clause[148] and was a proper incident to the treaty making power.[149] It was not decided whether the federal government had the power to enact the statute absent a treaty,[150] but the Court called the state ownership concept a "slen-

---

[140] 39 Fed. Reg. 27922, 27924-25 (Interior Department's Status Report on Marine Mammals) (1974) (United States v. The Kodiak, 53 F. 126 (D. Alaska 1892)).
[141] Convention between the United States and Great Britain Relating to Fur Seals in the Bering Sea (reprinted at 6 Am. J. Int'l L. Supp. 72 (1912)).
[142] Act of March 4, 1913, Ch. 145, 37 Stat. 828 (repealed 1918).
[143] 214 F. 154, 161 (E.D. Ark. 1914).
[144] "The Congress shall have power to dispose of and make all needful rules and regulations respecting the Territory or other Property belonging to the United States." U.S. Const. art. IV, § 3.
[145] 221 F. 288, 295-96 (D. Kan. 1915); 214 F. 154, 161 (E.D. Ark. 1914).
[146] Ch. 128, 40 Stat. 755 (1918) (current version at 16 U.S.C. §§ 703-711 (1976 & Supp. V 1981).
[147] Bean, *supra* note 7, at 20.
[148] U.S. Const. art. VI.
[149] Missouri v. Holland, 252 U.S. 416 (1920).
[150] *Id.* at 434.

der reed"[151] upon which the states leaned. Furthermore, Chief Justice Holmes recognized, in his opinion, that

> But for the treaty and the statute there soon might be no birds for any powers to deal with. We see nothing in the Constitution that compels the Government to sit by while a food supply is cut off and the protectors of our forests and our crops are destroyed. It is not sufficient to rely on the states. The reliance is in rain.[152]

Besides establishing the supremacy of the Federal treaty-making power, as a source for federal wildlife regulation, *Missouri v. Holland* rejected the doctrine of state ownership as a bar to federal regulation of wildlife.[153]

From passage of the Migratory Bird Treaty Act of 1918[154] until the mid-1960's Congress Concerned itself with Wildlife only to the extent of establishing a few grants-in-aid programs for state agencies, imposing minimal wildlife habitat planning requirements for federal water resource projects [155] and enacting legislation to protect the bald eagle.[156]

The migratory Bird Treaty Act is largely a nationwide hunting law, providing the mechanism for acquiring Wetlands and managing populationswith the Interior Department responsible for its implementation.[157]

The federal government had exercised the power of the property clause for some time. It prohibited all hunting in Yellowstone National Park in 1894, and in 1906 it prohibited the hunting of birds "on all lands of the United States which have been set apart or reserved as breeding grounds for birds by any law, proclamation, or Executive order" except under regulations of the Secretary of Agriculture.[158]

The states did not challenge this assertion of authority over federally owned lands. However, when the government sought to remove wildlife from such lands without complying with state law, several states challenged the action as being outside the scope of powers conferred by the property clause.

Such was the case in *Hunt v. United States*.[159] The Secretary of Agriculture had directed the removal of excess deer in Kaibab National Forests.

---

151 *Id.* at 434.
152 *Id.* at 434-35.
153 Bean, *supra* note 7, at 21.
154 16 U.S.C. §§ 703-711 (1970).
155 Fish and Wildlife Coordination Act of 1958, 16 U.S.C. § 661-67e (1970) as amended, 16 U.S.C. § 667b (Supp. IV 1974).
156 Bald Eagle Protection Act of 1940, Ch. 278, § 1, 54 Stat. 250, as amended, 16 U.S.C. § 668-68d (Supp. IV 1974).
157 Coggins & Hensley, *supra* note 11, at 1112.
158 Act of June 28, 1906, Ch. 3565, 34 Stat. 536 (current version at 18 U.S.C. § 41.
159 278 U.S. 96 (1928).

Their over-browsing threatened to harm the forests. State officials arrested persons carrying out the Secretary's orders charging the removal was in violation of State game laws. The United States brought suit to enjoin the state from enforcing its game laws with respect to the removal program. The state relied on state ownership doctrine as set forth in *Geer* and other cases, but the Supreme Court ruled that "the power of the United States to protect its lands and property does not admit of doubt . . . the game laws or any other statute of state . . . notwithstanding."[160] This holding was extended to include federal authority in acquired national forest lands in *Chalk v. United States*.[161]

Still, the dispute continued over the scope of the federal government's authority over wildlife on its own lands. The Public Land Law Review Commission, in response to a December 1, 1964 statement by the Solicitor for the Department of the Interior that the United States "has the constitutional power to enact laws and regulations controlling and protecting . . . [its] lands, including the . . . resident species of wildlife situated in such lands, and that this authority is superior to that of the State"[162] and concluded that "a clear showing of damage to Federal properly is required before action in violation of state law is sanctioned."[163]

In *New Mexico State Game Commissioner v. Udall*,[164] the court upheld the Secretary of Interior's directed killing of a number of deer in Carlsbad Caverns National Park for research purposes, without complying with state game laws and without any showing of existing depredation by the deer.[165] The court upheld the Secretary's research program because of his necessary power to determine which animals "may be detrimental to the use of the park."[166] The holding still left the requirement that the animals were regulable by federal authority only as they related to the authority bestowed by the property clause regarding the land.

The issue of whether, in fact, there had to be a clear showing of damage before wild animals could be federally regulated was addressed in *Kleppe v. New Mexico*.[167]

The Wild and Free Roaming Horses and Burros Act[168] was passed in 1976 to protect "all unbranded and unclaimed horses and burros on public lands of the United States "from" capture, branding, harassment, or death, "to accomplish which" they are to be considered in the area

---

160 *Id.* at 100.
161 114 F.2d 207 (4th Cir. 1940).
162 G. Swanson, Fish and Wildlife Resources on the Public Lands 15 (1969).
163 *Id.* at 32.
164 410 F.2d 1197 (10th Cir.), cert. denied sub nom., New Mexico State Game Comm'n v. Hickel, 396 U.S. 961 (1969).
165 *Id.* at 1201.
166 *Id.* at 1201.
167 426 U.S. 529 (1976).
168 16 U.S.C. § 1331 (1976).

where presently found, as an integral part of the natural system of the public lands of the United States as "loving symbols of the historic and pioneer spirit of the West". The Act provides that all such animals which are on the public lands administered by the Secretary of the Interior through the Bureau of Land Management (BLM) or by the Secretary of Agriculture through the Forest Service are committed to the jurisdiction of the respective Secretaries, who are "directed to protect and manage [the animals] as components of the public lands . . . in a manner that is designed to achieve and maintain a thriving natural ecological balance on the public lands," and if the animals stray from those lands onto privately owned land, the private landowners may inform federal officials, who shall arrange to have the animals removed.[169]

A three-judge Federal Court in *Kleppe* struck down the Act as unconstitutional thus setting the stage for the Supreme Court to make a definitive, pronouncement on the federal authority to regulate wildlife conferred by the Property Clause.

The *Kleppe* case began when a federal grazing permittee requested New Mexico authorities to remove certain of the protected burros from the federal land he was using as grazing for cattle because the wild burros were consuming his cattle's feed and were "molesting" the cattle. The New Mexico authorities removed the wild burros and sold them at auction. The Federal Bureau of Land Management then demanded that New Mexico recover and return them. Instead, the state sued the Secretary of the Interior to have the Federal Act declared unconstitutional. The Lower Court agreed with the state, distinguishing *Hunt*, *Chalk*, and *Udall* on the ground that in those cases the federal efforts were lawful only because they served to protect the federal lands, whereas the Act was designed solely to protect the animals.[170] Appellees argued that the property clause grants Congress two-kinds of power: (1) the power to dispose of and make incidental rules regarding the use of federal property; and (2) the power to protect federal property. Appellees argued the first power is not broad enough to support legislation protecting Wild animals that live on federal property; and that the second power is not implicated since the Act is designed to protect the animals, which are not themselves federal property, and not the public lands.[171] The Supreme Court however, unanimously reversed the lower court's decision, quoting *United States v. San Francisco*[172] which stated that although the Property Clause does not authorize "an exercise of a general control over public policy in a State, "it does permit an exercise of the complete power which Congress has over Particular public property entrusted to it." The Court held that the "complete power" that Congress has over

169  426 U.S. 529 (1976).
170  New Mexico v. Morton, 406 F. Supp 1237 (D. N.M. 1975).
171  426 U.S. at 536-37.
172  310 U.S. at 30 (1940).

public lands necessarily includes the power to regulate and protect the wildlife living there.[173]

The State's concern about loss of sovereignty was apparent in the argument set forth by appellees that if the Wild Free-Roaming Horses and Burros Act was upheld, under the Property Clause it would be an impermissible intrusion on the sovereignty, legislative authority, and police power of the State and would wrongly infringe upon the State's traditional trustee powers over wild animals.[174] The State argued this could only be done with the consent of the state. The Court rejected this argument, stating that the appellees had confused the Congress' derivative legislative powers, not involved in this case, with its powers under the Property Clause.[175] In either case, the Court pointed out that the legislative jurisdiction acquired may range from exclusive federal jurisdiction with no residential state power. . . to concurrent, or partial, federal legislative jurisdiction which may allow the State to exercise certain authority. [176] Absent consent or cession a State retains jurisdiction over federal lands within its territory, but Congress equally retains the power to enact legislation respecting those lands pursuant to the Property Clause. [177] When Congress so acts, the federal legislation necessarily overrides conflicting state laws under the Supremacy Clause.[178] The Court cited *Camfield v. United States*[179] which stated: "a different rule would place the public domain of the United States completely at the mercy of state legislation." Where those state laws conflict with the Wild Free-roaming Horses and Burros Act, or with other legislation passed pursuant to the Property Clause, the law is clear: The State laws must concede.[180]

The Court cited *Toomer*, *La Coste* and *Geer* in stating that the States unquestionably have broad trustee and police powers over wild animals within their jurisdictions. However, those powers exist only "in so far as [their] exercise may not be incompatible with, or restrained by, the rights conveyed to the Federal Government by the Constitution.[181] Thus, the Privileges and Immunities Clause,[182] precludes a State from imposing prohibitory licensing fees on non-residents shrimping in its waters;[183] the Treaty Clause[184] permits congress to enter into and enforce a treaty to protect migratory birds despite state objections;[185] and the Property Clause gives Congress the power to then overpopulated

---

173 426 U.S. at 540-41.
174 *Id*. at 541.
175 *Id*. at 542.
176 *Id*.
177 *Id*. at 543.
178 *Id*. at 543.
179 167 U.S. 518 (1897).
180 *Id*. at 543.
181 *Id*. at 545.
182 U.S. Const. art IV, § 2, cl. 1.
183 Toomer v. Witsell, 334 U.S. 385 (1948).
184 U.S. Const. art II, § 2.
185 Missouri v. Holland, 252 U.S. 416, 434 (1920).

herds of deer on federal lands contrary to state law.[186] The Court then held that "the Property Clause also gives Congress the power to protect wildlife on the public lands, state law notwithstanding".[187] The Court declined, however, to determine the extent, if any, to which the Property Clause empowers Congress to protect animals on private lands or the extent to which such regulation is attempted by the Act.[188]

Although the Supreme Court has not considered further the scope of federal authority over wildlife under the Property Clause, several lower courts have addressed questions left unresolved by the Kleppe decision.[189] In *United States v. Brown*[190] a National Park Service prohibition against hunting on state waters within, but not a part of, the National Park System was challenged. The Court held that the Property Clause empowers the United States to enact regulatory legislation protecting federal lands from interference occurring on non-federal public lands, or, in this instance, waters. Finding that the prohibition was needed to protect wildlife and visitors on federal lands, the court upheld it as a proper exercise of Property Clause powers.[191]

In *Palila v.Hawaii Department of Land and Natural Resources* the Court upheld the Endangered Species Act, as applied ton non-migratory species found on state lands, on the basis of the treaty power and Commerce Clause. The Court suggested that "The importance of preserving such a national resource [as an endangered species] may be of such magnitude as to rise to the level of a federal property interest. [192]

It is clear that the Constitution, in its Treaty, Property, and Commerce Clauses, contains ample support for the development of a comprehensive body of federal wildlife law and that, to the extent such law conflicts with state law, it takes precedence over the later. This does not completely divest the states of action as they will continue to play an important role in the implementation of federal wildlife programs.

The National Park Service clearly has plenary and pre-emptive power to manage for wildlife preservation within parks.[193] Except where authorized by Congress, sport and commercial hunting and trapping have long been prohibited, although fishing is sometimes allowed within parks.[194] The Park Service power over wildlife within parks supersedes and overrides any contrary state law or regulation.[195]

---

186  Hunt v. United States, 278 U.S. 96 (1928).
187  426 U.S. 546.
188  *Id.* at 546.
189  Bean, *supra* note 7, at 25.
190  552 F.2d 817, 822 (8th Cir. 1977).
191  *Id.* at 822.
192  471 F. Supp at 995, n.40.
193  Kleepe v. Mexico, 426 U.S. 529 (1976); New Mexico State Game Comm'n v. Udall, 410
      F.2d 1197 (10th Cir. 1969), cert. denied, 396 U.S. 961 (1970)
194  National Rifle Ass'n v. Potter, 628 F. Supp. 903 (D. D.C. 1986).
195  Kleepe v. New Mexico, 426 U.S. 529 (1976).

Courts in recent cases have upheld NPS regulations tightening controls over wildlife taking in Park System units. In *National Rifle Association v. Potter*[196] the Court ruled that unless Congress affirmatively commanded hunting and trapping in recreational areas of the Park System, those uses should be outlawed in all recreational areas.[197] A flat ban by NPS on commercial fishing in the Everglades National Park was upheld by the Eleventh Circuit Court.[198]

There are very few constitutional limits on the actions Congress can take to protect the national parks from external threats.[199] The question is one of political choice.[200] The Secretary of the Interior has the power, and arguably the duty, to consider whether projects on other lands under Interior Department jurisdiction will harm park resources and to factor that consideration into his discretionary decision-making.[201] The power question, therefore, does not concern NPS control over adjacent federally owned and controlled lands, but NPS power over activities on privately owned lands within and without park boundaries.[202] The main statutory command is that the NPS must use such measures as conform to the fundamental purpose of conserving park wildlife for the enjoyment of future generations.[203] Even though such power does exist to regulate private property as it affects National Park System, so far it has been used successfully only to abate or to punish closely-adjacent, nuisance-like activities.[204]

### Indian Treaty Rights

Indian treaty rights pertaining to wildlife vary from tribe to tribe, depending on the language and historical context of the treaties involved.[205]

One of the first cases before the Supreme Court to consider the relationships between the state's authority to regulate wildlife and the rights of hunting and fishing reserved by Indians in their treaty was *Ward v. Race Horse* in 1896.[206] Justice White, who had penned the opinion in *Geer v. Connecticut.*[207] the same year, also wrote the opinion of the Court in *Race*

---

196 628 F. Supp. 903 (D. D.C. 1986).
197 *Id.* at 910,192.
198 Organized Fishermen of Florida v. Hodel, 775 F.2d 1544 (11th Cir. 1985), cert. denied, 106 S. Ct. 2890 (1986).
199 Kleepe v. Mexico, 426 U.S. 529 (1976); New Mexico State Game Comm'n v. Udall, 410 F.2d 1197 (10th Cir. 1969), cert. denied, 396 U.S. 961 (1970)).
200 *See generally*, Coggins, Protecting the Wildlife Resources of National Parks From External Threats. 22 Land & Water L. Rev. 25 (1987).
201 The status outlining the preservation mandate for parks speak of the Secretary's duty to implement that mandate, *e.g.*, 16 U.S.C. § 3 (1982).
202 Coggins, *supra* note 200, at 16.
203 16 U.S.C. § 1 (1982 & Supp. III 1985).
204 United States v. Lindsey, 595 F.2d 5 (9th Cir. 1979); United States V. Brown, 552 F.2d 817 (8th Cir.), cert. denied, 431 U.S. 949 (1977).
205 Bean, *supra* note 7, at 48.
206 163 U.S. 504 (1896).
207 161 U.S. 519 (1896).

*Horse*. Keeping in mind the opinion in *Geer* was the state ownership doctrine, it is no surprise the Court's opinion in *Ward v Race* Horse mirrored that opinion.

In *Ward v. Race* Horse, Race Horse was a Bannock Indian convicted of killing elk in violation of Wyoming law. Race Horse pointed to a treaty of 1869 which reserved to the Bannocks "the right to hunt on the unoccupied land of the United States, so long as game may be found thereon." Wyoming was admitted to the Union in 1890, however, and claimed that state game laws enacted by it were applicable even on federal and within the state. Since Race Horse's offense was committed on such lands, the issue of treaty rights versus state law was presented.[208]

Because nothing in the treaty, in White's view, indicated congressional intent to have the treaty supersede state law, there was no constitutional issue to decide.[209] Justice White, in keeping with his decision in *Geer*[210] assumed that the federal government lacked authority to regulate wildlife within the state.

Justice White's interpretation of the Indian treaty in *Race Horse* was soon abandoned by the Supreme Court. In 1905, the Supreme Court in *United States v. Winans*[211] considered for the first time one of the so called "Stevens Treaties."[212] The Court decided that its reservation to the Jakima Indians of the right of taking fish at all usual and accustomed places, in common with the citizens of the Territory, entitled the Indians to use privately owned land for fishing at such usual places even though the landowner had been granted a license by the state to use a fish wheel there. The practicable effect was to exclude all others from fishing at the place.[213] Only Justice White dissented.

The Supreme Court continued to favor a rule of construction that attempted to give Indian treaties the meaning that was the probable understanding of them by the Indians at the time they were signed.[214]

In *Tulee v. Washington*[215] the Supreme Court upheld contrary to a Stevens treaty, a requirement of the state that Indians purchase fishing licenses. The Court also held that the state's regulation be "necessary for the conservation of fish."[216]

---

208 Bean, *supra* note 7, at 49.
209 *Id.* at 49.
210 161 U.S. 519 (1896).
211 198 U.S. 371 (1905).
212 Bean, *supra* note 7, at 50.
213 *Id.*
214 198 U.S. 371 (1905); Saufert Brothers Co. v. United States, 249 U.S. 194 (1919) (establishing the supremacy of Indian off-reservation treaty rights in relations to the rights of private landowners).
215 315 U.S. 681 (1942).
216 *Id.* at 684.

The Court recently refined its "necessary for conservation of fish" standard further when it decided *Puyallup Tribe v. Department of Game*.[217] In *Puyallup*, the state of Washington sued in a state court to enjoin certain Indians from violating state fishing regulations which restricted the use of nets for salmon and steelhead fishing. The state court entered an injunction requiring Indians to abide by all state fishing regulations. The injunction was modified by the state supreme court to require adherence only to those regulations that were "reasonable and necessary." The Supreme Court reviewed and affirmed the decision of the state supreme court, stating that the "manner of fishing, the size of the take, the restriction of commercial fishing, and the like may be regulated by the State in the interest of conservation, provided the regulation meets appropriate standards and does not discriminate against the Indians."[218] This left the "permissible standards" rule vague and unclear.

In 1973, the *Puyallup* case came back before the Supreme Court.[219] After the Court's first decision, the Washington Department of Fisheries relaxed its restrictions on net fishing for salmon, but continued its total ban on net fishing for steelhead trout, arguing that the catch of steelhead sports fishery alone in the Payallup River left only a sufficient number necessary for the conservation of steelhead fishery in that river.[220] This statutory allocation of all steelhead to sports fishery with no allocation to Indians was held by the Supreme Court to be unlawful discrimination against the Indians. The Court declared that the harvestable run of steelhead "must in some manner be fairly apportioned between Indian net fishing and non-Indian sport fishing".[221] The lower courts were left to decide the manner of apportionment.

On remand from the *Puyallup II* decision, the Washington state courts allocated 45 percent of the annual fishermen's net fishing, but included in the Indian share all fish taken by treaty fishermen on the Puyallup reservation.[222] The case came before the Supreme Court the third time, the Indians claiming that since the state had no authority to regulate Indian fishing on the reservation, fish caught there should not be counted against the Indian share.[223] The Supreme Court disagreed, basing its opinion on the fact that virtually all of the reservation had since been alienated. The Court stated that the language of the treaty which assured the Indians a share of the fishery resource also necessarily assured a share to non-Indian fishermen and that totally unregulated Indian harvest on the reservation could deprive the later of their share.[224] Quoting

---

217 391 U.S. 392 (1968).
218 *Id.* at 398.
219 414 U.S. 44 (1973).
220 *Id.* at 46.
221 *Id.* at 48.
222 Department of Game v. Puyallup Tribe, Inc., 86 Wash. 2d. 664, 548 P.2d 1058 (1976).
223 Puyallup Tribe Inc. v. Dep't of Game of Washington, 433 U.S. 165 (1977).
224 *Id.* at 175-76.

Justice Douglas from *Puyallup II*, the Court stated "The treaty does not give the Indians a federal right to pursue the last living steelhead until it enters their nets."[225]

In 1976, Senior District Judge Bolt, in the Western District of Washington applied the principles set forth by the Supreme Court in *Puyallup III* to his decision in *United States v. Washington*.[226] He declared that:

> every regulation of treaty right must be strictly limited to specific measures which before becoming effective have been established by the state, either to the satisfaction of all affected tribes or...of this court, to be reasonable and necessary to prevent demonstrable harm to the actual conservation of fish.[227]

As well as defining "reasonable and necessary" measures to include those which are "essential to conservation" and limited conservation to "the perpetuation of a particular run or species of fish",[228] he excluded such charges as assuring a maximum sustained harvest and providing for an orderly fishery.[229] Judge Bold also prohibited the state from any regulation whatsoever of the treaty rights to fishing of those tribes determined to be qualified for self regulation according to the criteria set forth in the opinion.[230] Judge Bolt determined that the treaty language "in common with" meant to share equally with, thus holding that Indians must be given the opportunity to take fifty percent of the fish (not counting the number necessary for perpetuation of the run).

Judge Belloni in Oregon modified a decree of five years earlier in *Sohappy v. Smith* to apply the fifty percent allottment the treaty Indians fishing in the Columbia River system.[231]

Judge Bolt's decision was short lived, however because the Supreme Court declared in *Puget Sound Gillneltir's Ass'n v. Moos*,[232] that his interpretation of the treaties was erroneous and that compliance with his ruling would violate the equal protection clause of the fourteenth amendment to the Constitution and exceed the authority of the state agencies under state law.[233] The Federal District Court then entered a series of orders by which it directly undertook the regulation of the fisheries at issue, displacing the state from any authority.[234]

---

225 414 U.S. at 49.
226 384 F. Supp. 312 (W.D. Wash 1974) aff'd, 520 F.2d 676 (9th Cir. 1975), cert. denied, 423 U.S. 1086 (1976).
227 384 F.2d at 342.
228 *Id.* at 342.
229 520 F.2d at 686.
230 Bean, *supra* note 7, at 54.
231 308 F. Supp. 899 (D. Or. 1969) aff'd as modified, 529 F.2d 570 (9th Cir. 1976).
232 88 Wash. 2d 677, 565 P.2d 1151 (1977).
233 *Id.* at 1151.
234 459 F. Supp. 1020 (W.D. Wash. 1978).

# WILDLIFE AND HABITAT

The Supreme Court had a choice between two interpretations of the Indian treaties regarding Indian fishing rights. One would allow the Indians the same opportunity to catch fish "at all usual and accustomed grounds and stations" as non-Indians enjoy. The other choice was to interpret the treaties to allow the Indians a qualified share of the fish available for taking at such places.[235] The Court interpreted the treaty to mean that Indians had a right to take a share of the available fish. As to the amount, the Court reasoned the treaties guaranteed "so much as, but no more than, is necessary to provide the Indians with a livelihood-that is to say, a moderate living."[236] But the amount may never exceed 50 percent of the available fish because the Indians' right to take fish "in common with" non-Indian settlers implied an equal division.[237]

Since the Court's decisions in *Puyallup III* and *Washington State Commercial Fishing Vessel Association* will influence the interpretation of treaties other than the Stevens treaties, the Court refused to review a case in which the Supreme Court of Minnesota upheld the right of the White Earth Indians to fish on their reservation completely free of state regulations.[238] The district court for the western district of Michigan held the state to be without authority to regulate even off reservation gill net fishing in Lake Michigan by Chippewa and Ottawa Indians.[239]

Although congress has the power to modify treaty rights,[240] the courts have generally been unwilling to do so, unless explicitly indicated by Congress.[241] Therefore, in *United States v. Cutler*, the Migratory Bird Treaty Act was held inapplicable to on reservation hunting by Shoshone Indians.[242] However, in at least one instance, the Supreme court has ruled that a tribe possessed no power to regulate the harvest of wildlife within certain portions of its reservations. In *Montana v. United States*,[243] the court held the Crow Tribe did not possess an inherent governmental authority to regulate hunting and fishing of non members of the tribe conducted on non-member fee-owned lands within its reservation. This was so because the tribe had not maintained its traditional authority over wildlife and because the record failed to show that non-member fishing and hunting "imperiled the subsistence or welfare of the Tribe".[244] Case law under the Bald Eagle Protection Act, however, is split as to whether it abrogates existing In-

---

235  Bean, *supra* note 7, at 57.
236  443 U.S. at 686.
237  94 U.S. 391 (1876).
238  State v. Clark, 282 N.W.2d 902 (Minn. 1979), cert. denied, 454 U.S. 904 (1980).
239  United States v. Michigan, 471 F. Supp. 192 (W.D. Mich. 1979), remanded, 623 F.2d 448 (6th Cir. 1980).
240  Lone Wolf v. Hitchcock, 187 U.S. 553, 564-67 (1903).
241  Pigeon River Co. v. Cox, Ltd., 291 U.S. 138, 160 (1934).
242  37 F. Supp. 724 (D. Idaho 1941).
243  450 U.S. 544 (1981)
244  *Id*. at 566.

dian treaty rights.[245] The extent of tribal sovereignty has lone been an intractable question.

Indian nations possess a unique sovereign status within the American polity. They possess all the attributes of nationhood except those which federal law has displaced.[246] Chief Justice Marshall held that the laws of the states have no force within Indian reservations because they are "distinct political communities having territorial boundaries, within which their authority is exclusive". The question of tribal jurisdiction to manage or control wildlife is fundamentally a federal question concerning the extent to which a tribe has been allowed to retain its inherent governmental power, through treaty or otherwise. In general, a tribes sovereign authority to regulate wildlife and Indian activities is limited to the geographical territory within its reservation. [247]

---

[245] Bean, *supra* note 7, at 289.
[246] Worcester v. Georgia, 31 U.S. (6 Pet.) 515, 557 (1832).
[247] New Mexico v. Mescalero Apache Tribe, 462 U.S. 324 (1983) (Mescalero tribe, rather than New Mexico, has authority to regulate hunting and fishing on the reservation); Mescalero Apache Tribe v. Jones, 1411 U.S. 145 (1973) (state laws apply to off-reservation activities of tribal members).

# CHAPTER THREE

## PROTECTION OF THE ENVIRONMENT

## NATIONAL ENVIRONMENTAL POLICY ACT

The first of the major environmental laws was enacted in 1969 and effective January 1, 1970.[1] The National Environmental Policy Act ushered in an era of concern for the nation's environment. Ample evidence could be found that the American society's development had reached a point where not only wildlife was in danger, but the wildlife habitat was destroyed and this phenomenon threatened to kill and reduce many species of animals.

Several attempts by the federal government to address specific issues had occurred in the early part of the 20th century. The Migratory Bird Treaty Act of 1918,[2] the Migratory Bird Conservation Act of 1929[3] which authorized the National Wildlife Refuge System, and the Federal Aid in Wildlife Restoration Program (Pittman-Robertson Program)[4] attempted to afford some protection for wildlife. But it was not until 1970 in the passage of the NEPA that the issue of wildlife and its habitat was made a part of an overall environmental concern.

In passing the NEPA, Congress made clear its purpose by declaring a national policy which would encourage productive and enjoyable harmony between man and his environment. Congress declared its purpose as follows:

> The Congress, recognizing the profound impact of man's activity on the interrelations of all components of the natural environment, particularly the profound influences of population growth, high density urbanization, industrial expansion, resource exploitation, and new expanding technological advances in recognizing further the critical importance of restoring and maintaining environmental quality to the overall welfare and development of man, declares that it is the continuing policy of the federal government, in cooperation with state and local governments, and other concerned public and private organizations, to use all practical means and measures, including financial and technical assistance, in a manner calculated to foster and promote the general welfare, to create and maintain conditions under which man and nature can exist in productive harmony, and fulfill the

1    42 U.S.C.A. § 4321 et seq.
2    16 U.S.C.A. § 710 et seq.
3    16 U.S.C.A. § 715 et seq.
4    16 U.S.C.A. § 669 et seq.

41

social, economic, and other requirements of present and future generations of Americans.[5]

In order to carry out the policy established by the NEPA, Congress declared that it was the continued responsibility of the federal government to improve and coordinate federal plans, functions, programs, and other resources so that the nation could (1) fulfill the responsibilities of each generation as trustee of the environment for succeeding generations; (2) ensure for all Americans safe, healthful, productive aesthetically and culturally pleasing surroundings; (3) obtain the widest range of beneficial uses of the environment without degradation, risks to health and safety, or other undesirable or unintended consequences; (4) preserve important historic, cultural, and natural aspects of our national heritage and maintain whenever possible, an environment which supports diversity and variety of individual choice; (5) achieve a balance between population and resource use which will permit high standards of living and a wide sharing of life's amenities; and (6) enhance the quality of renewable resources and approach the maximum attainable recycling of depletable resources.[6]

Under NEPA, Congress directs that public laws and regulations require all federal agencies to include in every recommendation a report on the proposes for the legislation and any other major federal action significantly affecting the quality of the human environment. This detailed statement must set forth (1) the environmental impact of the proposed action; (2) any adverse environmental effects which cannot be avoided should the proposal be implemented; (3) alternatives to the proposed action; (4) a relationship between local short-term uses of man's environment and the maintenance and enhancement of long-term productivity; and (5) any irreversible and irretrievable commitments of resources which would be involved in the proposed action should it be implemented.[7]

The fundamental concept underlying this recognized federal responsibility is one involving a systematic and interdisciplinary approach which would assure an integrated use of the natural and social sciences in planning and decision making. Prior to the making of any environmental impact statement, each federal official is to consult and obtain the comments of any federal agency which would have any jurisdiction by law or have any special expertise with respect to any environmental impact. Not only is a responsible federal official required to consult with federal agencies but such official is also required to solicit the comments and views of appropriate state and local agencies and members

5   16 U.S.C.A. § 4331.
6   16 U.S.C.A. § 4331(b).
7   16 U.S.C.A. § 4332(c).

of the general public who might have some interest in the protection of the environment.[8]

Section 2 of NEPA is responsible for the creation of the COUNCIL ON ENVIRONMENTAL QUALITY (referred to as CEQ). The council is composed of three members appointed by the President to serve at his pleasure by and with the consent of the Senate. The members of the council are to be appointed based on training, experience and qualifications to analyze and interpret environmental information of all kinds. One of the members is to be appointed as the chairman of the council.[9]

The functions and the duties of the council are (1) to assist and advise the President in preparation of the Environmental Quality Report (required to be transmitted to Congress by the President on July 1 of each year); (2) to gather timely and authoritative information concerning the conditions and trends in the quality of the environment both current and prospective, to analyze and interpret such information for the purposes of determining whether such conditions and trends are interfering or likely to interfere with achievement of the policy set forth underneath; (3) to review and appraise the various programs and activities of the federal government in the light of the NEPA policy; (4) to develop and recommend to the President national policies to foster and promote the improvement of the environmental quality and meet the conservation, social, economic, health and other requirements and goals of the nation; (5) to conduct investigations, studies, surveys, research, and analyses relating to ecological systems and environmental quality; (6) to document and define changes in the natural environment, including the plant and animal systems and to accumulate necessary data and other information for a continuing analysis of these changes or trends and an interpretation of their underlying causes; (7) report at least once each year to the President on the state and condition of the environment; and (8) to make and furnish such studies, reports thereon, and recommendations with respect to matters of policy and legislation the President may request.[10]

As previously mentioned the President under Section 2 of NEPA is required to report to Congress annually on July 1 of each year the status and condition of the major natural, man-made, or altered environmental classes of the nation including air, water, marine, estuarine, and fresh water and terrestrial environmental matters including forests, dry land, wetland, range, urban, suburban, and rural environment.[11]

NEPA in establishing the CEQ also places upon it the responsibility to consult with citizen's advisory committees on environmental quality

8    16 U.S.C.A. § 4332(c).
9    16 U.S.C.A. § 4342.
10   16 U.S.C.A. § 4344.
11   16 U.S.C.A. § 4341.

(established by Executive Order 11472, 1969), and with other groups such as science, industry, agriculture, labor, conservation organizations, and state and local governments.[12]

A provision of Section 2 of NEPA established that the CEQ is to serve fulltime.[13] The CEQ also is authorized to accept reimbursements from any private, non-profit organizations, and to make expenditures in support of its international activities.[14]

As part of the overall plan to afford the nation environment federal protection, President Nixon submitted to Congress Reorganization Plan No. 3 of 1970 which established the Environmental Protection Agency. The head of the agency referred to as the administrator was to be appointed by the President by and with the advice of the Senate.[15]

The accompanying letter to Congress stated that it was the intent of the President in recommending to Congress Reorganization Plan No. 3 "to promote the better execution of the laws, the more effective management of the executive branch and its agencies and functions, and the expeditious administration of the public business, and to increase the efficiency of the operations of the government to the fullest extent practicable."[16]

In effect the Reorganizational Plan transferred to the Environmental Protection Agency the functions of many other agencies previously charged with separate responsibilities. The Reorganization Plan resulted in the pulling together into one agency a variety of research, monitoring, standard setting, and enforcement activities which had heretofore been scattered throughout several departments and agencies. Included in the transfer to the EPA of the functions of various other agencies were matters relating to water quality, pesticides, air pollution, solid waste, radiation, and various agricultural activities.

In establishing the EPA, President Nixon stated that the principal roles and functions of the organization would include (1) the establishment and enforcement of environmental protection standards consistent with national environmental goals; (2) the conduct of research on the adverse effects of pollution and on methods and equipment for controlling it, the gathering of information on pollution, and the use of this information strengthening environmental protection programs and recommending policy changes; (3) assisting others through grants, technical assistance and other means in arresting pollution in the environment; and (4) assisting the Council on environmental quality

---

12  16 U.S.C.A. § 4345.
13  16 U.S.C.A. § 4346.
14  16 U.S.C.A. § 4346(a).
15  84 S.T.A.T. § 2086.
16  Message of the President to the Congress of the U.S., July 9, 1970, Richard Nixon.

and developing and recommending to the President new policies for the protection of the environment.[17]

The essential characteristic of the establishment of NEPA, and more importantly, the implementation of an overall environmental approach, is the Environmental Impact Statement process. The Council on Environmental Quality issued guidelines for the implementation of the Environmental Impact Statement process. The original guidelines issued shortly after CEQ was formed were in effect for a number of years, but it became obvious that the process needed some streamlining. In order to accomplish this purpose, CEQ was directed by Executive Order 11991 to issue binding regulations to federal agencies. The avowed purpose of this change was to "make the Environmental Impact Statement process more useful to decision makers and the public, and to reduce paperwork and the accumulation of extraneous background data in order to emphasize the need to focus on real environmental issues and alternatives." CEQ was required to develop these regulations after consultation with federal agencies and conducting public hearings in order to receive input from interested parties. It was certainly intended that the regulations issued by CEQ would require impact statements to be concise, clear, and to the point and to support by evidence that agencies have made the necessary environmental allowances.

## PURPOSE, POLICY, MANDATE AND PLANNING

The NEPA, the basic national charter for protection of the environment, establishes policies and sets goals to make certain that federal agencies act according to the spirit of the act. Section 102(2) contains provisions to make sure that all federal agencies act according to the letter of the act. The Council on Environmental Quality has promulgated regulations to implement the fundamental purpose in the NEPA. The purpose of the regulations is to tell federal agencies what they must do to comply with the goals of the Act.

It is obvious that the intention of the congressional act was not a mandate to pursue environmental policies to the exclusion of all others, but is rather a congressional reordering of priorities so that environmental costs and benefits will assume their proper place along with other considerations. This means, of course, that the federal agency need not in selecting a course of action elevate environmental concerns over other appropriate considerations.

NEPA does not by its express wording preclude federal actions that have adverse environmental impacts nor does it attempt to quantify severity of adverse environmental impacts that may be imposed by governmental action. The specific procedural requirements of NEPA

---

17    *Id.*

assume only that those government officials who must make final decisions on federal actions, before making such decisions, take a good faith, hard, objective look at adverse environmental impacts and consequences of such action to determine whether to proceed and whether the action will be consistent with the national policy expressed in the Act.

The underlying purpose of requiring any federal agency to prepare an Environmental Impact Statement is to force federal agencies proposing actions to provide a detailed statement of any impacts so that the decision maker will have sufficient information to decide whether to proceed on the project in light of the potential environmental consequences. In accomplishing this purpose, NEPA also serves as an environmental full disclosure law by furnishing the public with relevant environmental information. Also, NEPA serves the function of enabling those who did not have a part in the compilation of the EIS to understand and consider the factors involved and to force compliance with the Act in those cases where the agency is in violation.

In the case *In Action for Rationale Transmit v. Westside Hwy. Project by Birdwell*,[18] the court held that the purposes underlying the National Environmental Policy Act are to provide the public with full and active information about any significant environmental impact and to insure that the decision maker gives due considerations to such impact. It has been held that this mandate does not intend to require the pursuit of environmental policies to the exclusions of all others but rather it is a balancing between environmental costs and economical and technical benefits.

The basis thrust of the act is to provide assistance for evaluating the proposals for prospective federal actions in the light of their future effect upon environmental factors and not to serve as a basis for after the fact critical evaluation subsequent to substantial completion of any construction.[19]

Of course the crux of the matter is that NEPA procedures must ensure that environmental information is available to public official and others before decisions are made and actions taken. These procedures must utilize techniques and develop information that is of high quality. Accurate, scientific analysis and concentration on important issues are essential in order that appropriate decisions which are relevant to the environment can be made.

---

18  536 F. Supp. 1225. See also Sierra Club v. Block, 614 F. Supp. 134; Natural Resources Defence
    Council, Inc. v. Nuclear Regulatory Commission, 685 F. 2d 459.
19  Richard Park Homeowners Ass'n., Inc. v. Pierce, 671 F.2d 935.

# PROTECTION OF THE ENVIRONMENT

While process is important, of course the ultimate objective is to foster excellent decision making so that environmental consequences of any federal action can be appraised and measured against any impairment to the environment.

The Council on Environmental Quality has stated in its regulations that the policy underlying the regulations is intended to make the NEPA process more useful to decision makers, to reduce paperwork and the accumulation of extraneous background data, and to emphasize real environmental issues and alternatives.[20] The CEQ Policy also emphasizes that it is the intention of the procedural regulations to integrate the NEPA process with other planning in environmental review procedures, encourage and facilitate public involvement in decisions that effect the quality of the human environment, to ensure that the NEPA process is used to identify and assess reasonable alternatives to proposed actions, and to use all practical means to restore and enhance the quality of the human environment and to avoid and minimize any possible adverse effects of actions upon the quality of the human environment.[21]

It is important to note that these regulations promulgated by the Council on Environmental Quality are not discretionary with federal agencies, but are binding and mandated under a specific section of the regulations.[22]

The regulations promulgated by the CEQ are intended to simplify the process by which federal agencies analyze the impact on the environment of any proposed action, and also reduce the amount of paperwork that ordinarily accompanies federal reporting processes. As an example the regulations require all federal agencies in putting together their impact statements to prepare analytic rather than encyclopedic environmental impact statements, discuss insignificant issues only briefly, write the statements in plain English, and use various other techniques to make the statements clear and concise. In addition to reducing paperwork the regulations are intended to also reduce delay. According to the regulations this reduction of delay is to be accomplished by integrating the NEPA process into early planning and establishing appropriate time limits for the environmental impact statement process.

For time to time the CEQ deletes, amends, or adds to the regulations encumbered upon federal agencies in the implementation of NEPA. A good example of a change in the CEQ regulations is the matter of "worst case analysis".

---

20    40 C.F.R. § 1500 40 C.F.R. § 1500.2(a)(b).
21    40 C.F.R. § 1500.2 (e).
22    40 C.F.R. § 1500.3. See also The Steamboaters v. F.E.R.C., 759 F.2d 1382, National Audubon
      Society v. Hester, 627 F. Supp. 1419.

# WILDLIFE AND HABITAT

The Council in promulgating its regulations realized that in some situations an agency in evaluating reasonably foreseeable significant adverse effects on the human environment on the proposal would be faced with a situation in which there is incomplete or unavailable information. The question then became what to do in such situations and the CEQ responded by requiring agencies to apply a "worst case analysis". This regulation required the agency to speculate on the worst possible case that could happen and indicate some degree of probability or improbability of its occurrence. In 1986, however, the CEQ replaced the worst case requirement with a new requirement that federal agencies in the face of unavailable information concerning a reasonably foreseeable significant environmental consequence prepare a "summary of existing credible, scientific evidence which is relevant to evaluating the adverse impacts and prepare an evaluation of such impact based upon theoretical approaches or research methods generally accepted in the scientific community."[23] The change in the regulations therefore replaces a conjectural (worst case analysis) with a consideration of various evaluations of scientific opinions.

The CEQ brought about this change because of much criticism on the part of those reviewing the NEPA process.

Under the CEQ Regulations, the federal agency planning process is given specific guidelines as to how to incorporate the NEPA process into its planning. In addition to integrating the NEAPA process into the federal agency's early planning process, the regulations require a federal agency to utilize a systematic interdisciplinary approach, to study, develop and describe appropriate alternatives to any recommended courses of action, and to consult with appropriate state and local agencies of Indian tribes and with any other interested parties and organizations which might conceivably have input which would be valuable in the environmental process.[24]

The NEPA planning process begins after the consideration by a federal agency of some proposed action with a determination by the agency involved as to whether or not to prepare an environmental impact statement. In making such a determination federal agencies are required under the regulations to prepare an environmental assessment provided that the agency has not already decided to prepare an environmental impact statement.[25]

An environmental assessment is described in the regulations as a public document for which a federal agency is responsible that serves to (1) briefly provide sufficient evidence and analysis for determining

23  40 C.F.R. § 1502.22(b).
24  40 C.F.R. § 1501.1.
25  40 C.F.R. § 1501.3.

whether to prepare an environmental impact statement or a finding of most significant impact, (2) aid in agency's compliance with the Act when no environmental impact statement is necessary, (3) facilitate preparation of a statement when one is necessary.[26]

In practical terms the environmental assessment is evidence of a decision making process in which the federal agency has brief discussions on the need for the proposal or in the alternative the absence of any environmental impact and a listing of any agencies and persons consulted in making the decision.

An interesting question is how long will an E.A. last before either a new one must be issued or before an EIS is required. In *Pilchuck Audubon Society v. MacWilliams*,[27] the court held that an E.A. eight years old was subject to challenge in judicial review. The CEQ stated that E.A.'s more than five years old for implemented projects should be carefully reexamined to determine if a supplement is needed. In this case the U.S. Forest Service prepared an environmental assessment in 1979 which resulted in a finding of no sufficient impact and therefore negated the preparation of an E.I.S. The property involved was 166 acres on Olo Mountain in the Mount Baker-Snoqualmie National Forest, Washington. The track was to be logged by a particular company but that company ran into some economic problems and never finished the project. The Forest Service advertised for a successor to the contract previously let and it was awarded to another company. The second award was eight years after the first award and the Philchuck Aububon Society challenged the Forest Service because changed circumstances would require a new environmental review. The plaintiffs sought to halt a preliminary injunction in halting further logging activity on the Olo.

The basis for the challenge to the eight year old environmental assessment was that information developed since 1979 demonstrated the deleterious effect logging of old grown timber would have on the water quality in the fish habitat of Canyon Creek and on the habitat in the area for the Northern Spotted Owl. Plaintiff in its suit offered expert testimony to demonstrate that evidence not available in 1979 but presently available raised serious questions concerning the environmental impact of logging in the area.

The court agreed with plaintiffs and granted the injunction stating that the plaintiff had proven its case and that the U. S. Forest Service was enjoined, along with the new owner of the logging rights in the area, from carrying out any logging activities, until a new environmental assessment was issued.

---

26   40 C.F.R. § 1508.9.
27   No. C87-1707 R (W.D. Wash. Jan. 15, 1988).

# WILDLIFE AND HABITAT

In *Association Concerned About Tomorrow, Inc. v. Doyle*[28] it was held that the mere passage of time is insufficient to require the preparation of a supplemental EIS. The case also stated that a mere change in the quantity of land for a project does not by itself necessitate the preparation of a supplemental EIS.

In determining whether or not to prepare an environmental impact statement each federal agency is required under the regulations to decide whether the proposal under consideration is normally one which requires an environmental impact statement or is one which does not even require an environmental assessment.[29] If the decision is to prepare an environmental impact statement then of course the procedures required under the Council of Environmental Quality Regulations supplemented by the procedures established by the federal agency must be followed. If on the other hand the decision is made by the agency to not prepare an environmental impact statement then the agency must prepare a finding of no significant impact (F.O.N.S.I). The FONSI must be made public in sufficient time in order for any public review to express opinion contrary to the intention on the part of the federal agency not to make an environmental impact statement. Usually the F.O.N.S.I. must be made public thirty days prior to the final determination by the agency not to make an environmental impact statement.[30]

An interesting example of the process used by a federal agency to determine whether or not an Environmental Impact Statement needs to be issued is provided by the case *Cabinet Mountain's Wilderness v. Peterson*.[31] In that case the Sierra Club Legal Defense Fund, Inc. challenged a decision by the United States Forest Service approving a mineral exploration program by a private company, ASARCO, in the Cabinet Mountain's Wilderness area of northwest Montana. The Sierra Club based its challenge on an alleged violation of the Endangered Species Act as well as a violation of NEPA. The Endangered Species Act challenge, by the Sierra Club, was an allegation that the exploratory drilling would endanger a small isolated population of approximately a dozen grizzly bears, which is listed as a threatened species. The Sierra Club challenge was that NEPA required the Forest Service to prepare an Environmental Impact Statement before approving such a project.

---

28  610 F.Supp 1101.(1985)
29  40 C.F.R. § 1501.4(a)(1 & 2). An Environmental Impact statement must be prepared when substantial questions are raised as to whether or not a project may cause significant degradation of the enviroment. In making the threshold determination a federal agency has an affirmative duty to prepare a reviewable administrative record (see Citizen's Advocate for Responsible Expansion Inc. v. Doyle, 770 F.2d 423.
30  The process requires a consideration and discussion of all significant environmental effects, not merely adverse ones. The Environmental Defense Fund v. Marsh, 651 F.2d 983. (1983).
31  510 F.Supp 1186 (1981).

# PROTECTION OF THE ENVIRONMENT

Essentially, the Sierra Club wanted the court to engage in essentially a review of the agency action by assessing for itself whether there had been substantial compliance with the Act. The threshold question which the court had to discuss was whether or not the court should engage in agency environmental determinations or rather should the court use some other standard for assessing whether or not the agency action was in compliance with the various environmental acts.

The Court held that the arbitrary and capricious standard is appropriate when reviewing agency compliance with NEPA.[32] The Court after reviewing the NEPA process engaged in by the Forest Service concluded that the process engaged in by the Forest Service was not arbitrary and capricious.

The Forest Service in arriving at its decision that the exploration would have no environmental impact sought input from individuals and groups interested in the area, received comments from well over 100 parties, and held several public meetings. The specific drilling program proposed for the year 1980 was to drill 36 holes on 22 sites. The Forest Service prepared an environmental assessment in which input was had from the Fish and Wildlife Service of the Department of the Interior and many others. Included in the environmental assessment was a Biological Opinion from the FWS which contained a variety of mitigation suggestions to reduce any negative environmental impacts of the project. These suggestions as well as suggestions from others were incorporated into the final environmental assessment released by the Forest Service. Based on the environmental assessment the Forest Service issued a FONSI.

The court concluded that judges are not equipped to perform the task of making environmental decisions based on scientific data. It was clear to the Court that the Forest Service and the other participating agencies did take their responsibilities seriously and the resulting decision was accepted as amply supported by the record.

In another case, *Thomas v. Peterson*,[33] the Court applied what it called a "more searching standard of reasonableness." This Ninth Circuit holding stated that "an agency's determination that an E.I.S. need not be prepared will be upheld unless unreasonable." The Court concluded that the Forest Service had taken the requisite "hard look" at the environmental consequences of building the road, the court would not attempt to second guess the wisdom of the selected alternative.

---

32  5 U.S.C.A. § 706(2)(a).
33  589 F.Supp. 1139 (1984).

# WILDLIFE AND HABITAT

The Forest Service in connection with its decision intended to build a road, "Jersey Jack Road", in the Nezperce National Forest. The proposed road was to be a single lane gravel road located approximately 50 miles southeast of Grangeville, Idaho in the Red River Ranger District of the Nezperce National Forest. The Forest Service decided that the environmental assessment demonstrated that the impact on the environment was not significant and therefore the agency issued a FONSI.

In putting together the environmental assessment the Forest Service reasonably gathered and analyzed data relating to the effects of road construction in that portion of the Nezperce National Forest and from that data reasonably concluded that the road would not significantly affect the quality of the human environment. Plaintiffs, argued that the Forest Service omitted pertinent factors from the environmental assessment and that the environmental assessment understated the significance of several factors. One of the factors addressed by the plaintiffs was the failure of the Forest Service to include in its discussions a quarry and short haul road necessary to supply rock for the building of the major proposed road. In short, the plaintiff's attack on the environmental assessment concentrated on the scope, maintaining that the action contemplated by the Forest Service needed to be much broader than a mere decision to construct a forest road.

The crux of the plaintiff's challenge was that the Forest Service analyzed the environmental impact of the road and not the use of the road in later years. The Forest Service's environmental assessment did not contain an estimate of the amount of timber which would be harvested in future years. The Court agreed with the Forest Service stating that taking into account the future timber harvest in the area surrounding the proposed road, would require needless speculation in potentially duplicated effort. Timber sales plans would be reserved for the future and that at some future time when timber sales and timber harvest were contemplated the Forest Service would need to make a supplemental or additional environmental assessment or perhaps an Environmental Impact Statement.

The Court concluded that the Forest Service decision to build the road without first preparing an Environmental Impact Statement did not violate NEPA nor was the FONSI unreasonable in light of the environmental assessment scope or conclusions.

In the case *Save the Yak Committee v. Block*[34] the Courts arrived at a different decision as to the necessity for an EIS. In this case the Forest Service began reconstructing the Yak River Road in five separate sections. The road extends approximately 70 miles from U.S. Highway 2, west of

---

[34]    No. 86-3808 (9th Cir., March 1, 1988).

Libby, Montana to its junction with Montana Highway 37 & U.S. Highway 93, near Eureka, Montana.  The road winds through the Yak and Eureka range districts of The Kootenai National Forest located in Lincoln County, Montana. Environmental assessments were prepared for four of the five sections, but not on the fifth section called the Porcupine Sullivan Creek section of the road. An EA prepared for the Porcupine Sullivan Creek section some two years after the Forest Service decided to reconstruct the road.  No comprehensive EIS was ever prepared for the construction of the entire road.  In addition a Biological Assessment was never completed[35] prior to construction of any one of the road sections.

The plaintiffs challenged the eventually appearing EA for the Porcupine Sullivan Creek section of the road because the EA failed to analyze the project's impact on the environment. The Forest Service readily admitted that the Porcupine Sullivan EA was not prepared to examine the environmental impacts but rather to evaluate various techniques of maintaining the road. The environmental assessment's entire discussion of wildlife was comprised of five brief sentences and the only sentence that dealt with endangered species stated that "all alternatives proposed will temporarily displace wildlife particularly big game during construction activities."

The Forest Service, conceding that the was inadequate, countered that a biological assessment prepared under the Endangered Species Act cured the deficiency in the. The Court on this issue held that a biological assessment does not necessarily substitute entirely for an environmental assessment. The Court pointed out that the difference is that a Biological Assessment analyses the impact of a proposed action upon the endangered species while an EA analyses the impact of the proposed action on all facets of the environment. The court further held that even considering the EA and the BA together, the environmental analysis still had gaps. As an example the Court points to the fact that the biological assessment considered the effects of the project on endangered and threatened species, however, neither it nor the reviewed the potential impacts of the project on other wildlife.

In determining the inadequacies of the eventual EA the Court also pointed to two other factors that were not discussed in the E.A., connected actions and cumulative impacts. Connected actions are defined as those that are closely related and therefore should be discussed in the same impact statement. In this case the use of the road for logging operations and the construction of the road were connected actions.

---

35   A Biological assessment refers to information prepared by or under the direction of a Federal agency concerning listed and proposed species any designated and proposed critical habitat that may be present in the  action area and the evalation of potential effects of the action on such species and habitat -- 50 C.F.R. § 402, 02.

# WILDLIFE AND HABITAT

The Forest Service's EA did not analyze and discuss potential logging operations.

Cumulative actions are those which when viewed with other proposed actions have cumulative significant impacts. The Court held that the EA did not evaluate the environmental impacts of either the reconstruction or the ongoing and future accelerated timber harvest connected with the road.

The Court found the Forest Service in violation of NEPA and issued an injunction prohibiting the further reconstruction and any timber sales connected with the road.

Another case illustrating the agency's decision not to issue an EIS is the case *Connor v. Burford*.[36] The case involves both the United States Forest Service and the Bureau of Land Management and their decision to not issue an EIS for oil and gas exploration by two applicant companies.

The Flathead National Forest in northwestern Montana is a vast track of rugged mountain wilderness. It has many lakes and rivers and its ecosystem is a sustaining habitat for the bald eagle, the peregrine falcon, the grey wolf and the grizzly bear. The Galletin National Forest in south central Montana provides a diversity of natural resources with its rugged mountains, valleys and rivers supporting many wildlife populations including big game and the grizzly bear.

Both of these forests are located in a geological zone known as the Overthrust Belt, a formation running north/south from Canada to New Mexico and thought to be a rich source of petroleum deposits. Because of the potential for oil and gas exploitations, the explorations in this area have triggered an avalanche of applications to the Bureau of Land Management for oil and gas leases.

In February and March of 1981 the U.S. Forest Service issued EAs recommending that a total of 1,300,000 acres in these forests be leased for oil and gas development. Based on these environmental assessments the Forest Service also issued decision notices and findings of no significant impact (FONSI). Following the preparation of the EAs and the FONSI's, the Bureau of Land Management sold over 700 leases for oil and gas exploration, development and production on the 1,350,000 acres within the two forests. The leases fell under two basic categories, one labeled "No surface occupancy" (NSO) and the other "Surface occupancy leases" (Non-NSO).

The basis upon which the Forest Service and the Bureau of Land Management decided not to issue an EIS was that the mere sale of oil and

---

36    No. 85 - 3929 (9th Cir., January 13, 1988).

gas leases in the forest would have no significant impact on the human environment. The court after a review and an analysis of the EAs and the general situation disagreed with the U.S. Forest Service and the Bureau of Land Management.

The Court concluded that while the "no surface occupancy lease" is not an irreversible or an irretrievable commitment of resources that could have a significant impact on the environment since these leases prohibit disturbance of the surface without specific governmental approval, the "surface occupancy leases" fall into a different category. Therefore, the court decided that the no surface occupancy leases did not require an EIS, but that the surface occupancy lease did in fact require one.

The Court reasoned that the surface occupancy leases did not reserve to the government the absolute right to control all surface activity. This wasbased in part upon another case, *Sierra Club v. Peterson*,[37] which held that the government, for such leases, is limited in its control over post-leasing activities to reasonable regulations which are consistent with oil and gas development and production. The Court concluded that these leases therefore constitute a "point of commitment" after which the government no longer has the ability to prohibit potentially significant inroads on the environment.

In many proposed federal actions there are several agencies involved. The term "federal agency" means all agencies of the federal government, excluding however, Congress, the Judiciary, the President, and the President's staff.[38]

The agency preparing or taking primary responsibility for preparing the EIS is called the "lead agency."[39] A federal agency involved in the proposal other than the federal agency entitled the lead agency,is referred to as a "cooperating agency".[40]

As stated previously, the lead agency has responsibility to supervise the preparation of an EIS.[41] In rare cases where it is impossible to determine which agency is the lead agency the regulations provide for the federal agencies involved to file a request with the CEQ asking it to determine which federal agency shall in fact be the lead agency. The Council has a responsibility to determine very quickly which federal agency shall be the lead agency, the other federal agencies therefore are being designated as cooperating agencies.[42]

---

37   717 F.2d 1409 (1983).
38   40 C.F.R. § 1508.12.
39   40 C.F.R. § 1508.16.
40   40 C.F.R. § 1508.5.
41   40 C.F.R. § 1501.5.
42   40 C.F.R. § 1501.5(e.)

An important concept in the early planning requirements of federal agencies is the process entitled "Scoping." Scoping is defined as the open process for determining the scope of issues to be addressed and for identifying the significant issues related to a proposed action." The scoping process involves the responsibility of the lead agency to invite the participation of any affected federal, state and local agencies in the planning process. After inviting such participation, the lead agency then is required to make determinations as to the scope and the significant issues to be analyzed, to identify and eliminate non-significant issues and to generally allocate assignments for preparation of the EIS among the lead and cooperating agencies. In meeting its responsibilities the lead agency generally holds scoping meetings which are generally integrated with other planning meetings that the agency schedules.[43]

Although the Council has decided that it will not set time limits on the planning process or for that matter the entire NEPA process, nevertheless, the Council has encouraged federal agencies to set time limits appropriate to the quick and efficient implementation of the entire NEPA process.[44]

In addition to the specific procedures provided for by the CEQ Regulations, each federal agency is required to adopt procedures to supplement the Council's regulations. These agency procedures and regulations are not supposed to paraphrase the regulations established by the Council but rather must confine themselves to procedures which implement of the Council's regulations. Each agency is required to consult with the Council while developing its procedures and when finally put together the federal agency must publish the procedures in the federal register for comment under the process involved for the notification to the public. Generally speaking the procedures and regulations established by CEQ fol all federal agencies must be compatible with those established by the for all federal agencies. There is some limited leeway given to federal agencies in proposing their procedural regulations particularly in those situations where time periods may have to differ from those provided under the Council's regulations especially in those situations where particular statutory requirements are imposed.[45]

## THE ENVIRONMENTAL IMPACT STATEMENT

The underlying purpose of requiring any federal agency to prepare an EIS is to force federal agencies when proposing actions, to provide a detailed statement of any impacts so that the decision maker will have

---

[43]   40 C.F.R. § 1501.7.
[44]   40 C.F.R. § 1501.8.
[45]   40 C.F.R. § 1507.3.

sufficient information to decide whether to proceed on the project in light of the potential environmental consequences. In accomplishing this purpose NEPA also serves as an environmental full disclosure law by furnishing the public with relevant environmental information. Also NEPA serves the function of enabling those who do not have a part in the compilation of the EIS to understand and consider the factors involved and to force compliance with the act in those cases where the agency is in violation.

The regulations promulgated by the CEQ make it crystal clear that the EIS is more than just a document. The regulations provide that "the primary purpose of an environmental impact statement is to serve as an action-forcing device to ensure that the policies and goals defined in the Act (NEPA) are infused into the ongoing programs and actions of the federal government. The regulations ALS provides for full and fair discussion of significant environmental impacts, and inform decision makers and the public of the reasonable alternatives which would avoid or minimize adverse impacts or enhance the quality of the human environment. Agencies are instructed to focus on significant environmental issues and alternatives and to reduce paperwork and the accumulation of extraneous background data. Statements shall be concise, clear, and to the point, and shall be supported by evidence that the agency has made the necessary environmental analyses. An EIS is more than a disclosure document. It shall be used by federal officials in conjunction with other relative material to plan actions and make decisions".[46]

Implicit in this statement of purpose are several important concepts that are intended to underlie all government actions. It is clear that the EIS is not to be used to justify decisions that agencies have already made. Rather, the statements are to be used as means of assessing the environmental impact. Of equal importance is the concept that agencies are not to commit resources in any proposed action before making a final decision based on the full environmental impact statement process. In short, environmental impact statements are fully disclosed plans made prior to the commitment of resources, promulgated so that others may analyze the impact on the environment of the proposed agency action before the action is taken.[47]

---

46  40 C.F.R. § 1502.1. It has been held that an Environmental Impact Statement is in compliance with NEPA when its form, contents and preparation substantially provide decision makers with an enviromental disclosure sufficiently detailed to aid in the substantive decision whether or not to proceed with the project in light of its environmental impact and encourage public participation in the development of that information. Generally, the adequacy of the contents of an Environmental Impact Statement is determined by a "rule of reason" which requires only a reasonably thorough discussion of the significant aspects of the probable environmental consequences. See State of California by and Through Brown v. Watt, 520 F.Supp. 1359.
47  40 C.F.R. § 1502.2.

# WILDLIFE AND HABITAT

As to what kinds of activities conducted by or proposed by federal agencies need to have as part of the planning process the construction and promulgation of an environmental impact statement, the regulations are clear. First of all on EIS's are required for any proposal which is described as a agency goal which is actively under preparation preparatory to making a decision on one or more alternative means of accomplishing that goal.[48] Secondly, EIS's arerequired for any bill or legislative proposal developed by or with the significant cooperation and support of the federal agency which are sent to Congress. There are several tests for determining whether or not the proposal is in fact that which was predominately proposed by the agency rather than another source. The first test includes whether or not the agency was the primary moving body for the proposal. If the agency merely cooperated with Congress or a committee of Congress or was not instrumental in instigating the proposal in the first place, then the legislation would not be that of the agency but rather of some other source. The second test involves the process of drafting. Just because a federal agency drafts a piece of legislation does not necessarily mean that that agency has significantly cooperated in the piece of legislation.[49]

Finally and probably most importantly is the concept of major federal action. It is the intention of the N.E.P.A. process that any major federal action requires the preparation of an EIS. As a general rule a major federal action is one which is potentially subject to federal control and responsibility and is "significant". The phrase", major federal action", and the word, "significant", in combination mean that a proposed federal action must undergo the NEPA process if it affects society as a whole, and, the impact on society is severe.[50]

Timing is an important concept in the NEPA process. A federal agency is required to commence the preparation of an EIS as close as possible to the time the agency is developing or is presenting a proposal. Ideally, the EIS should be included in any recommendation or report on the proposal.[51]

The undertaking of a project by a federal agency may be triggered in one of two ways; either by the agency's own direct action or by proposals from an agency other than the federal agency which is to undertake the action. For all projects directly undertaken by the federal agency itself, the EIS process should begin at the feasibility analysis stage (go-no-go) and may be supplemented at a later stage if necessary. For applications to the agency from others appropriate environmental

---

48   40 C.F.R. § 1508.23.
49   40 C.F.R. § 1508.17.
50   40 C.F.R. § 1508.18.
51   40 C.F.R. § 1502.5.

assessements or statements should be commenced no later than immediately after the application is received.

In any event the final EIS should normally precede the final staff recommendation and that portion of the NEPA process involving a public hearing.

In order to insure that environmental impact statement are clear, and readable the regulations provide that normally the final EIS should not exceed 150 pages with an exception built in for those proposals of unusual scope or complexity, in which case the length of that EIS should not be more than 300 pages.[52]

Another requirement by the regulations to increase the readability of any EIS is the direction that all EIS's should be written in plain language. In order to increase this probability agencies are encouraged to employ writers or editors to write and review all data and material that are to be included in the final report. It is encouraged by the Council that appropriate graphics be used so that the decision makers and the public can readily understand the point being stated.[53]

Except for proposals for legislation, EIS's are to be prepared in two stages and may be supplemented. Stage One is entitled "The Draft Environmental Impact Statement" (DEIS). The draft statement is supposed to fulfill and satisfy all the requirements for a final statement except that it is prepared and promulgated before appropriate comments are received from others. In other words, the agency issuing the draft (DEIS) must make a concerted effort to disclose and discuss all major points of view on the environmental impacts and on the alternatives included in the proposed action.[54]

The final EIS is to be issued after the agency responsible for the issuance of the statement has received comments from various other organizations which either must or elect to make comments on the proposal.[55]

After the final EIS has been issued, agencies are encouraged to prepare supplements to the final EIS if the agency makes substantial changes in the proposed action, there are significant new circumstances or information relative to environmental concerns and bearing on the proposed

---

[52] 40 C.F.R. § 1502.7. The Courts have held that there are no pre-ordained number of pages, studies experts or criteria which must be included or satisfied in an Environmental Impact Statement, rather the adequacy so determined by a rule of reason. See Olmsted Citizens for a Better Community v. U.S. 606 F.Supp. 1964.

[53] 40 C.F.R. § 1502.8. In Oregon Environmental Council v. Kuntzman (817 F.2d 484) the Court held that an 8th to an 11th grade reading level was sufficient to communicate to intended readers the risk associated with intended action.

[54] 40 C.F.R. § 1502.9(a).

[55] 40 C.F.R. § 1502.9(b).

action, or in any other circumstance where the agency feels that the purposes underlying the NEPA will be furthered by the issuance of the supplemental EIS. It is mandated that any supplemental EIS be circulated in the same fashion as the draft or the final EIS.[56]

In another case involving the concept of a supplemental EIS, *State of California v. Lock,*[57] the court held that the National Forest Service violated NEPA by not circulating, for public comment, a supplemental draft EIS describing a proposed action where the proposed action was a radical departure from the alternatives considered in the draft EIS. Plaintiff in the case, the State of California, filed a suit challenging the Naional Forest Service decision to designate forty-seven areas in California as non-wilderness areas. The case stems from an action by the National Forest Service, which had the responsibility of managing 190 million acres of forest and which intended to promulgate a plan to manage 62 million acres of this. Beginning in 1972 and following in 1977 the Naional Forest Service attempted to evaluate programmatically the wilderness areas in the National Forest system. In a draft EIS, the National Forest Service applied this proposal to all roadless areas within the 62 million acres. What the draft EIS did not contain was a National Forest Service proposal which called for allocating 15 million acres of these lands located in California to wilderness.

When the Naional Forest Service issued a final EIS the plan for the 15 million acres was disclosed for the first time. The final EIS, unlike the earlier draft, was circulated only to Congress and to affected federal and state agencies. Its recommendations were sent to the President on May 2, 1979, approved them after making some minor changes in the allocations.

California challenged this National Forest Service action on the grounds that it violated NEPA, specifically in the requirement that circulating a supplemental draft EIS describing the proposed action. The Court, in addressing this challenge, reviewed the CEQ guidelines with respect to a proposed action. The court stated that NEPA requires an agency to provide the public with an opportunity to comment on a proposed action prior to the first significant point of decision in the agency review process. And, to the point in this case, the Court held that the Naional Forest Service should have circulated for public comment a supplemental EIS describing the proposed action when the proposed action could not have been anticipated from the alternatives considered in the draft EIS. Furthermore, the Court stated the proposed action here was a

---

56  40 C.F.R. § 1502.9(c). Supplemental Enviromental Impacts Statements changes in the proposed actions, the effected environment or the anticipated impacts. Mere passage of time is insufficient. See Humane Society of the U.S. v. Watt, and Association Concerned About Tomorrow, Inc. v. Doyle, 610 F.Supp. 1101.
57  690 F.2d 753 (1982).

radical departure from the alternatives considered in the draft EIS, thus requiring the circulation of a supplemental draft.

The agencies in soliciting information from the public and other interested organizations and groups must request public comment on site designations listed in any draft EIS. When the agency receives site specific comments, summaries of the site by site comments must be included in the final EIS. In addition, the agency must respond to any issues raised by the site specific comments.

The Council in its regulations has mandated that agencies should use a format for EIS which will encourage good analysis and a clear presentation of the alternatives including the proposed action. In order to promote this goal the Council has provided a standard format for environmental impact statements which is to be followed unless the agency determines there is a compelling reason to do otherwise. The format is as follows:

(a) Cover Sheet

(b) Summary

(c) Table of Contents

(d) Purpose of and need for action

(e) Alternatives including proposed action

(f) Affected environment

(g) Environmental consequences

(h) List of preparers

(i) List of agencies, organizations, and persons to whom the copies of the statement are sent

(j) Index

(k) Appendices (if any)[58]

There are some specifications for the various segments of the standard format. For example, the cover sheet of the EIS is restricted to one page. The content of that one page should include the title of the proposed action, the name, address and telephone number of the person at the agency who can supply further information, a designation as to

---

[58]   40 C.F.R. § 1502.10).

whether the statement is a draft, a final statement or a supplement, a one paragraph abstract of the statement, the date by which comments must be received, and a list of responsible agencies including the lead agency and any cooperating agency.[59]

The summary section of the EIS must contain a summary which adequately and accurately summarizes a statement. The summary must stress the major conclusions, areas of controversy, and the issues to be resolved. The summary should not exceed 15 pages.[60]

The purpose and need section of the EIS should specify the underlying purpose and the need to which the agency is responding and proposing the alternatives and the action.[61]

The heart of the EIS is the section relating to alternatives. In addition to presenting the environmental impact of the proposal itself, the section must also include the alternatives, so that the issues are sharply defined and so that the decision maker and perhaps the public in analyzing these statements, can have a clear basis for choice among the options. The mandate of this section is that the EIS must explore and objectively evaluate all reasonable alternatives. In addition, any alternative which was eliminated or passed upon unfavorably should be detailed in this section and be briefly discussed from the perspective of the reasons for the elimination.[62]

Also included in the alternatives section of the EIS is a statement and therefore an identification of the agencies preferred alternative or alternatives. In addition, this section should include an appropriate discussion of mitigation measures which may not have been already included in the proposed action of the alternatives.

Under the heading "Affected Environment" the agency preparing the EIS is required to briefly describe the environment of the area or the areas which would be affected by either the proposal or one of the alternatives. The agency is admonished to avoid useless bulk in the statements in this section and rather concentrate its effort and intention on the most important issues.[63]

While the section of the EIS which presents the alternatives to the proposed action may be the heart, following closely in importance is the section of the report in which the environmental consequences are treated. The EIS must present the discussions surrounding the alternatives including the proposed action and any adverse environmental ef-

59    40 C.F.R. § 1502.11.
60    40 C.F.R. § 1502.12.
61    40 C.F.R. § 1502.13.
62    40 C.F.R. § 1502.14.
63    40 C.F.R. § 1502.15.

fects associated with any of the alternatives or the proposed action. In addition the report must detail any adverse environmental effects which cannot be avoided should the proposal be implemented. Included in the discussion of the adverse effect should be references to direct effects and their significance, indirect effects and their significance, and possible conflicts between the proposed action and any objectives of the federal, regional, state, and local interests. Also the EIS should indicate the energy requirements and the conservation potential of various alternatives, the natural or depletable resource requirements and any affect on the urban quality, historic, and cultural resources affected by the proposal or its alternatives.[64]

The EIS also must contain a list of the preparers together with their qualifications, experience, professional disciplines. If a particular person is responsible for a particular analysis that shall be noted. It is obvious that the purpose underlying this particular section is to provide those who read the Report with contacts and pinpoint references so that particular people can be held accountable for their input into the EIS.[65]

The EIS may contain appendices. If it does, such appendices must consist of materials prepared in connection with the EIS, a reference to material used to substantiate any analysis fundamental to the entire Statement.[66]

Once the EIS is complete, then circulation becomes an important process. The Council has stated that the lead agency must circulate the entire draft and final EIS to those that may have an interest in participating in the process. Generally speaking, this means the statement must be circulated to any federal agency which has jurisdiction by law or special expertise with respect to any environmental impact involved and any federal, state, or local agency authorized to develop and enforce environmental standards. The EIS must also be circulated to any person, organization, or agency requesting the entire EIS as well, of course, to the applicant of the proposed action. Any person who contributed in a meaningful way to preparation of either the draft or the final EIS is also entitled to a complete copy of both of these documents.[67]

The Council has also provided some general direction for the preparation of the EIS. As an example, the Council encourages agencies to engage in a process called Tiering. Tiering, within the Council guidelines, refers to the coverage of general matters in broader EIS with sub-

---

64  40 C.F.R. § 1502.16.
65  40 C.F.R. § 1502.17.
66  40 C.F.R. § 1502.18.
67  40 C.F.R. § 1502.19. In order for the NEPA to be satisfied, an Environmental Impact Statement must be publicly circulated and available for public comment. See Com. of Mass. v. Watt, 716 F.2nd 946.

sequent narrower statements or environmental analyses incorporated by reference. In effect, this reserves the bulk of the EIS for the discussion of the most important aspects of the proposal and the potential alternatives, while leaving the less important ones for subsidiary documentation. However, in order that this other material not be lost, the Council urges agencies to incorporate such material by reference and cite in the EIS where this other material would be relevant. The Council also urges the agency to briefly describe this other material, however, it cautions that the overall intention underlying the EIS and its process is to reduce paperwork and keep the EIS as cogent and to the point as possible. [68]

The Council is aware that agencies in evaluating reasonably foreseeable significant adverse effects on the human environment in an EIS may not have sufficient information to make definitive statements. The Council mandates that the agency should note in the EIS that there is incomplete or unavailable information. It is understandable that incomplete information may arise from two possible reasons; the information is unavailable, or the information may be available, but, the overall cost of obtaining it is exorbitant. In such a situation the agency should indicate this in the EIS.

Where the information is incomplete because it is unavailable, or it is too costly, the agency in the EIS should discuss the relevance or the potential relevance of the incomplete or unavailable information to the best of its ability and an analysis of what impact this information may have on the final decision if the information were available or were used.[69]

In some situations a cost benefit analysis might be relevant to the choice among environmentally different alternatives. Where such is the case, the agency is mandated to incorporate by reference or append a statement of such cost benefit analysis. It is important to note that the Council does not mandate that a cost benefit analysis should be used, but where it is not used the agency is encouraged to indicate the considerations which led to the conclusion that the cost benefit analysis would not be relevant to the ultimate decision.[70]

The agency preparing the EIS is mandated to insure the professional integrity, including scientific integrity, of the discussions and analyses in EIS's. The agency must identify any methodologies used and must in a reference by footnote indicate the scientific and other sources relied upon for its conclusions.[71]

---

[68]　40 C.F.R. § 1502.23 & 1502.21.
[69]　40 C.F.R. § 1502.22.
[70]　40 C.F.R. § 1502.23.
[71]　40 C.F.R. § 1502.24.

# PROTECTION OF THE ENVIRONMENT

It was the intent of Congress in passing NEPA and the intent of the CEQ when promulgating its regulations to require that any E.I.S. be a detailed statement of the effect of a proposed action on the environmental quality. As part of the process the federal agency is mandated to consult with and obtain the comments of any federal agency or any other organization that would have valuable information to provide concerning any environmental impact involved. The fact situation in a case (*Citizens v. Bergland*, 428 F. Supp 908, 1979) involving the use of Phenoxy herbicides in the control of various growing plants in a forest can be cited to illustrate CEQ's requirement of full discussion. The Phenoxy herbicide was used to remove undesirable plants in the hope of fostering a group of more desirable plants. Plaintiffs challenged the use of this Phenoxy herbicide on the grounds that it injures not only other plants and trees but also animals and perhaps humans. A precise issue indicates what to do with divergent scientific opinions. The court held that where scientists disagree about possible adverse environmental effects the EIS must inform decision makers of the full range of responsible opinion on the environmental affects. The court stated that mere conclusory statements which do not refer to scientific or objective data supporting them do not satisfy NEPA's requirement for a detailed statement. The record of the court case indicates that there was considerable scientific disagreement concerning the effects of the Phenoxy herbicide on both agriculture and animals and that the EIS failed to properly detail all this information so that the public could be apprised of the precise basis for the agency decision.

The Court granted plaintiffs' motion for a permanent injunction prohibiting further application of the herbicides until such time as the National Forest Service remedied the defects in the EIS.

The Council urges the lead agency to prepare a DEIS concurrent with and integrated with environmental impact analyses in related surveys and studies required by various other agencies charged with the implementation of environmental laws and executive orders. Such other agencies customarily include the Fish and Wildlife Coordination Administration, the National Historic Preservation Act Administration, the Endangered Species Act Administration and others.[72]

One final Council mandate for draft EIS is that it shall list all federal permits, licenses, and other entitlements which must be obtained in implementing the proposal.[73]

After preparing a draft EIS and before preparing a final EIS, the Council urges each agency to obtain the comments of any federal agency which

---

[72]  40 C.F.R. § 1502.25(a).
[73]  40 C.F.R. § 1502.25(b).

might by law or special expertise have any jurisdiction with respect to the environmental impact of the proposal, and request comments from appropriate state and local agencies, Indian tribes when the effects may be on a reservation, and any agency which has requested that it receive statements on actions of the kind proposed. In addition, the lead agency is mandated to request comments from the public by general announcements and more directly by soliciting comments from those ersons or organizations who may be interested or effected.[74]

In the comment part of the NEPA process, the lead agency in preparing a final EIS is required to assess and consider comments, both individually and collectively, that have been received.[75] EIS may indicate that the agency accepted some of the comments as being valid and pertinent to the proposal and, in fact, was fundamental in causing the agency to modify some its alternatives based on the comment. Or, perhaps, the agency in its final EIS could discuss how the comment caused it to improve or modify its analysis. In those situations where the agency does not agree with the suggestions contained in the comments or determines that the comments are not relevant to its decision making process, the agency is required to explain why the comments do not warrant further agency response.[76]

The CEQ Guidelines for the lead agency speak of the requirements imposed on the agencies in general terms. As previously stated, the Council has mandated that each agency must adopt procedures to insure that the decisions it makes are in accordance with the policies and purposes of the NEPA.[77] One of the important procedures involves the implementation of the final decision made by the agency. The Council mandates that agency must provide for the monitoring of the process to assure that the decisions are carried out. This monitoring process includes putting appropriate conditions in any grants, permits, or other approvals, the conditional funding of actions predicated on mitigation, and the promulgating of information informing cooperating or commenting agencies on the progress in carrying out the measures.[78]

As stated in the purpose section of the CEQ Regulations, it is important that the NEPA procedures be carried through to their completion before any action is taken by federal agencies involving any proposal. The Council mandates that until an agency issues a record of decision (*i.e.*, final EIS) the agency cannot take any action concerning the proposal which would have an adverse environmental impact or limit the choice of any reasonable alternatives.

---

74    40 C.F.R. § 1503.1.
75    40 C.F.R. § 1503.3.
76    40 C.F.R. § 1503.4.
77    589 F. Supp. 1139 (1984).
78    40 C.F.R. § 1507.2.

# PROTECTION OF THE ENVIRONMENT

In order to streamline the NEPA process, federal agencies are encouraged to cooperate with state and local agencies to the fullest extent possible to reduce duplication between the NEPA and state and local requirements. This cooperation includes, among other things, joint planning processes, joint environmental research and studies, joint public hearings, and joint environmental assessments.[79]

Federal agencies are also required to cooperate with state agencies in those situations where state laws or local ordinances have environmental impact statement requirements. Federal agencies must fulfill those requirements so that the one EIS required of all federal agencies will comply with federal laws as well as applicable state and local laws.

If any inconsistency exists between federal and state requirements, the federal EIS must describe the extent to which the agency can reconcile its proposed action with any state or local plan.

Federal agencies are also required to cooperate with applicants which submit environmental information for possible use by the agency in preparing an EIS. This cooperation must take the form of helping the applicant to know and understand the types of information required. If the agency chooses to use the information submitted by the applicant in its own EIS, then the names of those independent persons supplying the information must be included in the EIS.[80]

Federal agencies may not accept as final and binding an environmental assessment submitted by an applicant. In these situations, the agency is required to make its own evaluation of the environmental issues and take the responsibility for the scope and content of the environmental assessment.

The preparation of EIS may be accomplished by the agency itself or by a contractor selected by the lead agency. It is also permissible for the lead agency to permit a cooperating agency to prepare the EIS. In those situations where the EIS is prepared by someone other than the lead agency under contract, the lead agency must furnish guidelines and participate in the preparation and independently evaluate the Statement prior to it approval.[81]

The NEPA process concentrates very heavily on public involvement. This public involvement includes efforts to integrate the public interest in preparing NEPA procedures, participation by the public in public hearings and meetings, and notification to the public of any action that the agency intends to take. In cases where an action would have an af-

---

[79] 40 C.F.R. § 1506.2.
[80] 40 C.F.R. § 1506.5(a).
[81] 40 C.F.R. § 1506.5(b).

fect of national concern, notice to the public shall include publication in the Federal Register as well as notice by mail to national organizations reasonably expected to be interested in the matter.

In those cases where the potential action affects primarily local or regional interests, notice must be given to the state and area-wide organizations. Each agency is encouraged to provide notice by publication in local newspapers where possible. Other methods of notification include a direct mailing to owners and occupants of nearby or affected property, posting of notice on and off sites in the area where the action is to be located. EIS are made available to the public pursuant to the provisions of the Freedom of Information Act (5 U.S.C. 552). This law makes it mandatory that every federal agency make available to the public the material requested pursuant to any proposal, unless the material falls into one of the limited exceptions stated in the Act.[82]

The CEQ is the primary organization through which a Freedom of Information Act request is processed. The Chairman of the Council has appointed a Freedom of Information Officer who is responsible for overseeing the Council's administration of the Act. The process to obtain the information from the Council is initiated by a letter addressed to the Freedom of Information Officer, Council on Environmental Quality, Executive Office of the President, 722 Jackson Place Northwest, Washington, D.C. 20006. The Council, through its Information Officer, has a ten day period for making a determination on the request and to make a response to the person who is making the request. Any denial by the Council on a request for information or any release of information which is inadequate can be appealed to the Council.

When the request for information has been approved by the Council, the person or organization requesting this information can make an appointment to inspect a copy of the material requested during regular business hours for which a reasonable fee may be charged. The fee may be waived in situations where the Freedom of Information Officer deems it to be either in the Council's interest or in the general public's interest.

As is the case with any other federal legislation, the NEPA and the required adherence to it, is reviewable by federal courts. The Courts role in reviewing decisions made pursuant to NEPA is restricted to the determination that the agency has or has not followed the chapter's procedure requirements. In a practical sense this means that the scope of review by a court is controlled by Title V (Administrative Procedure Act) and is restricted to a finding as to whether or not the action carried

---

[82]    40 C.F.R. § 1506.6.

out pursuant to the Act is "arbitrary, capricious, or an abuse of discretion."

## STANDING

In order for anyone to challenge federal action and to maintain a suit against a federal agency, a party must establish standing to sue. To establish this standing the party must generally allege that the challenged activity, that is, the activity about which the party is complaining about, will cause him injury in fact. This means that the injury incurred can be traced to the challenged action and that the injuries are likely to be redressed by a favorable decision.

In addition, any interest that a plaintiff claims to have must also be one which is arguably within the zone of interest to be protected by NEPA. Mere organizational interest in the environment are not sufficient to establish standing. Rather the plaintiffs must show that they have personally have suffered acts or threatened injury of the defendant's alleged illegal activity.

## EXHAUSTIVE ADMINISTRATIVE REMEDIES

Often the plaintiffs can show the threatened personal injury by showing that they or the members of their organization use the public land for recreational activities and for aesthetic enjoyment. Generally, the Courts are fairly lenient in allowing plaintiffs to show personal injury where the court feels that the action complained of might possibly violate NEPA.

In any challenge to an agency's decision on the part of a plaintiff with standing, the burden of proof is on the plaintiff to establish that an EIS is inadequate or that the Secretary or an official of the agency acted improperly in approving the action being challenged. In effect, what this means is that a plaintiff in any challenged action must show facts which, if true, would indicate that the proposed project would materially degrade any aspect of the environmental quality.

The Courts have stated three constitutional requirements for standing in cases involving statutory interpretation in the agency's compliance. First of all a party must establish actual or threatened injury in fact, second show that the injury is traceable to the challenged action, and third show that it is likely to be redressed by a favorable decree. The injury in fact can be aesthetic or environmental well being as well as economic interest. Purely ideological interest or an interest in compliance with law cannot be a basis for standing since standing presupposes a personal direct stake in the outcome of the suit. In most cases involving environmental challenges under NEPA, the plaintiff need only allege that he is a user of the resources that will be harmed if the challenged action is undertaken.

Generally plaintiffs who challenge the government's adherence to the requirements of NEPA are required to exhaust any administrative remedies they may have under the Act.

Judicial review of compliance with NEPA is covered under the Administrative Procedure Act (APA)[83] This section of the APA provides that the reviewing court shall . . . hold unlawful and set aside agency action, findings, and conclusions found to be . . . arbitrary, capricious, or abuse of discretion or otherwise not in accordance with law. . . . In general, the courts reviewing NEPA actions have interpreted the APA's arbitrary capricious standard to require a substantial inquiry and that the court take a "hard look" at both the factual and policy basis for the agency action. The "hard look" standard requires an agency to consider relevant factors bearing on its exercise of discretion and to ignore irrelevant factors; its decision must be justified on the record; and the agency must consider reasonable alternatives to the course it has chosen.

Once the Court is satisfied that the agency's decision is a product of reason and discretion and is justified by the record, it will rule for the agency. The reviewing court will not substitute its judgment or the judgment of a higher court for that of the agency.

Typically plaintiffs, after exhausting any potential administrative remedies they may have through the agency review procedure, file the suit under the APA in the district Court that would have proper jurisdiction of the case. Either the agency is upheld or the plaintiff's claim is allowed by the district Court and the agency is estopped from doing something or required to do something required under its regulations, in which case the losing side may appeal to a higher court which in the federal system would be the Circuit Court of Appeals. For the most part the case ends at this point except in those rare cases where a constitutional issue argued in the trial district court may be heard by the Supreme Court under its discretionary hearing powers.

Once a reviewing Court finds that an agency has failed to comply with NEPA, it grants remedies appropriate to the case. The usual form of relief in a NEPA suit is to enjoin the agency's project until it has complied with NEPA and in some cases remands the case to the agency for further procedures toward compliance. Damages are not available under NEPA and the usual remedy is injunctive relief. In many cases, if not most cases, injunctive relief appeals to plaintiffs because it stops the agency's project altogether until it complies with NEPA. The reviewing Court may issue a temporary injunction or a preliminary injunction and in some cases a permanent injunction. As in other cases involving injunctions, the test that the reviewing court uses is whether or not the

---

83    5 U.S.C.A. § 706.

plaintiff will suffer an irreparable injury if injunctive relief is not granted and, if the injunction is temporary or preliminary, whether or not the plaintiff is likely to succeed on the merits of the case when the Court has a full fledged review of all the facts.

There are several rules of thumb used by the courts in considering any plaintiff's challenge to the government's adherence to the requirements of NEPA. First and foremost the federal courts generally give "deference" to federal actions. This means that in close cases (those cases in which there may be some doubt that the federal action was inappropriate but not clear cut evidence) the court will rule in favor of the government action against the plaintiff's challenge.

The second standard used by Courts in analyzing any challenge to government action is that the courts in reviewing a decision generally attempt to determine merely that the agency involved has taken a "hard look" at environmental consequences and will not attempt to interject itself within the area of discretion of the agency as to the choice of action to be taken.

The NEPA and its procedures and processes constitute a basic national charter for protection of the environment. The policies and goals established and pursued establish action-forcing provisions designed to bring any federal activity impinging on the environment out into the sunshine. In the final analysis the President, the federal agencies, and the courts share the responsibility for the efficient working of the Act.[84]

[84]    40 C.F.R. § 1515.1 - 1515.15.

# CHAPTER FOUR

## ENDANGERED SPECIES

### BACKGROUND

For many years prior to the involvement of Congress, it had become increasingly apparent that some sort of protective measures would have to taken to prevent the further extinction of many of the world's animal species. Consideration of this need to protect the endangered species went beyond the value of the aesthetic. In hearings before Congressional committees on the environment, it was shown that many of the animals perform vital biological services in order to maintain a balance of nature within their environments. The need to maintain a balance of nature was accompanied by the recognition of a need for a biological diversity for scientific purposes.

Everyone recognized, at the time that Congress became involved in the matter, that the two major causes of extinction were hunting and destruction of natural habitat. In order to solve these problems, it was necessary for Congress to enact legislation that would develop law that would provide the kind of management tools needed to act early enough to save a vanishing species.

Based on all these considerations, Congress first started to address the issue by holding hearings in 1966.

The United States Congress in passing the Endangered Species Act of 1973, stated in its declaration of purposes and policy that (1) various species of fish, wildlife, and plants in the United States have been rendered extinct as a consequence of economic growth and development untempered by adequate concern and conservation; (2) other species of fish, wildlife, and plants have been so depleted in numbers that they are in danger of or threatened with, extinction; (3) these species of fish, wildlife, and plants are of aesthetic, ecological, educational, historical, recreational, and scientific value to the Nation and its people.[1] These findings were based on previous beliefs and understandings.

In order to alleviate these observed problems, Congress passed the first legislation enacted specifically to protect endangered species in 1966.[2] The 1966 act was entitled "Endangered Species Preservation Act of 1966" and it directed the Secretary of the Interior to "carry out a program in the United States of conserving, protecting, restoring and preserving selected species of native fish and wildlife," authorized the acquisition of endangered species habitat for inclusion in the National

---

1   16 U.S.C.A. § 1531 et seq..
2   Public Law 89-669, 80 Stat. 926.

# WILDLIFE AND HABITAT

Wildlife Refuge system, required the preparation of an official list of endangered species, and required the Departments of Interior, Agriculture, and Defense to protect species of fish and wildlife threatened with extinction and the habitat of these species to the extent consistent with the primary purpose of those departments.

In 1969 Congress passed the Endangered Species Conservation Act of 1969 which was designed to correct some weaknesses of 1966 Act.[3] The 1969 Act expanded the Secretary's habitat acquisition authority and redefined fish and wildlife to include any wild mammal, fish, wild bird, amphibian, reptile, mollusk, or crustacean. More specifically, however, the 1969 Act provided for the authorization to publish a list of species and subspecies of fish and wildlife threatened with worldwide extinction and to prohibit any importation of these species and subspecies into the United States.

In 1973 Congress enacted the Endangered Species Act of 1973.[4] This law broadened the definition of protection to include any member of the animal kingdom and for the first time authorized listing of plants. In addition, the 1973 Act provided a category for threatened species, designed to protect plant and animal species before they reached dangerously low numbers.

The 1973 Act also extended protection to habitat critical to the continued existence of threatened and endangered species. Also included in 1973 Act was a prohibition against the taking of endangered species and the placing of very strict requirements on all federal agencies to protect listed species in their habitat.

In 1978 the 1973 Act was amended by Congress.[5] These amendments provided for the establishment of an Endangered Species Interagency Committee to review federal agency actions that would jeopardize the continued existence of any threatened or endangered species or adversely modify habitat critical to such species and empowered the Endangered Species Interagency Committee previously established to determine, based on a review, whether the otherwise prohibited federal action should be allowed to proceed.

The 1978 Amendment included a requirement that the designation of critical habitat become part of the process of listing a species under the Act.

In the 1978 amendments to the Endangered Species Act Congress included, as part of the process of listing a species, the consideration of

---

3    Public Law 91-135, 83 Stat. 275.
4    16 U.S.C.A. § 1531 et seq.
5    Public Law 95-632, 92 Stat. 3751.

any economic consequences. By 1982 it was clear that the consideration of the economic impact in listing decisions unduly burdened the listing process and as a result Congress amended the Endangered Species Act to prohibit consideration of an economic impact in listing decisions.[6]

The Endangered Species Act of 1973, while maintaining its basic approach to the protection of wildlife and habitat, has expired on a number of occasions and it has been necessary to reauthorize the Act for specific time periods. The Act has been reauthorized on December 28, 1979, October 13, 1982, and most recently on October 7, 1988. The 1988 reauthorization is for five years. The 1988 Act authorized the appropriation of funds to carry out the Endangered Species Act through the fiscal year of 1992.[7]

## BASIC APPROACH

The Endangered Species Act not only requires the United States to improve the condition of various species of fish, wildlife, and plants in the United States but to do so as a sovereign state in the international community. The Act makes reference to various international agreements through which the United States has committed itself to cooperate with other nations in conserving various species of fish, wildlife, and plants. Specifically mentioned are: (1) migratory bird treaties with Canada and Mexico; (2) The Migratory and Endangered Bird Treaty with Japan; (3) the Convention on Nature Protection and Wildlife Preservation in the Western Hemisphere; (4) the International Convention for the Northwest Atlantic fisheries; (5) the International Convention for the High Seas Fisheries of the North Pacific Ocean; (6) the Convention on International Trade in Endangered Species of Wild Fauna and Flora; and (7) other international agreements.[8]

In addition to international cooperation, the United States, through its passage of the Endangered Species Act, has committed itself to cooperation with the states and other interested parties, through federal financial assistance and a system of incentives, to develop and maintain conservation programs which meet national and international standards.[9]

The bottom line in its approach to the conservation of various species of fish, wildlife, and plants is expressed by Congress as "a means whereby the ecosystems upon which endangered species and threatened species depend may be conserved, to provide a program for the conservation for such endangered species and threatened species, and to take such

---

6   Public Law 97-304, 96 Stat. 3751.
7   Public Law 100-478, 102 Stat. 2312.
8   16 U.S.C.A. § 1531(a)(4).
9   16 U.S.C.A. § 1531 (a)(5).

steps as may be appropriate to achieve the purposes of the treaties and conventions as set forth in the Act."[10]

Congress has declared a policy that all federal departments and agencies are mandated to seek to conserve endangered species and threatened species and must utilize their authorities in furtherance of this avowed purpose. Furthermore, federal agencies must cooperate with state and local agencies to conserve any endangered or threatened species.[11]

In addition to preserving its own interest in the conservation of species of fish, wildlife, and plants, the United States in passing the Endangered Species Act subserved another important interest - the execution of a commitment under the Convention on International Trade in Endangered Species of Wild Fauna and Flora.[12] This treaty to which the United States is a signatory is not self executing and it was necessary for the United States to pass implementing legislation in order to discharge its responsibilities under "C.I.T.E.S."

## CONSTITUTIONALITY

The constitutionality of the Endangered Species Act has been tested in several respects. One challenge to the Act rested on the ground that it was a taking of property in violation of the Fifth Amendment of the federal Constitution.[13] Another challenge was based on the Tenth Amendment, which reserves to the states powers not specifically allocated to the federal government. The Court, in this case,[14] threw out the challenge on the ground that Congress had the power to enact legislation based on valid treaties and also because Congress had the power to regulate commerce among the states.

Another constitutional challenge was presented by the case, *United States v. Billy*,[15] which was based on the First Amendment's free exercise rights. The case involved the hunting and the killing of a Florida panther by a Seminole Indian. The Indian challenged the Act under the free exercise clause, but the court held that the use of the panther parts was not critical or essential to the practice of the Seminole's religion and, therefore, the prohibitions of such action was not in violation of free exercise rights.

In one of the earlier constitutional challenge cases, *Tennessee Valley Authority v. Hill*,[16] the Supreme Court made it clear that it would sup-

---

10 16 U.S.C.A. § 1531(b).
11 16 U.S.C.A. § 1531(c).
12 27 U.S.T.; T.I.A.S. 8249.
13 U.S. v. Kepler, 531 F.2d 796.
14 Palila v. Hawaii Dep't of Land and Natural Resources, 649 F. Supp. 1070.
15 667 F. Supp. 1485.
16 437 U.S. 153.

port the intention of Congress to make the Endangered Species Act reflect the highest of priorities.

To date, therefore, the courts have upheld the constitutionality of the Endangered Species Act and have pushed aside any interest that might come in conflict with the purposes of the Act.

## ADMINISTRATION

The U.S. Fish and Wildlife Service (FWS) and the National Marine Fishery Service (NMFS) share responsibility for administering the Endangered Species Act. In regulations and in later amendments to the Endangered Species Act, these agencies are referred to by the designation of "Service."

The head of each of these Services is referred to as a director. When used, this term means the Assistant Administrator for Fisheries for the National Oceanic and Atmospheric Administration or his authorized representative or the Service Regional Director of the Fish and Wildlife Service. As an example, when consultation is required of federal agencies it means consultation with the appropriate director of the appropriate agency in each case.

The crux of the Act is 16 U.S.C.A. § 1533, which contains the concept of the determination of endangered species and threatened species. This section provides that the Secretary of the Interior shall determine whether any species is an endangered species or a threatened species because of such factors as: (1) the present or threatened destruction, modification, or curtailment of its habitat or range; (2) over utilization for commercial, recreational, scientific, or educational purposes; (3) disease or predation; (4) inadequacy of existing regulatory mechanisms; or (5) other natural or man made factors affecting its continued existence. In general the enforcement of the Act is vested in the Secretary of the Interior, however, in some cases the Secretary of Commerce and the Secretary of Agriculture have responsibilities under the Act. In cases where the Secretary of Commerce and the Secretary of Agriculture are permitted to make determinations concerning species, each of those secretaries is required to inform the Secretary of the Interior who performs the actual function of the listing of the endangered species or the threatened specie.[17]

## THE DETERMINATION OF THE SECRETARY

In making his determination as to whether or not a species is endangered or threatened, the Secretary must make his determination solely on the basis of the best scientific and commercial data available to him after conducting a review of the status of the species and after taking

[17]  16 U.S.C.A. § 1533(a.

into account those efforts, if any, being made by any state or foreign nation or any political subdivision of a state to protect said species. The Secretary must give consideration to species which have been identified as in danger of extinction or likely to become so within the foreseeable future by any state agency or by any agency of a foreign nation that is responsible for the conservation of fish and wildlife or plants. In addition, the Secretary must give consideration that is designed as requiring protection by a foreign nation pursuant to any international agreement.

Several cases are illustrative of the process by which the Secretary must make his determination as to whether or not a species is endangered or threatened.

In *Carson-Truckee Water Conservancy District v. Clark*,[18] the Ninth Circuit Court of Appeals upheld the district Court's findings concerning the Secretary's obligations under the Endangered Species Act.

In this case, a power company and a water conservancy district challenged the district court's refusal to issue in a declarartory judgment that the Secretary of the Interior violated the Endangered Species Act by refusing to honor a commitment under the federal act requiring the sale of water from the Stampee Dam and Water on the Little Truckee river for use in Reno and Sparks, Nevada.

The Secretary ruled that the Endangered Species Act required him to give priority to conserving the Cui-ui fish and the Cutthroat trout as they were on the Endangered and Threatened Species List. The Secretary found that there was no excess water to sell for municipal and industrial use under the federal water project statute after fulfilling the statutory obligations under the Endangered Species Act to the two fish.

Under the Endangered Species Act, the Secretary is required to give priority to the conservation of threatened and endangered species. The water conservancy and the power company argued that the Secretary abused his discretion with a proposed alternate plan. The plan included planting miles of shade trees along the river to reduce water temperatures, confine the river to a single channel, and constructing fish hatcheries. The purpose underlying the use of shade trees was reduction of water temperature so that the fish could spawn. The significance of the sixty-eight degree temperature is that it is too hot for the fish to reproduce successfully. The water conservancy and the power company's plan would, according to expert testimony, result in occasional but not constant sixty-eight degree water temperatures.

Notwithstanding this argument, the Secretary found that his obligations under the Act required him to conserve threatened and endan-

---

[18]   549 F. Supp 704.

gered species to the extent that they were no longer threatened or endangered. More importantly, the Secretary found that other sections of the Endangered Species Act required him to provide a program for conservation of such endangered species which requires not only the protection of the existing species in its current status, but to promote the species to a point where it no longer is endangered or threatened.

The appellate Court upheld the district Court in concluding that the Secretary discharged his responsibilities under the Endangered Species Act.

In *Friends of Endangered Species, Inc. v. Jantzen*,[19] the geographic area in question was the San Berno mountain area located on the Northern San Francisco peninsula. The mountain area is rich in wildlife and contains about 3,400 acres of undeveloped land and is considered by private interests for a development of approximately 7,655 residential units and two million square feet of office and commercial space.

The private companies purchased virtually all the land on the mountain and in a plan reached through a law suit by the county with the private companies sold or donated to the county in the State of California over 2,000 acres of the mountain for park land. This settlement was reached prior to the finding by the Fish and Wildlife Service that the Mission Blue Butterfly, which was on the Endangered Species List, inhabited the mountain.

Shortly after the finding that the Mission Blue Butterfly was inhabiting the mountain, various persons and organizations formed a committee to devise a plan that would protect the endangered species and allow some development of the mountain. The committee formed by this group consisted of representatives of the county, cities, the private developers, land owners, other prospective developers, the Fish and Wildlife Service, the California Department of Fish and Game, and a private citizens group which had opposed the earlier planned development. This committee initiated a two year biological study to determine the population and distribution of the Mission Blue Butterfly on the mountain and whether development would conflict with the butterfly's continued existence.

The study technique employed to determine this issue was a "mark-release-recapture" of the butterflies. This technique involves the capture of individual butterflies and giving each a unique wing identification mark. The butterfly is then released where it was captured. When the butterfly is recaptured its identify and characteristics are recorded. By observing the proportion of marked animals to unmarked animals in

---

19    589 F. Supp 113.

subsequent capture periods experts inferred the population size and distribution of the butterfly in the study area.

The biological study concluded that the Mission Blue Butterfly inhabited most of the grassland portions of the mountain, including areas planned for the development. The study also determined that if development did occur the butterflies' grassland habitat would inevitably be lost to the encroaching brush and the butterflies' continued existence would be seriously threatened.

Shortly after the conclusions were reached in the study, the committee developed a habitat conservation plan based on the biological study. According to the plan, the proposed private development would disturb only fourteen percent of the present habitat of the mountain's population of Mission Blue Butterflies.

To effectuate this agreement, the Endangered Species Act[20] required the Fish and Wildlife Service to issue a permit. Because the Service's approval of the permit required compliance with federal and California environmental statutes, the county involved and the service agreed to prepare jointly a combined Environmental Impact Report required under state law and an environmental assessment required under federal law.

Public hearings were held and the service received both favorable and adverse comments in its permit findings.

Later the Fish and Wildlife Service issued a biological opinion concluding that pursuant to the Endangered Species Act, the planned development under the permit would not jeopardize the continued existence of various species on the mountain, including the Mission Blue Butterfly. The Fish and Wildlife Service also issued a finding of no significant impact (FONSI) stating that the issuance of the permit would not significantly affect the quality of the human environment. This finding, therefore, obviated the need for an Environmental Impact Statement under the requirements of NEPA.

The permit issued by the Service allowed the incidental taking of Mission Blue Butterfly on the mountain. Shortly thereafter, the plaintiffs in this case filed an action in district court for declaratory and injunctive relief, contending that the field studies used by the Service were methodologically flawed because of low recapture rates of the Mission Blue Butterfly and some mistaken recaptures by the field crew in the mark-release-recapture phase of the field study were flawed.

20   17 U.S.C. § 1539.

# ENDANGERED SPECIES

The Court, applying the arbitrary and capricious standard required under the Administrative Procedures Act for review of the Service's conclusions, determined that the Fish and Wildlife Service's actions were not arbitrary and capricious. The Court pointed to the fact that the biological study acknowledged that populations estimates had a high variance when the recapture rate fell below fifty percent, but stressed that while the study did provide a sense of the overall population and that was all that was required of the Service.

In *Sierra Club v. Clark*,[21] the Eighth Circuit Court addressed the issue of whether or not the Secretary of the Interior could issue regulations preventing the sport trapping of Eastern timber wolves, which at that time was a threatened species, in Northern Minnesota.

Minnesota's grey wolf population was originally listed as endangered under the Endangered Species Act. However, a body of experts, based on a development plan, recommended that the grey wolf be reclassified to a threatened species rather than an endangered species under the Act.

This body of experts also recommended that "depredation" control be used where wolves were killing domestic animals. The Fish and Wildlife Service, based on this recommendation, issued regulations allowing the Minnesota Department of Natural Resources to permit persons to take a grey wolf in certain zones. The court did recommend, upon a review resulting from a filed suit, that this trapping or taking be restricted to within one-quarter mile of the place where the depredation occurred.

Later, the Fish and Wildlife Service caved in to a Minnesota request that it be allowed to grant public sport trapping of the wolf and after public hearings issued regulations permitting such trapping with certain restrictions. These regulations modified the existing predation control system by extending the trapping or taking to within one-half mile of the farm where the predation occurred and removing the limitation that wolves could be sport hunted only in the case of predator wolves. In other words, sport hunting of wolves was not restricted to predation circumstances.

Shortly after these new regulations were issued the Sierra Club along with numerous other organization filed an action to enjoin the trapping of the grey wolf.

The Secretary of the Interior argued in the case that he had discretion to determine whether to impose prohibition of the taking of threatened

21    577 F. Supp. 783.

species and to issue such regulations as he deems necessary and advisable to provide for the conservation of the species. The Sierra Club, on the other hand, argued that the terms conserving and conservation under the Endangered Species Act means to use all methods and procedures which are necessary to bring any endangered species or threatened species to the point at which the measures provided pursuant to the Act are no longer necessary. Further, the Sierra Club maintained that regulated taking may be permitted only "in the extraordinary case where population pressures within a given ecosystem cannot be otherwise relieved."

The Court adopted the Sierra Club's interpretation of the Act and ruled that the regulations permitting the sport trapping of the grey wolf were illegal.

In *Palila v. Hawaii Department of Land and Natural Resources*,[22] the Court had to make a determination as to the precise meaning of the word harm as it was involved in the prohibited act of taking under the Endangered Species Act. The facts of the case disclosed that the Palila bird endemic to Hawaii was found only in a small area on the upper slopes of Mauna Kea on the island of Hawaii. By the mid-twentieth century, the bird's historical range had shrunk to its present area. By 1979, the Palila bird had shrunk to an estimated population of between fourteen to sixteen hundred birds, which was dangerously close to the minimum number of individuals below which a population cannot drop if the species is to survive.

The bird had been placed on the Endangered Species List in 1967 and in a previous action Feral goats were declared harmful to the habitat of the Palila bird and were ordered to be moved by a court. At the time of that decision, scientific data on the impact of Moufloon sheep was not available and no decision was made at that time as to the effect that these sheep may have on the habitat of the Palila bird.

Since the removal of the feral sheep the numbers of Palilas in existence have increased somewhat to approximately twenty-two hundred by the time of the suit. The challenge of the suit was that the continued existence of the Moufloon sheep in the same area with the Palila bird constituted a threat to the critical habitat of the bird.

The crux of the case turned on a definition of harm. In 1981, the Secretary proposed to amend the definition of harm to read simply "an act which injures or kills wildlife." The Secretary explained that the word harm was being redefined from the original definition in the Act to "mean any action including habitat modification which actually kills or injures wildlife, rather than the present interpretation which might be

22   649 F. Supp. 1070.

read to include habitat modification or degradation alone without further proof of death or injury." He went on to explain that "habitat modification as injury would be only covered by the new definition if it significantly impaired essential behavior patterns of the listed species." The Secretary further explained that this redefinition did not limit harm to "direct physical injury to an individual member of the wildlife species . . . the purpose of the redefinition was to preclude claims of a taking for habitat modification alone without any attendant death or injury to the protected wildlife. . . ."

The plaintiffs in this case challenged this definition and asserted that the existence of the Moufloon sheep in the same habitat with the Palila harms and causes injuries to the Palila.

The defendants in the case, *Hawaii Department of Land and Natural Resources*, were very anxious to maintain the Moufloon sheep population for purposes of sport hunting. The claim by the defendants was that: (1) the existence of the Moufloon sheep along side the Palila bird had not resulted in a diminution of the numbers of the Palila bird and, therefore, could not constitute a harm, and (2) the area should be supportive of the concept of multiple use.

The multiple use approach has been embraced in many areas of environmental management. The defendants, in using this theory, argued that they have conflicting obligations to foster sport hunting and to protect endangered species.

The Court concluded: (1) that the Moufloon sheep were, in fact, harming the only remaining habitat of the Palila bird; (2) that the word harm did not mean only a reduction in numbers but could rather mean "an act which could significantly modify or degrade critical habitat which injures wildlife by significantly impairing essential behavior patterns, including breeding, feeding, or sheltering;" and (3) the Endangered Species Act does not allow a balancing approach for multiple use considerations. The Court, based on these conclusions, ordered that the Moufloon sheep be removed from the critical habitat of the Palila on Mauna Kea.

Each federal agency has a duty, under the Endangered Species Act, to insure that such action is not likely to jeopardize the continued existence of endangered or threatened species. In accomplishing this duty, the agency must make any assurance of "not likely to jeopardize" to be based on the best scientific and commercial data available. Such scientific and commercial data may, in many circumstances, necessitate tests or studies. In *Conservation Law Foundation v. Watt*,[23] the court held that the Secretary did not discharge his duty to use the best scientific data

23    560 F. Supp. 561.

available when he was aware that three research programs were in progress. These research programs were directly on point and pertinent to the action that the Secretary of the Interior was planning to act upon. The court held that the Secretary, proceeding without such information, did not do all that was practicable prior to approving the project with such potentially grave environmental costs.

## CRITICAL HABITAT

The Secretary is also mandated the responsibility to designate critical habitat based on the best scientific data available.

The original efforts to protect endangered or threatened species did not include any particular attention to critical habitat. Subsequent studies indicated that critical habitat perhaps was as important as protecting the species itself. Therefore critical habitat is subject to the listing process in addition to endangered and threatened species.

Ordinarily critical habitat is specified at the time a species is proposed for listing. However if the critical habitat is not determinable at that time, the reasons for not designating critical habitat must be stated in the publication of proposed and final rules listing a species.

It is necessary, before a final designation of critical habitat can be made, that adequate scientific data is available to assist in the decision making process. Included in any determination is the probable economic and other impacts of making such a designation. There are some situations in which critical habitat is not determinable. Generally this occurs when information is insufficient to perform required analysis on the impacts, if any, and/or the biological needs of the species that are not significantly well known to permit an identification of an area and its critical habitat.

In making such a determination the Secretary is required to consider the physical and biological features that are essential to the conservation of a given species and which may require special management considerations or protections. Generally such factors include space for individual and population growth for normal behavior, food, water, air, light, minerals or other nutritional or physiological requirements, cover or shelter, sites for breeding, reproduction, and rearing of offspring, germination or seed dispersal, and some general considerations relative to the historical or geographical or ecological distributions of a species.

When a critical habitat determination is made, it is necessary to define it by specific limits using reference points and lines as found on standard topographic maps of the area. In addition, each declared critical habitat area must be referenced by state, county, or other governmental unit.

# ENDANGERED SPECIES

It is possible for the Secretary to designate a critical habitat for a species even though such a critical habitat for that species has not been previously designated.

Critical habitats may be revised according to information as new data becomes available to the Secretary.[24]

## PROCESS OF LISTING

The process through which a species may be listed, delisted, or have its status changed may be initiated by the appropriate Secretary or by any interested person through a petition. The initial process established in the early years designated the Secretary as the only person who could carry out the listing and delisting functions. However, the 1973 Act provided for the initiation of listing by private petition. This change was designed to encourage public participation in the implementation of the entire program. The private petition initiation process was substantially revised by the 1982 amendments to give citizen participation even greater impact.[25]

The Secretary is required to act promptly, after receiving a petition of an interested person. Within ninety days of receiving such a petition, the Secretary is required (to the maximum extent practicable) to make a finding as to whether the petition presents substantial scientific or commercial information indicating that the petitioned action is warranted. Where the petition is found to present such information, the Secretary must promptly commence a review of the status of the species concerned. After making findings the Secretary must publish, in the Federal Register, the required notification.[26]

If the petition by an interested person does present the required information, the Secretary, after reviewing the information, must within twelve months, after receiving the petition make a finding either that the proposed action is not warranted (in which case the Secretary should publish such finding in the Federal Register) or that the petition is warranted (in which case the Secretary also should publish in the Federal Register such a general notice). The Secretary may also find that the proposed action might be warranted but that the immediate proposal is pending for further determinations. On occasion, the question to be determined is whether or not the species is an endangered species or a threatened species, and some additional time is needed to make this determination.[27]

---

24  16 U.S.C.A. § 1533(b); 50 C.F.R. §§ 424.01-.21.
25  Public Law 97-304, 96 Stat. 1426.
26  16 U.S.C.A. § 1533(b)(3)(A).
27  16 U.S.C.A. § 1533(b)(3)(B).

# WILDLIFE AND HABITAT

In addition to petitions relating to the listing of an endangered species or a threatened species, interested persons may also submit petitions to revise a critical habitat designation. The Secretary must follow the same time frame in these situations as he would be required to follow with respect to the listing of an endangered or a threatened species.[28]

In some cases an interested party may request that a critical habitat for an animal or a plant be designated where that animal or plant is on the endangered species list. Whether or not the Secretary is required to make such a determination depends in a large part on whether or not the information, available at the time the plant or animal was declared in danger, was sufficient to make such a determination as to the habitat.

When the Secretary makes a determination that the species should be listed or that the critical habitat should be designated, he formulates a regulation. Before the regulation can be effective the Secretary is required to publish a general notice and the complete text of the proposed regulation in the Federal Register. In addition, he must give any actual notice of the proposed regulation to any state agency in each state in which the species is believed to occur and/or to each county or equivalent jurisdiction in which the species is believed to occur and invite such agency or such jurisdiction to comment.[29]

The Secretary is also required to give, insofar as it is practicable, notice of the proposed regulation to any foreign nation in which the species is believed to occur, give notice to professional and scientific organizations who might conceivably have an interest, publish a summary of the proposed regulation in a newspaper of general circulation in each area of the United States in which the species is believed to occur and promptly hold at least one public hearing on the proposed regulation if any person requests such a hearing (within forty-five days after the date of publication of the general notice).[30]

After the public notice that a regulation has been proposed by the Secretary is published, another notice publication is required by the Secretary. This notice is in the form of a conclusion reached by the Secretary and states either that the final regulation is to be implemented declaring a species endangered or threatened or a critical habitat designated or that the proposed regulation is being withdrawn based on finding as to why the withdrawal has been determined. It is also possible that an extension to the one year requirement can being exercised by the Secretary.[31]

---

28   16 U.S.C.A. § 1533(b)(3)(C).
29   16 U.S.C.A. § 1533(b)(6).
30   16 U.S.C.A. § 1533(b)(5).
31   16 U.S.C.A. § 1533(b)(6)(B).

# ENDANGERED SPECIES

Included in the publication of any proposal or final regulation which is reached by the Secretary, is a summary of the data on which the regulation is based and in cases of critical habitat a brief description of the evaluation of activities which pose a threat to the habitat.[32]

The final outcome of a determination to list a species as endangered or threatened or a critical habitat as necessary to be designated is a list of all species and habitats so determined. The list is required to be published in the Federal Register and it must list all species determined by the Secretary of the Interior or the Secretary of Commerce to be endangered or threatened. The list must refer to the species contained therein by its scientific and common name or names if any. The list also must contain a specification with respect to each species over what portion of its range it is endangered or threatened and must specify any critical habitat within that range.

The list must be revised from time to time and at least once every five years the Secretary must review all species included in the list which is published. The review should address itself to whether or not the species should continue to be listed or removed.[33]

When a species is listed as a threatened species, the Secretary is required to issue regulations which he deems necessary and advisable to provide for the conservation of this species.[34]

An interesting case is presented when a species not listed, so closely resembles one that is listed that it would be extremely difficult to differentiate between the listed and unlisted species. In that case, the Secretary may pass a regulation even though the species is not listed until a determination is made at some future date that would allow the species in question to be released or removed from regulation.[35]

## RECOVERY PLANS

The primary purpose of the Endangered Species Act is of course to protect endangered or threatened species and critical habitat. Although the Endangered Species Act has enjoyed considerable success, it has been recognized by those with scientific knowledge that much more must be done. In order to go this extra mile, the Act has been amended to include a requirement that the Secretary must develop and implement so called "recovery plans." The purpose underlying this provision of the Endangered Species Act is to give endangered or threatened species an extra chance to benefit by conservation efforts. The Secretary is required, to the maximum extent practical, to give priority to those en-

---

32    16 U.S.C.A. § 1533(b)(8).
33    16 U.S.C.A. § 1533(c).
34    16 U.S.C.A. § 1533(d).
35    16 U.S.C.A. § 1533(e).

dangered species or threatened species that are most likely to benefit from such plans, particularly those species that are or may be in conflict with construction or other development projects or other forms of economic activity.[36]

In developing such a plan the Secretary must produce a plan with a description of sites specific management action as may be necessary to achieve the plan's goal for conservation and survival of the species, estimate the time required and the cost to carry out these measures needed to achieve the plan's goal and to achieve intermediate steps toward that goal.

The ultimate goal underlying the implementation of the recovery plans is to reach a point and time when the particular species in question could be removed from the threatened or endangered list. In formulating such a plan the Secretary is required to provide objective, measurable criteria which could result in a determination that the species be removed from the list.

In order to monitor the Secretary's work, he is required to report every two years to the Committee on Environment and Public Works of the Senate and the Committee on Merchant Marine and Fisheries of the House of Representatives on the status of efforts to develop and implement the recovery plans for all species listed and on the status of all species for which such plans have been developed.

In proposing a recovery plan, the Secretary is required to provide public notice and an opportunity for public review and comment on such plans. Of course he must include such comments and information received his determination and final proval of the plan.

When the recovery plan is successful then the particular species is removed from the endangered and threatened list. As a follow-up the secretary is required to monitor the process of the recovery plan by keeping track for a period of five years, of all species which have recovered and have beenremoved from the list.

In connection with the recovery plans, a system involving federal and state cooperation has been implemented which requires a monitoring of all species which have recovered to the point at which they no longer need to be listed as endangered or threatened. Each system of monitoring must last for not less than five years.[37]

---

36   16 U.S.C.A. § 1533(f).
37   16 U.S.C.A. § 1533(g).

# ENDANGERED SPECIES

In order to insure that the listing provisions of the statutes are achieved efficiently and effectively the Secretary is required to publish guidelines for the entire process.[38]

While this listing process is designed to solicit comment from the public, and in fact the Secretary is required at all times to consider any public comment, nevertheless public hearings are not required under the Endangered Species Act. [39]

## FEDERAL AGENCY ACTIONS AND CONSULTATIONS

The failure or success of the Endangered Species Act rests upon its application to those organizations and persons which might be in a position to insure the success or failure of any program. Looming large in this category would be federal agencies in pursuit of major actions which could conceivably impact upon the environment. Under § 7 of the Act each federal agency is required to insure that any action authorized, funded, or carried out by the agency is not likely to jeopardize the continued existence of any endangered species or threatened species or result in the destruction or adverse modification of the habitat of any such species. Each federal agency is required to consult with the Secretary in connection with any of its major actions and in addition to use the best scientific and commercial data available to determine what impact its actions might have on endangered species, threatened species, or critical habitat.[40]

After consultation between the federal agency and the Secretary has concluded, the Secretary is required to provide the federal agency and the applicant, if any, a written statement setting forth the Secretary's opinion and a summary of the information on which the Secretary's opinion is based. The Secretary's opinion must detail how the agency action affects the species or its critical habitat.

If any jeopardy or adverse modification is found, the Secretary must suggest reasonable and prudent alternatives which he believes would result in federal agency action which would not violate the Endangered

38  16 U.S.C.A. § 1533(h).
39  State Louisiana ex rel Guste v. Verity 681 F. Supp. 117.
40  16 U.S.C.A. § 1536. See also In Defenders of Wildlife v. Hodel, 707 F. Supp. 1082, the court addressed the issue of what kind of actions by federal agencies require adherence to the Endangered Species Act under U.S.C.A. § 1536. The language states that each federal agency must ensure that any action authorized or carried by the agency is not likely to jeopardize the continued existense of any endangered or threatened species or result in an adverse modification of the habitat of such species. Under 50 C.F.R. § 402.02 the definition of action contains the wording "by federal agencies in the U.S. or upon the high seas." The court found that the Secretary through regulations could not restrict federal agency actions to include the United States and high seas. The Court reasoned that the langue of the statute (16 U.S.C.A. § was all inclusive and that the regulations could not be more restrictive. The court ordered the regulations to be amended and that federal agency action included an action by a federal agency in a foreign land that might affect an endangered or threatened species there.

Species Act. The written statement must also contain any terms or conditions that must be complied with by the federal agency or the applicant to implement the measures articulated by the Secretary in his statement.

If the Secretary's statement to the federal agency states that based on the best scientific and commercial data available endangered or threatened species may be present in the area where the federal agency action is contemplated, the federal agency upon receipt of such statement must conduct a biological assessment for the purpose of identifying any endangered species or threatened species which is likely to be affected by any action that they might take. This biological assessment made be undertaken as part of the  federal agency's compliance with the Environmental Impact Statement requirements of NEPA.[41]

There are time limits both on the opinion issued by the Secretary and the conclusion of the biological assessment. The agency consultation with the Secretary must be completed within ninety days of the date on which it was initiated and in the case of the biological assessment within one hundred and eighty days after the date the consultation was initiated.

In those cases where the federal agency wishes to apply for an exemption (provided for in a subsequent section of the Act) such agency can conduct a biological assessment to identify any endangered or threatened species likely to be affected by the action. Any such biological assessment must be conducted in cooperation with the Secretary.[42]

An interesting case illustrating the procedural requirements of the Endangered Species Act is *Thomas v. Peterson*.[43]  In this case, the United States Forest Service planned a timber road in the Jersey Jack area of the Nezperce National Forest in Idaho. The purpose of the road was to implement a timber development plan in the area. In order to comply with NEPA, the Forest Service solicited public comments on the proposed plan, held a public hearing, and prepared an Environmental Assessment (EA) to determine whether an EIS would be required for the road.

Based on the EA, the Forest Service concluded that no EIS was required and issued a FONSI. The decision notice stated that "no known threatened or endangered plant or animal species has been found," within the area. It is significant that the EA did not contain a discussion of any endangered species.

41   16 U.S.C.A. § 1536(b).
42   16 U.S.C.A. § 1536(c).
43   589 F. Supp. 1139.

# ENDANGERED SPECIES

The plaintiffs in the case, who consisted of landowners, ranchers, outfitters, hunters, fishermen, recreation users, and conservation and recreation organizations, challenged the actions of the United States Forest Service on the ground that the Forest Service failed to comply with the Endangered Species Act in considering the effects of the road and the subsequent timber sales on the endangered Rocky Mountain Gray Wolf.

The Endangered Species Act contains both substantive and procedural provisions. The procedural provisions require what is essentially a three step process: (1) an agency proposing to take an action must inquire of the Fish and Wildlife Service whether any threatened or endangered species may be present in the areas of the proposed action; (2) if the answer is affirmative the agency must prepare a biological assessment to determine whether such a species is likely to be affected by the action; and (3) if the assessment determines that a threatened or endangered species is likely to be affected, the agency must formally consult with the Fish and Wildlife Service.

Under (3), above, the formal consultation process results in a biological opinion issued by the Fish and Wildlife Service. If the biological opinion concludes that the proposed action would jeopardize a species or destroy or adversely modify a critical habitat, then the action may not go forward unless the Fish and Wildlife Service can suggest an alternative that avoids this jeopardization, destruction, or adverse modification. If, on the other hand, the opinion concludes that the action will not violate the Act, the Fish and Wildlife Service may still require measures to minimize its impact.

The Court found in this case that the United States Forest Service did not follow the appropriate procedures required under the Endangered Species Act. The court reasoned that once an agency is aware that an endangered species may be present in the area of the proposed action, the Endangered Species Act requires the agency to prepare a biological assessment to determine whether the proposed action is likely to affect the species and, therefore, requires formal consultation with the Fish and Wildlife Service. The Forest Service in this case did not prepare such an assessment prior to its decision to build the Jersey Jack road. Without this biological assessment it cannot be determined whether the proposed project will result in any violation of the Endangered Species Act's substantive provisions. The Court further held that failure to prepare a biological assessment for a project in an area in which it has been determined that an endangered species may be present cannot be considered a de minimis violation of the Endangered Species Act, but rather is a major violation resulting in noncompliance.

## BIOLOGICAL ASSESSMENT

A biological assessment is the document that states the opinion of the appropriate service as to whether or not the federal action is likely to jeopardize the continued existence of listed species or result in the destruction or adverse modification of critical habitat. The biological assessment is intended to evaluate the potential effects of the action on listed or proposed species in designated and proposed critical habitat and determine whether any such species or habitat are likely to be adversely affected by the action and is used in determining whether formal consultation or a conference is necessary.

The biological assessment must be completed before any contract for construction is entered into and before construction is begun. The process through which the biological assessment is issued involves a contact by the federal agency of the appropriate director and a written request for a list of any listed or proposed species or designated or proposed critical habitat that may be present in the action area. Within thirty days of the receipt of this written notification from the appropriate agency, the director is required to provide the federal agency with a species list or in cases where no list has been provided by the federal agency that based on scientific and commercial data available either a proposed species or a proposed critical habitat may or may not be involved.

In addition to any listed and proposed species, the director must provide a list of candidate species that may be present in the action area. Candidate species means any species being considered by the Service for listing as endangered or threatened, but not yet subject to a proposed rule.

Although candidate species have no legal status and are accorded no protection under the Act, their inclusion will alert the federal agency of potential proposals for listings.

If the director advises that no listed species or critical habitat may be present, the federal agency need not prepare a biological assessment and further consultation is not required. If, on the other hand, only proposed species or proposed critical habitat may be present in the action area, then the federal agency must initiate a conference with the director. This conference consists primarily of informal discussions concerning an action that is likely to jeopardize the continued existence of the proposed species or will result in the destruction or adverse modification of the proposed critical habitat. During the conference the Service, through its director, will make advisory recommendations, if any, on ways to minimize or avoid adverse effects.

The consultation process between the federal agency and the Service can be designated either as formal or informal. An informal consultation is defined as an optional process that includes all discussions, correspondence, etc. between the Service and the federal agency. It is designed to assist the federal agency in determining whether formal consultation or a conference is required. If during the informal consultation it is determined by the federal agency with the written concurrence of the Service, that the action is not likely to adversely affect listed species or critical habitat the consultation is terminated and no further action is necessary.

However, where the informal consultation indicates that the agency's action may adversely affect either listed species or critical habitat or proposed or potential listed species or critical habitat then a formal consultation process is required.

Where a formal consultation process is required, the agency must submit a written request to the director of the appropriate Service and this request must contain descriptive materials that will enable the service in consultation with the federal agency to arrive at appropriate conclusions.

The natural conclusion of a consultation between the federal agency and the service is the publication, by the Service, of its opinion, called a biological opinion. The bottom line for any Service opinion is a statement as to whether or not the proposed action is likely to jeopardize the continued existence of a listed species or result in the destruction or adverse modification of critical habitat. If the service concludes that the action is not likely to endanger a listed species or result in the destruction or adverse modification of critical habitat the resulting conclusion reached by the service is "a no jeopardy biological opinion."

A condition for formal consultation is the preparation by the federal agency involved of the required biological assessment. This assessment must be completed and submitted to the director of the Service who will then use the results of the biological assessment in determining whether to request the federal agency to initiate a formal consultation or a conference, formulating a biological opinion or formulating a preliminary biological opinion.

The contents of a biological assessment are at the discretion of the federal agency and will depend on the nature of the action. But customarily the following are usually included in the assessment: (1) the results of an on site inspection of the area affected by the action to determine if listed or proposed species are present or occur seasonally; (2) review the recognized experts on the species at issue; (3) a review of the literature and other information; (4) analysis of the effects of the action on the species and habitat including consideration of cumulative effects and the results of any related studies; (5) analysis of alternative actions considered by the federal agency for the proposed action.

The federal agency must submit the completed biological assessment to the director of the appropriate service for review. The director has thirty days within which to respond in writing as to whether or not he concurs with the findings of the biological assessment.

After receiving a biological opinion from the Service, the federal agency involved must then determine whether and in what manner to proceed with the action it proposes. If the Service opinion is a jeopardy biological opinion, the federal agency must notify the Service of its final decision on the action. If the federal agency determines that it cannot comply with the requirements of the Endangered Species Act, after consultation with the Service, it may apply for exemption. The requirement that all federal agencies act in consultation with the Secretary of the Interior does not require acquiescence to the Secretary's opinion.

In *Village of False Pass v. Watt*,[44] the court held that the Secretary of the Interior did violate the Endangered Species Act where he merely issued orders to lessees in a proposed oil and gas lease-sale under the Outer Continental Shelf Act, requiring them to give him notice of any preliminary seismic activities they planned to conduct so that he might assess the environmental impact. The Secretary took this action in face of a biological opinion finding jeopardy from seismic activity for both gray and white whales. The court reasoned that the Secretary's order to the lessees only insured that any problem would be given attention at a later date and that this action was not sufficient in face of the biological opinion.

In order to insure that the endangered species process results in accomplishing the purposes of the Act, any federal agency and any permit or license applicant is prohibited from making any irreversible or irretrievable commitment of resources with respect to the action or to foreclose the potential implementation of any reasonable and prudent alternatives suggested by the Secretary.[45]

Where new information is developed which indicates that the agency action might indeed threaten an endangered species, the Endangered Species Act will prohibit further irreversible or irretrievable commitments of resources until consultation is reinitiated and a new biological opinion prepared. Under the Endangered Species Act, the irreversible or irretrievable commitment of resources is prohibited because the investment of such resources might very well preclude non-violative, reasonable, and prudent alternative measures. The theory is that investment of large sums of money in an endeavor, if at the time of the investment there was reasonable likelihood that the project at any stage of development would violate the Act, would create great pressures not to develop alternatives.

---

44   565 F. Supp. 1123.
45   16 U.S.C.A. § 1536(d).

# ENDANGERED SPECIES

## Endangered Species Committee

The Endangered Species Act establishes the Endangered Species Committee. The Committee is composed of seven members as follows:

(1) the Secretary of Agriculture;

(2) the Secretary of the Army;

(3) the Chairman of the Council of Economic Advisors;

(4) the Administrator of the Environmental Protection Agency;

(5) the Secretary of the Interior;

(6) the Administrator of the National Oceanic and Atmospheric Administration; and

(7) one individual from each affected state, as determined by the Secretary.

The Secretary of the Interior is designated as the Chairman of the Committee. The meetings and records of the Committee are open to the public. The primary purpose of the Endangered Species Committee is to process applications for exemption from the requirements imposed upon federal agencies to be formally aware of the impact on endangered or threatened species by any action or proposal contemplated.[46]

## EXEMPTIONS

The statutes and regulations provide for an exemption from the requirements imposed on federal agency with respect to endangered or threatened species. Any federal agency, the governor of the state in which an action will occur, and/or a permit or licensee applicant may apply for an exemption and relief from the requirements of the Endangered Species Act. Generally speaking, the application for an exemption must be submitted to the Secretary within ninety days following the termination of the consultation process. The application must be quite detailed so that the Committee making the decision as to whether or not to grant the exemption can make its decision based on relevant and adequate information. The federal agency or the applicant must provide information relevant to the value of the proposed action and why it cannot be altered so as to avoid interference with endangered or threatened species protected under the Act.[47]

---

[46]   16 U.S.C.A. §§ 1536(e)-(g).
[47]   16 U.S.C.A. § 1536(h); 50 C.F.R. § 451.02.

# WILDLIFE AND HABITAT

The Secretary, under the exemption process, is required to make a determination as to whether or not the exemption should be granted. Before such determination is made by the Secretary, he is required to undertake a substantial review process which includes an examination of all of the documents and records submitted with the exemption application and any evidence as to whether or not the federal agency or the permit applicant has carried out the consultation responsibilities required in good faith and has made a reasonable effort to modify the proposed action to comply with the requirements of the Endangered Species Act.

If the Secretary decides, based on his review, that the application for an exemption should be denied, he must notify the exemption applicant, whether it be private or a federal agency, in writing of his findings and the grounds upon which it is based. In such a case, the exemption process terminates and is subject to judicial review provided for by the United States Code.

If, on the other hand, the Secretary makes a positive finding on the threshold determination, he then notifies the exemption applicant in writing that the application qualifies for consideration by the Endangered Species Committee.[48]

If the Secretary's determination is positive, he must gather information and prepare a report for the Endangered Species Committee. As might be expected, the report to the Endangered Species Committee is a complete record and documentation of all that has been considered by the Secretary and that has been reported by the applicant.[49]

In addition to the record as it existed up to this point in time, the Secretary must also conduct a hearing in conjunction with the Endangered Species Committee. The purpose of the hearing is to perfect the record not only for the purposes of later judicial review but for the purpose of notifying everybody, including the public, the basis upon which the decision was made.

The person who conducts the hearing is an administrative law judge designated by the Secretary. The administrative law judge conducts a public hearing in which not only is the hearing open but also all records are open to the public. Of course, notices for this hearing are published in the Federal Register and intervenors are permitted to appear and make presentations at the hearing.

The hearing is conducted pretty much like most administrative hearings with a modified courtroom procedure in effect. The party bringing

48   50 C.F.R. § 452.03.
49   50 C.F.R. § 452.04.

the action, that is the party who is asking for the exemption from the Endangered Species Act, must bear the burden of going forward with evidence concerning the criteria for exemption.

Upon closing of the hearing, the administrative law judge certifies the record and transmits it to the Secretary for the preparation of the Secretary's report to the Endangered Species Committee. The Secretary is required to submit his report and a record of the hearing to the Committee within 140 days after making his original determination to recommend the approval of the exemption.[50]

The Endangered Species Committee then begins its review and the process toward making a final determination. The Committee has 30 days from the date of the receipt of the Secretary's report in which to make a decision. The criteria upon which a positive (a vote by at least 5 of its members) vote is based includes whether or not there are reasonable and prudent alternatives to the proposed action, whether or not the benefits of such action clearly outweigh the benefits of alternative courses of action consistent with conserving the species or its critical habitat and such action is in the public interest, the action is of regional or national significance, and neither the federal agency nor the applicant have made any irreversible or irretrievable commitment of resources prohibited under the Endangered Species Act.

The Committee also uses as a criterion whether or not the federal agency or the applicant has established reasonable mitigation and enhancement measures to minimize the adverse affects of the proposed action upon the endangered or threatened species or critical habitat concerned.

The Committee makes it final decision in writing. If the decision is positive (that is that the exemption should be granted), the Committee issues an order granting the exemption and specifies required mitigation and enhancement measures. This decision is then published in the Federal Register as soon as practicable.

In reaching its decision the Endangered Species Committee might very well solicit written submissions from interested persons and when the majority of the Committee so desire conduct a public hearing at which time the Committee would receive oral presentations.

The notification for either the written submissions or the oral submissions at a public hearing are advertised in the Federal Register. If a public hearing is conducted it is of course open to the public and conducted in an informal manner. All public hearings will be recorded verbatim and a transcript will be available for public inspection.[51]

---

[50]  50 C.F.R. § 452.05.

There is one exceptional case that would mandate the Committee to grant the exemption and that is a case where the Secretary of Defense finds in writing that an exemption for the agency action is necessary for reasons of national security. In this case the Committee grants the exemption notwithstanding any of the provisions required under the statutes and regulations.[52]

Another exemption under the Act is the authorization to the President to make determinations involving disaster relief and emergency assistance in the event of a major disaster. The Committee is required to accept the determination by the President.[53]

As might be expected, various acts are frequently involved with environmental protection including the Endangered Species Act, the Marine Mammal Protection Act, the Migratory Bird Act, etc. and sometimes conflict with each other and sometimes overlap. In the interest of clarifying the relationship between the Endangered Species Act and the Marine Mammal Protection Act, Congress has included in the Endangered Species Act a section which states that no provision of the Endangered Species Act shall take precedence over a more restrictive and conflicting provision of the Marine Mammal Protection Act.[54]

Any decision by the Endangered Species Committee is subject to judicial review. The petition must be filed in the United States Court of Appeals for any circuit wherein the agency action is concerned.[55]

## COOPERATION WITH THE STATES

In carrying out the provisions of the Endangered Species Act, the primary burden is on the federal government, however, it was recognized from early times that cooperation with the states would enhance federal efforts. In an attempt to involve the state's endangered species program processes, the Secretary is required to cooperate, to the maximum extent possible, with the state and this cooperation includes consultation with the states concerned in any matter related to the Endangered Species Act.

Cooperation may take the form of management agreements entered into between the federal government and the state involved and cooperative agreements proposed by a state. It is obviously in the best interest of everyone if federal responsibilities under the Act are assumed in part by state programs. When a state submits its program to the Secretary he is required to make a determination whether such program is

---

51  50 C.F.R. §§ 453.03-06.
52  16 U.S.C.A. § 1536(j).
53  16 U.S.C.A. § 1536(p).
54  16 U.S.C.A. § 1543.
55  16 U.S.C.A. § 1536(n). *See* Thomas v. Peterson, 753 F. 2d 754.

in accordance with the federal Endangered Species Act. If the Secretary determines that the state agreement is in accordance with the Endangered Species Act, he then is required to enter into a cooperative agreement with the state for the purpose of assisting in the implementation of the state program.

In making a determination that the state program is compatible with the federal program the Secretary must find that the state has established acceptable conservation programs consistent with the purposes and policies of the Endangered Species Act for all resident species of fish and wildlife in the state which are deemed by the Secretary to be endangered or threatened. In passing judgment on the state programs, the Secretary must review this plan that the state might have included in such programs and decide whether or not these plans will subserve the mandated under the Endangered Species Act for endangered and threatened species.

As part of this cooperative effort the Secretary is authorized to provide financial assistance to any state through the appropriate state agency, to assist in the development of programs for the conservation of endangered and threatened species. This allocation of funds to the states is based on the consideration of the number of endangered and threatened species within the state, the potential for restoring the endangered and threatened species within that state and the relative urgency to initiate a program to restore and protect an endangered or threatened species in terms of the survival of the species. The bottom line in any of these considerations, of course, is any benefits to be expected to be derived in connection with the conservation programs. The Secretary is required to review periodically (no more often than annual intervals) the allocation of funds to the state.

Occasionally state law regulation could come into conflict with federal laws with respect to endangered or threatened species. Such state law or regulation respecting the taking of the endangered or threatened species, may be permitted to stand if it is more restricted than the exemptions or permits provided for in the Endangered Species Act. However, any regulation which is less restrictive is void as it applies to any species listed by the Secretary as endangered or threatened.[56]

In *Manhing Ivory and Imports, Inc. v. Deukmejian*,[57] the court was faced with the problem of a California statute that made it a crime for any person to import into the state for commercial purposes a number of animals or animal parts including elephants. The defendant in the case, Manhing, was a wholesale importer of African elephant ivory products. He was charged with violating the California statute, which prohibited

---

[56] 16 U.S.C.A. § 1535.
[57] 702 F.2d 760.

such importation, and appealed to the federal courts on the ground that the California statute was in conflict with the Endangered Species Act and that Act preempted the California Act.

The Court analyzed the case from the perspective that the Endangered Species Act in 16 U.S.C. § 1535(f) states that "any state law or regulation which applies with respect to the importation or exportation of . . . endangered species or threatened species is void to the extent that it may effectively: (1) permit what is prohibited by this Act or by any regulation which implements this Act; or (2) prohibit what is authorized pursuant to the exemption or permit provided by this Act or in any regulation which implements the Act."

The Court found that, contemporaneous with the listing of African elephant, the Secretary adopted regulations permitting limited trade in elephant products. One of these regulations provided that the prohibition against importation did not apply to an African elephant or an elephant part which had been exported in compliance with one of the exceptions contained in the Convention on International Trade in Endangered Species of Wild Fauna and Flora. The court reasoned that there was another potential exception under 50 C.F.R. § 17.40(e), which provides that "a special purpose permit may be issued in accordance with the regulations which would exempt activity otherwise prohibited under the Act on submission of proof that says wildlife was already in the United States or that such wildlife was imported in accordance with any exception contained under the CITES."

Since *Manhing* fell within the scope of these exceptions, the California statute therefore violated the Endangered Species Act because it was a state law or regulation which violated the Endangered Species Act provision that provided for an authorized exception to the Act.

In another case involving an issue of conflict between state statutes related to endangered species and the Endangered Species Act, *H.J. Justin & Sons, Inc. v. Deukmejian*,[58] a manufacturer of boots brought action against the State of California challenging that state's statute forbidding the sale or possession for sale of products made from dead bodies of specified animals. As in the *Manhing* case, the Court found that the California statute was in conflict with the Endangered Species Act as to African elephant products and, therefore, the conviction against the defendant could not stand. However, in addition to prohibiting the sale or possession for sale of African elephant products, the state statute also prohibited trade in pythons and kangaroos. The court held that, since neither of these two animals were on the Endangered Species List, the California statute therefore could not be in conflict with the Endan-

---

58    702 F.2d 758.

gered Species Act and therefore refused to overturn the conviction against the defendant.

## PROHIBITED ACTS

An extremely important part of the Endangered Species Act is the section which covers prohibited acts.[59]  This section provides that with respect to any endangered species of fish or wildlife listed under the Act, it is unlawful for any person (subject to the jurisdiction of the United States) to import into or export from the United States any such species, take any such species within the United States, take any such species upon the high seas, possess, sell, deliver, carry, transport, or ship by any means whatsoever any such species, deliver, receive, carry, transport, or ship in interstate or foreign commerce by any means whatsoever in the course of a commercial activity of any said species, sell or offer for sale in interstate or foreign commerce any such species, or violate any regulation pertaining to such species or to any threatened species.

It is also a violation of the Act for any person to engage in the business as an importer or exporter of official wildlife or plants without first having obtained permission from the Secretary.  This prohibition applies only to those fish, wildlife, or plants listed as endangered species. In those cases where an exporter or importer does obtain permission to deal in the listed fish, wildlife, or plant, he must keep detailed records which disclose data concerning these importations or exportations, and afford to a duly authorized representative of the Secretary access to his records, his place or places or business, and any inventory reported fish, wildlife or plants.

A question arises as to the effect of the prohibition section of the Act on fish, wildlife, or plants held in a controlled environment on the date that said fish, wildlife or plants is listed as an endangered or threatened species.  The Act provides that a person holding such fish and wildlife is not in violation of the Act provided that the holding was not in the course of any commercial activity.  Therefore the person complying with this section is entitled to an exemption from the section on prohibited acts of the Endangered Species Act.

In addition to fish, wildlife, and plants listed under the Act, the exemption is made also for the holding in captivity in a controlled environment or any raptor or progeny of any raptor.  In this cases a continuing exemption is given to the holder of such raptor until such time as the raptor or its progeny is intentionally returned to a wild state.

---

[59]   16 U.S.C.A. § 1538.

# WILDLIFE AND HABITAT

The Endangered Species Act also prohibits any person (subject to the jurisdiction of the United States) to engage in any trade in any specimens contrary to the provisions of C.I.T.E.S. or to possess any specimens traded contrary to the provisions of this convention. This section is of course the implementation of the C.I.T.E.S. Convention which is described later on in this book.

In order to control traffic in species listed as threatened or endangered the Secretary is authorized under the Endangered Species Act to designate ports to be used in the importation or exportation of listed fish, wildlife or plant. Undoubtedly, this measure is important to the control of imported and exported fish, wildlife and plants listed under the Act.

In addition to being liable for committing any of the Acts listed in the Endangered Species Act prohibitions, it is also unlawful for any person to solicit another to commit any such prohibited acts.

## EXCEPTIONS

Where circumstances permit the Secretary may grant exceptions to persons or organizations which might commit acts which would be in violation of the prohibited acts section of the Endangered Species Act. One circumstance to encourage the Secretary to permit an exception would be in situations where the activities carried on are for scientific purposes or the purposes to enhance the propagation or survival of the affected species including the establishment and maintenance of experimental populations.

Also the Secretary may grant an exception where an action is lawful and the taking which is prohibited is incidental to its lawful activity.

Another situation in which the Secretary could declare an exception would be under circumstances of hardship. As an example, if a person or an organization entered into a contract with respect to a species of fish, wildlife or plant before the publication of notice that the species had been declared to be endangered and the enforcement of the Endangered Species Act Prohibition Section would cause undue economic hardship. In this case, the Secretary has the power and authority to grant the exemption for a limited period of time, not to exceed one year from the date the person or the organization violating the Endangered Species Act was on a notice. The term "undue economic hardship" means substantial economic loss resulting from inability to perform the contracts entered into before notice that the particular species had been placed on the endangered list. An example where this classification might be used is a situation in which a person suffers undue economic hardship because a substantial portion of the income enjoyed by that person was derived by the lawful taking of the species prior to the time it was listed as endangered.

# ENDANGERED SPECIES

It goes without saying that the Secretary may make as required whatever arrangements he thinks are appropriate under the circumstance.

The authority and power of the Secretary to grant these exceptions are not solely at his discretion. The Secretary must publish in the Federal Register each application for an exemption or permit and such notice shall invite submission from interested parties within 30 days after the notice. The information if any received by the Secretary must be part of his decision-making process and is available to the public as a matter of public record.

The policy underlying the exemption process is stated to be consistent with the purposes underlying the endangered species protection concept. In addition to the requirement of good faith on the part of the applicant for any exemption and the exemption if granted would not operate to the disadvantage of any endangered species.

An important exemption which is built into the Act runs in favor of Alaskan natives. The exemption covers an Indian, Aleut, or Eskimo who is an Alaskan native who resides in Alaska and any non-native permanent resident of an Alaskan native village. However, this exemption is conditioned upon the fact that the taking which is prohibited by the Act is primarily for subsistence purposes. Furthermore, non-edible by-products of any species taken may be sold at interstate commerce when made into authentic native articles or handicrafts and clothing provided that this classification of exemptions does not apply to a non-native permanent resident of an Alaskan native village unless that person is primarily dependent upon the taking and sale.

The term subsistence includes edible portions of fish and wildlife which are sold in native villages and towns in Alaska for native consumption within these villages and towns. The term authentic native articles or handicrafts and clothing means items composed wholly or in some significant respect of natural materials which are produced, decorated, or fashioned in the exercise of traditional native handicrafts without the use of pantographs, multiple cravers, or other mass copy devices. Traditional native handicrafts include weaving, carving, stitching, sewing, lacing, beading, drawing, and painting.

The Endangered Species Act does not require the Secretary to grant an exemption to Alaskan natives where a taking materially and negatively affects the threatened or endangered species. In such circumstances he may prescribe regulations, as he deems necessary, to accomplish the purposes of the Act.

Another exemption under the Act applies to *preact* endangered species parts. The Act prescribes two such (parts) - any sperm oil including any derivatives thereof which were held in the course of a commercial activity prior to December 28, 1973 and any finished shrimp shell product or the raw material from such product held in the course of a commercial activity prior to December 28, 1973.

The term scrimshaw product means any art form which involves a substantial etching or engraving of designs upon or the substantial craving of figures, patterns, or designs from, any bone or tooth of any marine animal of the order Cetacea.

The Act makes it unlawful for any person to sell in interstate or foreign commerce any *pre-Act* created scrimshaw product without a valid certificate and exemption issued by the Secretary.

One exception to this entire exemption process is that the Secretary may not approve an exemption and issue a certificate which would authorize a prohibited act if such act would be in violation of the C.I.T.E.S. Convention.

Also listed in the Endangered Species Act are several classifications of exemptions built automatically into the Act, not needing any discretion or action on the part of the Secretary. Included under this classification would be any article which could conceivably fall in or under the Act not less than 100 years of age, and importations into the United States of fish or wildlife where such fish or wildlife was lawfully taken and exported from the country of origin and/or the country of re-export.

Another exemption is built in for fish or wildlife under the Act where such fish or wildlife is in transport or transshipment through any place subject to the jurisdiction of the United States which is on route to a country where such fish or wildlife may be lawfully imported or received. A condition attached to this built in exemption is that it applies only while such fish or wildlife remain in the control of the United States Customs Service.[60]

A provision of the Endangered Species Act provides for rewards and certain incidental expenses. The Act provides that the Secretary of the Treasurer or the Secretary of the Interior must pay (from sums received as penalties, fines, or forfeitures of property for any violation of the Act) a reward to any person who furnishes information which leads to an arrest, a criminal conviction, a civil penalty assessment, or forfeiture of property for any violation of the Act or any regulation issued hereunder and the reasonable and necessary cost incurred by any person in providing temporary care for any fish, wildlife or plant pending the disposition of any civil or criminal proceeding alleging a violation of the Act with respect to that fish, wildlife or plant. The amount of the reward is to be designated by the appropriate Secretary.[61]

---

60 16 U.S.C.A. § 1539.
61 16 U.S.C.A. § 1540.

# ENDANGERED SPECIES

The appropriate Secretary is charged with the enforcement of the Act. The Secretary may use the personnel and services facilities of any federal agency or any state agency for the purposes of enforcing the Act.

The judges of the district courts of the United States and the United States Magistrates have authority under the Act to issue warrants or other processes that may be required for enforcement.

The Act also provides that the appropriate Secretary may detain for inspection and inspect any package, crate, or other container including its contents upon importation or exportation, for the purposes of enforcing the Act.

## FORFEITURE

The Act also contains a forfeiture provision which applies to all fish, wildlife or plants taken, all guns, traps, nets and other equipment, vessels, vehicles, aircraft, and other means of transportation used to aid the taking in violation of the Act and that these forfeited items may be disposed of and the monies acquired therefore apply for purposes of offering and rewards and to pay incidental expenses under the Act.[62]

## CITIZEN SUITS

Any person may commence a civil suit on his own behalf to enjoin any person including the United States and any other governmental instrumentality or agency (to the extent permitted by the 11th Amendment of the Constitution) who is alleged to be in violation of any provision of the Act, or to compel the Secretary to apply the prohibition set forth in the Act or against the Secretary where there is alleged a failure of the Secretary to perform any act or duty which is not discretionary under the Act.

Before such civil suit can be maintained, however the person bringing it must give a sixty day written notice of the violation to the Secretary and to any alleged violator of any provisions of the Act or of the regulations. This means that no action may be commenced prior to sixty days after the written notice has been given except that the action may be brought immediately after notification in any situation where the activity alleged to be in violation of the Act poses a significant risk to the well being of any species of fish, wildlife or plants.[63]

The court in issuing any final order in any suit brought pursuant to the section on civil suits may award cost of litigation (including reasonable attorney and expert witness fees) to any party whenever the court determines such award is appropriate.[64]

---

62    16 U.S.C.A. § 1540(f).
63    16 U.S.C.A. § 1540(g).  See Save the Yak Committee v. Block, 840 F.2d 714.

In determining the amount of fee awards under the Endangered Species Act it has been held that the starting point is a process involving a multiplication of the number of hours reasonably spent on litigation by the reasonable hourly rate of compensation. In *Palila v. Hawaii Department of Land and Natural Resources*[65] the court held that in arriving at this "lodestar," the district court should be guided by the following criteria: time and labor required, novelty and difficulty of questions involved, skill required to perform legal services properly, preclusion of other employment by attorney due to the acceptance of the case, customary fee, whether the fee is fixed or contingent, time limitations imposed by time or circumstances, amount involved and results obtained, experience, reputation, and ability of attorneys, undesirability of case, nature and length of professional relationship with client, and awards in similar cases.

The notice requirement is rather specifically enforced and requires a written notice to be sent to the Secretary of the Interior. In *Save the Yak Committee v. Block*,[66] the Court held that a letter sent to the supervisor of National Forests Service and to the regional director of the United States Fish and Wildlife Service with carbon copies sent to various state and federal legislators and environmental groups did not satisfy the Endangered Species Act's sixty day written notice requirement.

In *Maine Audubon Society v. Purslow*,[67] the Court discussed the meaning of the sixty day notice period required under the Endangered Species Act in a citizen's suit. In this case, the conservation society brought suit against a private party to enjoin the further development of the defendant's property as a residential subdivision. The development site contained two bald eagle nests, one active and the other inactive. The defendant's proposed road would run within a foot of the inactive nest tree and approximately six hundred and fifty feet from the active nest. Plantiff's claimed that this private development would interfere with the breeding pair and, thus, would violate the Endangered Species Act.

The plaintiffs in this case provided a written notice to the Secretary of the Interior of the violation of the Act by the defendant, but did not file a written notice to the defendant that a suit was going to be brought under the Act unless the action complained of was stopped.

The Court, in interpreting the statute, found that the sixty day notice requirement as to those other than the Secretary of the Interior was an ab-

---

64  16 U.S.C.A. § 1540(g). See also The Sierra Club v. Clark, 577 F. Supp. 783, the court applied the traditional rule in awarding attorney fees. An appropriate fee is awarded when the private party plainfiff achieves some success in the merit of his claims.
65  118 F.R.D. 125.
66  840 F.2d 714.
67  672 F. Supp. 528.

solute requirement of the Act and was not waived by any other provisions of the Endangered Species Act. The Court went on to state that with respect to the Secretary a waiver of notice is provided under emergency circumstances but nowhere in the Act is there a provision that the sixty day notice can be waived as to a non-Secretary party. The result of the conclusion reached by the court was a dismissal of plaintiff's suit on the procedural violation of the Endangered Species Act.

Citizen's suits are to be brought in the judicial district in which the violation occurs. The Attorney General at the request of the Secretary may intervene on behalf of the United States as a matter of right in any of these suits.

## VIOLATIONS AND PENALTIES

The penalty provision of the Act contains both civil penalties and criminal penalties.[68]

A civil penalty is assessed against any person who knowingly violates the act and any person engaged in business as an importer or exporter of fish, wildlife or plants who violates any provision of the Act. In such circumstances the Secretary may assess a civil penalty of not more than $10,000 for each violation.

It is undoubtedly true that the provision of civil penalties for violations of the Act was intended by Congress to serve as a efficient deterrent to would-be violators and to eliminate illegal trapping in endangered species by drying up the market for such endangered species.

A defendant who is charged with a violation of the Act may escape the imposition of civil penalty if he can show by a preponderance of the evidence that he committed the act based on a good faith belief that he was acting to protect himself or a member of his family or any other individual from bodily harm from any endangered or threatened species.[69]

The Act also contains criminal penalties. The Act provides that any person who knowingly violates any provision of the Act or violates any permit or certificate issued under the Act or any regulation related to the Act shall upon conviction be fined not more than $50,000 or imprisoned for not more than one year or both.

An interesting case involving a criminal violation of the Act is *United States v. Billy*.[70] In this case James Billy, a Seminole Indian, was charged in a two count information with the taking and subsequent possession,

---

68   16 U.S.C. § 540.
69   16 U.S.C. § 1540(a)(3).
70   667 F. Supp. 1485.

caring and transportation of a Florida panther in violation of the Endangered Species Act. The Florida panther at that time was listed on
the endangered species list. The defendant defended on the ground
that the Endangered Species Act does not apply to a non-commercial
hunting on the Seminole Indian reservation. He based this argument
on the premise that the Act does not evince a congressional intent to abrogate or modify the traditional right to hunt and fish on Indian reservations.

The Court disagreed with this theory stating that the Act is a reasonable, necessary, and non-discriminatory conservation statute which has
limited the Indian rights to take or possess species to the extent these
rights are inconsistent with the Act. The Court cited in its opinion another case from the Eighth Circuit, *United States v. Dion*,[71] in which that
court held that the Endangered Species Act did not apply to Indians exercising non-commercial hunting rights on Indian land. The Court reasoned that the decision was not binding on this Court which is in a
different circuit.

The Court in *United States v. Billy* took great pains to discuss the Endangered Species Act vis-a-vis Indian rights. The Court reasoned that Indian rights to hunt and fish are not absolute. While Indian rights to
hunt and fish may carry a great weight, they nevertheless must give
way to conservation measures which are necessary to protect endangered wildlife and that the government can intervene on behalf of these
federal interests.

The Court also called attention to the fact that Congress had drawn several extraordinarily narrow exceptions to the Act's prohibitions. Indians, Aluets, or Eskimos who are Alaskan natives residing in Alaska and
in some circumstances other non-native permanent residents of Alaskan native villages could be authorized to take endangered or threatened species but only if the taking is primary for subsistence purposes
and only subject to such regulations as the Secretary may issue upon
his determination that such taking materially and negatively affects the
species. The Court reasoned, however, that the Act did not specifically
provide exceptions for Indians in general, other than those specifically
mentioned in the Act.

As another defense, *Billy* argued that the criminal portion of the Endangered Species Act did not apply to his action because the government
did not prove beyond a reasonable doubt his knowledge that: (1) the
animal he shot was a Florida panther; (2) it was a crime to do so on the
Seminole Indian reservation. The court rejected the defendant's argument stating that Congress did not intend to make knowledge of the

71   752 F.2d 1261.

law an element of a criminal violation. The court stated that the Endangered Species Act used the word knowingly and that all this means is that the Act was done voluntarily and intentionally and not because of a mistake or accident.

The final argument the defendant used to attempt to escape his charges under the Act involved his right to freedom of religion under the First Amendment. The defendant's argument was that since the Endangered Species Act did not authorize the Secretary to permit the possession of this species for Indian religious purpose, the entire Act is invalid because it sweeps within its ambit his constitutionally protected religious practices and right. The Court, used an argument frequently applied in cases involving conflicts of acts and religion and stated that not all burdens on religion are unconstitutional. The Court stated that while the concept of freedom to believe under the free exercise clause is absolute, the freedom by act is not. The Court concluded that the interest in conservation must be balanced against Indian religious rights and that this balance involved a weighing of each interest. The Court after discussing in great length the balancing concept concluded that *Billy* had not adequately shown that the possession of panther parts was essential to an important religious ceremony or ritual.

In another case *United States v. St. Onge*[72] the Court had the opportunity to interpret the criminal provisions of the Endangered Species Act. Once again the questions centered around the meaning of the word "knowingly" contained in the criminal provisions of the Act. The Court cited the *United States v. Billy* case and approved that definition.

The Court identified the issue in the *St. Onge* case as being whether or not the government was required to prove that the defendant knew that he shot a grizzly bear which was on the endangered species list or rather whether it was only necessary for the government to prove that he shot a grizzly bear.

The Court concluded that in cases involving criminal violations of the Endangered Species Act the government must prove three elements beyond a reasonable doubt in order for the defendant to be convicted. The three elements identified were (1) that the defendant knowingly took an animal within the United States; (2) that the animal was a grizzly bear (or other listed endangered species); (3) that the defendant did not have permission from the United States Department of the Interior to take the bear (animal).

In several cases involving the criminal portion of the Act the questioned faced by a court was what the definition of a "person" was. In *United*

---

[72]   676 F. Supp. 1044.

*States v. Billy* previously cited, the Court stated that Indians were considered in the category of persons under the Endangered Species Act.

In *United States v. City of Rancho Palos Verdes*,[73] the Court faced the issue of whether or not a municipal corporation was a person subject to the requirements of the Endangered Species Act. The Court concluded that the Act does not give a clear answer to this question. A consideration of the legislative history of the Act does not give any clear indication that a municipal corporation was either included or excluded from the definition of person. Using the plain meaning approach to statutory interpretation, the Court concluded that at this time a municipal corporation was not a person under the Act.

The Court went on to note however that if Congress intended a different construction from the one the court is giving at this time, the statute is easily amendable. It is interesting to note that the Court held that enforcement of the Endangered Species Act is not lost in this case because city employees are subject to the Act and each could be sued within the person classification of the Endangered Species Act.

[73]   841 F.2d 329.

# CHAPTER FIVE

## NATURAL RESOURCES LAW AND POLICY

The well-being of wildlife is vitally dependent upon the health of its habitat. It is therefore clear that the management of federally owned lands, which comprise nearly twenty percent of the total land area in the United States, is of great significance for the health of much of the nation's wildlife. Without some mechanism for ensuring that the management of these lands protects their habitat values, the regulation of direct taking and the regulation of commerce in wildlife necessarily constitute an incomplete federal program of wildlife conservation.

In 1964, at the time Congress passed Wilderness Act,[1] it also established the Public Land Law Review Commission and directed it to undertake a comprehensive study and evaluation of the nation's laws affecting public lands and to come up with recommendations as to change, if any change were perceived to be necessary.

The report of the Commission was issued in 1970 (it was entitled "One-Third Of The Nation's Land")[2] and at that time the Commission estimated the total land area of all the states at over 2 billion acres, of which approximately 750,000 acres was federally owned. This figure did not include all submerged lands, but it did include the lands in Alaska which at that time were ninety-five percent federally owned.

The conclusions, which were in the form of recommendations, by the Commission included: (1) reversal of the then existing policy of large scale disposal of public lands; (2) Congress should authorize and require the public land agencies to condition the granting of rights or privileges to the public lands or their resources on compliance with applicable environmental control measures governing operations of public lands which are closely related to the right or the privilege granted; (3) to require by statute that users of public lands and resources conduct their activities in such a manner as to avoid or minimize adverse environmental impact and to make these users responsible for restoring areas to an acceptable standard; and (4) public land agencies should be required to plan land uses to obtain the greatest net public benefit.

The problem perceived by the Commission was predicated on a basic assumption; that the twin evils of population growth and economic growth will continue and cause potential damage to these federal lands.

---

1   16 U.S.C.A. § 1131 et seq.
2   U.S. Public Land Law Review Commission, One Third of the Nations Land: A Report, Washington, D.C. 1970).

# WILDLIFE AND HABITAT

The history of federal lands in the United States is, to say the least, interesting. Land grants to the original colonies were very vague and the fundamental purposes underlying the British government's theory and the Colonial theory were quite different. The British government intended to control land grants and acquire revenue for itself while the Colonies seemed more interested in converting land into private ownership as speedily as possible. In 1780 Congress adopted a general statement of its land policy which stated "that lands were to be disposed of for the common benefit of the United States." The states, apparently agreeing with this policy, ceded their lands to the central government. This process was completed about 1802.

In 1785, Congress passed the Land Ordinance of 1785. This ordinance resulted in authority being vested in the central government to sell public lands.

Shortly after independence, the United States began acquiring additional land areas. One was the Louisiana Purchase in 1803. Florida and the Oregon country were acquired in 1819, Texas in 1845, and the Southwestern area from Mexico in 1848. Alaska was purchased in 1867, Hawaii was annexed in 1898.

The vast addition of these public lands gave the new government prestige and the chance to promote progress. Roads, turnpikes, canals, and railroads were built and encouraged by land grants. State universities, agricultural and mechanical schools were encouraged and states were granted land to build their capitols.[3]

## FEDERAL LAND POLICY AND MANAGEMENT ACT

After many years of piecemeal attempts to develop and manage the nation's public lands, Congress addressed the matter from a coordinated and organized perspective in 1976. Fundamental to the concept of federal ownership, management, and control of public lands is the Federal Land Policy and Management Act of 1976.[4] The overall purpose underlying the Act was to modernize the vast number of public laws on the books at that time. In the House Report on the Bill, it was recognized that public lands had played a key role in the development of the economy and institution of the United States. More than three thousand public land laws were on the books at the time of the consideration of this Act. The Committee on Interior and Insular Affairs recognized that many of these public land laws were still viable and applicable under then existing present conditions, however, many were obsolete and when considered as a whole the vast number of public land laws did

---

3    Public Land Law, Practicing Law Institute, Course Handbook Series, Number 115.
4    43 U.S.C.A. § 1701 et seq.

not add up to a coherent expression of congressional policies adequate for national goals.[5]

The Committee recommended, as a major step toward modernizing the public land laws in existence, a bill which would accomplish the following major objectives: (1) establish a mission for the public lands administered by the Secretary of the Interior through the Bureau of Land Management; (2) clothe the Bureau of Land Management with sufficient authority to enable it to carry out the goals and objectives established by law for the public lands under its jurisdiction; (3) enact into law criteria, guidelines, and standards to be followed by the Bureau of Land Management and, in a more limited way, by the Forest Service in the administration of various resources under their jurisdiction consistent with statutory goals; (4) establish procedures to facilitate congressional oversight of public land operations entrusted to the Secretary of the Interior; and (5) weed out of the body of law those statutes and parts of statutes which are obsolete.

The Federal Land Policy and Management Act set up in the Department of the Interior the Bureau of Land Management. Specifically, the Act requires that the Secretary must carry out through the Bureau all of his functions, powers, and duties vested in him and relating to the administration of the Act.[6]

The Bureau is headed up by a director and he is assisted by various associate directors, assistant directors, and other employees.

The Secretary, acting through the Bureau of Land Management, is to conduct resource inventories and land use planning; sell public lands; issue licenses, leases, permits, and direct occupancy of public lands; acquire land for public use by purchase, donation, and exchange; record mining claims and terminate unrecorded claims; enforce all laws and regulations relating to public lands; perform a myriad of administrative type duties; create advisory boards and councils; issue rules and regulations; and issue certain rights of way and withdraw those rights of way when deemed appropriate.

The House Report, which was preliminary to the adoption of the House of Representatives' bill which finally became the law, identified a number of areas which were in urgent need of consideration. Included in this list were the need for a system to compute grazing fees which would be equitable and which would remove and relieve controversy, clarification of the tenure of grazing users, inclusion in the Bureau of Land Management lands in the wilderness system and appropriate procedures to bring this about, establishment of goals and a timetable for

---

5 House Report No. 94-1163, U.S. Code Congressional and Administrative News, 1976, p. 6175.
6 43 U.S.C.A. § 1731.

protection and management of the California desert area, liberalization of recreation and public purposes with respect to grants of recreational lands to states and local governments, and the use of motorized vehicles in the protection and management of wild horses and burros and transfer of title to these animals from federal lands.

In addition, the House Report expressed the necessity for certain oversight procedures. These procedures would vest in Congress the power to act by forcing the Bureau of Land Management to refer to Congress certain types of actions. Some of these actions included decisions to exclude one or more principal uses from areas of 100,000 acres or more of public lands, any proposed sale in excess of 2,500 acres, and any decision to withdraw and/or extend areas of 5,000 acres or more.

One other provision was of importance to the National Forest System, which was created out of the public domain. The House bill, which was finally enacted into law, made many of the provisions of the Federal Land Policy and Management Act applicable to the National Forest System.

In order to implement the policies and goals studied by Congress and embodied in the various committee reports the Act, when it finally was passed, contained a number of specific declarations of policy. The Act provides that it is the policy of Congress that:

(1) public lands be retained in federal ownership unless as a result of the land use planning procedure provided for by this Act it is determined that the disposal of a particular parcel will serve the national interest;

(2) the national interest would be best realized if the public lands and their resources are periodically and systematically inventoried and their present and future uses protected through a land use planning process coordinated with other federal and state planning efforts;

(3) public lands not previously designated for any specific use and all existing classifications of public lands that were affected by executive action or statute prior to the passage of this Act be reviewed in accordance with the provisions of the Act;

(4) that Congress exercise it constitutional authority to withdraw or otherwise designate or dedicate federal lands for specified purposes and that Congress delineate the extent to which the Executive may withdraw lands without legislative action;

(5) in administering public lands statutes and exercising discretionary authority granted by them the Secretary shall be required to establish comprehensive rules and regulations after considering the views of the general public and to structure adjudication procedures to assure ade-

quate third party participation and objective administrative review of initial decisions and expeditious decision making;

(6) that the public land law decisions be subject to judicial review;

(7) that goals and objectives should be established by law as guidelines for public land use planning and that management be on the basis of multiple use and sustained yield unless otherwise specified by the law;

(8) that public lands be managed in a manner that will protect the quality of scientific, scenic, historical, ecological, environmental, air and atmospheric, water resource, archaeological values, and that where appropriate will reserve and protect certain public lands in their natural condition, that will provide food and habitat for fish and wildlife and domestic animals, and that will provide for outdoor recreation and human occupancy and use;

(9) the United States must receive fair value of the use of the public lands and their resources;

(10) that uniform procedures for any disposal of public land, acquisition of non-federal land for public purposes, and the exchange of such land shall be established by a statute, requiring each disposal, acquisition, or exchange to be consistent with the prescribed mission of the department or agency involved and reserving to Congress review of disposals in excess of a specified acreage;

(11) regulations and plans for protection of public land areas of critical environmental concern be promptly developed;

(12) that public lands be managed in a manner which recognizes the nation's need for domestic sources of minerals, food, timber, and fiber from the public lands including implementation of the Mining and Minerals Policy Act of 1970 (30 U.S.C. 21a) as it pertains to the public lands; and

(13) the federal government should on a basis equitable to both the federal and local taxpayer provide for payments to compensate states and local governments for burdens created as a result of the immunity of federal lands from state and local taxation.[7]

There are several definitions which are essential to the understanding of the Act and those are provided by the Act itself. First of all, the term multiple use has an interesting and fundamental meaning to the entire concept of the use of public lands. The Act defines the term multiple use to mean "the management of the public lands and their various re-

7    43 U.S.C.A. § 1701.

source values so that they are utilized in the combination that will best meet the present and future needs of the American people; making the most judicious use of the land or some or all of these resources or related services over areas large enough to provide sufficient latitude for public adjustments in use to conform to changing needs and conditions; the use of some land for less than all of their resources; a combination of balanced and diverse resource uses that takes into account the long term needs of future generations for renewable and nonrenewable resources including recreation, range, timbers, minerals, watershed, wildlife and fish, and natural scenic, scientific, and historical values; and harmonious and coordinated management of the various resources without permanent impairment of the productivity of the land and the quality of the environment with consideration being given to the relative values of the resources and not necessarily to the combination of uses that will give the greatest economic return or the greatest unit output."[8]

Almost always included in the same sentence with the term multiple use is the term sustained yield. The Act defines this term to mean "the achievement and maintenance in perpetuity of a high level annual or regular output of the various renewable resources of the public lands consistent with multiple use."[9]

It is without doubt that the overriding and fundamental purpose of land management of the public lands is the concept embodied in the combined terms multiple use and sustained yield.

Of course of primary interest is a definition of "public lands." Under the Act, public lands is defined to mean "any land and interest in land owned by the United States within the several states and administered by the Secretary of the Interior through the Bureau of Land Management without regard to how the United States acquired ownership." Specifically excluded within this definition would be lands located on the outer Continental Shelf and lands held for the benefit of Indians, Aleuts, and Eskimos.[10]

In order to be compatible with the purposes expressed in Congress at the time of the introduction of the Bill, the Act when finally passed contained several provisions which implemented the intended policy. These provisions addressed the issues of land use planning, land acquisition and disposition, the administrative functions of the Bureau of Land Management including the setting into place the various advisory councils, range management, control by granting and eliminating

8   43 U.S.C.A. § 1702(c).
9   43 U.S.C.A. § 1702(h).
10  43 U.S.C.A. § 1702(e).

rights-of-way on public lands, and the specific designation of management areas.

A particularly important function of the Land Policy & Management Act is the process of land use planning. Congress mandated under the Act that the Secretary of the Interior should prepare and maintain on a continuing basis an inventory of all public lands and their resource and other values, giving priority to areas of critical environmental concern.

Included in the continuing inventory is a mandate upon the Secretary to ascertain the boundaries of public land, provide means of public identification of these lands through signs and maps, and provide state and local governments with data from the inventory for the purposes of planning and regulating the uses of non-federal lands in proximity of such public lands.

After the study of the public lands through the inventory the Secretary is mandated to develop, maintain and revise land use plans which provide by tracks or areas for the use of the public lands. In the development and revision of these land use plans, the Secretary of Agriculture must coordinate land use plans for lands in the National Forest Service with the Land Use Planning and Management Programs for Indian Tribes usually contained in Tribal Land Resource Management Programs.

The Act is rather specific as to the criteria for development and revision of these land use plans. Under the Act the Secretary must:

(1) Use and observe the principles of multiple use and sustained yield;

(2) Use a systematic interdisciplinary approach to achieve integrated consideration of physical, biological, economic and other sciences;

(3) Give priority to the designation and protection of areas of critical environmental concern;

(4) Rely to the extent that it is available on the inventory of the public lands and resources and other values;

(5) Consider present and potential uses of public lands;

(6) Consider the relative scarcity of the values involved and the availability of the alternative means and sites for realization of these values;

(7) Weigh long-term benefits to the public against short-term benefits;

(8) Provide for compliance with applicable pollution control laws including state and federal air, water, noise, or other pollution standards or implementation plans;

(9) Coordinate the land use inventory planning and management activities of these public lands with the same activities of other federal departments and agencies and of state and local governments.[11]

The Secretary of the Interior must issue management decisions to implement the developed or revised land use plan. These decisions, as it is characteristic in other portions of government environmental laws, require the Secretary to involve the public and in doing so establish regulations for procedures including public hearings, where appropriate input can be received from interested persons, including other federal agencies' state and local governments.

The Secretary of the Interior is permitted to sell public lands (except lands in units of the National Wilderness Preservation System, the National Wild and Scenic River Systems, and the National System of Trails), when the Secretary determines that the sale of such track is compatible with the purposes of public land management contained in the Act. Generally speaking the Secretary must determine that the track he is contemplating the sale of is difficult and non-economic to manage as part of the public land and is not suitable for management by another federal department or agency; that this track was acquired for specific purpose and the track is no longer required for that purpose; or the disposal of the track under consideration will serve important public objectives which cannot be achieved prudently or feasibly on land other than public land and which outweigh other public objectives and values.

In order to keep control over the sale of public land the statute provides when a track of public lands, in excess of 2,500 acres, is designated for sale by the Secretary he must notify both the Senate and the House of Representatives of such impending sale. The Congress then may adopt a resolution stating that it does not approve such designation.

The sale of public lands by the Secretary must be made at a price not less than the fair market value as determined by the Secretary. In addition the Secretary must make calculated determinations as to the size of the land to be sold based on the land use capabilities and development requirements of the land.

The sale of such public lands under the Act must be made under competitive bidding procedures which can be established by the Secretary. It is a public policy that certain users are given preference over others. The order of preference includes the state in which the land is located, the local government entities in such state which are in the vicinity of the land, adjoining landowners, and then individuals.[12]

---

11  43 U.S.C.A. § 1712.
12  43 U.S.C.A. § 1713.

An important section of the Act pertains to the process of withdrawal of federal lands. Under the statute the term withdrawal means withholding an area of federal land from settlement, sale, location, or entry under some or all of the general land laws for the purpose of limiting activities under those laws in order to maintain other public values in the area or reserving the area for a particular public purpose or program.

In making a determination to withdraw federal land the Secretary in notifying Congress of his intention must make a very clear explanation of the proposed use of the land involved which will lead to the withdrawal. Included in this explanation are such items as an inventory and evaluation of current and natural resources uses, identification of the present uses of the land involved and how they will be effected by the withdrawal, and some statement as to the expected length of time in which the withdrawal is to take place.

The Act limits withdrawal in excess of 5,000 acres to a period of not more than 20 years. Any withdrawal contemplated by the Secretary under the Act must be subjected to a public hearing.[13]

In addition to selling public lands, and withdrawing public lands from current use, the Secretary also has the authority to acquire public lands by purchase, exchange, donation, or eminent domain. Also, the Secretary of Agriculture under this Act has the authority to acquire access over non-federal lands to units of the National Forest System. The land so acquired is then designated as public land and in the case where land is purchased by the Secretary of Agriculture such lands become part of the National Forest System.[14]

The Secretary has the authority under the Act to exchange public land for non-public lands. Also the Secretary of Agriculture has authority under the Act to exchange non-federal lands for public lands contained in the National Forest System. In either of these cases the Act mandates that the value of the lands exchanged must be equal or if the value is not equal they shall be equalized by the payment of money to the grantor or to the Secretary provided that the payment does not exceed 25% of the total value of the lands or interest transferred out of the federal ownership. In the event that the Secretary determines that the exchange will be expedited without the payment of money he has authority under the Act to waive such cash equalization payment where the amount to be waived is not more than 3% of the value of the land being transferred out of federal ownership or $15,000 whichever is less.

---

13  43 U.S.C.A. § 1714.
14  43 U.S.C.A. § 1715.

# WILDLIFE AND HABITAT

All lands acquired through the exchange (when title passes through the United States) become part of the unit or area in which they are located. This means therefore that the land acquired through such exchange becomes a part of the National Forest System, the National Park System, the National Wildlife Refuge System, the National Wild and Scenic River System, the National Trail System, the National Wilderness System, the Wilderness Preservation System, or any other system established by the Act at a later time.[15]

In establishing the values of the lands for exchange both the Secretary and the owner of the non-federal lands are required to arrange for appraisals. In the event that the appraisals cannot agree or cannot be accomplished then an arbitrator appointed by the Secretary from a list of arbitrators submitted to him by the American Arbitration Association shall make such exchange evaluation.

Any title work which results from this exchange of land must be done simultaneously.

The land exchange provisions of the Act were beefed up in 1988. In expanding the possibility for exchange under the Act, Congress found that land exchanges are very important tools for federal and state land managers and private landowners for purposes of more efficient management and to secure important objectives including the protection of fish and wildlife, habitat and aesthetic values.

In order to ensure that there are increased funds and personnel available to the Secretaries of the Interior and Agriculture to consider and consummate land exchanges, Congress appropriated for the fiscal year 1989-1990 an annual amount not to exceed $4 million dollars which is to be used jointly or divided amongst the Secretaries as they determine appropriate for the consideration, processing and consummation of land exchanges pursuant to the Act.[16]

The Act provides authority to the Secretary to issue all documents of conveyance and further invests him with the authority to provide such terms, covenants, conditions, and reservations as he deems necessary.[17]

## BUREAU OF LAND MANAGEMENT

The Bureau of Land Management was established by the Reorganization Plan No. 3 of 1946. It is responsible for the management of over 270,000,000 acres the vast majority of which is located in ten western states and Alaska. The total amount of land under the jurisdiction of

---

15  43 U.S.C.A. § 1716.
16  Pub. L. 100-409, 102 Stat. 1087.
17  43 U.S.C.A. § 1718.

the Bureau of Land Management is approximately 60% of all the land under federal jurisdiction.

The importance of the lands under the Bureau of Land Management authority cannot be over emphasized with respect to the species of mammals, birds, reptiles, fish, and amphibians that call it home. It has been estimated that over 3,000 species inhabit the land under the control of the Bureau of Land Management. Furthermore these managed public lands contain large percentages of rare fish and wildlife habitats. It has been estimated that 85% of the desert big-horn sheep in the United States reside on public lands. However in addition to managing the habitat of fish and wildlife, the Bureau of Land Management also manages public lands used for energy resource development, mining, timber production, livestock grazing, utility rights-of-way, recreation, and protection of cultural resources and natural scenic and scientific values and as range for wild horses and burros. As it can be seen the underlying policy, governing the management authority of the Bureau of Land Management, is the Multiple Use Doctrine.

The Bureau of Land Management is an agency contained within the Department of the Interior. It is supervised by the Assistant Secretary for Land and Minerals Management and is headed by a director, politically appointed.

The BLM operates from twelve field offices and each office is headed by a state director. In addition there are 59 district offices each headed by a district manager. The 59 districts are further divided into resource areas which number approximately 146.[18] The authority vested in the Secretary of the Interior operating through the Bureau of Land Management requires him to manage the public lands under principles of multiple use-sustained yield. This management and authority involves regulation through easements, permits, leases, licenses, public rules, and the development of public land for habitation, cultivation, and the development of small trade or manufacture.

In accomplishing the purposes of the Act, the Secretary through the Bureau of Land Management is required to issue regulations necessary to implement all the provisions of the Land Policy & Management Act.[19]

The Secretary of the Interior has the authority to establish reasonable filing and service fees and reasonable charges of commissions with respect to his permitted use of public lands in whatever form he deems appropriate.[20]

---

18   Bureau of Land Management, Karen Franklin, Audubon Society, 1988.
19   43 U.S.C.A. § 1731(b), 43 U.S.C.A. § 1733.
20   43 U.S.C.A. § 1734.

# WILDLIFE AND HABITAT

In carrying out his duties under the Federal Land Policy Management Act the Secretary is authorized to establish advisory councils which may help him with respect to land use planning, classification, retention, management, and disposal of lands. These advisory councils must have a membership of at least ten persons and not more than 15 appointed by the Secretary from lists of persons who are representative of the various major citizen's interest groups concerned with the problems relating to land use planning or the management of the public lands located within a specific area.[21]

The Secretary of the Interior has the authority under the Land Policy & Management Act to issue regulations to implement the provisions of the Act.[22] The Act itself provides criminal penalties for any person who knowingly and willingly violates any regulation which is lawfully issued by the Secretary. The amount of penalty is a maximum of $1,000 and/or imprisonment for no more than twelve months. (In other words a misdemeanor penalty). The jurisdiction over such criminal matters is vested in the United States magistrate in the district in which the violation occurred.[23]

In addition to criminal penalties for violation of the provisions of the Federal Land Policy & Management Act, the Act also permits the Secretary to request from the Attorney General of the United States that a civil action in a United States District Court be brought in order to prevent any person from utilizing public lands in violation of the regulations. The remedy usually sought by the Attorney General in behalf of the Secretary is an order for an injunction. An interesting feature of the Act concerns the assistance of local law enforcement officials in enforcing the laws contained in the Federal Land Policy & Management Act and the regulations issued under it. The Act provides that the Secretary may contract with local officials having law enforcement authority within their respective jurisdictions to enforce federal laws and regulations. The Act vests in these local officials the authority to execute and serve warrants or other processes, make arrests, search, and perform any other activities customarily performed by law officials in carrying out their duties to enforce the law.[24]

The attempt to bring in local officials to enforce federal laws in the case of public lands is obviously intended to minimize and make more efficient law enforcement costs and to maximize enforcement of public land laws. One form the use of local officials may take is through federal reimbursement to a state or subdivision for expenditures incurred

21   43 U.S.C.A. § 1739.
22   43 U.S.C.A. § 1740.
23   43 U.S.C.A. § 1733(a).
24   43 U.S.C.A. § 1733(b.

by it in connection with activities which assists in the administration and regulation of use and occupancy of the public lands.[25]

One of the reasons that the Federal Land Policy & Management Act was passed in addition to reorganizing public land administration, was the matter of grazing on public lands. The Taylor Grazing Act[26] of 1934 was passed by Congress to preserve and protect the use of public lands for livestock grazing purposes and thereby to stabilize the livestock industry. The Act authorized the Secretary of the Interior to establish grazing districts and to issue grazing permits to graze livestock on such grazing districts.

Early on it became apparent that it would be necessary to reduce livestock grazing levels to be compatible with the land's carrying capacity.

When the Bureau of Land Management was created in 1946, one of its responsibilities was range management and this included the tasks of districting the public range lands and promulgating regulations to oversee the issuing of permits.

Livestock grazing is authorized on almost all of the 177,000,000 acres of public lands under the management of the Bureau of Land Management. The Bureau of Land Management issues permits or leases to almost 20,000 livestock operators for about 2.2 million cattle and 2.1 million sheep and goats on the public lands.[27] Under the FLMPA the Secretary of Agriculture for forest lands and the Secretary of the Interior for all other public lands are under mandates to determine the value of grazing on all the lands under their jurisdictions in the 11 western states and to establish a fee to be charged for domestic livestock grazing on such lands which is fair both to the United States (owners of these lands) and to the holders of the grazing permits.[28]

The Secretaries are required to take into consideration the cost of production normally associated with domestic livestock grazing, the differences in forage values, and such other factors as may relate to the reasonableness of such fees.

Congress is seriously interested in livestock grazing on public lands and requires both Secretaries to establish any grazing fees based on a study.

At the time of the passage of the FLMPA Congress was aware that a substantial amount of the federal range lands was deteriorating in quality and that it was necessary to arrest much of the continuing deteriora-

---

25   43 U.S.C.A. § 1733(c).
26   43 U.S.C. § 315.
27   Bureau of Land Management, Karen Franklin, Audubon Society, 1988.
28   43 U.S.C.A. § 1751(a).

tion and to better the forage conditions. Congress felt that not only would livestock grazing should be improved but also that the benefits would accrue to wildlife, watershed protection, and livestock production. In order to ensure such range improvement, Congress directed that 50% or a minimum of $10,000,000 per year, whichever was greater, of all the monies received by the United States as fees for grazing domestic livestock on public lands, should be credited to a separate account in the Treasury. One half of this amount was authorized to be appropriated and made available for use in the district or region from which such monies were derived for the purpose of on-the-ground range rehabilitation protection and improvements. The remaining one-half of such funds was to be used by the Secretary after consultation with district, regional, or national forage user representatives for a like purpose.[29]

The rehabilitation protection and improvement of the range was to take the form of range land betterment including seeding and re-seeding, fence construction, weed control, water development, and fish and wildlife enhancement.

This special fund to be used for land rehabilitation was to be in addition to the funds which would be generated under the Taylor Grazing Act. The Taylor Grazing Act provided that one-third of all the grazing fees received from each grazing district on Indian lands seeded to the United States was to be expended by the Secretary of the Treasurer in the state in which the land was situated for the benefit of public schools and public roads. The remaining two-thirds of all these grazing fees received was to be used for the benefit of Indians and deposited to the credit of these Indians pending a final disposition mandated by laws, treaties or agreements.

Under the FLMPA, grazing leases and permits for domestic livestock grazing on public land issued by the Secretary were limited to a term not to exceed ten years. The Secretary of Agriculture and the Secretary of the Interior are given discretion to impose such terms and conditions that each Secretary think necessary to implement the purposes of the Act. These discretionary actions might very well include modifying a grazing permit or lease in whole or in part, canceling or suspending one already issued or the imposition of any other term or condition thought necessary by the Secretary.

The Act provides that each Secretary may issue permits or leases for a period shorter than ten years provided that such Secretary determines that the land is either pending disposal, will be devoted to a public purpose prior to the end of ten years, or it is in the best interest of sound land management to specify a shorter term.

---

29   43 U.S.C.A. § 1751(b).

In basing his determination on whether or not to issue a permit or lease for domestic livestock grazing on public land, each Secretary is given the authority to incorporate an allotment management plan developed by the Secretary.[30]

All permits and leases for domestic livestock grazing may incorporate an allotment management plan developed by the Secretary. An allotment management plan means a document prepared in consultation with the lessees or the permittees involved which applies to livestock operations on the public lands. These plans prescribe (1) the manner and the extent to which livestock operations can be conducted in order to meet multiple use sustained yield objectives, (2) describes the type, location and ownership and general specifications for range improvements to be installed and maintained on the lands to meet the livestock grazing and other objectives of land management, and (3) contains such other provisions relating to livestock grazing and other objectives found by the Secretary concerned to be consistent with the provisions of the FLMPA.[31]

Each allotment management plan is required to be tailored to the specific range condition of the area to be covered by such plan and must be reviewed on a periodic basis to determine whether the plan has been effective in improving the range conditions of the lands involved.

The Secretary is given discretion to not complete an allotment management plan where the Secretary feels that such a plan is not necessary for management of livestock operations.

It is interesting to note that whether or not a Secretary decides to complete an allotment management plan, that decision has nothing to do with a requirement by a court that an environmental impact statement be developed prior to the incorporation of any such allotment management plan.

In cases where either Secretary does not complete an allotment management plan the Secretary must nevertheless specify the numbers of animals to be grazed and the seasons of use associated with any lease or permit. The term that's generally used to determine the number of livestock to be grazed on any particular piece of public land is an animal unit month (A.U.M.) of forage. This term is defined as the amount of forage consumed by one cow or five sheep in a month. The Secretary must re-examine the condition of the range periodically to make certain that the lease and permit numbers based on A.U.M.'s matches his determination as to what the range condition requires.[32]

---

30    43 U.S.C.A. § 1752(a,b,c).
31    43 U.S.C.A. § 1752(d).
32    See 36 C.F.R. Part 222.1 et seq. and 43 C.F.R. Part 4100-1 et seq.

The Act also provides that for each bureau or district office and each national forest headquarters office in the 16 contiguous western states the Secretaries upon petition of a simple majority of the livestock lessees and permittees under the jurisdiction of such office must establish and maintain at least one grazing advisory board of not more than 15 advisors. The function of these grazing advisory boards is to offer advise and make recommendations to the head of the office involved concerning the development of allotment management plans and the utilization of range betterment funds. The advisory board is appointed by the Secretary concerned in his discretion. The boards are required to meet at least once annually.[33]

Both the Secretary of the Interior with respect to public lands and the Secretary of Agriculture with respect to land within the National Forest System are authorized to grant and issue and where appropriate renew rights-of-way over public lands. The Act specifies that such rights-of-way are restricted to specific purposes which include reservoirs, canals, pipelines, systems for transmission of electrical energy, systems for transmission of radio, television, telephone and telegraph, roads, highways, trials, railroads, airways and any other necessary transportation or facilities which might be in the public interest.[34]

The Act also authorizes the Secretary of the Interior with respect to public lands to provide for the acquisition, construction, and maintenance of roads within and near the public lands. Generally the provision of these roads is intended to permit the harvesting of timber from the public lands and other resources. The financing of these roads can be accomplished by the Secretary using appropriate federal funds, by requirements imposed on those who are going to use public lands for purposes of timber harvesting. Included in such contract authorization are provisions for the amortization of these road costs, and, by various means, of cooperative financing with other public agencies and private agencies or persons.[35]

These documents associated with the provision of the roads must be filed in counties where the roads are located.[36]

The Secretary of the Interior is authorized to require of the users of any of these roads whatever measures he deems necessary to maintain the roads in a satisfactory condition. This maintenance may include reconstruction where circumstances require.[37]

---

[33] 43 U.S.C.A. § 1753.
[34] 43 U.S.C.A. § 1761.
[35] 43 U.S.C.A. § 1762(a).
[36] 43 U.S.C.A. § 1762(b).
[37] 43 U.S.C.A. § 1762(c).

With respect to the national forest lands, the Secretary of Agriculture has been provided by Congress with the same authority to administer all rights-of-way as the Secretary of the Interior has with respect to the public lands.

In exercising his authority to issue rights-of-way under the Act the Secretary is required to specify very carefully the precise boundaries of each right-of-way granted. In addition the Secretary is authorized to make decisions concerning the limitation of the right-of-way including its duration, and whether or not it is renewable, and whatever terms and conditions deemed necessary by the Secretary in connection with the use of the right-of-way.

The Act requires the holder of any right-of-way granted by the Secretary to pay in advance the fair market value of the right-of-way as determined by the Secretary. The Secretary also may structure any payment system concerning the right-of-way to meet any requirements that he deems necessary. However, as to private individuals, payments in excess of $100 may be, at the option of the private individual, either paid annually or include in one payment more than one year. Administrative and other costs associated with the granted right-of-way may be recovered by the Secretary from the holder of the right. This is subject, of course, to a power invested in the Secretary to waive any reimbursement where a cooperative cost share of right-of-way program between the United States and the holder of the right-of-way is in effect.[38]

The rights-of-way over public lands may be issued to a federal, state, or local government or, of course, to a private individual. Such rights-of-way issued are assignable with the approval of the Secretary issuing the right-of-way.

Rights-of-way may be issued or reviewed without rental fees for electric or telephone facilities financed pursuant to the Rural Electric Vocation Act of 1936.

In order to preserve the intention of the FLMPA to provide a balanced means of the use of public lands and the protection of the environment, the Act requires that each right-of-way contain provisions which will carry out the purposes of the Act. One category of terms and conditions required to be in each right-of-way is a requirement that damage to scenic and ethnic values, fish and wildlife habitat, and the environment in general be minimized. Under the Act the Secretary is given wide discretion to not only protect federal property and economic interests but to provide terms and conditions to protect lives, protect the in-

---

[38] 43 U.S.C.A. § 1766.

terest of individuals living in the general area traversed by the right-of-way who rely upon fish, wildlife, and other biotic resources of the area and to require the location of their right-of-way along a route that will cause the least damage to the environment.[39]

There are certain conditions which could cause the Secretary of the Interior to suspend or terminate a right-of-way. Generally speaking any non-compliance with a provision imposed by the Secretary at the time of the granting of the right-of-way or an abandonment of the right-of-way would be such grounds. Of course the Secretary must give due notice to the holder of the right-of-way including the grounds for his proposed action and must give the right-of-way holder a reasonable time to either resume use of the right-of-way or to comply with the conditions imposed by the Secretary at the time of its granting. What constitutes abandonment of course is an interesting question, but the Act provides that any failure of the holder of the right-of-way to use it for a continuous five year period creates a rebuttal presumption of abandonment.[40]

When the Secretary of the Interior makes a decision to convey public lands and these lands contain a right-of-way, the lands are to be conveyed subject to the right-of-way. It is possible for the Secretary to convey public lands and still retain the rights-of-way either to protect the interest of the United States or to protect the interest of the holder of the right-of-way.[41]

One of the provisions of the FLMPA is a requirement that within 15 years after its passage the Secretary through the Bureau of Land Management must review any roadless areas of 5,000 acres or more and roadless islands of the public lands which had the characteristics described in the Wilderness Act of 1964. The Secretary is to report to the President of the United States his recommendation as to the suitability or non-suitability of maintaining each of these areas as wilderness. However, prior to such recommendation the Secretary is required to cause a mineral survey to be conducted by the U.S. Geological Survey and the Bureau of Mines to determine the mineral value, if any, in those areas. In carrying out this mandate the Bureau is not required to immediately balance the mineral values against the wilderness values of a particular piece of land. Rather the Bureau may look first at potential wilderness characteristics and then proceed to study the area for all of its potential uses prior to making its final recommendations to the President.[42]

39   43 U.S.C.A. § 1765.)
40   43 U.S.C.A. § 1765.
41   43 U.S.C.A. § 1768.
42   43 U.S.C.A. § 1782.

As of this time the Wilderness Study is proceeding on schedule. The BLM has identified for study approximately 25,000,000 acres in almost 900 tracks. The BLM has completed draft environmental impact statements and made preliminary recommendations in almost 23 million acres and has recommended 9 million acres or about 39% as suitable for wilderness designation. After BLM completes the final impact statements the U.S. Geological Survey will study the areas recommended as suitable for wilderness in order to determine their mineral potential. After this is done the BLM will study the U.S. Geological Survey and make a determination as to whether or not any changes are needed in a wilderness suitability recommendation that will go to the President.

Finally the BLM will package its wilderness recommendations on a state-wide basis and then submit them to the President. These recommendations for most states are scheduled for submission by September 1990.[43]

The FLMPA specifically exempts from any Bureau of Land Management wilderness study any lands in Alaska. However the Secretary is given authority under the Act to make any recommendations to Congress he deems necessary for inclusion of any lands in Alaska in the National Wilderness Preservation System.[44]

In 1984 the Bureau of Land & Management promulgated regulations concerning range management.[45] The stated purpose of the regulations issued by the Secretary of the Interior was to provide uniform guidance for administration of grazing on the public lands. To accomplish this purpose the regulations intended to provide for the orderly use and treatment and development of the public lands, enhancement of their productivity by prevention of over grazing and soil deterioration, stabilization of the livestock industry dependent on the public range and to provide for the inventory and categorization of public range lands consistent with multiple use and sustained yield policy.

The authority for the regulations were listed as the Taylor Grazing Act, the Federal Land Policy & Management Act, the Public Range Lands Improvement Act, and various other executive orders.

Part of the regulations established the Cooperative Management Agreement Program (CMA). This regulation permitted the Bureau of Land Management to enter into special permit arrangements with selected ranchers who had demonstrated exemplary range land management practices. The expressed purpose of the CMA was to allow those

---

43 Bureau of Land Management, Kathleen Barton, Audubon Wildlife Report, 1987, Academic Press.
44 43 U.S.C.A. § 1784.
45 43 C.F.R. Part 4100-1. - et seq.

ranchers to manage livestock grazing on the allotment as they determined appropriate.

In the middle of 1984 the Bureau of Land Management issued its handbook which included amongst other things procedural direction and standards for CMA. The handbook defined a CMA as a formal written agreement between the BLM and the permittee that recognizes the co-operator as the steward of the allotment.

It is apparent that the BLM in issuing its plan for CMA did not intend the CMA to supersede or make unnecessary the allotment management plans called for by the FLMPA.

In *National Resources Defense, Inc. v. Hodell* [46] a dispute arose between the Bureau of Land Management and plaintiff's who were five environmental and wildlife organizations over whether or not the Bureau of Land Management's CMA violated the FLMPA with respect to the specificity required of a permittee under a permit with respect to livestock operations to be conducted on the public range lands.

Under the FLMPA the Secretary is required to prescribe the manner in and the extent to which livestock operations can be conducted on the public lands subject to the permit. In National Resources Defense Council the BLM issued a permit and entered into a CMA with a permittee that would prevent the Bureau of Land Management from canceling or suspending the ranchers permit even though he had failed to cooperate with the agreed upon plan for a period of ten years.

The CMA entered into by the Bureau of Land Management specified that for five years after the CMA was executed and not sooner the BLM and the permittee would conduct a joint evaluation of the range to determine whether or not the agreement's objectives had been realized. If it was found that the rancher had failed to cooperate to the extent required, the BLM was not empowered under the agreement to impose strict grazing guidelines for the remainder of the term. Rather the BLM was expressly directed to allow reasonable time within which the ranchers must comply before the agreement terminates. The only sanction available to the BLM under the agreement was to refuse to renew the ranchers permit after the expiration of the ten years.

The court determined that the regulation promulgated by the BLM which permitted this type of arrangement was not in substantial compliance with the permit issuance requirement of the grazing statute.

The significance of the case is that the regulations permitting such BLM abandonment of the responsibilities of the grazing statute is not permit-

---

[46]   618 F. Supp. 848.

ted in a case where a permittee would be in violation of the agreement reached between itself and the BLM.

## PUBLIC RANGE LANDS IMPROVEMENT ACT

In addition to the Federal Land Policy & Management Act, another act, the Public Range Lands Improvement Act,[47] also establishes policy with respect to range land under public control. This Act passed in 1978 declared a congressional policy that vast segments of the public range lands are in unsatisfactory condition. The term range land means lands administered by the Secretary of the Interior through the Bureau of Land & Management or by the Secretary of Agriculture through the Forest Service, in 16 continuous western states on which there is domestic livestock grazing or which may be determined to be suitable for domestic livestock grazing. Congress stated in the Act that it was the intention of Congress to address and correct the unsatisfactory condition by an intensive public range lands maintenance, management, and improvement program involving significant increases in levels of range lands management and improvement funding for multiple use value. Not only was Congress concerned about livestock grazing on the public lands, but it was also interested in improving the use of the land for wildlife, habitat, recreation, forage, water and soil conservation values.

The national policy established by Congress through the Act called for actions which would inventory and identify current public range lands conditions and trends, manage, maintain and improve the condition of the public range lands so that they become as productive as feasible for all range lands values in accordance with management objectives and land use planning, charge a fee for public grazing which is equitable and reflects the concerns addressed by the Act in stabilizing the economics of the western livestock industry, and to continue the policy for protecting wild and free roaming horses and burros from capture, branding, harassment or death.

Under the Act the Secretaries of the Interior and Agriculture for their respective responsibilities were mandated to maintain on a continuing basis an inventory of rain conditions and record acid rain conditions on public lands and to do this in conjunction with the Federal Land Policy & Management Act. Furthermore the Secretaries were required to manage the range lands in accordance with the Taylor Grazing Act and any other applicable law consistent with the range lands improvement programs.

In order to accomplish the purposes of the program, appropriations were made through the year 1999 on an increasing level of funding.

---

47    43 U.S.C.A. § 1901 et seq.

The funds appropriated were to be used for on-the-ground range reha-bilitation maintenance and the construction of improvements. In order to monitor the success of the application of the appropriated funds each Secretary was required to produce an environmental assessment record on each range improvement project.

The Secretaries were required under the Act to charge a fee for any do-mestic livestock grazing on the public range lands based primarily on the economic value of the use of the range lands to the user. Increases in the fees were limited to not more than plus or minus 25% of the pre-vious year's fee.

A significant part of the Range Lands Improvement Act was the Experi-mental Stewardship Program (ESP). Under this provision of the Act the Secretaries of the Interior and Agriculture were authorized to direct and develop and implement on an experimental basis in selected areas of public range lands, programs which would provide incentives or re-wards for the holders of grazing permits. The programs developed were intended to encourage the exploration of innovative grazing man-agement policies and systems which might provide incentives to im-prove the range conditions. Such policies and systems were identified as cooperative range management projects designed to foster a greater degree of cooperation and coordination between the federal and state agencies charged with the management of the range lands and with lo-cal private range users. The ESP program also provided for payments by the federal government of up to 50% of the amounts due the federal government from grazing permittees to improve the range and where appropriate such other incentives as the Secretaries might deem advis-able.

## NATIONAL FOREST SERVICE

The National Forest Service is lodged in the Department of Agriculture and is headquartered in Washington, D.C. with offices in various loca-tions around the country.[48]

The National Forest System consists of approximately 190 million acres of land in national forests, national grasslands, and other areas which have been transferred to the forest service for administration. The sys-tem provides habitat for about 3,000 species of fish and wildlife, con-tains half of the big game and cold water fish habitat in the nation, and supports 41% of the recreational use on all federal lands. It provides habitat for 129 species listed as endangered or threatened and some ad-ditional 682 species under consideration for listing.[49]

---

[48] See 36 C.F.R. Part 200.1 et seq. Under delegated authority from the Secretary of Agriculture the broad responsibilities of the Forest Service are; leadership in forestry, National Forest System Administration, cooperative forestry and forest research. See 36 C.F.R. Part 200.4.

[49] Audubon Wildlife Management Report - 1987.

National forests have been established throughout the history of federal involvement for the purpose of improving and protecting the forests and/or for the purpose of securing favorable conditions of water flows and to furnish a continuous supply of timber for the use in necessities of citizens.

Up to the end of World War II, the national forests were not in any particular jeopardy but shortly after the beginning of the 1950s, population and economic pressures created a problem for the maintenance of the National Forest System.

Wildlife and general conservation interests claim that the National Forest Systems' management leaned too heavily in favor of timber harvests and as a result some conflicts began to appear.

In 1976 in order to resolve some of these conflicts, Congress passed the National Forest Management Act of 1976.[50] In passing this Act Congress found that:

(1) The management of the nation's renewable resources is highly complex and the uses, demand for, and supply of the various resources are subject to change over time;

(2) The public interest is served by the Forest Service Department of Agriculture in cooperation with other agencies assessing the nation's renewable resources in developing and preparing a national Renewable Resource Program which is periodically reviewed and updated;

(3) To service the national interest, the Renewable Resource Program must be based on a comprehensive assessment of present and anticipated uses, demand for, and supply of renewable resources in the nation's private and public forest and rangelands, through analysis of environmental and economic impacts, coordination of multiple uses sustained yield opportunities as provided in the Multiple Use Sustained Yield Act of 1960, and public participation in the development of the program;

(4) The new knowledge derived from coordinated public and private research programs will promote a sound technical and ecological base for effective management and use of protection of the nation's renewable resources;

(5) Inasmuch as the majority of the nation's forest and rangelands is under private state and local government management and the nations major capacity to produce business services is based on these non-federally managed renewable resources, the federal government should be

---

50    16 U.S.C.A. § 1600 et seq.

a catalyst to encourage and assist these owners in the efficient long-term use and improvement of these lands and renewable resources consistent with principles of sustained yield and multiple use;

(6) The Forest Service by virtue of its statutory authority from the management of the National Forest System, research and cooperative programs, and its role as an agency in the Department of Agriculture, has both a responsibility and an opportunity to be a leader in assuring that the nation maintains a natural resource conservation posture level to meet the requirements of our people in perpetuity;

(7) Recycle timber product materials are as much a part of our renewable forest resources as are the trees from which they originally came and in order to extend our timber and timber fiber resources and reduce pressures for timber production from federal lands, the Forest Service should expand its research in the use of recycle and waste timber product materials, develop techniques for the substitution of these secondary materials for primary materials, and promote and encourage the use of recycled timber product materials.[51]

As a guide to accomplishing its purpose, Congress directed the Secretary of Agriculture through the Forest Service to prepare a RENEWABLE RESOURCES ASSESSMENT beginning in 1975 with an update in 1979 and renewable every 10th year thereafter. The assessment directed by Congress was to include an analysis of present and anticipated uses, demand for and supply of the renewable resources, together with an inventory of the present and potential renewable resources.[52] In arriving at any assessment of renewable resources the Secretary through the National Forest System was directed by Congress to examine forest mortality growth and also assess the economic demand for forest products.

Congress stated that its fundamental policy in passing the Renewable Resources Act was to insure that the National Forest System be maintained in appropriate forest cover with species of trees designed to secure the maximum benefits of the multiple use- sustained yield principle. In order to accomplish this purpose, the Secretary of Agriculture is required to report to Congress from time to time the status of all national forest lands and his plans for the management of the National Forest System.

The Secretary of Agriculture is required under the Act to develop and maintain resource management plans for units of the National Forest Systems. The essence of the plan is to provide for the multiple use and sustained yield of the forest and this must be done on a unit by unit ba-

---

51    16 U.S.C.A. § 1600.
52    16 U.S.C.A. § 1601.

sis. These plans must be embodied in appropriate written material, including maps and other descriptive documents reflecting proposed and possible actions including the plan for the Timber Sale Program and the proportion of probable methods of timber harvest within each unit necessary to fulfill the plan.[53]

The actual work of the Secretary of Agriculture is done by the Forest Service which provides overall leadership in forest and forest range conservation development and use. This leadership involves determination of forestry conditions and requirements and recommendations of policies and programs needed to keep the nation's private and public lands fully productive.[54]

The Forest Service conducts research into matters effecting forest conditions. This research is conducted on forest and range management into five basic areas of timber, forest soil and water, range forage, wildlife and fish habitat, and forest recreation. In addition, the Forest Service conducts research in the areas of forest protection from fire, insects and disease, forest products and engineering, forest research in economics including forest survey for its economics and forest products in marketing.[55] The federal government in protecting the nation's forest promulgates its procedures so that public scrutiny is possible. In addition to publishing regulations related to the general procedures involved in forest management,[56] the Secretary of Agriculture through the Forest Service publishes directives. These directives which relate to procedures for the conduct of the forest service include the FOREST SERVICE MANUAL AND THE FOREST SERVICE HANDBOOKS. These manuals and handbooks are available for public inspection and copying.[57]

In carrying out its responsibility under the National Forest and Management Act of 1976, the Forest Service has been mandated the responsibility to insure consideration of the economic and environmental aspect of various systems of renewable resource and management including the protection of forest resources to provide for outdoor recreation, range, timber, watershed, and wildlife and fish. In specifying guidelines for this land management, Congress has charged the Secretary of Agriculture with the responsibility of providing for diversity of plant and animal communities based on the suitability and capability of the specific land area in order to meet overall multiple use objectives.[58]

---

53   16 U.S.C.A. § 1604.
54   36 C.F.R. Part 200.3(b).
55   36 C.F.R. Part 200.3(b)(4).
56   Contained in 36 C.F.R. Chapter 200.1-299.
57   See 36 C.F.R. Part 200.4 - 200.11.
58   U.S.C.A. § 1604(e).

# WILDLIFE AND HABITAT

Congress has expressed a policy that the national forests are to be established and administered for outdoor recreation, range, timber, watershed, and wildlife and fish purposes.[59] Earlier in the Act Congress had expressed a policy that "no national forest shall be established except to improve and protect the forest within the boundaries or for the purpose of securing favorable conditions of water flows, and to furnish a continuous supply of timber for the use and necessities of the citizens of the United States."[60]

This earlier section on the National Forest Act was passed in 1897 and reflected congressional thinking of the time. The latter section referred to was passed by Congress in 1960 and established what has been referred to as the Multiple Use and Sustained Yield policy with respect to the national forest.

In the 1960 Act, Congress stated that the purposes established in this new section of the National Forest Act are declared to be supplemental to but not in derogation of the purposes for which the national forests were established back in 1897.

Perhaps the concept is best expressed by Section 16 U.S.C.A. 529 which states that "the Secretary of Agriculture is authorized and directed to develop and administer the renewable surface resources of the national forests for multiple use and sustained yield of the several products and services obtained therefrom. In the administration of the national forests due consideration shall be given to the relative values of the various resources in particular areas. The establishment and maintenance of areas of wilderness are consistent with the purposes and provisions of this section of the Act."

In the 1960 Amendment Congress stated that the Secretary of Agriculture is authorized to cooperate with interested and state and local governmental agencies and others in the development and management of the national forest. This spirit of cooperation runs throughout the various attempts by the federal government to enter the arena of the protection and control of the nation's natural resources.

In the 1960 Amendment Congress provided the following meanings:

(a) "Multiple use" means the management of all the various renewable surface resources of the national forests so that they are utilized in the combination that will best meet the needs of the American people; making the most judicious use of the land for some or all of these resources or related surfaces over areas large enough to provide sufficient latitude for periodic adjustments and use to conform to changing needs

---

59   16 U.S.C. § 528.
60   16 U.S.C. § 475.

and conditions; that some land will be used for less than all the resources; and harmonious and coordinated management of the various resources, each with each other, without impairment of the productivity of the land, with consideration being given to the relative values of the various resources, and not necessarily the combination of uses that will give the greatest dollar return or the greatest unit of output;

(b) Sustained yield of the several products and services means the achievement and maintenance and perpetuity of a high level annual or regular periodic output of the various renewable resources of the national forest without impairment of the productivities of the land.[61]

The concepts expressed in the 1960 Amendment to the National Forest Act make it clear that the national forests are to be used for a variety of purposes and that the United States Forest Service is given wide discretion in determining what these uses might be.

In *U.S. v. Means*[62] the United States Forest Service denied a special use permit to the Sioux Indians who sought to use 800 acres of national forest as permanent religious, cultural, and educational community purposes. The Forest Service denied this special use permit on the ground that these purposes as part of the established residential community would not conform with the requirements of the Multiple Use-Sustained Yield Act. The court upheld the United States Forest Service's determination and stated that the Service acted neither arbitrarily nor capriciously in denying this special use permit.

Under the 1960 Amendment establishing the multiple use-sustained yield concept with respect to the national forest, Congress did not give any indication as to the weight to be assigned each value. In *Sierra Club v. Hardin*[63] the court declared that any decision as to the proper mix or uses within any particular area is to be left to the sound discretion and expertise of the forest service.

In addressing the problem created by an emphasis on timber harvesting in the National Forest System, the Secretary of Agriculture is required to insure that timber will be harvested only where soil slope or other watershed conditions will not be irreversibly damaged, where there is assurance that such lands can be adequately restocked within five years after the harvest, and protection is provided for streams, streambanks, shorelines, lakes, wet lands, and other bodies of water.

A telling statement contained in the statute pretty well sums up the approach that Congress has used in passing the Act - "the harvesting sys-

---

61   16 U.S.C. § 531.
62   858 F.2d 404.
63   325 F. Supp. 99.

tem to be used is not selected primarily because it will give the greatest dollar of return or the greatest unit of output of timber."[64]

In authorizing the cutting of timber, the Secretary of Agriculture, through the National Forest Service, must approve such cutting only where the cuts are carried out in a manner consistent with the protection of soil, watershed, fish, wildlife, recreation and aesthetic resources and the regeneration of timber resource.[65]

In order to help the Secretary to made appropriate decisions, he is required in carrying out responsibilities created under the National Forest Management Act of 1976 to appoint committees of scientists which will give him advice and counsel on proposed guidelines and procedures to insure that an effective interdisciplinary approach is proposed and adopted.[66]

The Secretary must develop land management plans. These plans must involve the opportunity for public participation in their development, review and revision. The Secretary of Agriculture is required to publicize any management plan and to hold public meetings that foster public participation in the review of such plans or their revisions.[67]

The United States Department of Agricultural Forest Service has formalized a process of cooperation with private and state agencies. Under its promulgated regulations[68] a system is created whereby the Forest Service may organize associations with permittees (users of the national forests) or in the alternative may organize advisory boards which represent the permittee.

In addition, the regulations mandate that all forest officers must cooperate with state officials, insofar as that is practical, to enforce state, fire, game, and health laws. One of the ways in which this is accomplished is through a system whereby forest officers may become deputy state fire wardens, game wardens, or health officers and, function within those systems.

The Forest Service under these regulations also must enter into agreements with private owners of timber, with railroads and other industrial concerns operating in or near national forests so as to promote and foster mutual benefit in the preventions of or the suppression of forest fires.

---

64   16 U.S.C. § 531.
65   16 U.S.C.A. § 1604 (g).
66   16 U.S.C.A. § 1604(h).
67   16 U.S.C.A. § 1604(k).
68   36 C.F.R. Part 211.1 et seq.

# NATURAL RESOURCES LAW AND POLICY

The very essence of National Forest System Management is the concept of planning. The Forest and Rangeland Renewable Resources and Planning Act of 1974, requires the Forest System to develop a process for resource management plans for the national forest systems. The Forest Service develops regulations which prescribe how land and resource management planning is to be conducted on the national forest system lands. The bottom line is that the resulting plans must provide for multiple use and sustained yields of goods and services from the National Forest System in such a way that maximizes the long-term net public benefit in an environmentally sound manner.[69]

The plans guide all natural resource and management activities and establish management standards and guidelines for the National Forest System. These plans are intended to determine resource and management practice, levels of resource production and management, and the availability and suitability of lands for resource management.[70]

The regulations provide that forest planning must be based on principles which will, (1) establish goals and objectives for multiple use and sustain yield management of renewable resources without the impairment of the productivity of the lands; (2) consider the relevant values of all renewable resources including the relationship of non-renewable resources such as minerals to renewable resources; (3) recognize that the national forests are ecosystems and that their management requires an awareness and consideration of the interrelationships among plants, animals, soil, water, air, and other environmental factors within such ecosystems; (4) protect and where appropriate improve the quality of renewable resources; (5) preserve important historical, cultural, and natural aspects of our national heritage; (6) protect and preserve the inherent right of freedom of the American Indians to believe, express, and exercise their traditional religions; (7) provide for the safe use and enjoyment of forest resources by the public; (8) and to coordinate with land and resource planning efforts of other federal agencies, state, local governments, and Indian tribes.[71]

In practical terms the planning process requires a continuous flow of information and management direction among national, regional, and specific forest levels.

The planning process involves the use of teams representing several disciplines designed to insure coordinated planning of the various resources. The team is directed to integrate knowledge of the physical, biological, economic, and social sciences and environmental design arts in the planning process. The team is required to consider problems col-

---

69    36 C.F.R. Part 219.1.
70    36 C.F.R. Part 219.1(b).
71    36 C.F.R. Part 219.1(b)(1-14).

lectively rather than separately and to develop a broad range of alternatives which identify the benefits and costs of land and resource management according to the planning process required by the regulations.[72]

The regulations promulgated by the United States Department of Agriculture encouraged public participation.  As stated in the regulations[73] the intent of public participation is to broaden the information base upon which land and resource management planning decisions are made; to ensure that the Forest Service understands the needs, concerns, and values of the public; to inform the public of public service land and resource planning activities; and to provide the public with an understanding of Forest Service programs and proposed actions.

There are essentially three planning levels in the approach that the United States Department of Agriculture takes in its responsibility for the national forests, national, regional, and forest planning.  On the national level the Chief of the Forest Service is directed to develop the Renewable Resources Assessment and Program which includes an analysis of present and anticipated uses, demand for, and supply of the renewable resources of forest, range, and other associated lands.

On a regional level the planning procedure requires development of regional guides which are intended to provide standards and guidelines for addressing major issues and management concerns which need to be considered at the regional level to facilitate forest planning.

On the forest planning level the forest planning is within the scope and authority of the Forest Supervisor.  His responsibility is to prepare and implement a forest plan and to prepare an Environmental Impact Statement for the forest plan.  The Forest Supervisor must prepare a draft and final Environmental Impact Statement and involve the public in any recommendation that might be forthcoming from the planning process.

At the forest level the planning process involves the use of an interdisciplinary team which is charged with the responsibility of evaluating the significant effects of each management alternative that is considered in detail.  This evaluation must include a comparative analysis of the aggregate effects of the management alternatives and must compare present net value, social and economic impacts, outputs of good and services, and  overall protection and enhancement of the environmental resources.[74]

---

72   36 C.F.R. Part 219.5.
73   36 C.F.R. Part 219.6.
74   36 C.F.R. Part 219.12.

# NATURAL RESOURCES LAW AND POLICY

It is obvious that one of the alternatives for the use of forest lands is timber resource suitability.  Where such a possibility exists, the Forest Service is required to determine the appropriate long-term sustained yield capacities of the land and to provide schedules which indicate the allowable sale requirements and the quantity.[75]

Other potential uses of forest lands include the designation of forest lands for wilderness and primitive areas, recreation opportunities for the public, the possibility of mineral resource exploration, and the identification, protection, and management of significant cultural and historic resources.[76]

Management plans for national forest timbers resources are required to be prepared and revised in order to provide a continuous supply of national forest timber.  As with other matters concerning the use of forest lands, the principle of multiple use- sustained yield is paramount.[77]

One of the uses of national forest lands is the grazing of livestock.  Under the regulations the Chief of the Forest Service must develop allotment management plans which are designed to protect the range resources and permit and regulate the grazing uses of all kinds and classes of livestock on the National Forest System's lands.[78]

The allotment management plan is a program of action designed to control the extent to which livestock operations will be conducted on the National Forest System's lands.  These plans describe the type, location, ownership, and general specifications related to the particular lands designated as suitable for grazing.  The usual procedures for the Forest Service is to issue grazing permits which authorize the use of the National Forest System for the purpose of livestock production.  These grazing permits do not convey any title to the permittee in the lands, but merely allow the use of the lands by the permittee for livestock grazing.

In managing the grazing and livestock use on National Forest System's lands, the Forest Service is permitted to cooperate with and assist local livestock associations in managing the livestock and range resources. In addition, the Forest Service is permitted to establish grazing advisory boards in accordance with the provisions of the Federal Land Policy and Management Act of 1976.[79]  It is within the discretion of the Forest Service Manager to determine the number of such advisory boards.

---

75  36 C.F.R. Part 219.14.
76  See 36 C.F.R. Part 219.15 - 219.29.
77  36 C.F.R. Part 221.3.
78  36 C.F.R. Part 222.1 - 222.10.
79  36 C.F.R. Part 222.11.

# WILDLIFE AND HABITAT

The Forest Service is also charged under the regulations promulgated by the United States Department of Agriculture with the responsibility of protecting, managing, and controlling wild free roaming horses and burros on lands of the National Forest System. To the extent that these animals also use lands administered by the Bureau of Land Management as part of their habitat, the Forest Service is required to cooperate with the Department of the Interior through the Bureau of Land Management in administering the animals.[80]

The National Forest System is also concerned with minerals which may be found on National Forest System's lands. Under the United States mining laws[81] persons and organizations have a right to enter upon the public lands in search for minerals. The Forest Service has no control of whether or not these persons or associations can enter upon public lands to search for mineral resources since this is the responsibility of the Secretary of the Interior under the appropriate regulations. However, the regulations promulgated by the United States Department of Agriculture relating to National Forest Service Land which are issued pursuant to a special act of Congress[82] do apply to any operations conducted under the United States mining laws. The bottom line is that the Forest Service under the regulations have a responsibility of minimizing adverse environmental impacts on the national forest service resources as they effect surface resources.

The regulations provide that any person who intends to prospect, explore, develop, etc. on national forest lands must provide the Forest Service with a notice of intention to operate on the national forest lands. The plan required is rather comprehensive and covers sufficient information to allow the Forest Service Officer to implement controls which will in fact protect the land.[83]

The United States Department of Agriculture through the Forest Service has undertaken responsibility for the protection of wildlife under national forest system.[84] The Chief of the Forest Service through the regional foresters and the Forest Supervisors is charged with the responsibility to determine the extent to which national forests or portions thereof may be devoted to wildlife protection in combination with other uses and services of the national forests. He is responsible in cooperation with the fish and game department of a particular state to formulate plans for securing and maintaining desirable populations of wildlife species.

---

80   C.F.R. Part 222.20.
81   30 U.S.C. §§ 21-54.
82   16 U.S.C. §§ 482(a)-(q).
83   36 C.F.R. Part 228.4.
84   36 C.F.R. Part 241.1 - 241.3.

The Forest Service is encouraged to cooperate and interact with state authorities and organizations to help implement state laws which are designed to protect wildlife. Often this means that Forest Service personnel are appointed deputy game wardens under the laws of a particular state and operate under the same power as state game wardens to enforce the state laws in regulating fur bearing and game animals, birds and fish.

In addition to those uses previously mentioned, the National Forest System has other uses associated with it. Under promulgated regulations the Chief of the Forest Service is required to establish and permanently record a series of areas on national forest lands to be known as experimental forest or experimental ranges sufficient in number and size to provide adequately for the research necessary to serve as a basis for the management of forest and rangeland in each forest region.[85]

The regulations also provide for special uses.[86] These are defined as all uses other than timber, minerals, and grazing. The regulations provide, however, that certain other uses such as camping, picnicking, hiking, fishing, hunting, horse riding, boating or similar recreational activities do not require special use authorizations.[87]

In those situations where a special use is involved, the person or the organization seeking such special use must obtain a permit. This permit is an authorization which provides permission for specified use of the National Forest System Land and it does not convey any interest in the land other than occupancy. Such special use permits involve hotels, resorts, and other structures or facilities for recreation, easements for rights-of-way for pipeline for transportation of oil and gas products, the excavation of archeological sites, reservoirs, canals, systems for transmission of electrical energy, Nordic and Alpine ski areas, etc.

An interesting part of the National Forest System is the National Forest Wilderness. The National Forest Wilderness consists of units of the National Wilderness Preservation System.[88]

The administration of this National Forest Wilderness has as its purpose the promotion of recreation, scenic, scientific, educational, conservation, and historic uses.

Significantly in carrying out its management responsibilities the National Forest Service is mandated to encourage national ecological succession. The service is encouraged to make the wilderness available for

---

85   36 C.F.R. Part 251.23.
86   36 C.F.R. Part 251.50.
87   36 C.F.R. Part 251.50(c).
88   36 C.F.R. Part 293.1 - 293.16.

human use to the optimum extent consistent with the maintenance of primitive conditions. Where any conflicts exist the service is encouraged to give dominant effect to wilderness values.

Certain areas in the National Forest System are classified as "Primitive." With respects to these primitive areas the regulations provided that there shall be no roads or other provisions for motorized transportation, no commercial timber cutting, no occupancy under special use permits for hotels, stores, resorts, etc., and no hunting and fishing lodges.[89]

The National Forest Service is charged with the responsibility of protecting archeological resources located on forest lands. The Archeological Resources Protection Act of 1979 (16 U.S.C. 470(ii)) requires that the Secretaries of the Interior, Agriculture, and Defense and the Chairman of the Board of the Tennessee Valley Authority develop uniform rules and regulations for carrying out the purposes of the Act. The regulations provided by the United States Department of Agriculture pursuant to this federal statute implement the provisions of the federal act, and do not impose any new restrictions on the activities permitted under these laws.

An archeological resource defined under the federal act means any material remains of human life or activities which are at least 100 years of age and which are of archeological interest.

The regulations promulgated by the United States Department of Agriculture prohibits the excavation and removal, damage or otherwise altering or defacing of any archeological resource located on public lands or Indian lands unless such activity is pursuant to a permit issued under the regulations.[90]

A violation of these regulations which of course is also a violation of the Federal Archeological Act provide for stiff civil penalties and forfeitures.[91]

The United States Department of Agriculture Forest Service administers and manages the National Forest Lands to not only provide for the use and enjoyment of these lands but also to protect the lands in an environmental sense. As can be seen by reviewing the various provisions of the regulations promulgated by the United States Department of Agriculture the key factor in this stewardship is the concept of planning. The concept of planning is to be implemented in a public light. As part of this public involvement in the process, the regulations provide for an

---

89 36 C.F.R. Part 392.17.
90 36 C.F.R. Part 296.4.
91 36 C.F.R. Part 296.15 - 296.17.

appeal system whereby persons or other interested groups as part of the public may appeal any decision concerning the National Forest System. The regulations delineate a system of appeals involving all aspects of the management of the National Forest System.[92]

Initially these appeals are administrative which means that any person appealing the decision of the National Forest Service must appeal within the administrative structure of the National Forest System itself. The appeal process runs anywhere from an appeal of a District Ranger to the Forest Supervisor, through various different steps to a decision at the final level of review of the Department of Agriculture.

After exhausting the administrative appeal a person or a group as part of the public involvement may carry its appeal to the federal court system.

## THE WILDERNESS ACT

The National Wilderness Preservation System was enacted by Congress on September 3, 1964.[93] Its short title or its commonly referred to designation is the "Wilderness Act."

While the reservation and retention of some public lands to protect their mutual status has long been an objective in the management of the federal public lands, it was only in 1924 that the first area specifically designated for wilderness preservation was earmarked - the Gila National Forest, New Mexico.

In 1926 and shortly thereafter the Boundary Waters Canoe Area was established giving protection to these lands and to the superior national forests of Minnesota.

The Secretary of Agriculture in 1929, by regulation, established procedures for the designation of primitive areas in the national forests. This regulation established procedures for the designation of wilderness in wild areas.

Originally wilderness areas were required to be those areas in excess of 100,000 acres and were to be designated only by the Secretary of Agriculture while wild areas consisted of lands between 5,000 and 100,000 acres and were designated by the Chief of the Forest Service.

Between 1930 and 1964 at the time of the passage of the Wilderness Act, the Secretary of Agriculture and the Chief of the Forest Service set aside within a national forest 88 types of areas (wilderness, wild, primitive,

---

92    See 36 C.F.R. Part 211.16 - 211.18.
93    16 U.S.C.A. § 1131 et seq.

and canoe). The total of all of these areas prior to the passage of the 1964 Act was almost 15 million acres.[94]

In considering the 1964 Act, Congress decided that rather than to continue the process of preserving wilderness areas through regulations issued by the Secretary of Agriculture and the Chief of the Forest Service, it would be better organization to change the system to a legislatively authorized system. Congress felt that it would be fulfilling its obligation under the United States Constitution to exercise jurisdiction over public lands in this way.

In establishing the National Wilderness Preservation System, Congress declared, "In order to assure that an increasing population accompanied by expanding settlement and growing mechanization does not occupy and modify all areas within the United States and its possession, leaving no lands designated for preservation and protection in their natural condition, it is hereby declared to be the policy of Congress to secure for the American people of present and future generations the benefits of an enduring resource of wilderness."[95]

In this Act Congress established a National Wilderness Preservation System which was to be composed of federally owned areas designated by Congress as wilderness areas.

Congress defined a wilderness as "a wilderness, in contrast with those areas where man and his own works dominant the landscape, is hereby recognized as an area where the earth and its community of life are untrampled by man, where man himself is a visitor who does not remain."[96]

Congress intends to protect land which is undeveloped, without permanent improvements or human habitation and which generally appears to have been effected primarily by forces of nature with the imprint of man's works substantially unnoticed.

Congress intends to maintain in these lands the concept of solitude and a primitive and unconfined type of recreation.

While originally restricted to areas of land in excess of 100,000 acres, wilderness areas under the 1964 Act could be any area that had at least 5,000 acres of land or was in sufficient size to make it practicable to preserve its use in an unimpaired condition.

Within the provisions of the Act, the term wilderness was determined to be a technical term which served to classify areas containing primi-

---

94   See 1964 U.S. Code Congressional and Administrative News, 3615.
95   16 U.S.C.A. § 1131.
96   16 U.S.C.A. § 1131(c).

tive characteristics and had a meaning which was the same as "primitive."[97]

At the passing of the 1964 Act, all areas within the National Forest which had been classified at least thirty (30) days before the passage of the Act by the Secretary of Agriculture or the Chief of the Forest Service as "wilderness," "wild," or "canoe" were designated as wilderness areas.[98]

In order to correctly identify all the areas that had been designated as wilderness, wild or canoe prior to the passage of the Act, the Secretary of Agriculture was required within one year to file a map and legal description of each wilderness area with the President with correct descriptions of the area.

Also within 10 years after the passage of the 1964 Act, the Secretary of Agriculture was to review the suitability for preservation as a wilderness area, each area in the National Forest classified at the date of the passage of the Act as primitive.[99]

Thereafter the President was to advise the Senate and the House of Representatives of his recommendations with respect to the designation of wilderness and each recommendation by the President would result in an area being designated as wilderness only if so provided by an act of Congress.

Thus the creation of wilderness areas are through acts of Congress and these specific areas are designated as wilderness areas and are contained in a appendix to the Wilderness Act updated from time to time.

While the Secretary of Agriculture is the primary administrative official responsible for the Wilderness System, since the passage of the National Environmental Policy Act, the Secretary of the Interior is required to manage lands under the Wilderness Act so as to not impair the suitability of such areas for preservation as wilderness.[100] The reason for the involvement of the Secretary of the Interior is that he is the administrative officer who is to administer the policies, regulations, and public laws of the United States in accordance with the policies embodied in NEPA.

Prior to submitting any recommendations to the President, both the Secretary of Agriculture and the Secretary of the Interior are required to give a public notice of any proposed action that they deem appropriate. This notice is publication in the Federal Register and in a newspaper

---

97   Minnesota Public Interest Research Group v. Butz, 401 F. Supp. 1276.
98   16 U.S.C.A. §1132.
99   16 U.S.C.A. § 1132(b).
100  Getty Oil Co. v. Clark, 614 F. Supp. 904.

having general circulation in the area or areas in the vicinity of the affected land of their proposal. In addition the Secretaries are to hold a public hearing or hearings at a location convenient to the area, and notices of these hearings are to appear in the Federal Register and in newspapers of general circulation in the area.[101]

Prior to sending the recommendation to the President, the Secretaries must advise the governor of each state and the governing board of each county in which the lands are located and any federal departments and agencies concerned at least thirty (30) days before the date of any hearing and request them to submit their views on the proposed action. All such views submitted pursuant to this process must be included with any recommendations that go to the President and the Congress with respect to any area. In addition to designation of wilderness areas, it is possible that the boundaries of any wilderness area already designated could be modified or adjusted. In those circumstances the Secretary after public notice and public hearings, is required to send his recommendation to the President with the appropriate map and descriptions of the area.[102]

In passing the 1964 Wilderness Act, Congress specifically provided for use of the wilderness areas.[103] After stating that the purpose of the Act was to be within and supplemental to the purposes for which national forests, national parks, and national wildlife refuge systems were established and stating that this Act was not to interfere with the Multiple Use- Sustained Yield concept, Congress stated that each agency administering any area designated as wilderness must be responsible for preserving the wilderness character of the area.

The wilderness areas are determined to be devoted to the public purposes of recreation, scenic, scientific, educational, conservation, and historical uses.

With certain exceptions, certain kinds of activities are prohibited. These included commercial enterprise, establishment of permanent roads, temporary roads, prohibition against the use of motor vehicles, motorized equipment or motor boats, prohibition against landing of aircraft, and the prohibition against a structure or installation within such area unless required as emergencies involving health and safety apportions within the area.

With respect to aircraft or motor boats where uses have already been established these uses may be continued subject to control by the Secre-

---

101  16 U.S.C.A. § 1132(d).
102  16 U.S.C.A. § 1132(d)(1)(C)).
103  16 U.S.C.A. § 1133.

tary of Agriculture and of course vehicles may be used where necessary in the control of fire, insects diseases, etc.

Mineral activities in wilderness areas are restricted to either activities for the purposes of gathering information about mineral and other resources or those activities involving mining which were in effect prior to the year 1983. Regulations provide that after 1983 no patent shall be issued for such mining in wilderness areas.[104]

Commercial services may be performed within any of these wilderness areas to the extent necessary for activities which are proper for realizing the recreational or other wilderness purposes of the areas.

The regulations also provide that states still have jurisdiction and responsibility with respect to wildlife and fish in the national forest.[105]

It has been held that where there is a conflict between maintaining the primitive character of the area and between any other use including that of timber, the general policy of maintaining the primitive character of the area must be supreme.[106]

In some cases state owned or privately owned land is completely surrounded by national forest lands which have been designated as wilderness areas. In such cases the state or the private owner must be given such rights as may be necessary to assure adequate access to the state owned or privately owned land. In some cases it is necessary for the federal government to exchange federally owned land for state owned or privately owned land where it could accrue to the benefit of both parties provided that the exchange is deemed to be of equal value. One exception to this rule is where the United States land has mineral interests and in those cases the federal government may not transfer to the state or the private owner these mineral interests in any exchange.[107]

The Secretary of Agriculture may accept gifts or bequests of land within wilderness areas or the Secretary may accept bequests and gifts of land adjacent to wilderness areas provided that he notifies the President and the Congress of such intention to accept this gift or bequest. Where the land is accepted by the Secretary of Agriculture it becomes part of the wilderness area involved.[108]

The Secretaries of Agriculture and the Interior are expected to report to the President at the opening of each session of Congress on the status of

---

104  16 U.S.C.A. § 1133(d)(3).
105  16 U.S.C.A. § 1133(d)(7).
106  Minnesota Public Interest Research Group v. Butz, 401 F. Supp 1276.
107  16 U.S.C.A. § 1134.
108  16 U.S.C.A. § 1135.

the Wilderness System including a list and description of the areas and the system, what regulations happen to be in effect and any other pertinent information together with any recommendations they care to make.[109]

As in other areas of government activity the Secretary of Agriculture and the Director of Forest Service are subject to judicial review when their activities and directives constitute an abuse of their discretion under the Wilderness Act. Once such judicial challenge involved commercial logging within the Boundary Waters Canoe Area in Northern Minnesota.[110] The plaintiffs in the case challenged the Forest Service proposals to permit extensive logging in the Boundary Waters Canoe Area including the harvesting of previously unlogged forest areas. Under the Wilderness Act, previously logged land could continue to be logged provided that such activity was consistent with "maintaining the primitive character of the area." The Court in reaching its decision after an examination of all the facts found that an undisturbed forest was more primitive than areas where timber harvesting previously had taken place, and that logging within previously logged over areas does not have as much adverse effect on the primitive character of the area as does logging in virgin forest areas. Nevertheless, it enjoined logging within or adjacent to large tracks of previously unlogged forest.

The court of appeals reversed the district court's decision by holding that the Wilderness Act indicated that Congress had authorized logging in previously unlogged areas. In reading the district Court's and the Court of appeals' holdings together, in it obvious that insofar as the courts are concerned, the provisions of the Wilderness Act do accord primacy to the congressional directive to preserve the wilderness character.

Another case involving a judicial review of a forest service determination is the case of *Sierra Club v. Lyng*.[111] In this case the Forest Service determined that an extensive tree cutting program was necessary to halt the spread of the southern pine beetle infestation in four federal wilderness areas of Arkansas, Louisiana and Mississippi. The Forest Service felt that southern pine beetles which are endemic to these forests decrease the value of the commercial timberlands either by killing the trees before they are harvested or by forcing the premature harvest of timberlands threatened by these beetle infestations. The Forest Service argued that this cutting was proper under the Wilderness Act provision which permitted the Secretary of Agriculture to take such actions as may be necessary in the control of fire, insects and diseases.

---

109  16 U.S.C.A. § 1136.
110  Minnesota Public Research Group v. Butz, 401 F. Supp. 1276.
111  614 F. Supp. 488.

The Court wrestled with some interesting questions in the case. One question and a point made by the plaintiff was that the Secretary's discretion in taking this action was motivated by a desire to benefit commercial interest. The Court noted that if this were true, this action would be inconsistent with the Wilderness Act's primary directive to preserve wilderness character.

The Court placed an affirmative burden on the Forest Service to justify the beetle control efforts within the wilderness by demonstrating that they were necessary to effectively control the threatened outside harm that prompted the action being taken.

The final conclusion by the Court was that the Secretary used measures that were reasonably designed to restrain or limit the threatened spread of beetle infestations from wilderness land onto neighboring property and thus was a proper exercise of its discretion under the Wilderness Act. The Court articulated the customary standard by which courts view administrative action and that was the "arbitrary, capricious, or abusive discretion."

If there is a bottom line to any action by the Secretary of Agriculture or the Secretary of the Interior under the Wilderness Act it is that a healthy natural ecology is a vital component of the Wilderness character of the wilderness area. The wilderness character of such areas includes not only animal species but flora and fauna. The obvious intent of Congress in passing the Wilderness Act was to preserve America's last wild land areas, "where the earth and its community of life are untrampled by man."

## NATIONAL WILDLIFE REFUGE SYSTEM

The National Wildlife Refuge System was established by Congress in October 1966.[112] As stated in the legislative history accompanying the Bill[113] the purpose of the Bill is "to authorize and direct the Secretary of the Interior to initiate and carry out a program to conserve, protect, and restore selected species of native fish and wildlife including game and non-game migratory birds that are found to be threatened with extinction."

The need for the legislation was expressed as a consequence of expanding population and spreading urbanization which would require more working and living space, more highways, more lands under intensive agriculture, more rivers and streams harnessed, more forests cut, than had been experienced in previous time periods.

112 16 U.S.C.A. §§ 668dd - 668ee.
113 U.S. Code and Administrative News - 1966, p. 3342.

# WILDLIFE AND HABITAT

The legislation not only addressed the dire circumstance involving endangered species but also proposed that "the future would be far more appealing were there some assurance that it would be built in harmony with nature and tradition."

A recommendation coming out of the first world conference on national parks held in Seattle in 1962 stated that the first world conference on national parks recommended that for every kind of animal or plant threatened with extinction, an appropriate area of natural habitat should be provided in a national park, wildlife refuge, wilderness area, or equivalent reserve to maintain an adequate breeding population and took the view that any species so threatened which is not accorded official sanctuary proclaims the failure of the government concerned to recognize its responsibility to future generations and mankind.

In addition to consolidating the authorities relating to various categories of areas that are administered by the Secretary of the Interior for the conservation of fish and wildlife, the Act designated all lands, waters and interests administered by the Secretary of the Interior as wildlife refuges be designated as the "National Wildlife Refuge System."[114]

The Act provides that the Secretary of the Interior is to administer his responsibilities through the United States Fish and Wildlife Service. (FWS)

The general administrative authority for the Secretary includes the authorization to enter into contracts, to accept donations of funds and use those funds to acquire and manage lands or interests therein, and to acquire lands of interest by exchange or to acquire interests in lands.[115]

In order to provide some specifics for the protection of these wildlife refuges, the Act provides a major section detailing both prohibited and permitted activities.

As far as prohibitions are concerned the Act prevents any person from knowingly disturbing, injuring, cutting, burning, removing, destroying, or possessing any real or personal property in the United States including natural growth in any area of the system. In addition no person may take or possess any fish, bird, mammal, or other wild vertebrate or invertebrate animal, or part or nest of egg thereof, within any such area.

In the absence of any express permission no person can use or occupy any of the areas under the Act.

---

114   16 U.S.C.A. § 668dd(a).
115   16 U.S.C.A. § 668dd(b).

The Act does provide for certain permitted activities including hunting and fishing of resident fish and wildlife within the system, but only under regulations promulgated by the Secretary. Generally these regulations are consistent with state fish and wildlife laws and regulations. However, the Act provides that the states may continue to manage, control and regulate fish and resident wildlife under state law regulations in any area within the system.

In addition to hunting and fishing the Secretary may permit the use of any area within the system for public recreation accommodations.

The Secretary is also authorized to grant easements in or over the land for purposes such as power lines, telephone lines, ditches, pipelines, and roads provided that such easements are compatible with the purpose for which these areas were established.

The Secretary is under mandate to charge fees for the granting of the easement or the right-of-way which is equivalent to a fair market value for the right-of-way or the easement. The sums received by the Secretary in these endeavors are to be deposited in the migratory bird conservation fund after a reduction for any expenses incurred in the administration of the granting of the easement or the right-of-way.[116]

The Act contains a penalties section.[117] Penalties for violation of the Act assessed against any person can take the form of fines or imprisonment for not more than one year of both.

In order to enforce the provisions and mandates of the Act, the Secretary of the Interior may authorize persons to arrest any person violating the Act or regulations in his presence or view, without a warrant, and in addition may execute any warrant or other process issued by an officer of competent jurisdiction to enforce the provisions of the Act. In addition the Secretary may authorize persons within his employ to seize any property, fish, bird, mammal or other wildlife taken or possessed in violation of this Act with a proper search warrant. Persons authorized to make arrests and searches under warrants can seize property, fish, bird, mammal or other wildlife with or without a search warrant and hold these things until a determination is made as to whether or not the person charged is guilty under the penalty provisions of the Act. If the person charged under the Act is found guilty, all property seized from him is forfeited to the United States and may be disposed of by the Secretary.[118]

---

116 16 U.S.C.A. § 668dd(c).
117 16 U.S.C.A. § 668dd(e).
118 16 U.S.C.A. § 668dd(f).

# WILDLIFE AND HABITAT

Today the National Wildlife Refuge System contains more than 90 million acres of lands and waters set aside to protect and perpetuate wildlife. Most of the land in the refuge system is located in Alaska.

## WILDLIFE RESTORATION

A concept closely allied with the National Wildlife Refuge System is the congressional provision for Wildlife Restoration. The Act addressing this matter is entitled "A Federal Aid in Wildlife Restoration Act" or in the alternative the "Pitman-Robertson Wildlife Restoration Act".[119] It has been amended on several occasions not only with respect to the appropriations allocated to the implementation of the Act but also as to some of its fundamental provisions.

The fundamental purpose of the Act is to provide federal funds for allocation to the states when the state puts together a wildlife restoration project which would have as its purpose the restoration and rehabilitation and improvement of areas of land or water adaptable as feeding, resting, or breeding places for wildlife.[120]

The Act provides that the Secretary of the Interior is authorized to cooperate with the states through their respective state fish and game departments and wildlife restoration projects. Before the Secretary of the Interior can authorize the payment of funds to a state that state must have passed laws for the conservation of wildlife which would include a prohibition against the diversion of license fees paid by hunters for any other purpose than the administration of the state fish and game department and until the legislature of that state has formalized such a plan.[121]

The funds are to be used in acquisition by either purchase, condemnation, leases, or gifts of such areas as the states have interests therein which are suitable or capable of being made suitable for restoring or rehabilitating wildlife in the state. In addition funds may be used to construct such works that may be necessary to make them available for such wildlife restoration purposes and includes the provision of funds for appropriate research into the problems concerning wildlife and management.

Before a state can avail itself of any benefits under the act it must prepare and submit to the Secretary of the Interior a comprehensive fish and wildlife resource management plan which must insure the perpetuation of these wildlife resources for the economic, scientific, and recreational enjoyment and enrichment of the people. The plan must be for a period of not less than five years and based on projections of de-

---

119  16 U.S.C.A. § 669.
120  16 U.S.C.A. § 669a.
121  *Id.*

154

sires and needs of the people for a period of not less than 15 years. The plan must also include provisions for updating at intervals of not more than three years.[122]

When the Secretary finds that such a plan conforms to the standards established by him and he approves the plans, he may finance up to 75% of the cost of implementing segments of these plans provided that they meet the purposes of the Act.[123]

A state may also elect to avail itself of the benefits of the act by and through its state fish and game department by submitting to the Secretary of the Interior detailed statements of any wildlife restoration project proposed for that state.

The wildlife restoration projects, established and financed under the Act, must be maintained by the states in accordance with their respective laws.

Such projects as hunter safety programs, the construction, operation and maintenance of public target ranges are appropriate programs under this Act.

The Secretary of the Interior is authorized to make rules and regulations for carrying out the provisions of the Act.[124]

The Secretary of the Interior also is authorized to cooperate with the states through their respective state and fish game departments and wildlife restoration projects. A wildlife registration project is construed to mean and include the selection, restoration, rehabilitation and improvement of areas of land or water adaptable as feeding, resting, or breeding places for wildlife.[125]

These areas may be acquired by purchase, leased, or received as gifts provided they are suitable or capable of being made useful for the purposes of the Act.

Appropriations to the federal aid to wildlife restoration fund are generated by taxes assessed against bows and arrows and pistols and revolvers. The funds so accumulated may be expended to carry out the purposes of the Act.

If the funds are not expended in any fiscal year, the balance is made available for expenditure by the Secretary of the Interior in carrying out the provisions of the Migratory Bird Conservation Act.[126]

---

122   16 U.S.C.A. § 669e.
123   16 U.S.C.A. §669 g.
124   16 U.S.C.A. §669i.
125   16 U.S.C.A. § 669a.

A private right of action to enforce the provisions of this Act does not exist.[127]

## THE NATIONAL PARK SYSTEM

The National Park System began with the establishment of Yellowstone National Park in 1872. By 1970 the system had grown on an informal basis to include natural, historic, and recreational areas in every major region in the United States, its territories and island possessions.

Congress found in 1970 that these areas though distinct in character were united through their interrelated purposes and resources and therefore expressed a single national heritage.[128]

The 1970 act was passed to declare that all such areas were to be included in a "system" and to clarify the authorities applicable to that system.

Previously in 1916 Congress had created in the Department of the Interior a service which was to be called The National Park Service. This service was under the charge of a director who was to be appointed by the Secretary of the Interior. The purpose of the service so established was to promote and regulate the use of federal areas known as national parks, monuments and reservations. The underlying purpose of the charge to the service was to conserve the scenery and the natural and historic objects and the wildlife on these national parks and to provide for the enjoyment of the parks in such manner by such means as will leave them unimpaired for the enjoyment of future generations.[129]

Under the 1970 act, Congress specified that the Secretary of the Interior was authorized to carry out various activities in his charge to administer The National Park System. Included in these specified activities were the authority to establish advisory committees, purchase equipment, enter into contracts for the sale or lease to persons, states, or political subdivisions of the services or resources of The National Parks System, sell products or services produced in exhibits and demonstrations conducted in the national parks, erect and maintain fire protection facilities, water lines, etc. in the national parks, and construct, improve and maintain roads within any authorized boundaries of The National Park System.[130]

The Secretary of the Interior is authorized in his administration of The National Park Service to make and publish rules and regulations as he

---

126    16 U.S.C.A. § 715.
127    Illinois State Rifle Association v. State of Illinois, 717 F. Supp. 634.
128    16 U.S.C.A. § 1a-1.
129    16 U.S.C.A. § 1.
130    16 U.S.C.A. § 1a-2

may deem necessary for their proper use and management of the parks.[131]

As previously stated the first unit in The National Park System was created by Congress with the establishment of Yellowstone National Park in 1872. Additional units of the system were designated by Congress in subsequent legislative enactments. As part of each congressional enactment the geographic location and boundaries of each park are listed and any special restrictions and rules and regulations applicable to that park are contained in the establishing statute.[132]

## WILD AND SCENIC RIVERS

In 1968 Congress passed the Wild and Scenic Rivers Act.[133] The announced intention of Congress in passing the Act was to initiate "a national scenic rivers system, to name its first components of that system, and to prescribe the standards on the basis of which future additions to this system will be made and the methods by which this will be done."[134]

At the time of the passage of the Bill, Congress had before it 16 other wild and scenic rivers bills that were pending and the resulting act was a combining of the features of these 16 other bills into one final bill.

In 1960 the National Park Service pointed out, that particularly in areas of dense population and in arid regions, clear and natural running water was a rarity and under the pressure of anticipated future requirements could very well become nonexistent. The National Park Service recognized that if timely action could be taken, natural free-flowing streams remaining in various sections of the country could be preserved. On this basis the National Park Service recommended "that certain streams be preserved in their free-flowing condition because their natural scenic, scientific, aesthetic, and recreational values outweigh their value for water development and control purposes, and that a study be made to determine what streams in addition to the four listed in the report (the Allegash, the Current, the Elevenpoint, the Rogue) possess such values as these."

Following this recommendation several acts were passed designating specific water ways as ripe for control and protecting them with the passage of laws.

The comments appearing with the Bill pointed out that the federal government has paid attention to rivers as arteries of commerce and means of transportation almost from the beginning of the republic. The com-

131  16 U.S.C.A. § 3.
132  16 U.S.C.A. § 21 et seq.
133  16 U.S.C.A. § 1271 et seq.
134  U.S. Code Congressional and Administrative News, 1968, p. 3801.

mittee pointed out, however, that the one thing the federal government had not done up to that point in time was to protect the river ways by declaring them to be wild and scenic.

The Wild and Scenic Rivers Act rests upon some basic principles. The first principle is that just as the nation has set aside some of its land areas in national parks, national monuments, national historic sites, etc. so some of its streams which have exceptional values of the sorts mentioned above - scenic, recreational, aesthetic, and scientific - ought to be preserved for public use and enjoyment.

A second principle in passing the Act was that both the federal government and the states ought to be encouraged to undertake as much of the job of preserving these rivers as possible.

Thirdly, the principle was recognized that different streams needed to be protected and preserved for different reasons. These reasons would include natural beauty, recreational opportunity, and in some cases a combination of both of these reasons.

Six rivers or sections of rivers were recognized by the Congress at the time of the passage of the Bill as prime candidates for immediate designation. The six rivers recognized were the Rogue in Oregon, the Clearwater in the middle fork of the Salmon in Idaho, the Rio Grande in New Mexico, the Wolfe in Wisconsin, and the St. Croix in Minnesota and Wisconsin. In addition that part of the Wolfe which flows through Menominee County, Wisconsin would also be included if the governor of that state concluded that it be included in the list.

The Congress stated at the time of the passage of the Act that designation as a national scenic river means three things: (1) It means that it has been studied and appraised by competent experts and has been found to have in the words of the Bill "outstandingly remarkable scenic, recreational, geologic, fish and wildlife, historic, cultural, or other similar values; (2) It means that it has been decided that these values make preservation of the rivers themselves and the countryside through which they flow worthwhile and that to achieve this objective it has been decided to authorize the acquisition of the lands or of an interest in the lands bordering on them to a depth averaging a quarter of a mile on each side; (3) It means furthermore that it has been decided that in order to achieve the same objective, the licensing of projects under the Federal Power Act on or directly effecting these rivers segments should be forbidden, that no federal water projects should be constructed on them without being thoroughly reviewed both in the departments and in Congress, that no federal agency should make any loans or grants for or give any other form of assistance to such a project without assurance from the head of the department administering the scenic river that the project will not have a direct and adverse effect on the river and that in those cases in which the scenic river flows through public lands, these lands are withdrawn from disposition under the public land laws and that such mineral activities on them as remain permissible must be conducted in accord with regulations designed to effectuate the purposes of the Act.[135]

The protection of the rivers designated as national scenic rivers is restricted in the sense that the area through which a protective stream flows must be subject to a certain degree of control in order to achieve the objectives for which a river is designated as a component of the National Scenic River System, but the area need not be large and that in many instances much of the necessary control could be achieved through the use of conservation easements without acquiring, all the land bordering the streams, in fee simple.

In 1963 the Secretaries of the Interior and Agriculture in cooperation with a number of states had prepared a list of 650 or more rivers which were thought to be worthy of consideration for inclusion in a national scenic rivers system whenever that system was in fact established.

Section 1273 of the Act establishes the National Wild and Scenic River System. This system consists of rivers that are authorized for inclusion by an act of Congress or that are designated as wild, scenic, or recreational rivers by or pursuant to an act of the legislature of the state or states through which they flow.

Rivers so designated are permanently administered as wild, scenic or recreational rivers by an agency or political subdivision of the states concerned when they are designated as wild and scenic under the Act.

The procedure by which a river is declared to be wild or scenic under the Act usually starts with an application of the governor of the state concerned filed with the Secretary of the Interior. Once the Secretary of the Interior approves a river for inclusion in the system the he notifies the Federal Energy Regulatory Commission and publishes such application in the Federal Register.

After the river is designated as wild and scenic it is administered by the state or a political subdivision thereof without any expense accruing to the United States other than for administration and management of federally owned lands.

In order to be included in this system, a wild, scenic, or recreational river must be a free-flowing stream and the related adjacent land area to that river must possess one or more of the values detailed in that portion of the Act which is referred to as the Congressional Declaration of Policy. These values as stated in the Act include outstanding, re-

---

135 *Id.*, p. 3807.

markable scenic, recreational, geologic, fish and wildlife, historic, cultural, or other similar values.[136]

Every wild, scenic or recreational river that is included in the system shall be classified as one of the following:

(1) Wild river area - Those rivers or sections of rivers that are free of impoundments and generally inaccessible except by trail, with watersheds or shorelines essentially primitive and waters unpolluted.

(2) Scenic river areas - Those rivers or sections of rivers that are free of impoundments with shorelines or watersheds, still largely primitive and shorelines largely undeveloped, but accessible in places by roads.

(3) Recreational river areas - Those rivers or sections of rivers that are readily accessible by road or railroad, that may have some development along their shorelines, and that may have undergone some impoundment or diversion in the past.[137]

Within one year of the designation of a river as part of the national wild and scenic river system, the agency charged with the administration of this river much establish detailed boundaries and make a determination as to the classification of the river (i.e. wild river, scenic river, or recreational river).

In addition to making all maps of all boundaries and descriptions of the classification of the designated river available for public inspection, such boundaries and classifications must be published in the Federal Register and will not become effective until ninety (90) days after they have been forwarded to the President, Senate, and the Speaker of the House Representatives.[138]

The Act provides that for all rivers designated on or after January 1, 1986 the federal agency charged of the administration with each component of the National Wild & Scenic System must prepare a comprehensive management plan for such river segment to provide for the protection of the river values. Each management plan must address such issues as the protection of the designated river, the development of the lands and facilities associated with the river, user capacities of the river, and any other management practices necessary to achieve the purposes of the Act.

The resulting plan must be incorporated into any resource management planning for any effect on adjacent federal lands. These management plans must be prepared after consultation with state and local govern-

---

136  16 U.S.C.A. § 1271.
137  16 U.S.C.A. § 1273(b).
138  16 U.S.C.A. § 1274(b).

ments and the consideration of any interested public within three years after the date that the river is designated. The notice and the completion of availability of such plans must be published in the Federal Register.[139]

For any river designated before January 1, 1986 the boundaries, classifications, and plans must be reviewed within ten years of the designation by the regular agency planning and in control of the river.[140]

A provision of the Act covers the identification of potential national wild, scenic, and recreational areas. The Act provides that in all planning for the use of the development of water in related land resources consideration must be given by all federal agencies involved, to potential national wild, scenic, and recreational areas and all river basin and projected plan reports submitted to the Congress must consider and discuss any such potentials.

The Secretary of the Interior and the Secretary of Agriculture after receiving such lists of potentials must make specific studies and investigations to determine which additional wild, scenic, and recreational river areas within the United States must be evaluated in planning reports by all federal agencies as potential alternative uses of the water and related land resources involved.

The Secretary of the Interior must prepare the Nationwide Rivers Inventory as a specific study for possible additions to the National Wild and Scenic Rivers Systems.[141]

The boundaries for any river proposed for potential listing under the Act must generally comprise an area measured within one-quarter of a mile from the ordinary high water mark on each side of the river.[142]

The Act makes provisions for the acquisition of lands either in fee simple or any other interest, which are contained in the authorized boundaries of any component of the National Wild and Scenic Rivers System designated under the Act. Lands owned by a state meeting this description may be acquired only by donation or by exchange in accordance with provisions of the Act. Lands owned by an Indian tribe or a political subdivision of the state may be acquired with the consent of the appropriate governing body provided that the Indian tribe or the political subdivision is following a plan for management and protection of the lands which the Secretary finds protects the land and insures its use for purposes consistent with the Act.

---

139  16 U.S.C.A. § 1274(d)(1).
140  16 U.S.C.A. § 1274(d)(2).
141  16 U.S.C.A. § 1276(d).
142  16 U.S.C.A. § 1275.

# WILDLIFE AND HABITAT

The condemnation of such lands lying within the boundaries of the designation is one of the powers granted by the Act, and this condemnation can be used when it is necessary to clear a title or to acquire scenic easements or other such easements that are reasonably necessary to give the public access to the river and to permit its members to traverse the length of the area or selected segments of it.

As frequently happens, many of these lands which are going to be designated as wild and scenic rivers are under the administrative jurisdictions of a federal department or agency. The Act permits the head of any such federal department or agency to transfer to the appropriate Secretary jurisdiction over such lands for administration in accordance with the purposes of this Act. Where lands acquired by or transferred to the Secretary of Agriculture are involved, these lands within or adjacent to a national forest shall become national forest lands.[143]

In order to accomplish the purposes of the Act there are several provisions imposing restrictions on federal agencies where the duties of the federal agency might conflict with purposes of the Act. As a example the Federal Energy Regulatory Commission may not issue a license for the construction of a damn, water conduit, reservoir, powerhouse, transmission line or other project works under the Federal Power Act[144] on or directly effecting any river which is designated as a national wild and scenic river. This does not mean that the Federal Energy Regulatory Commission cannot issue licenses below or above a wild and scenic recreational river or any stream tributary thereto which does not invade the area or unreasonably diminishes the value of the area.[145]

Public lands within the authorized boundaries of any component of the National Wild and Scenic Rivers System are withdrawn from entry, sale, or other disposition under the public land laws of the United States.[146]

In addition, the Act imposes several restrictions on any federal mining and mineral leasing laws. The Act provides that while the Act does not prevent a continuation of the prospecting and mining operations on designated lands which are in or near the designated river, there are certain restrictions placed upon such continuations. The Act provides that the Secretary of the Interior or in the case of national forest lands the Secretary of Agriculture may prescribe regulations to protect the river. Furthermore the perfection or the issuance of the patten to any mining claim effecting lands within the system must confer or convey a right or title to own the mineral deposits and must restrict the use of the

---

[143] 16 U.S.C.A. § 1277.
[144] 16 U.S.C. § 791 et seq.
[145] 16 U.S.C.A. § 1278.
[146] 16 U.S.C.A. § 1279.

surface and the surface resources to that which are necessary to reasonably carry on prospect or mining operations and which do not substantially effect the value of the river.[147]

The Act states that the Secretary of the Interior or in cases where appropriate the Secretary of Agriculture are required to encourage and assist the states to consider formulating and carrying out their comprehensive statewide outdoor recreational plans and proposals. This assistance takes the form of advice and cooperation with states or their political subdivisions, landowners, private organizations, or individuals in planning, protecting and managing river resources. The assistance and advice can either be through written agreements or otherwise. The assistance referred to by the Act may take the form of financial assistance as well as non-financial.[148]

The Secretary is encouraged to utilize and make available any federal facilities, equipment, tools, and technical assistance to volunteers and volunteer organizations in carrying out the purposes of the Act. On federally owned land, the appropriate Secretary may use Volunteers in the Parks (16 U.S.C. 18 g-j) and Volunteers in the Forests (16 U.S.C. 558a-558d).

Any component of the National Wild and Scenic River System that is administered by the Secretary of the Interior through the National Park Service must become a part of the National Park System and any component that is administered by the Secretary through the Fish and Wildlife Service must become a part of the National Wildlife Refuge System.[149]

A river which is designated as a National Wild and Scenic River that is within the National Wilderness Preservation System as established by the Wilderness Act is subject to provisions of both the Wilderness Act and the Wild and Scenic Rivers Act.

In the interest of the integration of environmental provisions the Act provides that the head of any agency administering a component of the National Wild and Scenic Rivers System must cooperate with the administrator of the Environmental Protection Agency and with the appropriate state and water pollution control agencies for the purposes of eliminating or diminishing the pollution of waters of the river.[150]

The Act provides for the designation of rivers as components of the National Wild and Scenic Rivers System by name and description. Many of the designations merely list the name and the location of the river,

---

147  16 U.S.C.A. § 1280.
148  16 U.S.C.A. § 1282.
149  16 U.S.C.A. § 1281.
150  16 U.S.C.A. § 1283(c).

but many of the designations contain provisions for either allocations of specific monies for the development of the particular river or other matters which might relate to use. As an example, one of the rivers listed as a designated wild and scenic river is the Missouri River in Nebraska and South Dakota. In addition to its identification and geographic location the designation of the river provides that the Secretary of the Interior must enter into a written cooperative agreement with the Secretary of the Army acting through the Chief of Engineers for construction and maintenance of bank stabilization work and appropriate recreational development. In addition the particular designation requires the Secretary to permit access for pumping and associated pipelines as may be necessary to assure an adequate supply of water for owners of land adjacent to this river and for fish, wildlife, and recreational uses outside the river corridor which have been established. This plan not only provides for the maintenance of the values of the river but also for possible uses of the river which would fall outside the scope of the Wild and Scenic Rivers Act.

The Act provides several definitions which are useful. The river as used in the Act means "a flowing body of water or estuary or a section, portion, or tributary thereof including rivers, streams, creeks, runs, keels, reels, and small lakes.[151]

Free flowing as applied to any river or section of a river means "existing or flowing in natural condition without impoundment, diversion, straightening, rip-rapping, or other modifications of waterway. The existence, however, of low dams, diversion works and other minor structures at the time the river is proposed for inclusion in the National Wild and Scenic Rivers System shall not automatically bar its consideration for such inclusion provided that this shall not be construed to authorize or encourage future construction of such structures within components of the National Wild and Scenic Rivers System."[152]

Scenic easement means "the right to control the use of land (including the airspace above such land) within the authorized boundaries of a component of the Wild and Scenic Rivers System, for the purpose of protecting the natural qualities of a designated wild, scenic or recreational river area, but such controls are not in effect, without the owner's consent, and regular use exercised prior to the acquisition of the easement. For any designated wild and scenic river the appropriate Secretary shall treat the acquisition of fee title with the reservation of regular existing uses to the owner as a scientific easement for the purpose of this Act. Such acquisitions shall not constitute fee title ownership for purposes of this Act."[153]

---

[151] 16 U.S.C.A. § 1286(a).
[152] 16 U.S.C.A. § 1286(b).
[153] 16 U.S.C.A. § 1286(c).

Official designations for rivers as part of the Wild and Scenic Rivers System are made through congressional acts. 16 U.S.C. §1274 is the Section of the Act which contains the listing of the designations and it is amended from time to time.

## NATIONAL TRAILS

In order to provide for ever increasing outdoor recreational needs of an expanding population and in order to promote the preservation of public access to an enjoyment and appreciation of the open air outdoor areas and historic resources of the nation, Congress found that trails should be established (1) primarily near the urban areas of the nation and (2) secondarily within scenic areas and along historical tribal roots of the nation which are more remotely located. To accomplish this purpose Congress in 1968 passed the "National Trails System Act." [154]

The National System of Trails contemplated by the act consists of National Recreational Trails as established which will provide a variety of outdoor recreational uses in reasonably accessible urban areas and National Scenic Trails so located as to provide for maximum outdoor recreation potential and for the conservation and enjoyment of the nationally significance scenic, historic, natural or cultural qualities of the area through which such trails may pass.[155]

The National Scenic Trails are to be located so as to represent desert, marsh, grassland, mountain, canyon, river, forest, and other areas as well as landforms which exhibit significant characteristics of the physiographic regions in the nation.

National historic trails established under the act are to follow as closely as possible or practicable the original trail or routes of travel of national historical significance. These national historic trails have as their purpose the identification and protection of the historic route and its historic remnants and artifacts for public use and enjoyment. These national historic trails are only those located and selected which are on federally owned lands and which meet the national historic trail criteria established by the Act.

The Secretary of the Interior and the Secretary of Agriculture in consultation with appropriate governmental agencies and public and private organizations may certify lands as protected segments of a historical trail upon an application from a state or local government agency or private interest involved, if such segments meet the national historic trail criteria established under the act. In addition the appropriate Secretary must establish a uniform marker for the National Trail System.[156]

---

[154]  16 U.S.C.A. § 1241 et seq.
[155]  16 U.S.C.A. § 1242(a)(1&2).
[156]  16 U.S.C.A. § 1242(a)(3).

# WILDLIFE AND HABITAT

In addition to National Recreation Trails, National Scenic Trails, and National Historic Trails, connecting or side trails which will provide additional points of public access to national recreation, scenic, or historic trails which will provide connections between such trails are to be included in the system.

The Secretary of the Interior or the Secretary of Agriculture were lands administered by them are involved, may establish and designate National Recreation Trails with the consent of the federal agencies, states, or political subdivisions having jurisdictions of the lands involved, when either Secretary finds that such trails are reasonably accessible to urban areas and/or such trails meet the criteria established under the Act.[157]

In addition, trails within parks, forests, and other recreation areas administered by the Secretary of the Interior or the Secretary of Agriculture or in federally administered areas may be established and designated as "National Recreation Trails" by the appropriate Secretary when no federal land acquisition is involved. These National Recreation Trails must be reasonably accessible to urban areas, trails within parks, forest, and other recreation areas owned and administered by states or trails on privately owned lands.

National Scenic and National Historic Trails must be authorized and designated by an act of Congress. Under the act Natural Scenic Trails are required to be extended trails which are defined as trails or trail segments which total as least 100 miles in length. Historic trails of less than 100 miles may be designated as extended trails when these criteria established by the act are met. While it is desirable that extended trails be continuous, studies of such trails may conclude that it is feasible to propose one or more trail segments which in the aggregate constitute at least 100 miles in length.

Either the Secretary of the Interior or in appropriate cases the Secretary of Agriculture must make additional studies as either authorized by this act or by Congress to determine the feasibility and desirability of designating other trails as National Scenic or National Historical Trails. These studies must be made in consultation with the heads of other federal agencies administering lands through which such additional proposed trails would pass and in cooperation with interstate, state, and local government agencies, public and private organizations and land owners and land users concerned.[158]

The studies conducted by the Secretary of the Interior and/or the Secretary of Agriculture must include the discussion of the feasibility of des-

157 16 U.S.C.A. § 1243.
158 16 U.S.C.A. § 1244(b).

ignating a trail on the basis of an evaluation of whether or not it is physically possible to develop a trail along a route being studied and whether the development of a trail would be financially feasible. The studies conducted must be completed and submitted to Congress with recommendations as to the suitability of the trail designation. The studies must be printed as a House or Senate document and must include the proposed route of such trail including maps and illustrations, and the areas adjacent to such trails to be utilized. Characteristics which in the judgment of the appropriate Secretary make a proposed trail worthy of designation as a National Scenic or National Historic Trail, include the current status of land ownership and current potential use along the designated route, the estimated cost of acquisitions of lands or interest in lands if any, the plans for developing and maintaining the trail and the cost thereof, the proposed federal administering agency, the extent to which a state or its political subdivisions in public and private organizations might reasonably be expected to participate in the acquiring of necessary lands and in the administration thereof, the relative uses of the lands involved including the number of anticipated visitor days for the entire length of as well as for segments of such trail, the anticipated impact of public outdoor recreation use on the preservation of a proposed national, the historic trail and its related historic and archeological features and setting.[159]

To qualify for designation as a national historic trail a trail must meet the following three criteria:

(a) It must be a trail or route established by historic use and must be historically significant as a result of that use.

(b) It must be of national significance with respect to any of the several broad facets of American history such as trade and commerce, exploration, migration and settlement, or military campaigns. To quality as a nationally significant, and historic use the trail must have had a far reaching effect on broad patterns of American culture and this would include trails significant in the history of native Americans.

(c) It must have significant potential for public recreational use or historical interest based on historic interpretation and appreciation.[160]

The Secretary charged with the administration of each respective trail must within one year of the date of the addition of any National Scenic or National Historic Trail to the system, establish an advisory council for each trail.[161]

---

159  16 U.S.C.A. § 1244(b)(1-10).
160  16 U.S.C.A. § 1244(b)(11).
161  16 U.S.C.A. § 1244(d).

The advisory councils established under the act are to expire ten years from the date of their establishment. During their existence, however, the appropriate Secretary must consult with each Council from time to time with respect to matters relating to the Trail including the selection of rights-of-way, standards for the erection and maintenance of markers along the trail and administration of the Trail.[162]

Each Advisory Council will consist of not more than 35 members. Each term shall be for a period of two years and they are appointed by the appropriate Secretary. In making these appointments the Secretary must appoint the head of each federal department or independent agency administering lands through which the trail passes. A member appointed must represent each state through which the trail passes (made upon recommendation of the Governor of each state), and one or more members are to represent private organizations including corporate individual landowners and land users which in the opinion of the Secretary have an established and recognized interest in the trail (these appointments are made upon recommendations of the heads of such organizations). One of these members is designated by the Secretary to be the Chairman.

The act provides that within two complete fiscal years of the date of the enactment of legislation designating a National Scenic Trail, the Secretary must, after full consultation with effected federal land managing agencies, the Governor of the effected states, and the relevant advisory council established under the act, submit to the Committee on Interior and Insular affairs of the House of Representatives and the Committee on Energy and Natural Resources of the Senate a comprehensive plan for the acquisition, management, development, and use of the trail including the specific objectives and practices to be observed in the management of the trail, an acquisition or protection plan for all lands to be acquired, and insights specific to development plans including anticipated costs.[163]

The same procedure required of the National Scenic Trail Plan is also required for the National Historic Trail Plan.

The Secretary of the Interior and/or the Secretary of Agriculture may also establish a designated mark for connecting or side trails within a park, forest, or other recreational area as components of a national recreation, national scenic, or nationally historic trail. When no federal land acquisition is involved, connecting or side trails may be located across lands administered by interstate, state or local agencies, with their consent or where appropriate on privately owned lands with the consent of the landowner.[164]

---

162  *Id.*
163  16 U.S.C.A. § 1244 (e&f).

The Secretary who is charged with the overall administration of the trail designated under this act is required to consult with the heads of all other effected state and federal agencies. In addition, the appropriate Secretary may transfer the management of any specified trail segment of any designated trail to another appropriate Secretary pursuant to a joint memorandum of agreement containing such terms and conditions as the Secretaries consider most appropriate to accomplish the purposes of the act.[165]

The appropriate Secretary must select the rights-of-way for National Scenic and National Historic Trails and publish notice of the availability of appropriate maps or descriptions in the Federal Register. After publication of the notice on the availability of appropriate maps or descriptions in the Federal Register, the appropriate Secretary may relocate segments of a National Scenic or National Historic Trail right-of-way with the concurrence of the head of the federal agency having jurisdiction over the lands involved. This determination by the Secretary must be made on the basis that such a relocation is necessary to preserve the purposes for which the trail was established or the relocations necessary to promote a sound management program in accordance with established multiple use principles. Any substantial relocation of the rights-of-way for any such trail must be by an act of Congress.[166]

A National Scenic or National Historic Trail may contain campsites, shelters, and related public use facilities. Other uses along the trail which do not substantially interfere with the nature purposes of the trail may be permitted by the Secretary charged with the administration of the trail. While reasonable opportunities to have access to such trails are mandated, the use of motorized vehicles by the general public along any such national scenic trail is prohibited by the act. An exception can be made by the Secretary where the use of such motorized vehicles is necessary to meet emergencies or to enable adjacent landowners or land users to have reasonable access to their lands or timber rights.[167] Heads of federal agencies may use lands for trail purposes and may acquire lands or interests in lands by a written cooperative agreement with another party, a donation, purchase with appropriate funds or exchange. The appropriate Secretary may acquire these lands or interests therein from local governments. In addition the appropriate Secretary may utilize condemnation proceedings without the consent of the owner to acquire private lands or interests therein in cases where in his judgment all reasonable efforts to acquire such lands or interests by negotiations have failed. There are some limitations on the amount of land that can be acquired under condemnation proceedings. Generally

164 16 U.S.C.A. § 1245.
165 16 U.S.C.A. § 1246(a).
166 16 U.S.C.A. § 1246(b).
167 16 U.S.C.A. § 1246(c).

condemnation proceedings may not be utilized to acquire fee title or even lesser interests to more than an average of 125 acres per mile.[168]

The money with which the appropriate Secretary is able to acquire an interest in a land for purposes of a designation of a trail is obtained from money appropriated for federal purposes from the Land and Water Conservation Fund.

The Secretary charged with the administration of a National Recreation, Scenic, or Historic Trail must provide for the development and maintenance of such trails within federally administered areas and must cooperate with and encourage the states to operate, develop, and maintain portions of such trails which are located outside the boundaries of federally administered areas. In carrying out this responsibility the Secretary is authorized to enter written cooperative agreements with the states or their political subdivisions, land owners, private organizations, or individuals, to operate, develop and maintain any portion of such trail within or outside a federally administered area. These agreements may provide for limited financial assistance to encourage participation and the acquisition, protection, operation, development or maintenance of such trails.[169]

In carrying out his responsibility under the act the appropriate Secretary after consultation with the heads of other federal agencies who administer the lands through which one of these trails run may issue and revise from time to time regulations governing the use, protection, management, development and administration of the trails of the National Trails System.[170]

Potential trail uses allowed on designated components of the National Trail System may include bicycling, cross-country skiing, day hiking, equestrian activities, jogging, or similar fitness activities, trail biking, overnight and long distance backpacking, snowmobiling, and surface water and underwater activities. Vehicles which may be permitted on certain trails include motorcycles, bicycles, four-wheeled drive or all terrain off-road vehicles. In addition trail access for trail handicapped individuals may be provided.[171]

Under a provision of the act[172] various Secretaries are directed to encourage various entities (states, state and local agencies, private interests) to consider in any comprehensive outdoor recreation plan or proposal, needs and opportunities for establishing park, forest, and

---

168   16 U.S.C.A. § 1246(e,f,g).
169   16 U.S.C.A. § 1246(h).
170   16 U.S.C.A. § 1246(i). See also 43 C.F.R. 8300.1 et seq.
171   16 U.S.C.A. § 1246(j).
172   16 U.S.C.A. § 1247.

other recreation and historic trails on lands owned or administered by states and recreation or historical trails on lands in or near urban areas.

Congressional appropriations are made from year to year for the purposes of supplying the funds necessary to carry out the purposes of the act.[173]

In order to help with the planning, development, maintenance and management of trails and in the interest of cutting down on federal costs, the act provides for the Secretary of the Interior and the Secretary of Agriculture to encourage volunteers and volunteer organizations to help with these tasks.[174] The Secretary of the Interior is required each odd numbered fiscal year to submit to the Speaker of the United States House of Representatives and to the President of the United States Senate a revised National Trails System Plan. This comprehensive plan must indicate the scope and extent of the completed nationwide system of trails to include desirable national, significant and historic components which are considered necessary to complete a comprehensive national system and other trails which would balance out a complete and comprehensive nationwide system of trails. In preparing this plan the Secretary of the Interior must consult with the Secretary of Agriculture, and the Governor of the various states in the trails community.[175] In 1968 when the act was first passed new trails were designated in the initial Act - the Appalachian Trail and the Pacific Crest Trail. Subsequently additional trails were added. Some of the more important and well known trails established under this act include the Appalachian National Scenic Trail (a trail of approximately 2000 miles extending generally along the Appalachian Mountains from Mount Katahdin, Maine to Springer Mountain, Georgia), the Pacific Crest National Scenic Trail (a trail of approximately 2350 miles extending from the Mexican California border northward generally along the mountain ranges of the east coast to the Canadian Washington border near Lake Ross), the Oregon National Historic Trail (a route of approximately 2000 miles extending from near Independence, Missouri to the vicinity of Portland, Oregon), the Mormon Pioneer National Historic Trail (a route of approximately 1300 miles extending from Nauvoo, Illinois to Salt Lake City, Utah) the Continental Divide National Scenic Trail (a trail of approximately 3100 miles extending from the Montana/Canadian border to New Mexico/Mexico border) the Iditarod National Historic Trail (a route of approximately 2000 miles extending from seaward Alaska to Nome, Alaska) the Pony Express Trail, (extending from St. Joseph, Missouri through Kansas, Nebraska, Colorado, Wyoming, Utah, Nevada, to Sacramento, California) etc.

173  16 U.S.C.A. § 1249.
174  16 U.S.C.A. § 1250.
175  16 U.S.C.A. § 1242(c).

# WILDLIFE AND HABITAT

The National Trails System has been established in order to maintain, develop, and promote an important aspect of our environment - national, scenic, recreational and historic trails.

## OCEAN AND COASTAL RESOURCES

There is a growing national recognition of the significance of our ocean and costal resources. Various activities can impact upon the coastal ecosystem and cause serious and permanent damage to the nation's ocean and coastal resources.

Such activities as recreation, commercial fishing (a billion dollar a year business), industrial activities (oil and mineral exploration), and ocean pollution through such activities as garbage dumpage, have such potential for ecologic damage to the coastal waters ecosystem that it is necessary to provide a federal structure of laws, in cooperation with various coastal states, in order to mitigate these potentially adverse effects.

Various federal statutes have been passed which address these vital issues. Such statutes as the Outer Continental Shelf Lands Act, the Coastal Zone Management Act, the Federal Wetlands Protection Act, Coastal Barriers Resources Act, Marine Sanctuaries Act, Ocean Dumping Act, and such fishery conservation acts as the Fishery Conservation and Management Act, and various salmon and tuna acts are all designed to involve the federal government as the leader, with the help of the coastal states, in affording some protection to our ocean and coastal regions.

## COASTAL ZONE MANAGEMENT ACT

In 1972, Congress passed the Coastal Zone Management Act.[176] At the time of its passage there were various bills designed to establish a national policy and develop a national program for the management, protection, and development of land and water resources of the nation's coastal zone.

The main purpose underlying the Act was to encourage and assist the states, in preparing and implementing management programs to preserve, protect, develop, and restore the resources in the coastal zone of the United States. Essentially, the bill authorizes federal grants in aid to coastal states who develop these coastal zone management programs and additional grants to help coastal states implement these management programs, once approved. A vital part of this program is the encouragement of the states to acquire and operate estuarine sanctuaries.

---

176    16 U.S.C.A. § 1451 et seq.

The theory is that this system of providing grants in aid to states provides financial incentives for them to undertake the responsibility for setting up management programs in the coastal zone.

It was stated at the time of the passage of the Act by Congress that there was no intention to diminish state authority through any federal pre-emption program but rather to enhance state authority by encouraging and assisting the states to assume the primary responsibility for planning and regulating their own coastal zones.

The need underlying the purpose was apparent by the time of the passage of the Act in 1972. There had developed, by 1972, a world-wide interest in the world's coastal zones. A report entitled "Man in the Living Environment" was promulgated by the Institute of Ecology in 1971 based on a workshop concerning global ecological problems. The report stated that:

> about seventy percent of the earth's population lives within an easy days travel of the coast and many of the rest live on the lower reaches of rivers which empty into estuaries. Furthermore, coastal populations are increasing more rapidly than those of the continental interiors . . . . Settlement and industrialization of the coastal zone has already led to extensive degradation of highly productive estuaries and marshlands. For example, in the period 1922 to 1954 over one-quarter of the salt marshes in the United States were destroyed by filling, diking, draining, or by constructing walls along the seaward marsh edge. In the following ten years a further ten percent of the remaining salt marsh between Maine and Delaware was destroyed. On the west coast of the United States the rate of destruction is almost certainly much greater for the marsh areas and the estuaries are much smaller.

Congress further found that problems confronting the coastal zone are characterized by burgeoning populations congregating in even larger urban systems creating growing demands for commercial, residential, recreational, and other development often at the expense of natural values that include some of the most productive areas found anywhere on earth. In 1972 about fifty-three percent of the population of the United States, some 106,000,000 people, lived within those cities and counties within fifty miles of the coast of the Atlantic and Pacific Oceans, the Gulf of Mexico, and the Great Lakes. Estimates projected that by the year 2000 eighty percent of our population would live in that same area, perhaps 225 million people. Research by congressional committees found that the demand for the limited coastal zone space would increase dramatically in future years. In 1972 there were only 88,000 miles of shoreline on the Atlantic, Pacific, and Arctic coastlines and another 11,000 miles of lake line on the Great Lakes. Congress speculated that with that expanded population there would be increased demand for recreation. Large numbers of people will use the coast for swimming, sport fishing, pleasure boating, and general recreation a majority of which would be in parks and recreational areas along the coast.

Congress further found that about seventy percent of the 1972 United States commercial fishing took place in coastal waters.[177]

Coastal and estuarine waters and marshlands then provided and now still do provide nutrients, nursing areas, and spawning grounds for a large percentage of the world's entire fisheries harvest.

Recognizing the importance of the coastal zone, the Commission on Marine Science, Engineering and Resources devoted the first chapter of its publication "Our Nation and the Sea" to the management of the coastal zone.[178]

The opening paragraph of the first chapter in that publication stated:

> The coast of the United States is, in many respects, the nation's most valuable geographic feature. It is at the juncture of the land and sea that the great part of this nation's trade and industry takes place. The waters off the shore are among the most biologically productive regions of the nation.

> The uses of valuable coastal areas generate issues of intense state and local interest, but the effectiveness with which the resources of the coastal zone are used and protected often is a matter of national importance. Navigation and military uses of the coast and waters off shore clearly are direct federal responsibilities: economic development, recreation, and conservation interests are assured by the federal government and the states.

> Rapidly intensifying use of coastal areas already has outrun the capabilities of local governments to plan their orderly development and to resolve conflicts. The division of responsibilities among the several levels of government is unclear, and the knowledge and procedures for formulating sound decisions are lacking.

At the national governor's conference in 1971, a policy was developed relative to coastal management and it read in part:

---

177 See U.S. Code Congressional and Administrative News, 1972, p. 4776.
178 "Our Nation and the Sea" G.P.O. 1969 Washington, D.C.

The coastal zone represents one of the most perplexing environmental management challenges.  The thirty-one states which border on the oceans and the Great Lakes contain seventy-five percent of our nation's population.  The pressures of population and economic development threaten to overwhelm the balanced and best use of the invaluable and irreplaceable coastal resources in natural, economic, and aesthetic terms.

To resolve these pressures . . . an administrative and legal framework must be developed to promote balance among coastal activities based on scientific, economic, and social considerations. This would entail mediating the differences between conflicting uses and overlapping political jurisdictions.  The ultimate success of the coastal management program would depend on the effective cooperation of federal, state, regional, and local agencies.

The National Advisory Committee on Oceans and Atmosphere, through its vice-chairman, stated "the coastal zone is the key or gate to the oceans.  Effective management in the coastal zone almost automatically assures control over quality of ocean environment and quality of resources."[179]

At the time of the passage of the Act, Congress recognized that some states had already taken strong action.  In 1961, Hawaii had undertaken the first and most far reaching reform of land use regulations, placing state wide zoning power in the State Land Use Commission.

Similar situations existed in other states which had attempted to manage utilization of their land and shore areas.  The concern of the states was recognized as being very important, however, the several coastal states needed assistance in assuming responsibility for the management of the coastal zone.  Congress expressed the hope that the states would accept the assistance designed by the Act and move forward forthrightly to find a workable method for state, local, regional, federal, and public involvement in the regulation of non-federal land and water use within the coastal zone.

Congress, in passing the Act, concluded that in light of the competing demands and the urgent need to protect the coastal zone, the existing institutional framework in the United States was too diffuse, unfocused, neglected in importance, and inadequate in the regulatory authority needed to do the job.

179 _Id_.

175

# WILDLIFE AND HABITAT

Congressional findings, located at the beginning of the Act, are as follows:

(a) There is a national interest in the effective management, beneficial use, protection and development of the coastal zone;

(b) The coastal zone is rich in a variety of natural, commercial, recreational, ecological, industrial and aesthetic resources of immediate and potential value to the present and future well being of the nation;

(c) The increasing and competing demands upon the lands and waters of our coastal zone occasioned by population growth and economic development including requirements for industry, commerce, residential development, recreation, extraction of mineral resources and fossil fuels, transportation and navigation, water disposal and harvesting of fish, shellfish, and other living marine resources, have resulted in the loss of living marine resources, wildlife, nutrient rich areas, permanent and adverse changes to ecological systems, decreasing open space for public use and shoreline erosion;

(d) The coastal zone and the fish, shellfish, other living marine resources and wildlife thereon are ecologically fragile and consequently extremely vulnerable to destruction by man's alterations;

(e) Important ecological, cultural, historic, and aesthetic values in the coastal zone which are essential to the well being of all citizens are being irretrievably damaged or lost;

(f) New and expanding demands for food, energy, minerals, defense needs, recreation, waste disposal, transportation, and industrial activities in the Great Lakes, territorial sea, and the Outer Continental Shelf are placing stress on these areas and are creating the need for resolution of serious conflicts among important and competing uses and values in coastal and ocean waters;

(g) Special natural and scenic characteristics are being damaged by the ill planned development and threatens these values;

(h) In light of competing demands and the urgent need to protect and to give high priority to natural systems in the coastal zone, present state and local institutional arrangements for planning and regulating land and water use in such areas are inadequate;

(i) The key to more effective protection and the use of land and water resources of the coastal zone is to encourage the states to exercise their full authority over the lands and waters in the coastal zone by assisting the states in cooperation with federal and local government and other vitally affected interests in developing land and water use programs for the coastal zone, including unified policies, criteria, standards, methods, and processes for dealing with land and water use decisions of more than local significance;

(j) The national objective of obtaining a greater degree of energy self sufficiency would be advanced by providing federal financial assistance to meet state and local needs resulting from new or expanded energy activity in or affecting the coastal zone.[180]

Based on these findings, Congress declared the following national policy:

(1) To preserve, protect, develop, and where possible to restore and enhance the resources of the nation's coastal zone for this and succeeding generations;

(2) To encourage and assist the states to exercise effectively their responsibilities in the coastal zone through the development and implementation of management programs to achieve wise use of the land and water resources of the coastal zone, giving full consideration to the ecological, cultural, historic, and aesthetic values as well as to needs for economic development which programs should at least provide for --

(A) The protection of natural resources, including wetlands, flood plains, estuaries, beaches, dunes, barrier islands, corral reefs, and fish and wildlife and their habitat within the coastal zones,

(B) The management of coastal development to minimize the loss of life and property caused by improper development in flood prone, storm surge, geological hazard, and erosion prone areas and in areas of subsidence and salt water intrusion and by the destruction of natural protective features such as beaches, dunes, wetlands and barrier islands,

(C) Priority consideration being given to coastal dependent uses and ordinary processes for citing major facilities related to the national defense, energy, fisheries development, recreation, ports and transportation, and the location of, to the maximum extent practical, new commercial and industrial developments in or adjacent to areas where such development already exists,

(D) Public access to the coast for recreational purposes,

---

[180] 16 U.S.C.A. § 1451.

(E) Assistance in the redevelopment of deteriorating urban water fronts and ports and sensitive preservation and restoration of historical, cultural, and aesthetic coastal features,

(F) The coordination of and simplification of procedures in order to insure expedited governmental decision making for the management of coastal resources,

(G) Continued consultation and coordination with and the giving of adequate consideration to the views of affected federal agencies,

(H) The giving of timely and effective notification of and opportunities for public and local government participation in coastal management decision making, and

(I) Assistance to support comprehensive planning, conservation and management for living marine resources, including planning for the siting of pollution control and aquaculture facilities within the coastal zone, and improved coordination between state and federal coastal zone management agencies and state and wildlife agencies. . . .[181]

In order to completely comprehend the effect of the Act it is necessary to know some of the definitions contained in the Act. The term coastal zone, is defined to mean the coastal waters (including the lands thereon and thereunder) and the adjacent shore lands (including the waters therein and thereunder), strongly influenced by each other and in proximity to the shorelines of the several coastal states and includes islands, transitional and intertidal areas, salt marshes, wetlands and beaches.[182]

Included in the definition of coastal waters is the Great Lake area (the water within the territorial jurisdiction of the United States) and includes any connecting waters, harbors, roadsteads, and estuary type areas such as bays, shallows, and marshes. In the actual coastal areas of the United States, costal waters mean any water adjacent to the shoreline which contains a measurable quantity or percentage of sea water and these ordinarily include sounds, bays, lagoons, bayous, ponds, and estuaries.[183]

---

[181] 16 U.S.C.A. § 1452.
[182] 16 U.S.C.A. § 1453(1).
[183] 16 U.S.C.A. § 1453(3).

An important exclusion under the definition of coastal water is the one relating to lands the use of which is by law subject solely to the discretion of the federal government.

The crux of the Coastal Zone Management Act is the provision for the development of management programs. Under the Coastal Zone Management Act the Secretary of Commerce may make grants to any coastal state for the purpose of assisting that state in the development of a management program for the land and water resources for the coastal zone and in addition make grants for the purpose of assisting a state in the completion of the development and the initial implementation of its management program before the state qualifies under the eighty percentum of the cost provided for in another section of the Act.[184]

In order to qualify for any grant, a state's management program must include the following:

(1) An identification of the boundaries of the coastal zone subject to the management program;

(2) A definition of what shall constitute permissible land uses and water uses within the coastal zone which have a direct and significant impact on the coastal waters;

(3) An inventory and designation of areas of particular concern within the coastal zone;

(4) An identification of the means by which the state proposes to exert control over the land uses and water uses referred to in the uses listed above, including a listing of relevant constitutional provisions, laws, regulations, and judicial decisions;

(5) Guidelines on priorities of uses in particular areas including especially those uses of lowest priority;

(6) A description of the organizational structure proposed to implement such management program including the responsibilities and interrelationships of local, area wide, state, regional, and interstate agencies in the management process;

(7) A definition of the term beach and a planning process for the protection of and access to public beaches and other public coastal areas of environmental, recreational, historical, aesthetic, ecological or cultural value;

---

184   16 U.S.C.A. § 1454(a).

(8) A planning process for energy facilities likely to locate in or which may significantly affect the coastal zone, including a process for anticipating and managing the impacts from these facilities;

(9) A planning process for assessing the effects of shoreline erosion, and studying and evaluating ways to control or lessen the impact of such erosion and to restore areas adversely affected by erosion.[185]

The Secretary may make grants to any coastal state for the purpose of administering that state's management program if the state matches any such grant according to a ratio one to one after 1988. In effect this means that the government's grant is a matching contribution and can be made only if the Secretary finds that the program planned meets the requirements set forth under the Act.[186] In order to insure that coastal states applying for grants meet the program requirements contained in the Act, the Secretary is required to establish and promulgate regulations which set forth the requirements for a state to qualify under the Act.[187]

In addition to complying with the requirements of the Act and the regulations promulgated by the Secretary of Commerce, a state, in order to qualify for a grant, must prove that it has coordinated its program with local, area wide, and interstate plans applicable to any areas within the coastal zone and that the state has held public hearings in the development of the management program.[188]

Under the Act, the governor of the state must review and approve the management program and must designate a single state agency to receive and administer the grants for implementing the management program.[189]

The Secretary of Commerce also must find that the program submitted by the state for a grant contains a process by which the state provides criteria and standards for local implementation subject to administrative review and enforcement of compliance.

The state, after having the grant approved by the Secretary of Commerce, may allocate to a local government or an area wide agency a portion under the grant for purposes of carrying out the management plan. The state is under an obligation to insure that the allocation is used according to the approved state plan.[190]

---

185  16 U.S.C.A. § 1454(b).
186  16 U.S.C.A. § 1455.
187  See 15 C.F.R. Part 923.90 et seq.
188  16 U.S.C.A. § 1455(c).
189  16 U.S.C.A. § 1455(c).
190  16 U.S.C.A. § 1455(f).

There are provisions under the Act whereby a state may amend or modify its management program with the approval of the Secretary of Commerce.

While the grants, once approved by the Secretary of Commerce, are in effect they cannot be canceled. New grants under the Coastal Resource Improvement Program may not be made where the Secretary finds that the coastal state has failed to make satisfactory progress in the activities described under its management plan.

In addition to grants under the Act for the administration of a management program involving a coastal area, the Secretary may also make coastal resource improvement program grants. These grants are designed to meet one of the following objectives:

(1) the preservation or restoration of specific areas of the state that are designated under the management program procedures that, because of their conservation, recreational, ecological, or aesthetic values, have resources of national significance;

(2) the redevelopment of deteriorating and under-utilized urban waterfronts and ports that are designated in the state's management program as areas of particular concern; and

(3) the provision of access of public beaches and other public coastal areas and to coastal waters in accordance with the planning process required under the management plan.[191]

The terms of these grants can be dictated by the Secretary of Commerce and are essentially matching grants for each fiscal year after the fiscal year of 1988.

A primary value under the Coastal Zone Management Act is the concept of coordination and cooperation. The Secretary of Commerce, under the Act, must cooperate with interested federal agencies and cannot approve a management program without consulting these federal agencies.

Under the Act, a federal agency which undertakes any development project in the coastal zone of a state must insure that its project is, to the maximum extent practicable, consistent with the approved state management program.[192]

After approval by the Secretary of a state's management program, any person or agency that is seeking a federal license or permit to conduct

---

191 6 U.S.C.A. § 1455a.
192 16 U.S.C.A. § 1456.

an activity affecting land or water uses in the coastal zone of that state must provide, in its application for the license or the permit, a certification that the proposed activity complies with the state's approved management program and that such activity will be conducted in a manner consistent with the program. The applicant, at the time of its submission, must also submit to the coastal state involved a copy of the certification with all necessary information and data.[193]

In order to implement this program, each coastal state is required under the Act to establish procedures for public notice in the case of any such certification and to provide, where possible, procedures for public hearings.

This certification procedure must also be followed by any person who submits to the Secretary of the Interior any plan for exploration or development of production from any area which has been leased under the Outer Continental Shelf Lands Act (43 U.S.C. 1331 et seq.). This certification, as in other types of certification, must also describe in detail how the plan for exploration or development complies with the coastal state's approved management program.

It is conceivable that the requirements under the Act may potentially conflict with other laws applicable to the coastal zone resources. The Act provides that nothing in the Act should diminish either federal or state jurisdictions responsibilities or rights in the fields of planning, development, or control of water resources, submerged lands, or navigable waters. Nor is the Act intended to supersede, modify, or repeal any existing laws applicable to the various federal agencies having jurisdiction over the same subject matter or affect any requirements under the Federal Water Pollution Control Act (33 U.S.C.A. 1251 et seq.) or the Clean Air Act (42 U.S.C.A. 7401).[194]

It is possible that a coastal state's management plan might be in serious disagreement with a federal agency's plan or requirement and in such a situation the Act provides for mediation. Under the Act the Secretary is required to mediate the differences involved in any such disagreement. This process of mediation does include public hearings, which are to be conducted in the local area concerned.[195]

Another important part of the Coastal Zone Management Act is the provision for the funding of coastal energy impact programs. The program is intended to assist the coastal states in developing energy resources.[196]

---

193  16 U.S.C.A. § 1456(c).
194  16 U.S.C.A. § 1456(e).
195  16 U.S.C.A. § 1456(h).
196  16 U.S.C.A. § 1456a.

The Secretary is authorized to make grants to any coastal state for the construction, expansion, or operation of new or expanded energy facilities. Included in the grants are amounts for the purposes of study and planning. The limit of such grants is not to exceed eighty percent of the cost of such study and planning.[197]

In addition to grants the Secretary of Commerce under the Coastal Zone Management Act is authorized to make loans to any coastal state for the purpose of developing energy.

To provide a repository for funds for the purposes of carrying out the intentions of the energy development plan under the Act, Congress established within the Treasury of the United States the Coastal Energy Impact Fund. The funds available to the Secretary must be paid from that Fund.[198]

As a monitoring devise the Act provides for a continuing review of the performance of the coastal states with respect to coastal management by the Secretary. This review must be a written evaluation with an assessment and detailed findings concerning the extent to which the state has implemented and enforced the program approved by the Secretary. Included in the process of making evaluations is a requirement that the Secretary conduct public meetings and provide an opportunity for oral and written comments by the public. The evaluation, when prepared by the Secretary, must be made available to the public.[199]

The Act authorizes the Secretary to withdraw approval of the management program of any coastal state and also withdraw any financial assistance available to the state (including any unexpended portion of a grant) if the Secretary determines that the coastal state is failing to adhere to the management program approved by the Secretary or is violating any of the terms of the grant as conditioned upon the approval of the management program. This withdrawal of management program approval and financial assistance may not be implemented until the coastal state has received notice and has had an opportunity for a public hearing on the proposed action.[200]

A further provision of the Act establishes the National Estuarine Reserve Research System. Included in the National Estuarine Reserve Research System are all those estuarines designated by the Secretary upon the nomination of the governor of any coastal state in which the area is located and upon the finding by the Secretary of Commerce that an area is a representative estuarine ecosystem that is suitable for long

---

197  16 U.S.C.A. § 1456b.
198  16 U.S.C.A. § 1456a(h).
199  16 U.S.C.A. § 1458.
200  16 U.S.C.A. § 1458(c,d).

term research and contributes to the geographical and topological balance of the system. The Secretary must develop guidelines for the conduct of research within the systems and in developing these guidelines he must consult with prominent members of the estuarine research community.

The Secretary is required to promote and coordinate the use of the system for research purposes, including requiring that the National Oceanic and Atmospheric Administration in conducting or supporting estuarine research give priority consideration to research that uses this system and consult with other federal and state agencies to promote use of one or more reserves within the system by such agencies when conducting estuarine research.

In order to promote the interests of estuarines, the Secretary may make grants to a coastal state for purposes of acquiring lands and waters or for purposes of operating or managing a natural estuarine reserve and constructing the appropriate reserve facilities or for the purposes of conducting educational or interpretive activities. In addition, the Secretary may make grants to public or private persons for purposes of supporting research and monitoring within a national estuarine reserve.

The amount of financial assistance available for estuarine research is limited to fifty percent of the cost of the land, waters, and interests or four million dollars, whichever amount is less.

The Secretary, under the Act, must periodically evaluate the operation and management of each national estuarine reserve and if while doing this evaluation determines that the research being conducted within the reserve is not consistent with the research guidelines he may withdraw the designation of the area as a National Estuarine Reserve.[201]

The Act requires the Secretary to establish a Coastal Zone Management Committee consisting of not more than fifteen persons. The Committee is to advise, consult with, and make recommendations concerning the coastal zone.[202]

The Secretary of Commerce is under an obligation to consult with Congress on a regular basis concerning the administration of the Coastal Zone Management Act and to make a report to Congress on a two fiscal yearly basis. In addition to identifying the programs in the coastal states involved and providing information as to the effectiveness of these programs, the Secretary must also make recommendations for additional legislation as he deems necessary to achieve the objectives of the Coastal Zone Management Act. In making recommendations and

---

[201] 16 U.S.C.A. § 1461.
[202] 16 U.S.C.A. § 1460.

in informing Congress of his evaluations, the Secretary must conduct a systematic review of federal programs other than those programs under the Coastal Zone Management Act for the purposes of identifying conflicts between the objectives and administration of such other programs and the purposes of this Act.

Another section of the Act provides for the establishment by the Secretary of Commerce of the National Coastal Resources Research and Development Institute. This Institute is under an obligation to conduct research and carry out educational and demonstration projects designed to promote the efficient and responsible development of ocean and coastal resources, including Arctic resources. These projects must be based on biological, geological, genetic, economic, and other scientific research applicable to the purposes of the study and must also include studies on economic diversification and environmental protection of the nation's coastal areas.

The policies of the Institute are determined by a Board of Governors composed of representatives from the states of Oregon, Alaska, Washington, California, and Hawaii. The governors, in turn, are required to establish an advisory council composed of specialists in ocean and coastal resources from the academic community. The Institute is administered by a director and the Institute must report to the Secretary of Commerce on its activities.[203]

Congress appropriated forty million six hundred thousand dollars for grants and the Coastal Resource Improvement Program, and seventy-five million dollars for the Coastal Energy Impact Program both for the fiscal year 1990.[204]

## OUTER CONTINENTAL SHELF LANDS ACT

In 1953 Congress passed the Submerged Lands Act,[205] which established that the seabed and subsoil in the Outer Continental Shelf beyond state boundaries of the United States was subject to the jurisdiction and control of the federal government. There were no provisions for any leasing or development of the area by the federal government nor any provisions made for the exchange of state leases for federal leases in the same area.

Later in 1953, Congress decided to correct these perceived deficiencies in the Submerged Lands Act and passed the amendment to the Submerged Lands Act entitled the Outer Continental Shelf Lands Act.[206]

---

[203] 16 U.S.C.A. § 1463(b).
[204] 16 U.S.C.A. § 1461(g).
[205] 43 U.S.C.A. § 1301-1315.
[206] 43 U.S.C.A. § 1331 et seq.

# WILDLIFE AND HABITAT

A continental shelf has been defined as a slightly submerged portion of the continent that surrounds all the continental areas of the earth. They are considered to be a part of the continental mass that forms the lands above water. As a practical matter they are part of the continent temporarily

(measured in geological time) overlapped by the oceans.

The outer boundary of the shelf is marked by a sharp increase in the slope of the sea floor. It is the point where the continental mass drops off steeply toward the ocean deeps. Generally, this abrupt drop occurs where the water reaches a depth of 100 fathoms or 600 feet and, for convenience, this depth is used as a rule of thumb in defining the outer limits of the shelf.[207]

Along the Atlantic coast the maximum distance from the shore to the outer edge of the shelf is 250 miles and the average distance is about 70 miles. In the Gulf of Mexico the maximum distance is 200 miles and the average is about 93 miles. The total area of the shelf of the United States is estimated to contain about 290,000 square miles. The area of the shelf off Alaska is estimated to contain 600,000 square miles. That part of the shelf which lies within historic state boundaries, in most cases three miles, is estimated to contain about 27,000 square miles.[208]

The primary purpose of the Outer Continental Shelf Lands Act amendment to the Submerged Lands Act was to authorize the leasing by the federal government of the remainder of the shelf extending beyond historic state boundaries.[209]

The Outer Continental Shelf Lands Act amendment to the Submerged Lands Act was passed at the urging of not only off-shore operators but also by the federal government and the states in order to enable the federal government to lease for oil and gas operations the vast areas of the continental shelf outside the state boundaries. Prior to the passing of the amendment there was not any law in existence whereby the federal government could lease those submerged lands and this Act was intended to correct that defect.

On September 8, 1945, the President, by Proclamation, asserted on behalf of the United States, jurisdiction and power of dispensation over the natural resources of the subsoil and seabed of the continental shelf.[210]

---

207 U.S. Code Congressional and Administrative News, 1953, p. 2178.
208 *Id.*
209 43 U.S.C.A. § 1332.
210 U.S. Code Congressional and Administrative News, 1953, p. 2178.

# NATURAL RESOURCES LAW AND POLICY

The Outer Continental Shelf amendment to the Submerged Lands Act provided for the leasing of the Outer Continental Shelf area by the Secretary of the Interior under circumstances where there would be a demand for the purchase of leases. The sale of the leases are to be made to the responsive and qualified bidder bidding the highest cash bonus per leasing unit.[211]

The Secretary, under the Act, is given the authority to describe the tract to be leased, the minimum bonus per acre accepted for each leasing unit, the amount of royalty, the rental per acre per annum, and the time and place for opening of bids in public.[212]

Originally, the Act fixed the term of the lease as a primary term of five years, which is to continue so long thereafter as oil or gas was produced in paying quantities. Provisions in each lease are required to insure that the lessee exercises reasonable diligence in the operation of the lease and is conducting his operations in a sound and efficient oil field practice so as to prevent waste.

Further provisions of the Act stipulate that after discovery of gas or oil the royalty is to be fixed at a minimum of 12-1/2% in the amount or value of the production saved or removed or sold from a leasing unit with a minimum of $1.00 per acre per annum in lieu of any rental for each lease year commencing after discovery.

The Act provides that if, at the end of the primary term, oil or gas is not being produced in paying quantities on the leasing unit the operations can be stopped and the lease canceled upon proper notice to the lessee by the Secretary.

Under the Act, the holders of state leases are entitled, as a matter of equity and right, to the issuance by the federal government of exchange leases for state leases. All payments, rentals, royalties, and other sums payable under a lease to the United States are to be deposited in the Treasury of the United States.

There were several reservations under the amended Act. One of these is a reservation of power in the United States in time of war to have the right of first refusal to buy any of the oil or gas produced from the area and/or to terminate any lease or suspend operations under the lease for necessary national defense. Another reservation is to the effect that persons and agencies of the United States could continue to conduct or start conducting geological or geophysical explorations in the Outer Continental Shelf area so long as they did not interfere with or endanger any lease issued under the Act.[213]

---

211  43 U.S.C.A. § 1337(a).
212  43 U.S.C.A. § 1337(a)(1).

# WILDLIFE AND HABITAT

As previously stated, the primary purpose of the Act is to vest in the Secretary of the Interior the authority to prepare and periodically revise and maintain an oil and gas leasing program to accomplish the purposes of the Act.[214]

In discharging his responsibilities, the Secretary is required to conduct his management program in a manner which considers economic, social, and environmental values of the renewable and nonrenewable resources contained in the Outer Continental Shelf and to consider the potential impact of oil and gas exploration on the resource values of the Outer Continental Shelf and the marine, coastal, and human environments.[215]

The procedures involved in this management require the Secretary to invite and consider suggestions for any management program from any interested federal agency, from the governor of any state which may become affected under a proposed program, from the executive of any affected local government in a state, and from other persons. In order to insure that these persons who could potentially give advice and suggestions would be aware of the program, the Secretary is required to publish the proposed leasing program in the Federal Register.[216]

Procedural regulations are established for the management of any program and they require the Secretary to establish procedures for the receipt and consideration of nominations for any area to be offered for lease or to be excluded from any such leasing, public notice of and participation in development of the leasing program, review by state and local governments which could be impacted by the proposed leasing, periodic consultation with state and local governments, oil and gas lessees and permittees, and representatives of other individuals or organizations engaged in activity in or on the continental shelf, including those involved in fish and shellfish recovery, and recreational activities and consideration of a coastal zone management program being developed and administered by an affected coastal state pursuant to the Coastal Zone Management Act.[217]

In order to minimize or at least be aware of the impact of such leases on the environment, the Secretary is required to conduct studies of any area or region included in any oil and gas lease sale in order to establish information needed for the assessment and management of any environmental impact on the human, marine, and coastal environments of the Outer Continental Shelf and the coastal area which might be affected by the oil and gas development in the area or region. These envi-

213  43 U.S.C.A. § 1341.
214  43 U.S.C.A. § 1344.
215  *Id.*
216  43 U.S.C.A. § 1344(c).
217  43 U.S.C.A. § 1344 (d,e,f,g).

ronmental studies are required to be conducted not later than six months prior to the holding of a lease sale with respect to any area or region.[218]

The Act also provides that the Secretary must conduct additional environmental studies subsequent to the leasing and developing of any area or region.[219]

As a monitoring device the Act provides that at the end of each fiscal year the Secretary must submit to Congress and make available to the general public an assessment of the cumulative effect of activities conducted under the Act, concentrating especially on human, marine, and coastal environments.

The Act also requires that the Secretary study the adequacy of existing safety and health regulations and submit a plan for the promotion of such values to Congress. The Secretary is also required to promulgate regulations or standards that apply to hazardous working conditions.[220]

The Act provides for citizen suits to enforce the provisions of the Act, in the event that a person with a valid legal interest thinks that the Secretary or any of the people working under the auspices of the Act are not adhering to the requirements. The citizen suit actions are to be filed in the appropriate United States district court having jurisdiction over a particular area.[221]

The award of attorney fees under the Continental Shelf Lands Act is appropriate. In *Conservation Law Foundation of New England, Inc. v. Secretary of the Interior*,[222] the Court awarded attorney fees to a conservation foundation which obtained a preliminary injunction against the sale of offshore drilling leases. The Court held that the conservation foundation was entitled to the award of attorney fees for work done in assisting the state of Massachusetts in a successful claim under the Act, even though the foundation did not seek relief for violations of these statutes on its own behalf.

A significant section of the Act provides for remedies and penalties. Under this section, the Secretary of the Interior, the Secretary of the Army, the Secretary of the department under which the Coast Guard is operating, or the Attorney General of the United States is authorized to institute similar action against any person who shall violate any provisions of the Act. Penalties include not only civil penalties of $10,000 for each day of the continuance of such violation of the Act but also crimi-

---

218  43 U.S.C.A. § 1345.
219  43 U.S.C.A. § 1346.
220  43 U.S.C.A. § 1347.
221  43 U.S.C.A. § 1349.
222  790 F.2d 965.

nal penalties with a limit of $100,000, imprisonment for not more than ten years, or both.[223]

In 1978, Congress passed the Outer Continental Shelf Lands Act Amendments of 1978.[224] The purposes underlying the Amendment are expressed by Congress as follows:

(1) establish policies and procedures for managing the oil and natural gas resources of the Outer Continental Shelf which are intended to result in an expedited exploration and development of the Outer Continental Shelf in order to achieve national economic and energy policy goals, assure national security, reduce dependence on foreign resources and maintain a favorable balance of payments in world trade;

(2) preserve, protect, and develop oil and natural gas resources in the Outer Continental Shelf in a manner which is consistent with the need to make resources available to meet the nation's energy needs as rapidly as possible, to balance orderly energy resource development with protection of the human, marine, and coastal environments, to insure the public a fair and equitable return on the resources in the Outer Continental Shelf and to preserve and maintain free enterprise competition;

(3) encourage development of new and improved technology for energy resource production, which will eliminate or minimize risk of damage to the human, marine, and coastal environments;

(4) provide states and through states local governments which are impacted by the Outer Continental Shelf and oil and gas exploration, development, and production with comprehensive assistance in order to anticipate and plan for such impact, and thereby to assure adequate protection of the human environment;

(5) assure that states and through states local governments have timely access to information regarding activities in the Outer Continental Shelf and an opportunity to review and comment on decisions relating to such activities in order to anticipate, ameliorate, and plan for the impact of such activities;

(6) assure that states and through states local governments which are directly affected by exploration, development, and production of oil and natural gas are provided an opportunity to participate in policy and planning decisions relating to management of the resources of the Outer Continental Shelf;

223  43 U.S.C.A. § 1350.
224  43 U.S.C.A. § 1801 et seq.

(7) minimize or eliminate conflicts between the exploration, development, and production of oil and natural gas and the recovery of other resources such as shellfish;

(8) establish an oil spill liability fund to pay for the prompt removal of any oil spilled or discharge as a result of activities on the Outer Continental Shelf and for any damages to public or private interests caused by such spills or discharges;

(9) insure that the extent of oil and natural gas resources of the Outer Continental Shelf is assessed at the earliest practical time; and

(10) establish a fisherman's contingency fund to pay for damages to commercial fishing vessels and gear due to Outer Continental Shelf activities.[225]

These purposes are based on certain congressional findings, which include the following:

(1) the demand for energy in the United States has been increasing, domestic production of oil and gas has declined in recent years and the United States has become increasingly dependent upon imports of oil from foreign nations;

(2) technology is or can be made available which will allow significantly increased domestic production of oil and gas without undue harm or damage to the environment;

(3) the Outer Continental Shelf contains significant quantities of oil and natural gas and is a vital national resource reserve which must be carefully managed so as to realize fair value, to preserve and maintain competition and reflect the public interest;

(4) legal and technological problems presently in existence which retard the development of oil and natural gas reserves of the Outer Continental Shelf and that need to be corrected;

(5) the development, processing, and distribution of oil and gas resources of the Outer Continental Shelf impact very heavily on coastal states and communities of the states and need to be evaluated;

(6) funds must be made available to pay for the prompt removal of any oil spill or discharge as a result of activities on the Outer Continental Shelf and for any damages to public or private interests caused by such spills or discharges; and

---

225  43 U.S.C.A. § 1802.

(7) because the oil and gas resources of the Outer Continental Shelf are limited, nonrenewable resources which must be developed in a manner which takes into consideration the nation's long range energy needs and also ensures adequate protection of renewable resources of the Outer Continental Shelf.[226]

One of the major provisions of the 1978 amendments is the establishment of the Off Shore Oil Pollution Compensation Fund. The Fund is to be composed of all fees levied by the Secretary of Transportation and collected by the Secretary of the Treasury from the owners of the oil facilities which are producing oil found on the Outer Continental Shelf. The fee initially assessed is one not to exceed three cents per barrel. In addition, the Fund is to include monies collected on behalf of the Fund from all persons who were liable because they contributed to oil pollution on the Outer Continental Shelf.[227]

Except where the action which caused the damage to the Outer Continental Shelf was caused by an intentional act, liability of owners of oil facilities on the Outer Continental Shelf is limited to $250,000 or $300 per gross ton, whichever was greater. This was related primarily to vessels operating within the Outer Continental Shelf. A total limit of $35 million dollars for all damages caused by an off shore facility was also imposed under the Act.[228]

While there are some exceptions to liability, namely acts of war, civil war, insurrection, or an unanticipated grave national disaster, otherwise owners and operators of oil facilities on the Outer Continental Shelf are liable for damages that they may have caused.[229]

Claimants for compensation under the Fund are identified as the federal government, state or political subdivisions of a state, foreign claimants where the oil pollution had occurred in or on the territorial sea of a foreign country, and any group (asserted through the Attorney General) who could adequately establish any injury.

The monies from the Fund can be used for removal costs and amounts necessary to compensate for the loss of or damage to natural resources and all administrative and personnel costs associated with any activity involved in cleaning up the damage caused.[230]

In order to insure that there is appropriate financial responsibility, the Act provides that the owner or operator of any vessel which uses any off shore facility must establish and maintain some evidence of finan-

---

226  43 U.S.C.A. § 1801.
227  43 U.S.C.A. § 1812.
228  43 U.S.C.A. § 1814(b).
229  43 U.S.C.A. § 1814(c).
230  43 U.S.C.A. § 1814(d).

cial responsibility sufficient to satisfy the maximum amount of liability to which the owner or operator of that vessel would be exposed. This financial responsibility can be established by evidence of insurance, a guarantee or surety bond, or qualification as a self-insurer. The Secretary of Transportation had authority under the Act to deny entry to any port or place in the United States and/or to detain at a port or place in the United States from which it was about to depart any vessel which does not produce certification that it is in compliance with the financial responsibility provisions of the Act.[231]

The Act also provides that any person in charge of a vessel or off shore facility which is involved in an incident which could result in damage must immediately notify the Secretary of Transportation as soon as he has knowledge of it. As soon as the source of the potential damage is located either the owner of the vessel or the off shore facility or the Secretary must advertise a designation of the potential damage and identify the procedures by which claims may be presented. After the designation and advertisement, any person may present a claim to either the owner or the operator or the guarantor of the owner or operator.[232]

The Act provides various procedures for appraisal and settlement of the claims against the Fund. One of these procedures is the possibility that the Secretary of Transportation may appoint one or more panels to hear and decide disputes under the Act.[233]

The United States district courts have been accorded original and exclusive jurisdiction over all controversies arising under the Act and the venue shall be determined to be in any district wherein the injury complained of occurred.[234]

The Act provides penalties for any person who fails to comply with the requirements of the Act. The civil penalty of $10,000 will be assessed to anyone who fails to provide evidence of financial responsibility under the Act. A criminal penalty of a fine of not more than $10,000 or imprisonment for not more than one year or both is assessed against a person who fails to notify and designate the oil spill or other damage that would be a cause for damage to the environment under the Act.[235]

Another major provision of the 1978 amendments is the establishment of the Fisherman's Contingency Fund.[236] This Fund is established in the Treasury of the United States and consists of fees assessed against

---

231  43 U.S.C.A. § 1815.
232  43 U.S.C.A. § 1816.
233  43 U.S.C.A. § 1817(h).
234  43 U.S.C.A. § 1819.
235  43 U.S.C.A. § 1822.
236  43 U.S.C.A. § 1841.

each holder of an exploration permit, an easement or right-of-way for the construction of a pipeline in any area of the Continental Shelf, and monies collected by the Secretary of Commerce from those responsible for damages recovered under the Act.

Claims against the Fund are permitted by commercial fishermen who own, operate, or derive income from commercial fishing. These claims are based on hazards to commercial fishing caused by Outer Continental Shelf oil and gas exploration, development and production activities including all obstructions on the bottom, throughout the water, and on the surface.[237]

The Secretary of Commerce must prescribe and promulgate regulations for filing, processing, and settlement of claims pursuant to the Act.

An interesting section of this portion of the Act provides a presumption that any damage to commercial fishing was caused by oil and gas exploration, development, or production if the claimant (the commercial fisherman) can establish that: (1) the commercial fishing vessel was being used for fishing and was located in the area affected by the Outer Continental Shelf activities; (2) a report on the location of the material, equipment, tool, container, or other item which caused the damage was made within fifteen days after the date on which the vessel first returned to a port after discovering such damage; (3) there was no record on the latest nautical charts or notice to mariners in effect at least fifteen days prior to the date that the damage was sustained that such material, equipment, tool, container, or other item existed where such damages occurred . . .; and (4) there was no proper surface marker or lighted buoy which was attached or closely anchored to such material, equipment, tool, container, or other item.[238]

There are some miscellaneous provisions of the 1978 amendments which are of interest. One of those provisions relates to the notification by the Secretary of the Interior to the Comptroller General of the United States of all shut-in oil and gas wells and wells flaring natural gas on leases issued under the Outer Continental Shelf Lands Act. The report submitted by the Secretary must indicate whether or not the Secretary intends to require production on such a shut-in well or order cessation of flaring.[239]

Another interesting provision relates to natural gas distribution. This provision encourages expanded participation by local distribution companies in acquisition of leases and development of natural gas resources on the Outer Continental Shelf by facilitating the transportation

237  43 U.S.C.A. § 1843.
238  43 U.S.C.A. § 1844.
239  43 U.S.C.A. § 1861.

and interstate commerce of natural gas which is produced from a lease located on the Outer Continental Shelf. This section of the Act empowers the Federal Energy Regulatory Commission to publish a statement of policy which sets forth the standards under which the Commission will consider applications for the transportation and interstate commerce of natural gas which is produced from a lease located on the Outer Continental Shelf.[240]

One additional provision of the 1978 amendments provides for the investigation of reserves of oil and gas on the Outer Continental Shelf.[241]

Congress found that there was a serious lack of adequate basic information available to the Congress and the Secretary of the Interior with respect to the availability of oil and natural gas on the Outer Continental Shelf. This section of the Act mandates that the Secretary of the Interior must, on a continuing basis, gather data and information which will bear on the question of oil and natural gas located on the Outer Continental Shelf. The Secretary is required to report to Congress each year on his findings.[242]

## FISHERY CONSERVATION AND MANAGEMENT

In 1976 Congress passed the Fishery Conservation and Management Act.[243] It is commonly referred to as the Magnuson Fishery Conservation and Management Act, named after the main sponsor of the bill.

In passing the Act, Congress found the following:

(1) That fish off the coast of the United States, highly migratory species on the high seas, the species which dwell on the continental shelf appertained to the United States and the anadromous fish which spawn in the United States rivers or estuaries constitute valuable and renewable natural resources;

(2) Increased fish pressure and inadequacy of fishery conservation and management practices result in the survival of certain stocks of fish as threatened and other stocks have been reduced in number so that they could become similarly threatened;

(3) Commercial and recreational fishing constitutes a major source of employment and contribute significantly to the economy of the nation. Many coastal areas are dependent upon fishing and related activities and their activities have resulted in an over fishing of the resources. Activities of massive foreign fishing fleets in waters adjacent to our coastal areas have contributed to the damage, have interfered with do-

---

240   43 U.S.C.A. § 1862.
241   43 U.S.C.A. § 1865.
242   43 U.S.C.A. § 1865(c)(e).
243   16 U.S.C.A. § 1801.

mestic fishing efforts and caused destruction of the fishing gear of the United States fisherman;

(4) International fishing agreements have not been effective in preventing or terminating the over fishing of these valuable fishing resources and there is a danger that irreversible effects of over fishing will take place before an effective international agreement on fishery management can be negotiated, signed, ratified, and implemented;

(5) Fishing resources are finite but renewable, if placed under sound management before over fishing has caused irreversible effects;

(6) A national program for the conservation and management of the fishery resources of the United States is necessary to prevent over fishing, to rebuild over fished stock, to insure conservation, and to realize the full potential of the national's fishery resources;

(7) A national program for the development of fisheries which are under utilized or not utilized by the United States Fishing Industry including bottom fish off of Alaska it is necessary to insure that our citizens benefit from the employment, food supply and revenue which could be generated thereby.[244]

Based on these findings, Congress declared that the purposes of the Act where as follows:

(1) To take immediate action and conserve and manage the fishery resources found off the coast of the United States and the anadromous species in continental shelf fishery resources of the United States by establishing:

> (A) The Fishery Conservation Zone which the United States will assume exclusive fishery management authority over all fish except highly migratory species and;

> (B) Exclusive fishery management authority on said zone over such anadromous species and continental shelf fishery resources;

(2) To support and encourage the implementation and enforcement of international fishery agreements for the conservation and management of highly migratory species and to encourage negotiation and implementation of additional sets of agreements as necessary;

(3) To promote domestic, commercial, and recreational fishing under sound conservation and management principles;

---

[244]  16 U.S.C.A. § 1801(a).

(4) To provide for the preparation and implementation in accordance with national standards of fishery management plans which will achieve and maintain on a continuing basis the optimum yield from each fishery;

(5) To establish regional fishery management counsels to prepare, monitor, and revise such plans under circumstances which will enable the states, the fishing industry, consumer and environmental organizations, and other interested persons to participate in the advise on the establishment and administration of such plans and which take into account the social and economic needs of the states; and

(6) To encourage the development by the United States fishing industry of fisheries which are currently under utilized or not utilized by the United States fishermen including both bottom fish off Alaska and to that end to insure that optimum yield determinations promote such development.[245]

In order to accomplish these purposes, Congress declared certain policies were necessary. These policies as stated by Congress include the intention to maintain without change the existing territorial or other ocean jurisdiction in the United States for all purposes other than the conservation and management of fishery resources; to not interfere or fail to recognize legitimate uses of the high seas except as necessary for the conservation and management of fishery resources; to insure that national fishery conservation and management programs utilize and are based upon the best scientific information available including responses from the public and the academic community; to permit foreign fishing consistent with the provisions of the Act; and to support and encourage continued act of the United States efforts to obtain an international acceptable treaty at the Third United States Conference of the Law of the Sea which will provide for effective conservation and management of fishery resources.[246]

The Act establishes what is known as the Fishery Conservation Zone which is defined as a zone contiguous to the territorial sea of the United States. The inter-boundary of the Fishery Conservation Zone is a line co-terminus with the seaward boundary of each of the coastal states and the outward boundaries of such zone is a line drawn in such a manner that each point on it is 200 nautical miles from the baseline from which the territorial sea is measured.[247]

As a backdrop to this concept, it is interesting to note that for a number of years nations had disputed just what constituted the territorial sea of

245  16 U.S.C.A. § 1801(b).
246  16 U.S.C.A. § 1801(c).
247  16 U.S.C.A. § 1811.

a particular coastal nation. Many nations including the United States considered three miles from the coast as constituting the territorial sea, but this was eventually increased to 12 miles. With the passage of the Magnuson Act, the United States extended its jurisdiction from 12 miles to 200 miles offshore. Of this 200 miles, 197 miles constitutes the United States Exclusive Economic Zone (E.E.Z.).

It might be noted that there is an exception to the three mile rule in the cases of Texas, Florida, and Puerto Rico whose seaward boundaries extend to approximately 9 miles.

Under the Act the United States claims and intends to exercise, sovereign rights and exclusive fishery management authority over all fish and all continental shelf fishery resources within the Exclusive Economic Zone. It is also provided that beyond the Exclusive Economic Zone the United States will exercise exclusive fishery management authority over all anadromous species throughout the migratory range of each such species beyond the Exclusive Economic Zone and all continental shelf fishery resources beyond the Exclusive Economic Zone.[248]

Congress did exempt from the Exclusive Fishery Management Authority under the Act highly migratory species of fish.[249]

## INTERNATIONAL FISHING AGREEMENTS

An essential part of the Magnuson Act is the monitoring of foreign fishing and the promotion of international fishing agreements. In order to control the amount of foreign fishing which was damaging to the fish resources in the United States, the Magnuson Act prohibited foreign fishing after February 28, 1977 except fishing which was subject to an international fishing agreement which was in effect on April 13, 1976, and any "governing international fishing agreement" which would come into effect after the passage of the Magnuson Act. In the latter case any agreement entered into by Congress with a foreign nation would include commitments by any foreign nation to abide by all regulations promulgated by the Secretary of Commerce and to permit up front when the occasion demands to allow and authorize an officer under the provisions of the Act to broad, search or inspect any vessel at any time and to make arrests and seizures whenever the officer has reasonable cause to believe as a result of the search or inspection that any vessel has committed an act which is prohibited by the Magnuson Act.

Further provisions of the Act require foreign fishing vessels, before they engage in fishing within the fishery conservation zone or the continental shelf to apply for a permit for each of its fishing vessels that wishes to engage in any fishing controlled under the Act. These permits can-

---

248  16 U.S.C.A. § 1812.
249  16 U.S.C.A. § 1813.

not be valid for any longer than one year and must be applied for through the Secretary of State.[250]

The appropriate authorities including the Secretary of State and the Secretary of the Department in which the Coast Guard is operating are required to prescribe the forms for permit applications pursuant to this Act. The application for the permit is required to contain in addition to the name an official identification number of each fishing vessel. Such additional facts as a complete description of the vessel including tonnage, capacity, speed, equipment, etc. the fishery in which each vessel wishes to fish, the estimated amount of tonnage of fish that will be caught, and the ocean area in which the fishing will be conducted are required.[251]

After receiving the application the Secretary of State is required to publish a notice of the receipt of the application the Federal Register together with a summary of the contents of the application, and to transmit the application with its contents to the Secretary of Commerce. In addition to the Secretary of Commerce who must receive a copy of the application, the appropriate Regional Fishery Management Council must also receive a summary of the application.[252]

The Regional Fishery Management Council after receiving the application and examining it can prepare and submit to the Secretary of Commerce any written comments as it deems appropriate. Included in the regional fishery management counsel's recommendations may be included comments by any interested person who chooses to make comments on the application.

After the receipt of the recommendation by the Council, the Secretary of Commerce after consulting with the Secretary of State, in taking into consideration all the views and recommendations and comments received may approve the application results in the issuing of the permit.[253]

A control is placed on the approval of the application for the permit in the form of establishing a maximum taking of fish which will not exceed the optimum yield of the fishery concerned. Other matters which may be appropriate may be taken in consideration by the Secretary before he approves any application for a permit.

After the approval of the application by the Secretary of Commerce he is required under the Magnuson Act to transmit a copy of the permit and any conditions and restrictions that he has established to the Secre-

250  16 U.S.C.A. § 1821.
251  16 U.S.C.A. § 1824(a).
252  16 U.S.C.A. § 1824(a)(4).
253  16 U.S.C.A. § 1824(a)(6).

tary of State who will in turn transmit the permit to the foreign nation involved; to the secretary of the department of which the coast guard is operating; and to the Regional Fishery Management Council which has authority over any fishery specified in the application.[254]

In the event the Secretary of Commerce after receiving the application with comments and recommendations decides not to approve the application for the permit, he must promptly inform the Secretary of State of his disapproval and the reasons therefore. The Secretary of State thereafter must notify the foreign nation involved and transmit the reasons why the application was not approved. The foreign nation involved may after consideration of the reasons for disapproval submit a revised application, which will be handled in the same manner as the original application.[255]

The Magnuson Act provides that the Secretary of Commerce in consultation with the Secretary of State must establish a schedule of fees for the issuance of the permit provided for by the Act. The Act provides that the fees which are established must be non-discriminatory as to each foreign nation and must be at least in an amount sufficient to return to the United States an amount which bears some relationship to the total cost of carrying out the provisions of the Magnuson Act during each fiscal year.[256]

The cost ordinarily associated with the carrying out of the provisions of the Magnuson Act include fishery conservation and management activities, research, the overall administration and enforcement of the Act, etc., but does exclude the cost for observers covered by surcharges within that provision of the Act.

The amounts collected by the Secretary of Commerce are then placed in a special fund which is used for the purposes of making loans covered under another portion of the Act.

The Act provides for sanctions, in the form of the revocation of any permit issued under the Act, against any foreign fishing vessel which has been used in the commission of any act which is prohibited by any section of the Magnuson Act. The Act provides that the Secretary of Commerce may temporarily deny or suspend any permit of such foreign fishing vessel pending the outcome of any administrative proceeding instituted for the purposes of determining a violation as provided by the Act.[257]

254  16 U.S.C.A. § 1824(a)(8).
255  16 U.S.C.A. § 1824(a)(9).
256  16 U.S.C.A. § 1824(a)(10).
257  16 U.S.C.A. § 1824 (a)(12).

## GOVERNING INTERNATIONAL FISHERY AGREEMENT

Under the Magnuson Act fishing is authorized provided for under a "governing international fishery agreement." The fishing agreement is customarily between the United States and a foreign government which intends to engage either collectively or through some of its nationals in fishing in the zone protected by the Magnuson Act.

The Magnuson Act provides that each governing international fishing agreement requires that the foreign nation involved must acknowledge the Exclusive Fishing Management Authority of the United States as set forth under the Act. In addition to that general provision, each agreement must include the following terms and conditions:

(1) The foreign nation and the owner or operator of any fishing vessel fishing in the protected zone will abide by all regulations promulgated by the Secretary of Commerce including any fishery management plan or preliminary fishery management;

(2) The foreign nation and the owner or operator of any fishing vessel must agree to permit a boarding and searching of the vessel for purposes of the Act (and agree that if any observer is to be stationed aboard a vessel, then all costs incurred in such stationing be paid for by the owner or operator of the vessel);

(3) Apply for and obtain the permit required, prominently display the permit in the wheel house of any vessel involved, pay the required fees required by the Magnuson Act in advance, and assume responsibility for reimbursement of any United States citizens for any loss or damage to their fishing vessels, gear, or catch caught by the fishing vessel of that nation;

(4) Agree that the nation and the owners and operators of the vessels will not in any year harvest an amount of fish which exceeds such nation's allocation.[258]

## ALLOWABLE LEVEL OF FOREIGN FISHING

An important part of the Magnuson Act is the concept of the total allowable level of foreign fishing and an allocation of that allowable level to any particular nation. The Act defines the total allowable level of foreign fishing with respect to any United States fishery for each harvesting season at the level representing that portion of the optimum yield of such fishery that will not be harvested by vessels of the United States as determinined in accordance with the procedures to be followed under the Act.

---

258   16 U.S.C.A. § 1821(c).

# WILDLIFE AND HABITAT

The actual amount of the fishing permitted under the Act is determined by the appropriate fishery management counsel for each United States fishery. These Fishery Management Councils determine and certify to the Secretary of State and the Secretary of Commerce the annual fishing level for that fishery for each harvesting season. Thereafter the Secretary of Commerce in consultation with the Secretary of State determines the amount of harvesting of any United States fishery which may be allocated for that season to foreign fishing vessels. An exception can be found under the Act where the Secretary of Commerce finds that any such portion as recommended by the counsel for that harvesting season might be detrimental to the development of the fishing industry. He may thereafter decline to approve any harvest by foreign vessels.

From the total allowable level of foreign fishing the Secretary in State in cooperation with the Secretary of Commerce then may make allocations to foreign nations.

The allocation to any foreign nation is to be based on several factors including the following:

(1) Whether and to what extent such nation imposes tariff barriers or non-tariff barriers on the importation or otherwise restricts the market access of both United States fish and fishery products particularly fish and fishery products for which the foreign nation has requested an allocation;

(2) Whether and to what extent such nation cooperating with the United States in both the advancement of existing and new opportunities for fishery exports in the United States through the purchase of fishery products from the United States processors and the advancement of fishery trade through the purchase of fish and fishery products from United States fishermen particularly fish and fishery products for which the foreign nation has requested an allocation;

(3) Whether and to what extent the nation and the fishing fleets of such nation have cooperated with the United States in the enforcement of the United States fishing regulations;

(4) Whether and to what extent such nation requires the fish harvested from the fishery conservation zone for its domestic consumption;

(5) Whether and to what extent such nation otherwise contributes to a process of growth of a sound and economic United States fishery industry including minimizing gear conflicts with fishing operations of the United States fishermen and transferring the harvesting or processing technology which will benefit the United States fishing industries;

(6) Whether and to what extent fishing vessels of such nation have traditionally engaged in fishing in such fishery;

(7) Whether and to what extent the nation is cooperating with the United States in making substantial contributions to fishery research and identification of fishery resources;

(8) Any other matters that the Secretary of the State in cooperation with the Secretary of Commerce might deem appropriate.

In establishing total allowable levels of foreign fishing the Magnuson Act provides that the annual fishing level for any United States fishery during any harvesting season is the "base harvest." From this base harvest there is subtracted a "reduction factor amount" which is either 5, 10 or 15% and any increase in the amount of harvest by vessels of the United States.

In order to emphasize the United States agreement with the purposes underlying the International Convention for the Regulation of Whaling the Magnuson Act provides that the Secretary may issue a certification with respect to any foreign country that conducts fishing operations or engages in trade or taking of any fishery which diminishes the effectiveness of the Convention. When the Secretary so certifies that that nation has engaged in such conduct the allocation of that particular country must be reduced by not less than 50% for that particular harvest season.

In order to keep track of the effectiveness of the Magnuson Act the Act provides that the Secretary of Commerce and the Secretary of State must prepare and submit a report to the Congress and the President not later than July 1st of each year on such matters as a list of species of all allocations made to foreign nations pursuant to the Act and the permits issued, and all tariff and non-tariff trade barriers imposed by such nations on the importation of such species from the United States.[259]

An essential part of the Act provides that foreign fishing will not be authorized for any foreign fishing vessel before a nation satisfies the Secretary and the Secretary of State that such nation extends substantially the same fishing privileges to fishing vessels of the United States.[260]

The Secretary of Commerce and the Secretary of State are required to prepare preliminary fishery management plans. The fishery management plan must be prepared, if no prior fishery management plan has been prepared, when any foreign nation applies for a permit to fish in the United States protected zone.

---

259  16 U.S.C.A. § 1821(e).
260  16 U.S.C.A. § 1821(f).

The content of the plan requires a description of the fishery, a preliminary determination as to the optimum yield for such fishery, that portion which will be harvested by vessels of the United States, and the total allowable level of foreign fishing with respect to that fishery.[261]

In addition to international fishing agreements which are not treaties, there are international fishing agreements which are in fact treaties. The Act provides that the Secretary of State may not only negotiate international fishing agreements which do not rise to the level of treaties, but also negotiate treaties. In addition the Secretary of State may negotiate boundary agreements with any adjacent foreign nation to establish a fishery conservation zone in the United States applicable to such nation.

The Secretary of Commerce may begin the whole process by requesting the Secretary of State to initiate and conduct negotiations for the purposes of entering into an international fishing agreement which would allow fishing vessels in the United States equitable access to fish in foreign nations' exclusive fishing zones.

The Secretary of State in cooperation with the Secretary of Commerce is authorized under the Act to renegotiate any treaty which pertains to fishing in the Exclusive Economic Zone or on or near the continental shelf.

As to international fishing agreements which do not rise to the level of a treaty, the Act forbids the renegotiation of such agreements unless they comply with the Act and, specifically that portion of the Act which relates to governing international fishery agreements.[262]

One section of the Act entitled "non-recognition" provides that the Congress of the United States will not recognize a claim of any foreign nation to an Exclusive Economic Zone beyond such nation's territorial sea, if that nation fails to consider and take into account traditional fishing activities of fishing vessels of the United States or fails to recognize and accept that highly migratory species are to be managed by applicable international fishery agreements or imposes on fishing vessels in the United States any conditions or restrictions which are unrelated to fishery conservation or management.[263]

Governing international fishing agreements as provided for by 16 U.S.C. 1821 are agreements entered into by the United States and a foreign country which are not designated as treaties. Congress as part of the rule making power of both the House of Representatives and the

261  16 U.S.C.A. § 1821(g).
262  16 U.S.C.A. § 1822.
263  16 U.S.C.A. § 1822(e).

Senate has declared an intention to oversee these governing international fishing agreements and has provided a mechanism for control. The procedure called for under the Act provides that the President must submit to both the House of Representatives and the Senate a document setting forth the text of any governing international fishing agreement. Thereupon the agreement is placed upon the appropriate calendar and a stay period of sixty (60) days prevents the agreement from becoming effective.

Sections of the Act provide for Congressional consideration of the agreement and as a result of the debate and final consideration the resolution may either be approved or prohibited as a result of Congressional consideration.[264]

In those situations in which Congress does in fact approve the governing international fishery agreement, the wording of such approval invariably starts off with "notwithstanding any other provision of law the governing international fishing agreement entered into between the government of the United States and the government of . . . . pursuant to the Magnuson Fishery Conservation and Management Act of 1976[265] signed at Washington on . . . . is approved and shall become effective on . . . ."[266]

In 1987 Congress passed the "Drift Net Impact Monitoring Assessment and Control Act." This Act was part of an international fishery agreement and was based on findings by Congress that the use of long plastic drift nets was a fishing technique that may result in entanglement and death of enormous numbers of marine resources and that there was a pressing need for detail and reliable information on the numbers of marine resources that became entangled.

Marine resources were defined to include fish, shellfish, marine mammals, sea birds, and other forms of marine life or water fowl. Congress stated its intention that the Secretary of Commerce through the Secretary of State and in consultation with the Secretary of the Interior should immediately initiate negotiations with foreign governments that conduct or authorize there nationals to conduct drift net fishing that results in the taking of marine resources in the United States in waters of the North Pacific Ocean outside the Exclusive Economic Zone in territorial sea of any nation.

Congress stated that it was necessary for these agreements to provide for the use of a sufficient number of vessels from which scientists of the

---

264 16 U.S.C.A. § 1823.
265 16 U.S.C. § 1801 et seq.
266 A listing of various agreement including the effective date can be found following 16 U.S.C. § 1823.

United States and foreign governments could observe and gather reliable information.

In addition a part of the Act provided that the Secretary must report to the Congress facts concerning the extent and the effects of drift net fishing in waters of the North Pacific Ocean on marine resources of the United States. Congress further directed that the Secretary of Commerce through the Secretary of State should request foreign governments to provide information relative to draft net fishing. The Act further provides that the Secretary of Commerce should evaluate the effects of drift net fishing and make recommendations for tracking drift net fishing, develop and propose alternate drift net materials, offer bounties for persons who may retrieve from the Exclusive Economic Zone abandoned and discarded drift net and other plastic fishing material and make a report to Congress on the need for additional research in such matters.[267]

The Magnuson Act encourages the entering into of agreements by the United States and foreign countries with respect to fishing matters. It is of course possible that the Secretary of State may not be able to enter into these agreements either because he has not had a reasonable time to do so or because a foreign nation refuses to enter into such an agreement. In those situations where the foreign nation is not allowing the fishing vessels of the United States to engage in fishing for highly migratory species in their fishing zones, or where the Secretary of States finds that a foreign nation is not complying with its obligations under any international fishing agreement or where a foreign nation has seized a United States fishing vessel within its territorial sea, he may certify to the Secretary of the Treasury that such action has taken place. Upon receipt of this certification from the Secretary of State, the Secretary of the Treasurer must immediately take action to prohibit the importation in the United States of all fish and fish products from the fishery involved or from any fishery of the foreign nation concerned. This prohibition may be removed when the Secretary of State finds that the reasons for the imposition of this import prohibition no longer prevails.[268]

In an attempt to control and supervise foreign fishing in American waters the Secretary of Commerce must establish a program under which a United States observer will be stationed aboard each foreign fishing vessel while that vessel is in the waters that are within the protected United States zone. The purpose of such observers is to carry out such scientific and other duties as may be deemed necessary to protect the United States interest, as defined under the Magnuson Act.

---

[267] See Pub. L. 100-220, 101 Stat. 1477.
[268] 16 U.S.C.A. 1825. This is called the "Packwood Amendment."

In order to pay for this observer program each owner or operator of a foreign fishing vessel that fishes in the United States waters must pay a fee that is sufficient to cover all the costs of providing an observer aboard that vessel. The funds so accumulated are deposited by the Secretary of the Treasury and a fund entitled the "Foreign Fishing Observer Fund." The fund is to be used to pay the cost of providing the observers

In order to put teeth into the observer program, the Act provides that any owner or operator of a foreign fishing vessel who refuses to permit an individual to authorize to act as an observer is subject to a civil penalty as defined under 16 U.S.C. § 1858.

Under the Act, the Secretary of Commerce is authorized to issue regulations as may be needed to carry out the provisions of the Act.[269]

In addition to the control of foreign fishing in the Economic Fishery Zone a major portion of the Act concerns fishery conservation and management. This section involves the articulation of national standards for fishing conservation and management. These standards as stated by Congress include the following:

(1) Conservation and management measures shall prevent over fishing while achieving on a continuing basis the optimum yield from each fishery for the United States fishing industries;

(2) Conservation and management measures shall be based upon the best scientific information available;

(3) To the extent practicable and an individual stock of fish shall be managed as a unit throughout its range and interrelated stocks of fish such be managed as a unit or enclosed coordination;

(4) Conservation and management measures shall not discriminate between residents of different states. If it becomes necessary to allocate or assign fishing privileges among various United States fishermen, shall allocation shall be fair and equitable to all such fishermen . . . .;

(5) Conservation and management measures shall where practicable promote efficiency in the utilization of fishery resources, except that no such measures shall have economic allocations as a sole purpose;

(6) Conservation and management measures shall take into account and allow for variations among and contingencies in fisheries, fishery resources and catches;

---

269  16 U.S.C.A. § 1827.

(7) Conservation and management measures shall where practicable minimize costs and avoid unnecessary duplication.[270]

Fishery conservation and management under the Magnuson Act calls for the establishment of Regional Fishery Management Councils. The regions established include New England Council, Mid-Atlantic Council, South Atlantic Council, Caribbean Council, Gulf Council, Pacific Council, North Pacific Council, and Western Pacific Council.

Each council has voting members which include the principal state official with marine fishery management responsibilities and expertise in each constituent state, the regional director of the National Marine Fishery Service for the geographic area concerned and additional members of each council appointed by the Secretary of Commerce from a list of individuals submitted by the governor of each applicable constituent state. Conditions and stipulations for length of term, appointment of successors, removal, and other matters relating to the membership of the counsel are provided for in the Act.

Each regional counsel is required to appoint committees and panels to perform the functions dictated to it by the Act.

The counsels are required to prepare and submit to the Secretary of Commerce a fishery management plan with respect to each fishery within its geographical area of authority that requires conservation and management, prepare comments on any application for foreign fishing transmitted to it under a prior section of the Act, conduct public hearings at appropriate times and places so as to allow all interested persons an opportunity to be heard in the development of fishery management plans, submit to the Secretary of Commerce such periodic reports as its counsel deems appropriate, review on a continuing basis the assessment and specifications made in any previous time period, and any other activities which are required or provided for by the Act.

Each counsel is subject to procedural matters as provided for in the Act.[271]

A major portion of the Magnuson Act is the concept of fishery management plans. These plans are those which are prepared by a council or in the appropriate circumstances by the Secretary of Commerce with respect to any fishery.

Such plans must (1) contain the conservation and management measures applicable to foreign fishing and fishing by vessels of the United States which are necessary and appropriate for the conservation and

---

270  16 U.S.C.A. § 1851.
271  16 U.S.C.A. § 1852.

management of the fishery and which are consistent with the national standard as provided under the Magnuson Act; (2) contain a description of the fishery including the number of vessels involved, the type and quantity of fishing gear used, the species of fish involved, their location and the costs likely to be incurred in management and potential revenues from the fishery, and the nature and extent of foreign fishing and Indian fishing rights if any; (3) access and specify at a present and probable future condition of and the maximum sustainable yield and optimum yield from the fishery including a summary of information utilizing and making such specifications; (4) access and specify the capacity and extent to which fishing vessels of the United States on an annual basis will harvest the optimum yield, the portion of such optimum yield would on an annual basis will not be harvested by fishing vessels in the United States, and the capacity and extent to which the United States fish processors on an annual basis will process that portion of such optimum yield that would be harvested by fishing vessels in the United States; and (5) specify the pertinent data and transmit it to the Secretary of Commerce with respect to the fishery including the information regarding the type and quantity of fishing gear used, catch by species in numbers of fish or weight thereof, areas in which fishing was engaged in, time of fishing, number of hauls, and the estimated processing capacity of United States fish processors.

In addition to these requirements a fishery and management plan may require a permit to be obtained, and fees paid with respect to any fishing vessel of the United States fishing or wishing to fish in the Fishery Conservation Zone, designate zones where and periods when fishing shall be limited or not permitted or specified types and quantities of fishing gear, established specified limitations on the catch of fish, prohibit or limit the types and quantities of fishing gear, fishing vessels or equipment to be used including devices, establishing a system for limiting access to the fishery in order to achieve the optimum yield, and assess and specify the effect which the conservation and management measures of the plan will have on the stocks of naturally spawning anadromous fish in the region.

The regional council management plans are submitted to the Secretary of Commerce who must after receipt of the plan immediately commence a review of the management plan to determine whether it is consistent with the national standard, and immediately publish in the Federal Register a notice stating that the plan is available and that written data or views or comments of interested persons on the plan may be submitted to the Secretary and within thirty (30) after receipt of the plan make such changes in the proposed regulations as will be necessary for the implementation and publish such proposed regulations including any changes within the Federal Register together with an explanation of these changes which are substantive.

These regional management plans will take effect and be automatically implemented if the Secretary of Commerce does not notify the counsel in writing of his disapproval or partial of the plan before the close of the 95th day after receipt of the plan.

If the Secretary of Commerce disapproves of the plan, then the regional counsel may submit a revised plan or amendment to the Secretary. Upon receipt of this revised plan or amendment the Secretary must undertake the same review as for the original plan.

In addition to the regional management plans the Secretary of Commerce may also prepare a fishery management plan provided in accordance with the national standards. He is authorized to do this where the appropriate counsel fails to develop and submit to the Secretary a fishery management plan for any fishery or the Secretary of Commerce partially disapproves of any counsel plan and the counsel involved fails to submit a revised or further revised plan or amendment.

Whenever the Secretary of Commerce prepares a fishery management plan he must submit the plan or any amendments to a counsel plan to the appropriate counsel for consideration and comment and in addition publish in the Federal Register a notice stating that the plan is available and encourage public comment.

After a plan is finally approved the Secretary of Commerce is required to promulgate regulations that are necessary to carry out the plan. The regulations promulgated by the Secretary are subject to judicial review for the purpose of determining whether or not the plan or the amendment violates the national standards determined under the Act or any other applicable law. The standard for this judicial review is the customary, arbitrary, and capricious standard.[272]

The Congressional intent with respect to all natural resources is to involve the states in cooperation with the government as much as possible. This theory is carried forward in the Magnuson Act by an expression by Congress that "nothing in this Act shall be construed as extending or diminishing the jurisdiction or authority of any state within its boundaries." State jurisdiction and authority is extended to any body of water that is adjacent to the state and totally enclosed by lines delineating territorial sea of the United States pursuant to the Geneva Convention on the territorial seas and contiguous zones. The jurisdiction of the authority of the state is confined to the boundary of the state and a state may not directly or indirectly regulate any fishing vessel outside its boundaries unless the vessel is registered under law of that state. Even the jurisdiction and authority of the state may be curtailed under certain circumstances. If the Secretary of Commerce finds that fishing which is covered under a fishery management plan is en-

---

[272] U.S.C.A. § 1853-1855. See also Alaska Factory Trawler Assn. v. Baldridge, 831 F.2d 1456.

gaged in primarily within the Exclusive Economic Zone or beyond such zone or if any state has taken any action or admitted to have taken any action the results of which are substantial and which adversely affect the carrying out of such plans, then the Secretary must promptly notify the state and appropriate counsel of such finding and he may proceed to regulate the applicable fishery within the boundaries of such state provided that he does so within the requirements of the fishery management plan and any regulations promulgated to implement such plans.[273]

In order to promote the interests covered under the Act, a later provision lists prohibited acts for which penalties may be accessed. As might be expected the prohibited acts include all those acts which might be in derogation of the purposes of the Magnuson Act. However in addition to the prohibition of acts directly related to the concerns of the Magnuson Act, the prohibition provision also prohibits the shipping, and transport, offer for sale, purchase, or import or export of any fish taken or retained in violation of any of the provisions of the permit granted under the Act or any agreement reached under the Act. In addition the Act prohibits the knowing and willful giving of to any counsel, the Secretary, or the governor of the state false information regarding the capacity and extent to which any fish processor will process a portion of the optimum yield of fish that will be harvested by fishing vessels of the United States.[274]

Later provisions of the Act provide for civil penalties, criminal penalties, and civil forfeitures. Any person who is found to have committed an act which is in violation of the prohibition section of the act is subject to a civil penalty of $25,000 for each violation. In accessing this civil penalty the Secretary of Commerce must take into account the nature, circumstances, and extent of the gravity of acts committed and in addition any history of prior offenses and the ability to pay and such other matters as justice may require.

A person against whom a civil penalty has been assessed may obtain a review of this penalty in the United States District Courts for the appropriate district.

Under the civil penalties portion of the Act, the Secretary of Commerce has subpoena authority.

There are also criminal penalties applied under the Act and against anyone who has violated any of the provisions of the Magnuson Act. The criminal penalties include a fine of not more that $50,000 or imprisonment for not more than six months or both. The criminal section also

---

273  16 U.S.C.A. § 1856.
274  16 U.S.C.A. § 1857.

provides that if a person committing one of the prohibited acts engages in conduct that either involves the use of a dangerous weapon or causes bodily injury to any officer are authorized to enforce the provisions of the Act, the offense is punishable by a fine not more than $100,000 or imprisonment for not more than ten years or both. The punishment of persons committing acts in violation of the Magnuson Act is within federal jurisdiction.

The Magnuson Act also provides for civil forfeitures. Where a fishing vessel commits acts in violation of the Magnuson Act including fishing gear, furniture, appurtenances, stores and cargo may be seized and declared forfeited. As a practical matter this process is begun in a United States District Court which has jurisdiction of the Act and the parties.[275]

The process is usually begun by the Attorney General who may seize any property or interest declared forfeited through the United States.

The penalty provisions of the Act are enforced by the Secretary and the Secretary of the department in which the coast guard is operating. The officers authorized by the Secretary may make an arrest without a warrant for any offense against the United States committed in his presence or for a felony cognizable under the laws of the United States if he has reasonably grounds to believe that the person to be arrested has committed or is committing a felony.

The district courts of the United States have exclusive jurisdiction over any case or controversy arising under the provisions of the Act.[276]

In order to carry out the purposes and the functions of the Magnuson Act, Congress each year makes appropriations. Appropriation for fiscal year 1989 was $75 million dollars.[277]

## FISHERMAN'S PROTECTIVE ACT OF 1967

The Fisherman's Protective Act of 1967 had as its original intention the protection of American vessels from foreign actions.[278] Specifically, the Act provided that the Secretary of State would take appropriate actions when a United States vessel was seized by a foreign country and under appropriate circumstances provided for the reimbursement of the owner of any direct charges paid to secure release of any vessel and crew.

In addition to these provisions, however, later provisions of the Act provide for a type of retaliatory action by the Secretary of Commerce in those situations where nationals of foreign countries directly or indi-

275 16 U.S.C.A. § 1858-60.
276 16 U.S.C.A. § 1861.
277 16 U.S.C.A. § 1882.
278 22 U.S.C.A. § 1971.

rectly conduct fishing operations in a manner or under circumstances which diminish the effectiveness of an international fishery conservation program.[279]

The Act requires the Secretary of Commerce or the Secretary of the Interior, when they find that nationals of a foreign country directly or indirectly are engaging in trade or a taking which diminishes the effectiveness of either an international fishery conservation program to which the United States is a party or which diminishes the effectiveness of an international program for endangered or threatened species, to certify such finding to the President of the United States.

Upon receipt of any such certification from one of the Secretaries, the President may direct the Secretary of the Treasury to prohibit the bringing or the importation into the United States of fish products (or wildlife products) from the offending country for such duration as the President determines appropriate to the extent that such prohibition is sanctioned by the General Agreement on Tariffs and Trade.

Within sixty days after the certification by either one of the Secretaries, the President must notify Congress of any action taken by him pursuant to this certification.

The Congress or Secretary of the Interior, depending on the appropriate jurisdiction, must review the activities of nationals of the defending country to determine whether the reasons for such certification continue to prevail. Where the Secretary finds that such reasons no longer prevail, the Secretary must terminate the certification and publish the notice of such termination in the Federal Register.

A provision of the Act stipulates that it is unlawful for any person subject to the jurisdiction of the United States knowingly to bring or import into the United States any fish products or wildlife products prohibited by the Secretary of the Treasury pursuant to this Act.[280]

A person who violates the provisions of the Fisherman Protection Act is subject to a fine of not more than $10,000 for the first violation and not more than $25,000 for any subsequent violation. The enforcement of the penalty provision is within the jurisdiction of the United States district courts and the United States Magistrates.[281]

The Secretaries of the Treasury, Commerce, or Interior are each authorized to prescribe regulations necessary to carry out the Act.

---

[279] 22 U.S.C.A. § 1978.
[280] *Id*.
[281] 22 U.S.C.A. § 1978(e).

# WILDLIFE AND HABITAT

In addition to the provision to protect values promoted by the Magnuson Act, the Fisherman's Protection Act also provides for a Fisherman's Protection Fund. This Fund is created by any claim collected by the Secretary of State from any foreign country as reimbursement for damage to the United States resulting from a seizure of a United States ship. Such funds are available for purposes of reimbursing vessel owners who have suffered monetary damages because of the foreign country's seizing.[282]

In addition, owners and operators of United States vessels are eligible for compensation for loss or destruction of commercial fishing vessels or gear when such vessel is engaged in any fishery subject to the exclusive Fishery Management Authority of the United States under the Magnuson Act. Subsequent provisions of the Act provide for the procedure for application of compensation and restrictions on the amount of money that can be forthcoming to the United States owner of the vessel or gear.[283] The funds used to compensate United States vessel owners for loss or destruction of the fishing vessel or gear where that damage has occurred when the vessel was engaged in a fishery subject to the Magnuson Act come from a fund entitled the Fishing Vessel and Gear Damage Compensation Fund. This Fund is created not only by amounts of money obtained from foreign countries who have seized American vessels after a protest by the Secretary of State but also by a surcharge on foreign fishing vessels in the amount of twenty percent on the permit fees charged foreign nations and owners and operators of vessels under the Magnuson Act.[284]

## COASTAL BARRIER RESOURCES

Congress found in 1982 that coastal barriers along the Atlantic and Gulf Coasts of the United States and adjacent wetlands, marshes, estuaries, inlets, and near-shore waters provided habitats for migratory birds and other wildlife and habitats which are essential spawning, nursery, nesting, and feeding areas for commercially and recreationally important species of pinfish and shellfish as well as other aquatic organisms such as turtles.

In addition, Congress found that coastal barriers contain resources of extraordinary scenic, scientific, recreational, natural, historic, archeological, cultural, and economic importance which are being irretrievably damaged and lost due to development on, among, and adjacent to such barriers.[285]

---

282  22 U.S.C.A. § 1979.
283  22 U.S.C.A. § 1980.
284  22 U.S.C.A. § 1980(f).
285  16 U.S.C.A. § 3501(a).

Although Congress found that coastal barriers serve as natural storm protective buffers, they are generally unsuitable for development because they are vulnerable to hurricane and other storm damage, and because natural shoreline recession and the movement of unstable sediments undermine man-made structures. Nevertheless, certain actions and programs by the federal government have subsidized and permitted development on coastal barriers resulting in the loss of these barriers and the creation of threats to human life, health, and property.

Based on these findings, Congress declared when it passed the Coastal Barrier Resources Act that its purpose was to minimize the loss of human life, wasteful expenditure of federal revenues, and the damage to fish, wildlife, and other natural resources associated with the coastal barriers along the Atlantic and Gulf Coasts and along the shores of the Great Lakes by restricting future federal expenditures and financial assistance which had the effect of encouraging development of coastal barriers.[286]

The resulting Act established a Coastal Barrier Resources System. The final statement of the purpose underlying the establishment of this System was to provide a system whereby the federal government could consider the means and measures by which the long term conservation of fish, wildlife, and other natural resources could be achieved.

The Coastal Barrier Resources System consists of those undeveloped coastal barriers that are located on the Atlantic and Gulf Coasts of the United States and those undeveloped coastal barriers along the shore areas of the Great Lakes that are designated by Congress by law after recommendation by the Secretary of the Interior.[287]

The term "undeveloped coastal barrier" under the Act means a depositional geological feature (such as a bay, barrier, tombolo, barrier spit, or barrier island) that consists of unconsolidated sedimentary materials, is subject to wave, tidal, and wind energies, and protects landward aquatic habitats from direct wave attack. In addition, the term includes all associated aquatic habitats including the adjacent wetlands, marshes, estuaries, inlets, and near shore waters.[288]

The designation was restricted, however, to include only such feature and associated habitats which contain few man-made structures and/or which are not included within the boundaries of areas established under federal, state, or local law and reserved primarily for wildlife refuge, sanctuary, recreational, or natural resource conservation purposes.

---

286  16 U.S.C.A. § 3501(b).
287  16 U.S.C.A. § 3503.
288  16 U.S.C.A. § 3502(1).

# WILDLIFE AND HABITAT

The term "Great Lakes," which was added in a later amendment to the Act, was defined to mean Lake Ontario, Lake Erie, Lake Heron, Lake St. Clair, Lake Michigan, and Lake Superior to the extent that those lakes are subject to the jurisdiction of the United States.[289]

Under the Act, the Secretary of the Interior must recommend to Congress and prepare maps identifying the boundaries of those undeveloped coastal barriers along the shore areas of the Great Lakes that the Secretary considers appropriate for inclusion in the Coastal Barrier Resources System. Excluded from these recommendations by the Secretary would be any undeveloped coastal barrier that is publicly owned and protected by federal, state, or local government law or held by a qualified organization as defined in the Tax Reform Act of 1986[290] primarily for wildlife refuge, sanctuary, recreational, or natural resource conservation purposes.

Before the Secretary of the Interior can recommend to Congress any undeveloped coastal barriers, he is required to consult with and provide an opportunity for comment to appropriate United States government agencies, state agencies (including the Coastal Zone Management Agencies) of the states bordering the Great Lakes and the public and, in addition, update on the basis of aerial photographs and consider the draft coastal barrier inventory maps prepared by the Secretary of the Interior in January 1985 for the states of Michigan, Wisconsin, Ohio, New York, and Minnesota.

The maps that the Secretary of the Interior must provide to Congress must also be made available to each appropriate state and county or equivalent subdivisions in which the system units are located and the Coastal Zone Management Agency in each appropriate state that has a coastal zone management program approved under the Coastal Zone Management Act in addition to each United States government agency.

All maps that are prepared under this Act must be made available for public inspection by the Director of the United States Fish and Wildlife Service.

After the System had been established, the Secretary of the Interior must conduct a review of the System maps at least once every five years and make any minor or technical modifications to the boundaries of any System unit that are necessary solely to reflect changes that have occurred in the size or location of that unit as a result of natural forces.

---

289   16 U.S.C.A. § 3502(4).
290   26 U.S.C. § 170(h)(3).

In conducting these reviews of the boundaries, the Secretary must consult with appropriate state coastal zone management agencies, each appropriate United States government agency, and the public.

All maps which are appropriate to the purposes of the Act are to be kept by the Director of the United States Fish and Wildlife Service, Department of the Interior. These maps must be made available for public inspection.[291]

An appropriate federal officer, after consultation with the Secretary, may make federal expenditures or make financial assistance available within the Coastal Barrier Resources System for the following purposes:

(1) exploration, extraction, or transportation of any energy resources which can be carried out only on, in, or adjacent to the coastal water areas;

(2) maintain existing channel improvements and related structures such as jetties, and including the disposal of dredge materials relating to such improvements;

(3) maintain, replace, reconstruct, or repair, but not expand, publicly owned or publicly operated roads, structures, or facilities that are essential links in a larger network or system;

(4) conduct military activities essential to national security;

(5) construct, operate, maintain, and rehabilitate Coast Guard facilities and access thereto; and

(6) the provision for actions or projects consisting of air and water navigational aids, projects under the Land and Water Conservation Fund Act and the Coastal Zone Management Act, scientific research, assistance for emergency actions essential to the saving of lives and the protection of property and the public health and safety, roads, structures, or facilities which are necessary, and projects for shoreline stabilization that are designed to mimic, enhance, or restore natural stabilization systems.[292]

In order to insure the primacy of the Coastal Barrier Resources Act, the Act provides that the Director of the Office of Management and Budget shall, on behalf of each federal agency concerned, make a written certification that each such agency has complied with the provisions of the Act during each fiscal year beginning after September 30, 1982. The

---

291  16 U.S.C.A. § 3503(a,b,c).
292  16 U.S.C.A. § 3505.

certification must be submitted to the House of Representatives and to the Senate on an annual basis.[293]

## MARINE SANCTUARIES

In 1972 Congress found that certain areas of the marine environment possess qualities which give them special national significance. Marine environment was and is defined as those areas of coastal and ocean waters, the Great Lakes, and their connecting waters and submerged lands over which the United States exercises jurisdiction consistent with international law.[294]

Prior to the passage of the Marine Sanctuaries Act, Congress had enacted resource-specific legislation to control the effects of particular activities impacting on the marine environment. But Congress felt, in 1972, that additional legislation was needed to identify special areas of the marine environment with a view toward the conservation and management of marine resources.[295]

Congress identified the purposes and policies of the Act to be:

(1) to identify areas of the marine environment of special national significance due to their resource of human use value;

(2) to provide adequate authority for comprehensive and coordinated conservation and management of these marine areas that will complement existing regulatory authority;

(3) to support, promote, and coordinate scientific research on and monitoring of the resources of these marine areas;

(4) to enhance public awareness, understanding, appreciation, and wise use of the marine environment; and

(5) to facilitate, to the extent compatible with the primary objective of resource protection, all public and private uses of the resources of these marine areas not prohibited pursuant to other authorities.[296]

The Act provides that the Secretary of Commerce may designate any discrete area of the marine environment as a national marine sanctuary and promulgate regulations implementing the designation.

Before the Secretary may so designate, he must find that the area is of specific national significance due to its resources or human use value, that existing state and federal authorities are inadequate to insure coor-

293 16 U.S.C.A. § 3506.
294 16 U.S.C.A. § 1432(3).
295 See U.S. Code Congressional and Administrative News, 1972, p. 4234.
296 16 U.S.C.A. § 1431(b).

dinated and comprehensive conservation and management of the area, including resource protection, scientific research, and public education, that the designation of the area as a national marine sanctuary will facilitate the objectives of the Act, and that the area is of a size and nature that will permit comprehensive and coordinated conservation and management.

In exercising his authorities under the Act, the Secretary of Commerce is required to consider the area's natural resource and ecological qualities, including its contribution to biological productivity, maintenance of ecosystem structure, maintenance of ecologically or commercially important or threatened species or species assemblages, and the biogeographic representation of the site.

The Secretary must also take into consideration the area's historical, cultural, archeological, or paleontological significance and the present potential uses of the area that depend on the maintenance of the area's resources including commercial and recreational fishing, subsistence uses, other commercial and recreational activities, and research and education.

One of the considerations the Secretary of Commerce must include in his determination includes the manageability of the area as a counter-balance to the public benefits to be derived from declaring the area to have sanctuary status.

In making his determination the Secretary of Commerce must consult with the Committee on Merchant Marine and Fisheries of the House of Representatives and the Committee on Commerce, Science, and Transportation of the Senate, the Secretaries of State, Defense, Transportation, and the Interior, and the administrator and heads of other interested federal agencies. In the interest of coordination and cooperation, the Secretary of Commerce is also required to consult with relevant agency heads of appropriate state and local government entities including Coastal Zone Management agencies, appropriate officials of any regional Fishery Management Council, and any other interested persons.

In making his determinations, the Secretary of Commerce must draft, as part of an Environmental Impact Statement, a resource assessment report documenting present and potential uses of the area.[297]

The Act establishes procedures for designation and implementation of marine sanctuaries. In proposing to designate a national marine sanctuary, the Secretary of Commerce must:

---

[297] 16 U.S.C.A. § 1433.

(1) issue in the Federal Register a notice of the proposal, proposed regulations that would be necessary and reasonable to implement the proposal, and the summary of the draft management plan;

(2) provide notice of the proposal in newspapers of general circulation or electronic media in the communities that may be affected by the proposal; and

(3) submit to the Committee on Merchant Marine and Fisheries of the House of Representatives and the Committee on Commerce, Science, and Transportation of the Senate a prospectus on the proposal.[298]

The Secretary of Commerce must prepare a draft environmental impact statement as required under NEPA. This impact statement must include the resource assessment report required under the Act, maps depicting the boundaries of the proposed designated area, and the existing and potential uses and resources of the area. This draft environmental impact statement must be made available to the public.

In addition, the Secretary of Commerce must hold at least one public hearing in the coastal area or areas that would be most affected by the proposed designation of the area as a national marine sanctuary.

The Act requires the Secretary of Commerce to provide the appropriate regional Fishery Management Council with the opportunity to prepare draft regulations for fishing within the United States Fishery Conservation Zone as the Council may deem necessary to implement the proposed designation.[299]

The Act provides that the House and Senate special committees, after receiving the prospectus required by the Act, may each hold hearings on the proposed designation and on the matters set forth in the prospectus.

After the public hearings, the public notice, and a consideration of any appropriate comments, the Secretary must publish in the Federal Register a notice of the designation together with the final regulations to implement the designation and submit such notice to Congress.[300]

The designation may be withdrawn either by the Secretary of Commerce himself, when he considers that the goals and objectives of the sanctuary cannot be fulfilled, or by joint resolution of the Congress.[301]

---

298  16 U.S.C.A. § 1434.
299  16 U.S.C.A. § 1434(a)(5).
300  16 U.S.C.A. § 1434(b)(1).
301  16 U.S.C.A. § 1434(b)(2).

The designation may be approved by Congress but some of the terms of the designation may be disapproved. In such a situation, Congress may disapprove one or more terms of the designation by a joint resolution.[302]

The regulations issued by the Secretary of Commerce under the Act must be applied in accordance with generally recognized principles of international law and in accordance with treaties, conventions, and other agreements to which the United States is a party.[303]

The Secretary is mandated to conduct research and educational programs as are necessary and reasonable in carrying out the purposes and polices of the Act.[304]

The Act clothes the Secretary with enforcement powers that are necessary and reasonable to carry out the purposes of the Act. The Act empowers any person who is authorized to enforce the Act to board, search, inspect, and seize any vessel and any equipment, storage, and cargo of the vessel suspected of being used to violate the Act or any regulation or permit issued under the Act.

In addition, authorized persons may seize, wherever found, any sanctuary resource taken or retained in violation of the Act, seize any evidence of a violation of the Act, and execute any warrant or other process issued by any court of common jurisdiction.[305]

The Act provides for civil penalties of not more than $50,000 for each violation of the Act. After assessment, the Secretary may refer the matter to the Attorney General of the United States for recovery of the amount assessed. This action must be brought in the appropriate district court of the United States.

In addition to civil penalties, the Act also contains a forfeiture provision. The Act provides that vessels or other items used in any sanctuary resource taken or retained in connection with or as a result of any violation of the Act or a permit issued under the Act is subject to forfeiture to the United States.

The Secretary may issue subpoenas for the attendance and testimony of witnesses and the production of relevant papers, books, and documents that he deems appropriate and in doing so may administer oaths.

---

302  16 U.S.C.A. § 1434(b)(3).
303  16 U.S.C.A. § 1435.
304  16 U.S.C.A. § 1436.
305  16 U.S.C.A. § 1437.

The Secretary also may ask the Attorney General to seek and obtain injunctive relief in situations where there is an imminent risk of destruction, loss, or injury to a sanctuary resource.[306]

The monies that the Secretary of Commerce receives under the Act in the form of civil penalties, forfeitures of property, etc., may be used to defray the reasonable and necessary costs incurred by the Secretary in providing temporary storage, care, and maintenance of any sanctuary resource or other property seized under the Act and to provide rewards to people who furnish information leading to an assessment of a civil penalty or to a forfeiture of property for a violation of the Act.[307]

The Act was amended in 1988 to require the Secretary to promote and coordinate the use of national marine sanctuaries for research purposes including requiring that the National Oceanic and Atmospheric Administration, in conducting or supporting marine research, give priority to research involving national marine sanctuaries and consulting with other federal and state agencies to promote use by such agencies of one or more sanctuaries for marine research.[308]

Included within the 1988 amendments to the Act were provisions authorizing the Secretary of Commerce to issue special use permits and enter into cooperative agreements with non-profit organizations.[309]

The Secretary can issue special use permits which authorize the conduction of special activities in a national marine sanctuary if the Secretary determines that the permit is necessary to establish conditions of access to and use of any sanctuary resource or to promote public use and understanding of the resource. In issuing the special use permits, the Secretary may assess and collect fees which are related to the costs incurred by the Secretary in issuing the permit and/or the costs incurred by the Secretary in monitoring the conduct of the activities. The fees collected under this provision of the Act may be used by the Secretary for the process of issuing and administering permits and for expenses of designating and managing national marine sanctuaries.[310]

The Act provides authority for the Secretary to suspend or revoke any permit without compensation to the permittee for a violation of a term or condition of the permit and in addition assess a civil penalty in accordance with the civil penalty provision of the Act.

The Act also authorizes the Secretary to enter into cooperative agreements with non-profit organizations for purposes of aiding and pro-

306  16 U.S.C.A. § 1437(b).
307  16 U.S.C.A. § 1437(e).
308  16 U.S.C.A. § 1440.
309  16 U.S.C.A. § 1441.
310  16 U.S.C.A. § 1441(c)(3).

moting interpretive, historical, scientific, and educational activities and for solicitation of private donations for support of such activities.

The 1988 amendments also provided for the assessment of liability against any person who destroys or causes loss of or injuries to any sanctuary resource. The liability extends to response costs and damages which include the costs of repairing, restoring, or acquiring the equivalent of a sanctuary resource, the value of the lost use of a sanctuary resource pending its restoration or replacement, and the value of a sanctuary resource if the resource cannot be restored, replaced, or the equivalent if such resource cannot be acquired.[311]

The recovery of response costs and damages is in the hands of the Attorney General, upon a request by the Secretary of Commerce, who may commence a civil action in the United States district court for the appropriate district against any person or vessel who may be liable under this section of the Act.

An interesting amendment to the Act in 1988 provided for the recognition of the historical significance of the wreck of the United States ship Monitor to coastal North Carolina and to the area off the coast of North Carolina known as the Graveyard of the Atlantic. Under this provision of the Act, Congress directed that a suitable display of artifacts and materials from the United States ship Monitor be maintained permanently at an appropriate site of coastal North Carolina. The responsibility for putting together a plan for interpretation and display of artifacts of the Monitor was given over to the Committee on Merchant Marine and Fisheries of the House of Representatives.[312]

## OCEAN DUMPING

In 1972 Congress found that unregulated dumping of material into ocean waters endangers human health, welfare, and amenities and the marine environment, ecological systems, and economic potentialities. In response to this finding, Congress passed the Marine Protection Research and Sanctuaries Act of 1972.[313]

Congress declared that it was the policy of the United States to regulate the dumping of all types of materials into ocean waters and to prevent or strictly limit the dumping into ocean waters of any material which would adversely affect human health, welfare, and amenities or the marine environment, ecological systems, or economic potentialities.[314]

Based on this policy, the Act was passed "to regulate the transportation by any person of material from the United States and in the case of

---

311 16 U.S.C.A. § 1443.
312 16 U.S.C.A. § 1445.
313 33 U.S.C.A. § 1401 et seq.
314 33 U.S.C.A. § 1401(b).
315 33 U.S.C.A. § 1401(c).

United States vessels, aircraft, or agencies, the transportation of material from a location outside the United States when in either case the transportation is for the purpose of dumping the material into ocean waters and the dumping of the material transported by any person from a location outside the United States when the dumping occurs in the territorial sea or the contiguous zone of the United States."[315]

In its essential part, the Act prohibits any person from transporting any material for the purpose of dumping it into the ocean waters unless authorized by permit.[316]

There are some interesting definitions accompanying the Act. Ocean waters is defined to mean "those waters of the open seas lying seaward of the base line from which the territorial sea is measured as provided for in the Convention on the Territorial Sea and the Contiguous Zone." Material is defined as any kind or description including dredge material, solid waste, incinerator residue, garbage, sewage, sewage sludge, munitions, radiological, chemical and biological warfare agents, radioactive materials, chemicals, biological and laboratory waste, wrecked or discarded equipment, rock, sand, evacuation debris, and industrial, municipal, agricultural and other waste. Dumping means a disposition of material.[317]

The Act provides that the Administrator of the Environmental Protection Agency may issue EPA Agency permits for the transportation from the United States of material for the purpose of dumping it into ocean waters where the Administrator determines that such dumping will not unreasonably degrade or endanger human health, welfare, or amenities or the marine environment, ecological systems, or economic potentialities. The Act contains an exception which prohibits the Administrator from issuing a permit for dredged material, radiological, chemical and biological warfare agents, high level radioactive waste, and medical waste.[318]

In making the determination of whether or not to issue a permit, the Administrator must consider the need for the proposed dumping and the effect that such dumping may have on human health, welfare, or amenities.[319]

In reviewing an application for a permit, the Administrator is mandated under the Act to consult with interested federal and state agencies as he deems useful and necessary.

---

[315] 33 U.S.C.A. § 1401(c).
[316] 33 U.S.C.A. § 1411.
[317] 33 U.S.C.A. § 1402.
[318] 33 U.S.C.A. § 1412.
[319] *Id.*

The Administrator may not issue permits for a dumping of material which will violate applicable water quality standards.

Originally, under the Act, the Administrator is absolutely prohibited to allow and is required to end the dumping of sewage, sludge, and industrial waste into ocean waters, but a 1988 amendment provided that the Administrator could issue a permit for such dumping in an emergency situation where he has determined that there has been demonstrated to exist an emergency requiring the dumping of such waste which poses an unacceptable risk relating to human health and admits of no other feasible solution. The Act defines an emergency to require action with a marked degree of urgency.[320]

In addition to the emergency provision, the Act also contains a provision which would permit the Administrator to issue a permit for the dumping of industrial wastes into ocean waters if he determines that the proposed dumping is necessary to conduct research on new technology related to ocean dumping or whether the dumping of such substance will have an unreasonable or an endangering effect on the marine environment, ecological systems, or economic potentiality. In issuing this permit, the Administrator is required to insure that the dumping will have minimal adverse impact and that the potential benefits of such research will outweigh any such adverse impact.[321]

The Act defines sewer sludge to mean "any solid, semi-solid, or liquid waste generated by a municipal waste water treatment plant the ocean dumping of which may unreasonably degrade or endanger human health, welfare, or amenities or the marine environment, ecological systems, and economic potentialities." The Act defines industrial waste to mean "any solid, semi-solid, or liquid waste generated by a manufacturing or process plant the ocean dumping of which may unreasonable degrade or endanger human health, welfare, or amenities, or the marine environment, ecological systems, and economic potentialities."[322]

In another provision of the Act the Secretary of the Army is authorized to issue permits after notice and opportunity for public hearing for the transportation of dredge material for the purpose of dumping into ocean waters where the Secretary determines that the dumping will not unreasonably degrade or endanger the values associated with the ocean waters considered to be important under the Act.[323]

Prior to the issuing of the permit, the Secretary of the Army must notify the Administrator of the EPA of his intentions to do so and in a case

---

[320]  *Id.*
[321]  *Id.*
[322]  33 U.S.C.A. § 1412(d).
[323]  33 U.S.C.A. § 1413(a).

where the Administrator disagrees with the Secretary as to the compliance with the criteria established, the determination of the Administrator must prevail. Under such circumstances, the Secretary of the Army may request from the Administrator a waiver and if it is issued it is based upon the determination that there is no economically feasible method or site available other than a dumping site the utilization of which would result in noncompliance with the criteria established under the Act.[324]

When the Administrator (or in a case where the Secretary of the Army is authorized) issues permits under the Act, each permit must designate and include the type of material authorized to be transported for dumping, the amount of material authorized to be transported for dumping, the location where such transport for dumping will be terminated or where such dumping will occur, the length of time for which the permit is valid with an expiration date, and any special provisions deemed necessary by the Administrator or the Secretary after consultation with the Secretary of the Department under which the Coast Guard is operating for the monitoring and surveillance of the transportation or dumping.[325]

The Administrator or the Secretary, as the case may be, may prescribe processing fees for permits.

The Administrator and/or Secretary must require the applicant for a permit under the Act to provide such information as may be deemed necessary to review and evaluate such application. The application must be made available to the public as a matter of public record at every stage of the proceedings. The final determination of the Administrator or the Secretary likewise must be made available to the public.[326]

Any permit issued under the Act must be reviewed periodically and if appropriate revised so as to reflect new conditions.

The Act prohibits the Administrator from issuing a permit under the Act for the disposal of radioactive waste material unless the applicant for the permit prepares, with respect to the site at which the disposal is proposed, a Radioactive Material Disposal Impact Assessment which must include a listing of all radioactive materials in each container to be disposed, an analysis of the environmental impact of the proposed action, any adverse environmental effects at the site which cannot be avoided, an analysis of the resulting environmental and economic conditions if the containers fail to contain the radioactive waste material, a

---

324  33 U.S.C.A. § 1413(d).
325  33 U.S.C.A. § 1414.
326  Id.

plan for the removal or containment of the disposed material if the container leaks or decomposes, a determination by each affected state where the proposed action is consistent with approved coastal zone management programs, an analysis of the economic impact upon other uses of marine resources, alternatives to the proposed action, comments and results of consultation with state officials and public hearings held in the coastal states that are nearest to the affected area, and a comprehensive monitoring plan to be carried out by the applicant to determine the full effect of the disposal on the marine environment.[327]

Upon a determination by the Administrator that a permit to dump radioactive material should be issued, the Administrator must transmit such a recommendation to the House of Representatives and the Senate. The Senate and the House thereafter must authorize the Administrator to grant a permit by a joint resolution.[328]

In 1988 the original Act was amended to include some special provisions regarding certain dumping sites. One of the provisions contained a prohibition, which stopped the Administrator from issuing a permit for transportation for the purposes of dumping municipal sludge within the Apex, defined to mean the New York Bight Apex, unless the person was an "eligible authority." Eligible authority was defined to mean any sewage authority or other unit of state or local government that was authorized under court order to dump municipal sludge at the Apex site on November 2, 1983.[329]

The same restriction applicable to the New York Bight Apex was also applicable to the "106 Mile Ocean Waste Dump Site."

Another provision of the 1988 amendments related to outright prohibitions on dumping in the New York Bight Apex after December 31, 1991. An exception, under the 1988 amendments, permits the Administrator to enter into a compliance agreement with an eligible authority up to December 31, 1991.[330]

One additional provision of the 1988 amendments to the Act was a prohibition on disposal of sewage sludge at landfills on Staten Island, New York.

The Act contains both civil and criminal penalties. The civil penalty assessed against any person who violates a provision of the Act is limited to $50,000 for each violation. A civil penalty for a person who violates the Act by dumping medical waste is set at $125,000 for each violation.[331]

---

[327]  33 U.S.C.A. § 1414(h).
[328]  33 U.S.C.A. § 1414(e).
[329]  33 U.S.C.A. § 1414a.
[330]  Id.

In addition to civil penalties, the Act contains a criminal provision which carries criminal penalties of $50,000, imprisonment for not more than one year, or both for a person who knowingly violates the Act.[332]

The criminal penalty for a person who dumps medical waste into the oceans is listed at $250,000, imprisonment for not more than five years, or both.[333]   In addition to both civil and criminal penalties, the Act authorizes the Attorney General of the United States to bring an action for equitable relief to enjoin an imminent or continuing violation of the Act.

An exception to civil and criminal penalties under the Act is a provision which accords a person relief from any civil or criminal liability under the Act who dumps materials from a vessel in an emergency situation to safeguard life at sea, provided that the person reports the dumping to the Administrator.

The Administrator or the Secretary of the Army are given the authority to utilize services and facilities of other federal departments, agencies, instrumentalities, or state agencies or instrumentalities for purposes of enforcing the Act.

The Act also contains express authority for the Administrator and the Secretary to issue regulations as they may deem appropriate to implement the purposes of the Act.[334]

An important section of the Act concerns itself with the concept of research.  The Act provides that the Secretary of Commerce, in coordination with the Administrator of the EPA, must initiate a comprehensive and continuing program of monitoring and research regarding the effects of the dumping of material into ocean waters, coastal waters where the tide ebbs and flows, and the Great Lakes or the connecting waters.  This monitoring and research program must also cover the possible long range effects of pollution, fishing, and man-induced changes of ocean ecosystems.  The responsibilities for the monitoring and research program includes the scientific assessment of damages to the natural resources from spills of petroleum or petroleum products.[335]

The Administrator of the EPA, in cooperation with the Secretary of Commerce, is required to assess the feasibility in coastal areas of regional management plans for the disposal of waste materials.  The plans would integrate waste disposal activities into a comprehensive regional disposal strategy.  These plans would address things such as

---

331  33 U.S.C.A. § 1415(a).
332  33 U.S.C.A. § 1415(b).
333  *Id.*
334  33 U.S.C.A. § 1418. See 40 C.F.R. Part 2.100 et seq.
335  33 U.S.C.A. § 1442.

the sources, quantities, and types of materials that require disposal, the environmental, economic, social, and human health factors (and the methods used to assess these factors) associated with disposal alternatives, the improvements in production processes, methods of disposal, and recycling to reduce the adverse effects associated with such alternatives, the applicable laws and regulations governing waste disposal, and the improvements in permitting processes to reduce administrative burdens.[336]

The Act provides that the Secretary of Commerce must report in March of each year to the Congress an evaluation of the short term ecological affects and the social and economical factors involved with the dumping, the results of activities undertaken pursuant to the Act, long term research requirements associated with activities under the Act, and a description of how federal research under the Act will meet those requirements.

International cooperation is encouraged by the Act through a provision which mandates that the Secretary of State, in consultation with the administrator must seek effective international action and cooperation to insure protection of the marine environment and may formulate, present or support specific proposals in the United Nations and other international organizations in support of the purposes underlying the Act.[337]

## FISHERY RESOURCES

In 1938 Congress passed an act which provided that the Secretary of Commerce could direct and establish one or more salmon cultural stations in the Columbia River Basin in each of the states of Oregon, Washington and Idaho.[338]

The act authorizes the Secretary of Commerce to conduct investigations and engineering and biological surveys and experiments in order to direct and facilitate a conservation of the fishery resources in the Columbia River and its tributaries. This includes the authority to construct and install devices in the Columbia River Basin for the improvement of feeding and spawning conditions for fish, for the protection of migratory fish from irrigation projects, and for facilitating free migration of fish over obstructions.[339]

The act has been amended from time to time and in 1965 Congress amended the Fishery Resources Act to include a section which is entitled the "Anadromous Fish Conservation Act."[340] The stated purpose of

---

336  33 U.S.C.A. § 1443.
337  33 U.S.C.A. §1419.
338  16 U.S.C.A. § 755.
339  16 U.S.C.A. § 756.
340  16 U.S.C.A. § 757a.

this act is the conservation, development and enhancement within the several states of the anadromous fishing resources of the nation.[341]

In fulfilling his obligations under the act, the Secretary of the Interior is authorized to enter into cooperative agreements with one or more states that concern development and conservation or enhancement of such fish and when deemed feasible to enter agreements with non-federal interests.[342]

The agreements authorized under the act must cover the actions to be taken by the Secretary of the Interior and cooperating parties and the benefits and costs to be derived from such agreements.

This Act provides that the federal government may share in the cost of operating and maintaining any facility accomplishing the purposes of the act provided that the federal government's share shall not exceed 50% of such costs exclusive of the value of any federal land involved. Where two or more states having a common interest in any basin jointly enter into a cooperative agreement with the Secretary of the Interior, the federal share of the program cost can be increased to a maximum of 66 2/3%.[343]

Where a state has implemented an interstate fishery management plan for anadromous fish or resources prepared by an interstate commission, the federal share of the grant to carry out the activities required by such a plan can amount up to 90% of the total cost. The definition of an interstate commission means a commission established by the Atlantic States Marine Fisheries Compact (Public Law 80-77), the Commission established by the Pacific Marine Fishery Compact (Public Law 80-232), and a Commission established by the Gulf States Marines Fisheries Compact (Public Law 81-66).[344]

The act also provides that the Secretary of the Interior may (1) conduct such investigations, engineering, biological surveys and research as may be desirable to carry out the act; (2) carry out stream clearance activity; (3) construct, install, maintain and operate devices or structures for the improvement of feeding and spawning conditions for the protection of fish or resources and for facilitating the free migration of fish and for the control of sea lamprey; (4) construct, operate and maintain fish hatcheries whenever necessary to accomplish the purposes of the act; (5) conduct such studies and make such recommendations as the Secretary determines to be appropriate regarding the development and management of the mainstream or other body of water for the conservation and enhancement of anadromous fishing resources and the fish

341 The definition of an "anadromous fish" is one which ascends streams to spawn.
342 Id.
343 16 U.S.C.A. § 757a(c).
344 Id.

in the Great Lakes and Lake Champlain that ascends streams to spawn.[345]

A 1979 provision of the act (amended in 1984) concerns striped-bass population studies. Under the act the Secretary is mandated to cooperate with states and other non-federal interests in conducting studies on the size and distribution of the population of striped-bass (Morone saxatilis).[346]

The studies are to include the amount in geographical location of annually spawning and the factors responsible for the decline in the number of striped-bass that are available to the public for recreation and commercial use. The Secretary must make annual reports to Congress concerning the progress and findings of these studies. These studies are funded separately and must not exceed $1 million dollars for each of the fiscal years 1988 - 1991.[347]

There are additional provisions of the act which authorize for exploration, investigation, development and maintenance of fishery resources in the Pacific Ocean, Kentucky, Montana, Pisgah National Forest, Pittsburgh, Vermont, Virginia, West Virginia, Pennsylvania, and South Carolina.[348]

A 1950 provision of the act mandates the Secretary of Commerce to undertake a comprehensive continuing study of species of fish of the Atlantic Ocean including bays, sounds, and tributaries for the purposes of recommending, to the states of the coast, appropriate measures for the development and protection of such resources and their wisest utilization.[349]

In 1959 the Secretary of Commerce was directed to undertake a comprehensive continuing study of the migratory marine fish of interest to recreational fishermen in the United States including species inhabiting the offshore waters of the United States and species which migrate through or spend part of their lives in the inshore waters of the United States.[350]

Another 1959 amendment to the act authorized the Secretary of Commerce to acquire lands, construct laboratories or other buildings, to purchase boats, acquire such other equipment and apparatus, and to place such offices and employees as he deems necessary to cooperate or contract with state and other institutions and agencies to make public

---

345  16 U.S.C.A. § 757b.
346  16 U.S.C.A. § 757g.
347  Id.
348  16 U.S.C.A. § 758 - 760-12.
349  16 U.S.C.A. § 760a.
350  16 U.S.C.A. § 760e.

the result of research conducted in the study of migratory game and game fish.[351]

The act provides for the appropriation of funds for the carrying out of the purposes of the act. The appropriation for 1989 was $8,152,000 with a limitation of not more than $1,250,000 of funds for any one state.[352]

## ANTARCTICA CONSERVATION

In 1959 the United States entered the Antarctic Treaty with various nations to promote international cooperation and scientific investigation of Antarctica. In 1978 Congress passed the "Antarctica Conservation Act of 1978" in order to provide for the conservation and protection of the fauna and flora of Antarctica and upon the ecosystem on which such fauna and flora depend. This act was passed to perpetuate studies of Antarctica fauna and flora, there adaptation to the rigorous environment and the interrelationships of the fauna and flora with that environment and the impact this may have on scientific research of fauna and flora throughout the world.[353]

The Act contains a provision which specifically prohibits United States citizens from taking any native mammal or native bird within Antarctica, to possess, sell, or offer for sale, deliver, receive, carry, transport, ship by any means whatsoever or import into the United States or export from the United States any native mammal or native bird taken from Antarctica or native plant collected in any especially protected area 'unless under a permit issued by the director of the National Science Foundation.[354]

The Act provides civil and criminal penalties for a violation of the act.[355]

In 1984 another convention was entered by the United States, the Conservation of Antarctic Marine Living Resources, which purported to establish international mechanisms and create legal obligations necessary for the protection, conservation of Antarctic Marine Living Resources. Congress found in passing the act that the convention served important United States environmental or resource management interests. Listed among these interests were political objectives (maintenance of Antarctica as an area of peaceful international cooperation); research objectives (protecting Marine Living Resources of Antarctica); and security, economic, and environmental interests in developing and maintaining a fleet of ice-breaking vessels capable of operating effectively in the heavy ice regions of Antarctica.

---

351 16 U.S.C.A. § 760f.
352 16 U.S.C.A. § 757d.
353 16 U.S.C.A. § 2401 et seq.
354 16 U.S.C.A. § 2403.
355 See 16 U.S.C.A. §§ 2407 & 2408.

The act was passed to provide the legislative authority necessary to implement, the obligations of the United States, the Convention on the Conservation of Antarctic Marine Living Resources of 1984."[356]

The violation of this act by any person also subjected him to civil and criminal penalties.[357]

## FEDERAL WETLANDS PROTECTION ACT

At one time there were probably over 200 million acres of wetlands in the United States. It is estimated that less than one half of these acres still exist. The greatest loss was during the period between 1950 and 1970 and occurred in Louisiana, Mississippi, Arkansas, North Carolina, North Dakota, South Dakota, Nebraska, Florida and Texas. The U.S. Fish and Wildlife Service estimates that we are continuing to lose wetlands at a annual pace of nearly one half million acres, an area approximately 12 times the size of the District of Columbia.

In 1986 Congress, after reviewing the condition of wetlands in the United States, passed "The Emergency Wetlands Resources Act of 1986." [358]

In passing the Act Congress found that: (1) wetlands play an integral role in maintaining the quality of life through a material contribution to our national economy, food supply, water supply and quality, flood control, and fish, wildlife, and plant resources, and thus to the health, safety, recreation, and economic well being of all of our citizens in the nation; (2) wetlands provide habitat essential for the breeding, spawning, nesting, migration, wintering, and ultimate survival of a major portion of the migratory and resident fish and wildlife in the nation, including migratory birds, endangered species, commercially and recreationally important fin fish, shellfish and other aquatic organisms that contain many unique species of communities of wild plants; (3) the migratory bird treaty obligations of the nations with Canada, Mexico, Japan, Union of Soviet Socialists Republic, and with various countries in the Western Hemisphere require federal protections of wetlands that are used by migratory birds for breeding, wintering or migration and needed to achieve and maintain optimum population levels, distributions and patterns of migration; (4) wetlands and fish, wildlife, and plants dependent on wetlands provide significant recreational and commercial benefits . . . .; (5) wetlands enhance the water quality and water supply in the nation by serving as ground water recharge areas, nutrient traps, and chemicals sinks; (6) wetlands provide a natural means of flood and erosion control by retaining water during periods of high runoff thereby protecting against loss of life and property; (7) wet-

356  16 U.S.C.A. § 2431 et seq.
357  16 U.S.C.A. §§ 2437 & 2438.
358  16 U.S.C.A. § 16 U.S.C.A. § 3901 seq.

lands constitute only a small percentage of the land area of the United States and are estimated to have been reduced by half in the contiguous states since the founding of our nation and may continue to disappear by hundreds of thousands of acres per year; (8) certain activities of the federal government have inappropriately altered or assisted in the alteration of wetlands, thereby unnecessarily stimulating and accelerating the loss of these valuable resources in the environmental and economic benefits that they provide; (9) the existing federal, state, and private cooperation of wetlands conservation should be strengthened in order to minimize further losses of these valuable areas and to insure their management in the public interest for this and future generations.[359]

Based on these findings Congress stated that the purpose of the Act was to promote in concert with other federal and state statutes and programs the conservation of wetlands of the nation in order to maintain the public benefits that they provide and to help fulfill international obligations contained in various migratory bird treaties and conventions with Canada, Mexico, Japan, the Union of Soviet Socialists Republics, and with other various countries in the Western Hemisphere by intensifying cooperative efforts among private interests and local, state, and federal governments for the management and conservation of wetlands and intensifying efforts to protect the wetlands in the nations through acquisitions in fee, easements, or other interests and methods by local, state, and federal governments and the private sector.[360]

In its essential parts the Act provides for revenue development, federal wetlands acquisition, and a program that covers wetlands inventory and trend analysis.[361]

The primary concern for wetland conservation stems from migratory bird conservation related responsibilities. However the wetlands of the nation provide other equally important benefits to wildlife other than birds. The Act refers to irrigation of crops and drinking water, to agricultural interests, to the protection of the top soil which could be lost through erosion, to a protection of the rivers and streams through the settling of sediment and pollutants in wetland basins, and to general recreational interests such as hunting and bird watching.

The Act defines wetland to means "land that has a predominance of hydric soils and that is inundated or saturated by surface or ground water at a frequency and duration sufficient to support, and that under normal circumstances does support, a prevalence of hydrophytic vegetation typically adapted for life in saturated soil conditions." The term

---

359  16 U.S.C.A. § 3901(a).
360  16 U.S.C.A. § 3901(b).
361  16 U.S.C.A. § 3931.

hydric-soil means soil that in its undrained condition is saturated, flooded or ponded long enough during a growing season to develop an anaerobic condition that supports the growth and regeneration of hydrophytic vegetation.[362]

Many of the terms used in the Wetlands Resource Act are based on definitions previously used by the U.S. Fish and Wildlife Service and their classification of wetlands for the "National Wetlands Inventory."

One section of the Act provides revenues for refuge operations and the Migratory Bird Conservation Fund.[363] Under this provision the Secretary of the Interior is authorized with respect to the National Wildlife Refuge System to charge fees for fishing permits, sell Golden Eagle Passports and Golden Age Passports, and issue at no charge lifetime admission permits.[364]

The Secretary must determine, when he intends to charge fees, that the level of visitation for recreation purposes is high enough to justify the collection of the fee for admission permits, that there is a practical mechanism in existence for implementing and operating a system of collecting fees for admission permits, and that the imposition of a fee for admission permits is not likely to result in undue economic hardship for a significant number of visitors to the National Wildlife Refuge System each year.[365]

In order to reduce confusion and conflicts of interests, the Secretary under the Act, may not require an admission permit (and therefore cannot charge a fee) to any person who holds a valid migratory bird, hunting and conservation stamp (16 U.S.C. § 718b - commonly known as the Duck Stamp Act), or to any person holding a valid Golden Eagle Passport (under 16 U.S.C. §§ 460L-6a), or to anyone holding a valid Golden Age Passport (16 U.S.C. § 460L).[366]

The permit fee that can be charged for a single visit to any designated unit of the National Wildlife Refuge System cannot exceed $3.00 for individuals or $7.50 per vehicle. This fee is charged for the purposes of a single visit and include privileges for reentry during a given time period.[367]

In addition to individual fees charged for a single visit, the Secretary is authorized to issue admission permits to groups and may establish a fee for that permit.

---

362 16 U.S.C.A. § 3902.
363 16 U.S.C.A. § 3911.
364 16 U.S.C.A. § 3911(a).
365 16 U.S.C.A. § 3911(b).
366 Id.
367 Id.

# WILDLIFE AND HABITAT

The fees collected for admission permits under the Act are to be distributed and made available to the Secretary of the Interior (30 percent) for the purpose of deferring the cost of collection, operation, maintenance of the collecting unit, and other costs of the maintenance of the National Wildlife Refuge System, and for purposes of administering to the needs of migratory birds under the Migratory Bird Conservation Act[368]. As previously stated wetland protection and the protection of the interest of migratory birds are integrally interwoven.[369]

A second major section of the Act concerns state and federal wetlands acquisition. This provision authorizes the Secretary to purchase wetlands or interests in wetlands (which are not acquired under the authority of the Migratory Bird Conservation Act) consistent with a wetlands priority conservation plan established under another provision of the Act.[370]

The Act requires the Secretary to establish and periodically review and revise a national wetlands priority conservation plan which must specify on a region-by-region basis or any other basis considered appropriate by the Secretary, the types of wetlands and interest in wetlands which should be given priority with respect to federal and state acquisition.

In establishing this plan the Secretary is required to consult with the administrator of the Environmental Protection Agency, the Secretary of Commerce, the Secretary of Agriculture, and the chief executive officer of each state involved.

In establishing the plan the Secretary is required to consider: (1) the estimated proportion remaining of the respective types of wetlands which exist at the time of the European settlement; (2) the estimated current rate of loss and the threat of future losses of the respected types of wetlands; (3) the contributions of the respective types of wetlands to wildlife, endangered species, migratory birds, the resident species, commercial and sport fisheries, surfacing ground water quality and quantity and flood control, outdoor recreation, and other areas of concerns that the Secretary considers appropriate.[371]

The Act eliminates the possibility of condemnation or eminent domain in the acquisition of wetlands.[372]

Another section of the Act requires the Secretary, acting through the Director of the United States Fish and Wildlife Service, to continue the

---

368  16 U.S.C. § 715 et seq.
369  16 U.S.C.A. § 3911(c).
370  16 U.S.C.A. § 3922.
371  16 U.S.C.A. § 3921.
372  16 U.S.C.A. § 3923.

National Wetlands Inventory Project and produce national wetlands inventory maps for the areas that have been identified by the service as top priorities for mapping.

The Act specifies certain areas which are to be accorded top priorities including the entire coastal zone of the United States, flood plains of major rivers, and the Prairie Pothole Region.[373]

In addition to updating the inventory maps already contained in the national wetlands inventories, the Secretary is also required to produce inventory maps for those portions of the contiguous United States for which final maps have not been produced earlier, produce inventory maps for Alaska and other non-contiguous portions of the United States, produce at 10 year intervals after September 30, 1990 reports to update and improve the information contained in a report dated September 1982 entitled, "Status and Trends of Wetlands and Deep Water Habitat in the Coterminous United States, 1950s to 1970s," and to produce a report by September 30, 1990 (that date is already past and is assumed that the report has been published) that provides an assessment to the total estimated number of acres of wetland habitat as of the 1780s in the areas that now comprise each state and, in addition, an assessment of the estimated total number of acres of wetlands in each state as of 1980 and the percentage of loss of wetlands in each state between the 1780s and the 1980s.[374]

Prior to the actual beginning of the creation of the maps required under the Act, the Secretary must notify the appropriate state or local units of government as to the identification of the area to be mapped, the proposed schedule for completion, and the identification of a source for further information.[375]

In carrying out his responsibilities for the Wetlands Inventories Project, the Secretary of the Interior must consult with the Secretary of Agriculture and prepare and submit to the Committee on Merchant Marine and Fisheries, the Committee on Interior and Insular Affairs of the House of Representatives, the Committee on Environment and Public Works, and the Committee on Energy and Natural Resources of the Senate, a report regarding the status, conditions and trends of wetlands in the lower Mississippi Alluvial Plain and the Prairie Pothole Regions of the United States and a report regarding trends of wetlands in all other areas in the United States.[376]

The reports required under the Wetlands Inventories Project section of the Act must contain an analysis of the factors responsible for various

373  16 U.S.C.A. § 3931(a).
374  Id.
375  16 U.S.C.A. § 3931(b).
376  16 U.S.C.A. § 3932.

wetlands destruction, degradation, protection and enhancement; a compilation and analysis of federal statutory regulatory mechanisms, including expenditures, financial assistance, and tax provisions; a compilation and analysis of federal expenditures resulting from wetlands destruction, degradation, protection or enhancement; a compilation and analysis of the environmental and economic impact of eliminating and restricting future federal expenditures and financial assistance and what effect this elimination would have on the destruction, degradation, protection or enhancement of the wetlands; an analysis of the environmental and economic impact of failure to restrict future federal expenditures; and recommendations for the conservation of wetland resource based on an evaluation of comparison of all management alternatives and combination of management alternatives such as state and local actions, federal actions, and initiatives by private organizations and individuals.[377]

An analysis of the Wetland Resources Act prompts the conclusion that as stated in the Senate report (number 99-445) the Act promotes the conservation of wetlands through state and federal wetland acquisition and cooperative efforts among private interests and local, state and federal governments for the conservation and management of wetlands.

As can to seen, the primary intention of the Act is to protect the nation's wetlands. The approach taken by the Act concentrates on the concept of government purchase. Another method of trying to protect the wetlands is to acquire a conservation easement, although these usually require some form of government acquisition and frequently are in effect only for a short time. While all of these methods are in some small measure a protection of American wetlands, without doubt the most far reaching and effective method of protecting the nation's wetlands is Section 404 of the Clean Water Act.[378]

When originally passed the Clean Water Act[379] stated that it was a national goal that the discharge of pollutants into the navigable waters be eliminated by the year 1985. When enacting the legislation Congress expressed a desire to "restore and maintain the chemical, physical, and biological integrity of the nation's waters."

In the many years that followed the original passage of the Act there was a controversy over whether the Act applied to only navigable waters or all waters. There was an ongoing conflict between the Army Corps of Engineers and the Environmental Protection Agency on many matters but the chief bone of contention was what kind of approach should be taken under the permit section of the Act. The permit section

---

377  Id.
378  33 U.S.C.A. § 1344.
379  33 U.S.C.A. § 1251 et seq.

under the Clean Water Act is referred to as Section 404 and it is entitled "Permits for Dredged or Filled Material."[380] This section of the Clean Water Act provides a procedural system whereby the Secretary of the Army acting through the Chief of Engineers may issue permits after notice and an opportunity for public hearings for the discharge of dredged or filled material in the navigable waters at specified disposal sites.[381]

The controversy between EPA and the Corps of Engineers can be characterized as a difference of opinion as to what kinds of permits should be issued under the Clean Air Act. The EPA's long standing view is that harm to wetlands should be avoided entirely while the Corps of Engineers position is that harm to wetlands should simply be mitigated.

On November 15, 1989 the EPA and the Department of the Army signed a memorandum of agreement providing that mitigation alone cannot serve as a basis for issuing a 404 permit. The memorandum addresses the problem of how much mitigation would be required in order for the permit to be issued by the Secretary. The concept adopted by that memorandum was a "no net loss."

Generally the procedures requires the Corps of Engineers to make a determination that potential impacts to the wetlands have been avoided to the maximum extent practical, that remaining unavoidable impacts would then be mitigated to the extent appropriate and practicable by requiring steps to minimize impacts and, finally the activity carried on must compensate for aquatic resources losses.

The memorandum establishes a preference for an in-kind compensation system for any loss in the existing wetlands in the environment.

As an example on the type of issue involved, the case of _Bersani v. United States Environmental Protection Agency_[382] centered around the proposed construction of a shopping center that would have altered or filled 32 of 50 acres of wetlands while creating an on-site, nine replacement acres of wetlands, and altering 13 acres of wetlands to enhance the ecological value of the area. Additionally the developer planned to create 36 acres of replacement wetlands nearby. This plan by the developer would be an effort on his part to compensate for the wetlands that would be lost.

The Army Corps found that in its opinion the project, with its compensation system, satisfied the public interest and that therefore a permit

---

380   33 U.S.C.A. § 1344.
381   33 U.S.C.A. § 1344(a).
382   674 F. Supp. 405.

should be issued. The EPA vetoed the Army Corps' permit and the final result was decided by the federal courts which upheld the EPA's veto of the permit.

This dispute between the Department of the Army and the EPA highlights a concern that the federal government has over the nation's wetlands. As is the case with many environmental protection statutes, there is a balancing interest. The final chapter with respect to wetland policy has not yet been written.

In 1985 Congress by statute withdrew price supports under the Commodity Credit Corporation Charter Act (15 U.S.C.A. 714 et seq.) for any person who in a crop year produces an agricultural commodity on a field on which highly erodible land is predominant.[383]

Also the same ineligibility for price supports applies to any person who produces an agricultural commodity on converted wetland. The term "converted wetland under the act means "wetland that has been drained, dredged, filled, leveled or otherwise manipulated for the purpose of making the production of agriculture possible."[384]

## NORTH ATLANTIC SALMON

The United States entered a convention in 1982 entitled "Convention for the Conservation of Salmon in the North Atlantic Ocean." This act was signed in Reykjavik, Iceland and had as its purpose the protection, control and management of salmon in the North Atlantic Ocean.

In 1982 Congress passed the "Atlantic Salmon Convention Act of 1982" in order to discharge its obligations under the treaty.[385] The primary purpose of the act was to provide for the appointment by the President of three United States commissioners to serve on the commissions of the organization that had been established by the Convention. Under the act the commissioners are required to be (1) one official of the United States government and (2) two individuals who are not officers of the United States government but who are knowledgeable or experienced concerning the conservation and management of salmon of United States origin.[386]

Under the act the Secretary of State may receive and transmit any reports or recommendations and proposals or other communications of the Commission, and with the concurrence of the Secretary of Commerce and the Secretary of the Interior approve, object, to or withdraw objections to regulatory measures proposed in accordance with the treaty.[387]

---

383  16 U.S.C.A. § 3811.
384  16 U.S.C.A. §§ 3821 & 3801(a)(4)(a).
385  16 U.S.C.A. § 3601 et seq.
386  16 U.S.C.A. § 3602.

In carrying out the functions under the convention, the United States commissioners may consult with the appropriate regional Fishery and Management Council as provided by the Magnuson Act and may consult with such other interested parties as they consider appropriate.[388] In addition, the Secretary of Commerce in carrying out the provisions of the convention may arrange for the cooperation of agencies of the United States and of the states and of any private institutions and organizations.[389]

The act provides civil and criminal penalties and forfeitures for any person who is found to violate any provision of the act, or any vessel subject to the jurisdiction of the United States who has violated any provisions of the act and of the convention.[390]

## THE NORTHERN PACIFIC HALIBUT CONVENTION AND ACT

In 1953 the United States and Canada entered into a Convention for the preservation of the Halibut Fishery of the North Pacific Ocean and Bering Sea. That Convention was then amended in 1979. Regulations were subsequently promulgated. In 1982 Congress passed the Northern Pacific Halibut Act of 1982 for the purposes of carrying out the responsibilities of the United States under the Convention.[391]

The Convention established a "Commission" for the purposes of implementing the provisions of the Convention. The 1982 Act provided for the appointment by the President of the United States of three commissioners to represent the United States on the Convention Commission. The commissioners, under the Act, were to consist of one official of the National Oceanic and Atmospheric Administration and two other persons who should be knowledgeable or experienced concerning the Northern Pacific Halibut Fishery. One of these two knowledgeable and experienced persons was to be a resident of Alaska and the other a nonresident of Alaska. Of the three commissioners appointed by the President only one was to be a voting member of the North Pacific Fishery Management Council.[392]

Article Three of the Convention contained a provision whereby each country could accept or reject recommendations made by the Commission. The 1982 Act provided that the Secretary of State, with the concurrence of the Secretary of Commerce, could exercise this acceptance or rejection.[393]

---

387 16 U.S.C.A. § 3603.
388 16 U.S.C.A. § 3602(d).
389 16 U.S.C.A. § 3605.
390 16 U.S.C.A. § 3606.
391 16 U.S.C.A. § 773 et seq.
392 16 U.S.C.A. § 773a.
393 16 U.S.C.A. § 773b.

# WILDLIFE AND HABITAT

Under the Northern Pacific Halibut Act, the Secretary of Commerce was delegated the general responsibilities of carrying out the Convention and the Act. In carrying out these responsibilities, the Secretary of Commerce is required to consult with the Secretary of the department in which the Coast Guard is operating and adopt such regulations as may be necessary to carry out the purposes and objectives of the Convention and the Act. In addition, the Secretary of Commerce, in concurrence with the Secretary of State, is authorized to cooperate with officials of the government of Canada.

Since a Regional Fishery Management Council has authority for the geographic area concerned, this Council may develop regulations governing the United States portion of Convention waters, including limited access regulations applicable to nationals or vessels of the United States, which are not in conflict with the regulations adopted by the Commission established by the Convention.[394]

The Act provides that if it becomes necessary to allocate or assign Halibut fishing privileges among various United States fisherman such allocation shall be fair and equitable to all such fisherman based on the rights and obligations in existing federal law, and such allocations shall be reasonably calculated to promote conservation and carried out in such a manner that no particular individual, corporation, or other entity acquires an excessive share of Halibut fishing privileges.[395]

The Act contains a listing of prohibited acts. The Act makes it unlawful for any person to violate any provision of the Convention, to refuse to permit any enforcement officer to board a fishing vessel subject to such person's control for purposes of conducting any search or inspection in connection with the enforcement of the Convention, to forcibly assault, resist, oppose, impede, intimidate, or interfere with any enforcement officer in the conduct of any search or inspection authorized under the Act and Convention, to resist a lawful arrest or detention for any act prohibited by this Act, to ship, transport, offer for sale, purchase, import, export, or have custody, control, or possession of any fish taken or retained in violation of the Convention, and to interfere with enforcement of the provisions of the Act.[396]

The Act contains both civil and criminal penalties. The Act provides for a civil penalty of not in excess of $25,000 for each violation for any person who is found by the Secretary, after an administrative hearing, to have committed any violation of this Act. Any person who has been assessed a civil penalty under the Act may obtain a review thereof in the appropriate United States district court.[397]

---

394  16 U.S.C.A. § 773c.
395  *Id*
396  16 U.S.C.A. § 773e.

The Act also contains criminal penalties in the amount of $50,000, imprisonment for not more than six months, or both for the committing of any act prohibited by the Act.[398]

The Act also contains forfeiture provisions. The forfeiture sections provide that a fishing vessel used and any fish taken or retained in violation of the Act shall be subject to forfeiture to the United States. This forfeiture is pursuant to a civil proceeding initiated in any district court of the United States by the Attorney General on behalf of the United States. When the judgment is entered for the United States in this civil forfeiture proceeding, the Attorney General may seize any property or other interest declared forfeited to the United States.[399]

The Act contains a bonding provision whereby a person charged under the Act may post a satisfactory bond as security. The bond or other security must be delivered to the appropriate court upon an order issued by the court.

The Act contains a rebuttable presumption that all fish found on board a fishing vessel which is seized in connection with any act prohibited by the Act were taken or retained in violation of the Convention and the Act.[400]

The Act also authorizes any officer authorized by the Secretary of Commerce to arrest any person, with or without a warrant, if he has reasonable cause to believe that such person has committed an act prohibited by the Act, board to search or inspect any fishing vessel suspected of a violation of the Act; at reasonable times enter and search or inspect shore side facilities in which fish taken subject to this Act are processed, packed, or held; seize any fishing vessel, together with its gear, used or employed in any act prohibited by this Act; seize any fish taken or retained in the course of an act prohibited by the Act; and seize any other evidence related to an act prohibited by the Act.[401]

One of the provisions of the Act relates to cooperation with Canadian authorities. The Act authorizes officers and employees of the Coast Guard, the National Oceanic and Atmospheric Administration, or any other agency of the United States to attend as a witness and peruse such available records and files or duly certified copies thereof as may be necessary by the prosecution in Canada of any violation of the Convention or any Canadian law relating to the enforcement thereof.[402]

---

397   16 U.S.C.A. § 773f.
398   16 U.S.C.A. § 773g(b).
399   16 U.S.C.A. § 773h.
400   16 U.S.C.A. § 773h(d)(2).
401   16 U.S.C.A. § 773i(b).
402   16 U.S.C.A. § 773i(e).

# WILDLIFE AND HABITAT

## PACIFIC SALMON TREATY ACT

On January 28, 1985 the United States government and the government of Canada entered into a treaty concerning Pacific Salmon. In March of 1985 Congress passed the Pacific Salmon Treaty Act of 1985.[403] This act was necessary in order for the United States to fulfill its obligations under the treaty with Canada and to establish responsibility and procedures commensurate with the requirements of the treaty.

The treaty establishes the Pacific Salmon Commission and under the Act the United States is represented on the Commission by four United States commissioners who are knowledgeable or experienced concerning Pacific Salmon and who are appointed and serve at the pleasure of the President.[404] The four commissioners as specified under the act include an official of the United States government who is a non-voting member; a resident of the state of Alaska appointed from a list of at least six qualified individuals nominated by the governor of Alaska; a resident of the states of Oregon or Washington who is appointed from a list of at least six qualified individuals nominated by the governors of these states; and a person nominated by the Treaty Indian Tribes of the states of Idaho, Oregon or Washington from a list of at least six qualified individuals submitted by the Indian Tribes of those states.[405]

The treaty establishes various panels and the act details the composition and appointment procedures.[406]

Under the treaty the United States has a single vote within the Commission established by the treaty. The Act states as a policy that United States section must operate with the objective of obtaining consensus decisions in the development and exercise of its vote. The Act specifies what procedures are required in the event that a consensus decision is not possible.[407] In order to coordinate the work of the United States Commission and the panels established under the treaty, the Secretary of State is authorized to receive and transmit on behalf of the United States any reports, requests, recommendations, proposals, and other communications up to the Commission and the panel.[408]

The Secretary of Commerce is also involved in the coordination required in order to insure United States participation on the Commission under the treaty. He must consult with the Secretary of the Interior for cooperation with the agencies of the United States, the states, the Treaty Indian tribes, private institutions and organizations.[409]

---

403  16 U.S.C.A. § 3631 et seq.
404  16 U.S.C.A. § 3632(a).
405  Id.
406  16 U.S.C.A. § 3632 (c,d,e).
407  16 U.S.C.A. § 3632(g).
408  16 U.S.C.A. § 3633(a).
409  16 U.S.C.A. § 3634(a).

The act also provides that agencies in the United States may cooperate in the conduct of scientific and other programs and may furnish facilities and personnel for the purposes of assisting the Commission and the panels in carrying out the responsibility under the treaty.[410]

The act expresses very clearly the preemption exercised by the United States in fulfilling its obligations under the treaty with Canada. The Secretary of Commerce can issue federal regulations which shall supersede any state or treaty Indian tribal law, regulation, or order determined by the Secretary that places the United States in jeopardy of not fulfilling its international obligations under the treaty. There are provisions for timely notice and for voluntary cooperation that signal that in the final analysis the Secretary of Commerce has preemptive power.[411]

The Secretary of Commerce in consultation with the Secretary of the Interior is empowered, under the Act, to promulgate such regulations as may be necessary to carry out the United States international obligations under the treaty and under this Act. The regulations are subject to judicial review by the district courts of the United States.[412] The geographic panels established by the treaty are empowered to promulgate regulations and these regulations are paramount in their application to the authority vested in them under the treaty. The Secretary of Commerce in cooperation with the Regional Fishery Management Councils, states, and treaty Indian tribes may promulgate regulations applicable to nationals or vessels of the United States or both which are not in conflict with the fishery regimens and the regulations adopted under the treaty.[413]

The act contains a section listing prohibited acts and penalties. Generally the prohibited acts and penalty provisions make it unlawful for any person or vessel subject to the jurisdiction of the United States to violate any provision of the act or any regulation adopted under the authority of the act or approved by the United States under the treaty. In addition, this provision makes it unlawful for any person to refuse to permit an authorized officer or vessel to broad a fishing vessel subject to such person's control for purposes of conducting any search or inspection in connection with enforcement of the act, or to resist, oppose, impede, intimidate or interfere with any authorized officer in the conduct of any search or inspection provided for in the act and to generally interfere and delay any enforcement under the act.[414]

The prohibited acts and penalty provision of the act provide for both civil penalties, criminal penalties, and forfeiture. The civil penalty is

---

410  16 U.S.C.A. § 3634(b).
411  16 U.S.C.A. § 3635.
412  16 U.S.C.A. § 3636(c).
413  16 U.S.C.A. § 3636(b).
414  16 U.S.C.A. § 3637(a).

listed as a maximum of $25,000 for each violation of the act (the same as provided under the Magnuson Act). The criminal penalty is listed as a fine of not more than $50,000, imprisonment for not more than six months or both (the same as under the Magnuson Act). The forfeiture provisions are comparable to those provided under the Magnuson Act (16 U.S.C. § 1860).[415]

The Secretary of Commerce, and the Secretary of the Department in which the Coast Guard is operating are entitled under the act to enforce the provisions relating to civil penalties, criminal penalties and forfeiture. The district courts of the United States are accorded exclusive jurisdiction over any case or controversy arising under the act.[416]

The Act in, conformity with the requirements of the treaty, contains standards which must be taken into account by any authority under the act. Generally speaking the standards require the use and consideration of the best scientific information, in the consideration of the measures necessary and appropriate for the conservation, management, utilization, and development of the Pacific Salmon Resource.[417]

The act provides for the appointment of an advisory committee of not less than twelve and not more than twenty members who are knowledgeable and experienced with respect to the fisheries concerned under the Act. One half of the membership of the Committee must be residents of the state of Alaska and one member of the Committee must be a resident of the state of Idaho. The committee is authorized to attend all public meetings of the Commissions and the Panels and are given the opportunity to examine and to be heard on any non-administrative matter under consideration.[418]

## TUNA CONVENTIONS AND AGREEMENTS

Various tuna conventions and agreements have been signed by the United States since 1949. The first convention entered into by the United States was the Convention for the Establishment of an International Commission for the Scientific Investigation of Tuna signed in Mexico City January 25, 1949 by the United States and the United Mexican states.

On May 31, 1949 the United States and the Republic of Costa Rico entered a convention for the purpose of controlling and studying the rich tuna fish regions of the eastern Pacific Ocean.

These conventions established two commissions, the International Commission for the Scientific Investigation of Tuna, and the Interameri-

415  16 U.S.C.A. § 3637(b,c,d).
416  16 U.S.C.A. § 3637(e).
417  16 U.S.C.A. § 3638.
418  16 U.S.C.A. § 3639.

can Tropical Tuna Commission which were to administer the provisions of the Treaties and make pronouncements for the control of tuna fishing.

In order to implement the two tuna conventions Congress in July 1950 passed the Tuna Conventions Act of 1950.[419]

In addition to providing the procedures through which the United States would be represented on the Commissions established by the treaty, the Act appointed Advisory Committees which authorized the Secretary of State to act for the United States in this country's participation in the conventions, and provided for penalties and forfeitures for violations of the conventions and the Act by any persons.[420]

In May 1966 the United States entered the International Convention for the Conservation of Atlantic Tuna with Canada, Brazil, Cuba, France, Portugal, Spain, Ghana, The Ivory Coast, Morocco, Senegal, South Africa, Japan and Korea. The convention was a response to the increasing exploitation of tuna resources of the Atlantic Ocean by a great number of nations from around the world. Evidence began to accumulate in the early 1960s that several stocks of tuna-like fishes were declining. The fact of over fishing became obvious and the convention was conceived.

In 1975 Congress passed the "Atlantic Tunas Conventions Act of 1975."[421] The purpose of this Act was to permit the United States to (1) implement the provisions of the convention which it had entered in 1966 (2) to provide an advisory committee for the purposes of participating in the convention and (3) provide for the appropriate administration of the Act.[422]

The authority to represent the United States was vested in the Secretary of State and penalties and forfeitures were provided for violations of both the convention and the Act.[423]

In 1983 the United States entered into the "Eastern Pacific Ocean Tuna Fishing Agreement." The parties to the agreement were the United States, Costa Rico and Panama. Guatemala and Honduras also signed the accord (which was designated by them as an interim agreement pending the negotiation of a more comprehensive management regimen).

In 1984 Congress passed the "Eastern Pacific Tuna Licensing Act of 1984."[424]

---

419 16 U.S.C.A. § 951 et seq.
420 16 U.S.C.A. § 953-957.
421 16 U.S.C.A. § 971 et seq.
422 16 U.S.C.A. § 971(a&h).
423 16 U.S.C.A. §§ 971(c)-(e).
424 16 U.S.C.A. § 972 et seq.

The Act was passed in order to implement the participation by the United States in the Eastern Pacific Ocean Tuna Fishing Agreement, and to provide the necessary representation and enforcement provisions customarily associated with such Conventions.

In 1987 the United States entered a treaty entitled "Treaty on Fisheries Between the Government of Certain Pacific Island States and the Government of the United States of America."

The treaty contained three major initiatives. First the treaty provided the United States' tuna fishermen with access to over 10 million square miles of rich fishing waters in the South Pacific Ocean. Second, the treaty defined procedures for regulating fishing activities in enforcing treaty provisions. Basically it required that licenses be obtained, that observers be carried on the tuna fishing boats, and that the parties to the treaty had a right to enforce regulations and prosecute violations of the treaty.

The problem created which necessitated the convention was that tuna migrate through broad oceanic expanses, traversing the coastal waters of many nations. In the South Pacific fishery disputes arose between the United States and several Pacific Island nations which resulted from conflicting jurisdictional positions with respect to the migrating tuna. On some occasions the United States tuna boats had been seized by island nations causing retaliatory United States trade embargoes. In an attempt to resolve these problems and secure a reliable access to South Pacific Tuna resources for the United States fleet, the United States initiated negotiations with sixteen Pacific nations (including Australia and New Zealand) and approved a method whereby a regional tuna licensing agreement could be developed.

In 1988 Congress passed the "South Pacific Tuna Act of 1988."[425]

The Act in addition to authorizing the United States to participate in the treaty (Treaty on Fisheries Between the Government of Certain Pacific Island States and the United States) also established a description of prohibited Acts, provided penalties for the violation of the terms of the convention or of the Act, and provided for a licensing procedure for tuna boats.

An important provision of the Act was (the implementation of a requirement of the treaty) that observers be placed on tuna boats. The Act requires both the operator and the member of the crew of a vessel to allow and assist any individual identified as an observer under the treaty to board the vessel for scientific, compliance, monitoring, and

---

425   16 U.S.C.A. § 973 et seq.

other functions and to have full access to, and use of, the facilities and equipment on board the vessel which the observer may determine necessary to carry out observer duties.[426]

In the Act Congress authorized appropriations which from 1988 through 1992 are not to exceed $350,000 annually.[427] Responsibility for the administration of the Act and for United States participation in the treaty is vested in the Secretary of Commerce.

## CONTROL OF JELLYFISH OR SEA NETTLES

In 1966 Congress passed an act to conserve and protect fish and shellfish resources in the coastal waters of the United States and the Commonwealth of Puerto Rico.[428] In order to do this Congress found that it was necessary to control and eliminate jellyfish commonly referred to as sea nettles, and other such pests in the ocean habitat occupied by fish and shellfish. In addition the act provided for the conducting of research for the purposes of controlling floating seaweed in such waters.

The Secretary of Commerce is vested with authority in cooperation with the States and the Commonwealth of Puerto Rico to: conduct investigations, directly by contract, studies, and research, as he deems necessary and desirable to determine the abundance and distribution of jellyfish and other such pests and their effects on fish and shellfish on water based recreation; to conduct studies or control measures of such pests or of the floating seaweed; and to carry out studies made for a program to control and eliminate such pests and such seaweed.[429]

In addition to providing appropriations for the act, Congress also provided, that it would consent to any compact or agreement between any two or more states for the purposes of carrying out a program of research, study, investigation and control of jellyfish and other pests in the coastal waters of the United States.[430]

426  16 U.S.C.A. § 973e.
427  16 U.S.C.A. § 973r.
428  16 U.S.C.A. § 1201.
429  16 U.S.C.A. § 1202.
430  16 U.S.C.A. § 1204.

# CHAPTER SIX

## PROTECTION OF WILDLIFE

### EAGLES, BURROS AND HORSES

Once upon a time, before Horace Greely urged young men to move west, birds and beasts existed in harmony with the land. As man expanded his settlements, land became precious. Animals that once roamed the plains and mountains suffered the same fate as the Indians who also occupied those lands. Animals such as the buffalo, big horn ram, grizzly bear and gray wolf were hunted to the point of near extinction. Land was valuable and anything on that land had to be cleared. Also, ranchers shot anything that resembled a predator to protect their herds.

As these settlements developed, industry and farming took hold. Pesticides were used to insure a better harvest. Unfortunately the effects of these pesticides on wildlife were not known until they showed up. The pesticides got into the digestive system of small animals that ate the crops and in fish in nearby streams into which rainwater drained. From there the pesticides gradually worked their way up the food chains settling with the top level predator. Once there, the pesticides began to poison that individual animal and wreak havoc with its genes; and consequently this affected future generations.

Industry also had a drastic impact on wildlife. Skies that were once azure blue became black from the smoke and smog caused by man's increasing use of technology. Lungs of animals that inhabited the skies as well as the lungs of nearby land animals and man became clogged with particles that shortened their collective lives.[1] Industry also caused another problem similar to that caused by pesticides. Wastes and chemicals were emptied into lakes and streams. Once there, it was one step at a time up the food chain.

Not only were there the problems associated with industrialization, but there was also the problem of unregulated hunting. Many animals died purely in the name of sport. Wildlife was in dire straits.

Three such animals that faced all of the above mentioned problems, the bald eagle, the wild horse and the burro were accorded the distinction of being designated this country's national symbols. These animals therefore occupied a special place in the array of wildlife affected by man's contamination. This chapter is devoted to an exposition of the efforts made by dedicated wildlife advocates through legislation to pro-

---

[1]   The pollution of the skies continues to wreak destruction today in the form of acid rain.

tect these animals made special by their designation as national symbols.

## I. The Bald Eagle

The bald eagle (Haliaetus leucocephalus) is the only North American representative of the fish or sea eagles.[2] It inhabits the continent from the Gulf of Mexico to the Arctic and is usually found near the seacoast, inland lakes and rivers.[3] The bald eagle is a large, long-lived bird of prey. Adults, with their dark brown bodies, white heads and white tails are easily recognizable both in the wild and as our nation's symbol.[4]

Nesting bald eagles are associated almost exclusively with lakes, rivers or sea coasts. Fish are the main item in their diet.[5]

Adults tend to use the same breeding area, and often the same nest, each year. The nests are primarily in trees, and to a lesser extent on cliffs or (rarely) on the ground.[6] Nesting phenology depends largely on latitude; egg-laying ranges from November in Florida to May in Alaska and northern Canada.[7]

The breeding range has receded during the 19th and 20th centuries. Historic records indicate that bald eagles formerly nested in at least 45 of the contiguous 48 states. As of 1981, however, occupied nests were known in only 30 states, and approximately 90 of the 1,250 or so known pairs were in just 10 states.[8] In contrast, large numbers of pairs, perhaps ten times the number in the contiguous states continue to nest in parts of Alaska and Canada south of the Arctic tundra.[9] The winter

2 M. Grossman & J. Hamlet, Bird of Prey of the World 27 (Potter Inc., New York, NY).
3 J. Abbot, "Bald Eagle Nest Survey," 29 (4) Atlantic National 161-163.
4 However, the adult plumage is not required until the age of four, at the earliest. Bald eagles go through a series of plumages prior to attaining adult coloration, and in some plumages the young, fledgling eagles bear a superficial resemblance to the golden eagle (Aquilla chrysaetos. U.S. Fish and Wildlife Service, 1983. Recovery plan for the Northern Bald Eagle. United States Fish and Wildlife Service, Twin Cities, Minnesota. Page 2 of 121 pp. Sexual maturity is reached at four to six years of age, but the birds may be considerably older before they breed for the first time. Eagles in the wild have been found to have bred as early as four and as late as seven. Id. at 4. The average life span is not known, but 30 years is a reasonable estimate of potential longevity under natural conditions. S. Sherrod, "Biology of the Bald Eagle on Amchitka Island, Alaska," 13 The Living Bird 143 (1976). Mortality is thought to be relatively high in the immature age classes, but much lower for the birds that manage to survive their first year or two. Id. at 45
5 Hence, the nickname fish or sea eagle. It is an unproven myth that eagles are monogamous. Birds are likely to replace lost mates and there may be changes of mates.
6 Clutch sizes range from one to three eggs. Successful pairs usually raise one to two young, or occasionally three per nesting attempt. Northern Bald Eagle Recovery Plan, Supra note 4, at 11.
7 The time between egg-laying and fledging is approximately four months. The entire breeding cycle, from initial activity at a nest through the period of fledgling dependence, is about six months. Northern Bald Eagle Recovery Plan, Supra note 4, at 11.
8 Florida, Minnesota, Wisconsin, Washington, Michigan, Oregon, Maine, California, Maryland, and Virgina.
9 N. Green, Status and Distribution of the Bald Eagle in Continuous United States (August 14, 1982) (unpublished manuscript, presented at Bald Eagle Days, Rochester, N.Y., 1982).

range includes most of the breeding range but extends mainly from southern Alaska and southern Canada southward. [10]

A few adult bald eagles in the temperate latitudes and far north remain in association with nesting areas throughout the year. However, most bald eagles in the interior Canadian provinces and northern United States move south in the fall, probably in response to changes in prey availability and weather conditions. As a result, thousands of bald eagles (approximately 13,000 were counted during the 1981 nationwide midwinter survey sponsored by the National Wildlife Federation) are present in the contiguous 48 states from November through March, which is referred to in the Plan as the "wintering period." Because nesting phenology varies with latitude, the wintering period overlaps with the initial weeks of the nesting season in some areas.

Wintering bald eagles occur throughout the country but are most abundant in the West and Midwest. An abundant, readily available food supply, in conjunction with one or more suitable night roost sites, is the primary characteristic of winter habitat.[11] The majority of wintering eagles are found near open water and they feed on fish and waterfowl, often taking those which are dead, crippled, or otherwise vulnerable. Mammalian carrion is an important alternate source of food at some locations. Also, many bald eagles spend a substantial portion of the wintering period in terrestrial habitats far from open water, relying on prey they can catch easily or scavenge, such as big game or livestock carrion and small mammals.

As man civilized and tamed North America, the consequences on flora and fauna were not noticed or taken into account. It was not until the late 1930s that man noticed the decline in the bald eagle population.[12]

---

10  Statistics available American Ornithologist Union, 1983.
11  At night, wintering eagles often congregate at communal roost trees, in some cases traveling 20 km or more from feeding areas to a roost site. The same roosts are used for several years. Many are in locations that are protected from the wind by vegetation or terrain, providing a more favorable thermal environment. The use of these protected sites helps minimize the energy stress encountered by wintering birds. It also has been suggested that communal roosting facilitates food-finding. In addition to natural factors, roost sites generally provide isolation from humans. When human disturbance of a night roost occurs, birds may abandon the location. In some locations the absence of a suitable night roost could limit the use of an otherwise suitable habitat. The tendency for bald eagles to congregate at certain locations during the wintering period is well known, and for years it had been assumed that most of the birds were at concentration areas. However, recent analyses of data collected during the National Wildlife Federation's nationwide midwinter surveys indicate that perhaps only about 50% of the bald eagles present in the Region are in concentration areas; others are present in hundreds of locations that are used regularly by one to 20 birds. Collectively, the smaller groupings and individuals are probably equal in importance to the larger concentration areas. G. Keister, "Characteristics of Winter Roosts and Populations of Bald Eagles in Klamath Basin," at 56 (unpublished Master's Thesis, available at Oregon State University, Corvallis, Oregon).
12  B. McClelland, "The Bald Eagle Concentration in Glacier National Park, 19 The Living Bird 133 (1982).

# WILDLIFE AND HABITAT

Throughout the continent the number of eagles dwindled to the point that, in certain areas, breeding populations disappeared entirely.[13] These declines or disappearances were attributed primarily to a loss of habitat, plus mortality from shooting and trapping. In some areas, throughout the early 20th century, these problems continued and even accelerated. In the mid-20th century a new and even more dangerous variable entered the equation; environmental contamination, which caused further significant declines in the remaining nesting populations.

Loss of habitat is perhaps the most serious negative factor and it is certainly the most difficult to halt and reverse. Habitat alterations and encroachment by man have resulted in a slow eagle population decline for many decades. Today, the migration of people to the "sun belts" of the Southeast and West is resulting in extensive alterations of land use. This urban and recreational development combined with logging, mineral exploration and extraction, industry, farming and all other forms of human activities are adversely affecting the suitability of breeding, wintering and foraging areas. While individual and small scale actions may not appear to jeopardize the species as a whole, the cumulative effect of habitat loss, continues to pose a severe threat to the eagle.

Shooting has long been known as a major factor in the mortality of bald eagles. Reduction in shooting mortality is the current trend. The following figures indicate the percentage of total reported mortalities which were caused by shooting: 62 percent from 1961-65,-[14] 41 percent from 1966-68,[15] 46 percent from 1969-70,[16] 35 percent from 1971-72[17] 25 percent from 1973-74,[18] 20 percent from 1975-77,[19] and 18 percent from 1975-81.[20] Thus, during a 21-year period, 30 percent of the documented bald eagle mortality has been a result of shooting.[21]

For more than two decades eagles found dead or moribund have been sent to research laboratories of the U.S. Fish and Wildlife Service for necropsies and chemical analyses to determine cause of death. Published

13 Pitt, "Eagles and Indians: The Law and the Survival of a Species," 5 Public Land L. Rev. 100, 103 (1984).
14 N. Coon, "Causes of Bald Eagle Mortality 1960-1966," 6 Journal of Wildlife Diseases 72-76 (1970).
15 B. Mulhern, "Organochloride Residues and Autopsy Data from Bald Eagles 1966-68," 4 Journal of Pesticide Monitoring 141-144 (1970).
16 A. Belisle, "Residues of Organochloride Pesticides, Polychlorinated Biphenyls and Mercury and Autopsy Data for Bald Eagles 1969-70," 6 Journal of Pesticide Monitoring 133-137 (1972).
17 E.- Cromartie, "Residues of Organochloride Pesticides, Biphenyls and Autopsy Data for Bald Eagles 1971-72," 9 Journal of Pesticide Monitoring 11-14 (1975).
18 R. Prouty, "Organochloride Poisoning in Bald Eagles 1973, 1974," 11 Journal of Pesticide Monitoring 85-94 (1976).
19 T. Kaiser, "Autopsy Data for Bald Eagles from 29 States 1975-77," 13 Journal of Pesticide Monitoring 145-149 (1980).
20 L. Locke, Bald Eagle Mortality 1975-1971, at 55-77 (T. N. Ingram ed. 1980).
21 While this downward trend is encouraging, the current level of mortality is unacceptable and may be limiting, particularly in areas of remnant nesting populations.

summaries of data through the mid 1970s reveal that shooting and trauma were leading causes of death. Poisoning, electrocution, disease, and trapping injuries were other important causes in varying proportions from year to year.[22]

A unique problem that contributes to eagle mortality rates is electrocution. Electrocutions may occur on any unsafe powerlines in eagle use areas, and young birds whose flight skills are not fully developed are most vulnerable. In general, collisions with power lines seem to occur with less frequency than electrocutions; Olendorff and Lehman (in press) documented only 15 confirmed cases of bald eagle collisions with utility lines.[23]

The most dramatic declines in eagle populations nationwide are probably due to environmental contaminants. Direct toxic effects of organochlorine insecticides such as DDT and its metabolites have had severe adverse impacts on bald eagle populations.[24]

Many other environmental contaminants represent potentially significant threats to bald eagles. For example, two immature bald eagles were confirmed to have died recently in California from ingestion of an organophosphate insecticide used by systemic treatment of warble fly in cattle. Dioxin, endrin, heptachlor, epoxide, mercury, and polychlorinated biphenyls (PCB's) still occur in eagle food supplies; however, their overall effects on eagle populations are poorly understood.[25]

---

22  Bald eagle mortality data from 1975 to the present recently were computerized by the U.S. Fish and Wildlife Service. These data (N = 754) disclose the following distribution: trauma, 21%; shot, 17.6%; rotten (too decomposed for a diagnosis), 12.3%; emaciation, 9.7%; electrocution, 9.3%; poisoned, 8.4%; infectious diseases, 8.0%; open (no diagnosis determined), 5.7%; trapped, 5.2%; drowned, 0.7%; and other, 2.1%. These figures try to give FWS an insight to try and manage the eagle population. Northern Recovery Plan, *supra* note 4, at 5.

23  However, in certain areas where bald eagles concentrate, transmission lines can represent a threat. In the Klamath Basin for example, collisions with transmission lines may cause more injuries and mortalities than electrocutions on distribution lines. U.S. Fish and Wildlife Service, 1986. Recovery plan for the Pacific Bald Eagle. United States Fish and Wildlife Service, Portland, Oregon. Page 21 of 160 pp.

24  Dieldrin and endrin were implicated most often in acute poisonings, that is, those resulting in deaths of individual birds. However, it is DDE, a metabolite or breakdown product of DDT, that caused gravest contaminant problems for eagle welfare. Heavy DDT applications were implicated in massive acute kills of birds and other non-target fish and wildlife. By the late 1960s pesticide researchers had discovered and proven experimentally that chronic exposure to even low levels of DDE inhibits reproduction in many bird species. The inhibition results primarily from thinning of eggshells causing failure to hatch. B. McClelland, *supra* note 12, at 136. Through physiological mechanisms not fully understood, DDE interferes with calcium metabolism. Eggshell thinning occurs most commonly in flesh-eating birds, especially those that feed heavily on birds or fish at the ends of long food chains. Pitt, *supra* note 13. Eagles living even part of the year in areas with high background levels of DDT absorb amounts sub-lethal to adults but sufficient to cause eggshell thinning and loss of annual production. Since a ban on DDT in the U.S. by Congress in 1972, a slow recovery in eagle productivity has occurred. U.S. Fish and Wildlife Service, 1984. Recovery plan for the Southeast Bald Eagle. United States Fish and Wildlife Service, Atlanta, Georgia, Page 5 of 164 pp. Most populations appear to be producing chicks at the expected rate.

25  **Id.**

A more severe type of secondary poisoning has recently surfaced. Secondary lead poisoning is a significant problem where eagles feed on crippled or wounded waterfowl. The waterfowl may also be poisoned by being wounded with lead pellets used by hunters.[26] The result   lead poisoning.

With all of the above factors contributing to the decline of the eagle population, it was obvious that something needed to be done to protect the nation's symbol.  In response, Congress first acted in 1940 and accordingly passed the Eagle Protection Act.[27]  The amended Act now states in part:

> Whoever, within the United States or any place subject to the jurisdiction thereof, without being permitted to do so as provided (elsewhere in the Act) shall knowingly, or with wanton disregard for the consequences of his act take, possess, sell, purchase, barter, offer to sell, purchase or barter, transport, export or import, at any time or in any manner any bald eagle commonly known as the American eagle, or any golden eagle, alive or dead, or any part, nest, or egg thereof of the foregoing eagles . . . shall be fined . . . imprisoned . . . (or) assessed a civil penalty . . . (emphasis added).[28]

The language in the Act regarding the golden eagle was added in 1962.[29]  Thus, the blanket of protection was expanded to include both the Bald and Golden Eagle.[30] Notably, the 1962 amendments also allowed Indian tribes to take eagles for religious purposes.[31]  Aroused by reports of unabated destruction, and of possible extinction, Congress amended the Act in 1972 by increasing penalties to include higher fines and loss of grazing on public lands.[32]  The Act and man's overall understanding of wildlife and environment has helped stem the tide of possible extinction, but there are critical questions that still must be answered.

---

26   B. Mulhern, *supra* note 15. If lead shot is embedded in a bird's muscle tissue, an eagle will swallow the pellets with the flesh. During the period that a pellet remains in an eagle's stomach, its digestive acids cause some lead to dissolve and enter the bird's blood stream. The lead pellet can also become lodged in the folds of an eagle's crop and fail to regurgitate. This causes more lead to enter the blood stream. J. Feirrabend, "A National Summary of Lead Poisoning in Bald Eagles and Waterfowl," 1984 National Wildlife Federation Report, 11-13.
27   Eagle Protection Act, Pub. L. No. 76-567, 54 Stat. 250 (codified as amended at 16 U.S.C. § 668(a)-(d) (1976)).
28   16 U.S.C. § 668(a) (1976).
29   Pub. L. No. 87-884, 76 Stat. 1246 (codified as amended at 16 U.S.C. § 668 (1976)).
30   This necessary protection was added because immature bald and golden eagles are virtually indistinguishable to the untrained eye. Pitt, *supra* note 13, at 104.
31   Pub. L. No. 87-884, 76 Stat. 1246 (codified as amended at 16 U.S.C. § 668(a) (1976)).
32   Pub. L. No. 92-535, 86 Stat. 1064 (codified as amended at 16 U.S.C. § 668(b) (1976)).

# PROTECTION OF WILDLIFE

## II. The Eagle as a National Symbol

On June 20th, 1782 the Continental Congress adopted the design of Charles Thomson as the official seal of the fledging United States of America. Thomson's report describing the seal was full of symbolism. The bird on the seal was to have its wings opened out and its head and neck feathers erected in anger. There were to be thirteen stars above its head and on its chest was to be a red and white shield. In its right foot, the great bird was to clasp the olive branch of peace; while in its left were to be the warlike thunderbolts of Zeus. In its beak was the motto "E Pluribus Unum." To be sure there was no mistaking what type of bird was on the seal, Thomson added one last line: "The Head and Tail of the American Bald Eagle are White, the Body and Wings are of a Lead or Dove Color."[33]

The federal eagle that represents the nation is symbolic of the people that compose that nation. It is a new world creature with no history and no heritage, yet is composed of the ideas and ideals of all the civilizations that preceded it. Because it was a fitting symbol for the United States, Congress enacted, in 1940, the Bald Eagle Protection Act. This legislation was a direct recognition of the need to preserve the animal as a symbol of the nation.. [34]

Congress seized upon the dubious inherent federal authority to preserve the symbol of the nation[35] when it passed the Bald Eagle Protection Act (BEPA) in 1940.The Act originally protected the bald and golden eagles within the United States or in any place subject to its jurisdiction except Alaska.[36] It expressly prohibited the taking, possession, sale, purchase, barter, transportation, export and import of bald and golden eagles, their parts, nests and eggs except as the Secretary of the Interior may, in limited circumstances, permit.[37] The Act did not interfere with the possession or transportation of bald eagles lawfully acquired prior to June 8, 1940 or golden eagles lawfully acquired prior to October 24, 1962. However, these birds could not be purchased, sold, imported or exported. Any person violating this Act, if convicted, could be fined not more than $5,000, one year in jail or both, for the first offense, and $10,000, two years in jail or both, for any subsequent offenses.[38]

---

33 P. Redford, Raccoons & Eagles 123-145 (Detton & Co., Inc., New York, N.Y.). The federal eagle is a strange bird - half real, half myth, full of glory and patriotism, emotion and confusion. The symbol has not changed since 1884. It is a royal bird that bears a republican escutcheon; its head and tail are those of an American erne, while the position of its wings is taken from the golden eagle of heraldry; its right talon grasps an ancient Assyrian olive branch and its left the lightning arrows of Zeus; in its beak carries the Latin motto of an English-speaking nation that means all things to men. *Id*.

34 Bean, The Evolution of National Wildlife Law 411 (Praeger Publishers, New York, N.Y.).

35 T. Lund, American Wildlife Law 50 (University of California Press, Los Angeles, Cal.).

36 W. Sigler, Wildlife Law Enforcement 57 (Brown Co. Publishers, Dubuque, Iowa).

37 16 U.S.C. §§ 668-668(a,d) (1976 & Supp. V 1981).

The 1972 amendment authorized the assessment of a civil penalty of not more than $5,000 per violation.

The original form of the Act contained several prominent exceptions. The Secretary of the Interior could permit the taking and possession of bald eagles "for scientific or exhibition purposes of museums, scientific societies and zoos." He was also empowered to permit taking of the birds "for the protection of wildlife or of agricultural or other interests in any particular locality."[39] The Secretary could permit such takings only "after investigation" and upon his then making a determination "that it is compatible with the preservation of the bald eagle."[40] The original exceptions, including the possession of any bald eagle, or part, nest or egg thereof lawfully taken before the passage of the Act, continue today. The only other original exception that was eliminated in 1959, provided that the terms of the Act did not apply within the boundaries of Alaska.[41] Today, the Act encompasses all land and territory within the jurisdiction of the United States.

Since 1940, Congress has substantially amended the Act twice. In 1962, the Act was broadened to include golden eagles.[42] This was done to enhance the protection of immature bald eagles which are indistinguishable from the golden eagle. The 1962 amendments include two new exceptions. The new provisions allowed some taking by special groups,[43]. (1) Indians would be allowed to possess and take eagles for religious purposes, and (2) the only other time the Act would permit takings to occur is when the Secretary, after a request from the governor of any state, finds it necessary to authorize takings "for the purpose of seasonally protecting flocks and herds of domestic animals within such a state."[44] Although the Act still makes it theoretically possible to obtain a blanket permit of this nature, the Secretary established as a matter of administrative policy in March, 1970, that no further blanket permits would be issued.[45] Despite this change in policy, administrative regulations continue to provide for issuance of blanket depredation control orders. These regulations provide for publication in the Federal Register and notice to the requesting governor after the Director of the Bureau of Sports Fisheries and Wildlife's decision. With respect to other types of permits for taking bald or golden eagles, no public notice is required at any time.[46] Regulations of the Fish and Wildlife Service make it clear that only sport hunting is absolutely prohibited by statute. Although depredating bald and golden eagles may be taken under the

---

38 Ch. 278, § 1, 54 Stat. 250 (1940) (current version at 16 U.S.C. § 668(a) (Supp. V 1981)).
39 16 U.S.C. § 668(a) (1981).
40 50 C.F.R. Part 22.21 (1981).
41 Act of June 25, 1959, Pub. L. No. 86-70, § 14, 73 Stat. 143.
42 Act of Oct. 24, 1962, Pub. L. No. 87-884, 76 Stat. 1246.
43 Id
44 16 U.S.C. § 668(a).
45 Bean, *supra*note 35, at 91.
46 50 C.F.R. Part 22.31.

Act, FWS regulations limit how these birds may be taken. These regulations strictly prohibit hunting or taking of depredating eagles from any form of aircraft.

The second substantial amendment to the Act came in 1972.[47] The amendment was the result of widely publicized deaths of several dozen eagles due to the use of predator (coyote) control poison, thallium sulfate, and the accounts of the deliberate shooting of hundreds of eagles from helicopters by ranchers.[48] These notorious killings were not prosecuted and were hedged because of a governmental fear that the Act was unconstitutional,[49] and also because of the problem of interpretation. The Act was interpreted as requiring scienter or "guilty mind." This was interpreted to mean that before any prosecution could be brought under the Act, a person must have actually intended to kill eagles. This interpretation made a wall of proof next to impossible to climb. Congress, through the 1972 amendment, did away with the scienter requirement, and took more of a strict liability stance. The Act was amended to provide that whoever "shall knowingly or with wanton disregard for the consequences of his act, take any eagle shall be subject to penalties prescribed."[50] The Act also broadened the definition of "take" to encompass poisoning.[51] The motive behind these amendments was to strengthen the protection of the eagle and to impose a more stringent burden on anyone who attempted to take an eagle.

Going hand in hand with the broadened protection were increased penalties for violations of the Act. For first violations, maximum penalties were set at $5,000, one year's imprisonment, or both; for subsequent violations, the applicable maxima were $10,000 and two years imprisonment. [52] In addition to increasing the existing criminal penalties, the 1972 amendments also authorized two additional types of sanctions. First, civil penalties of up to $5,000 per violation could be assessed against any person taking or possessing eagle, part, nest or egg thereof.[53] Second, the federal grazing privileges of any person convicted of a violation of the Act were made subject to immediate cancellation.[54]

The strengthened protection of the eagle also extended to their nests. This possible conflict led Congress to add another exception in 1978.[55] That exception authorizes the Secretary of the Interior to permit, by

---

47  Act of Oct. 23, 1972, Pub. L. No. 92-535, § 1, 86 Stat. 1064.
48  *supra*note 51.
49  Coggins, "Constitutional Limits on Federal Power to Protect and Manage Wildlife: Is the Endangered Species Act Endangered?" 61 Iowa L. Rev. 1099, 1112-13 (1976).
50  *supra*note 50.
51  16 U.S.C. § 668(c) (Supp. IV 1974).
52  16 U.S.C. § 668(b) (1976).
53  *supra*note 49.
54
55  Bean, *supra*note 35, at 93.

regulation, "the taking of golden eagle nests which may interfere with resource development or recovery operations."[56]  Although the Act does not define what standards were to be applied in making a determination, the legislative history and purpose of the Act make it clear that the preservation of the species will receive priority.  Thus, through the increase of protection and imposition of more stringent burdens, the Act has become an effective tool in protecting a symbolic species.

Throughout the history of the Act, there have been two constant streams of litigation.  One is litigation involving the BEPA and other wildlife statutes, such as the Lacey Act[57] and the Migratory Bird Treaty Act (MBTA).[58]  The other course of litigation involves Indian treaty rights.

*Andrus v. Allard* was the case in which the Supreme Court addressed the application of both the BEPA and the MBTA to eagle parts acquired prior to the enactment of either law.[59]  The Court found that the restrictions of both Acts did so apply.  With respect to the Bald Eagle Act, its holding was facilitated by a limited exception in that Act for the possession or transportation (but not the sale) of eagles taken prior to its enactment.  From this narrow exception the Court drew the negative inference that no exception for sale of such eagles was intended.[60]

The one key element that keeps the acts from being superimposed over one another is intent.  Prior to the 1972 amendments of the BEPA only "willful" violations of the Act were punishable.  Under the MBTA, scienter is not an element of a violation.[61]  In *United States v. Hetzel*,[62] the Court stated that "rules of decision developed under the Migratory Bird Treaty Act may not automatically be applied to a prosecution under the Bald Eagle Protection Act."[63]  The *Hetzel* decision is a good example of the axiom that bad cases make bad law.[64]  In that action, the defendant was charged with a violation of the Bald Eagle Act because of his possession of a pair of bald eagle talons.  He apparently removed them from a dead bald eagle that he found while hunting on a national wildlife refuge, intending to give them to a Boy Scout organization.  The defendant was convicted before a United States Magistrate and fined one dollar.  Despite the nominal fine, the defendant appealed.  On appeal, the Court emphasized the change in the degree of intent required for a violation as a result of the 1972 amendments.  The Court reasoned that

---

56  Fish and Wildlife Improvement Act of 1978, Pub. L. No. 95-616, 92 Stat. 3114 (codified at 16 U.S.C. § 668(a) (Supp. V 1981)).
57  16 U.S.C. § 701, 18 U.S.C. § 42 (1976 & Supp. V 1981).
58  16 U.S.C. §§ 703-711 (1976 & Supp. V 1981).
59  444 U.S. 51 (1979).
60  *supra* note 64.
61  18 U.S.C. § 1(3) (1976).
62  385 F. Supp. 1311 (W.D. Mo. 1974).
63  Id. at 1312.
64  Bean, *supra* note 35, at 94.

since prior to 1972 only "willful" violations were punishable, the defendant's act, which occurred prior to the 1972 amendments, could not be punished, lest "thousands of Boy Scouts who have innocently obtained and now possess eagle feathers would also be subject to criminal prosecution by the government. The holding strongly suggests that the requirement of "willfulness" would be met if it could be shown that the defendant knew he was violating the law.

This attitude started to change with the 1972 amendments which did away with the willfulness requirement. The change became evident when a different, and more convincing, result was reached in *United States v. Allard*.[65] This case involved an Indian charged with selling a war bonnet containing golden eagle feathers. The defendant claimed that he was unaware that such a sale was unlawful because the practice was commonplace among Indians. The court rejected the *Hetzel* decision and drew a distinction by stating:

> The effect of the word 'knowingly' is to require that . . . the defendant (know) that the feathers were golden eagle feathers, and I think it clear that a conviction would not be had were a person to sell golden eagle feathers thinking them to be turkey feathers .
> . . . The Act does not, and no statute that I recall seeing, makes the defendant's knowledge of the law an element of the crime.[66]

In differentiating knowledge of the law and knowledge of the facts, the court recognized the purpose and aim of the 1972 amendments, as the stopping of any actions that, although done without knowledge of violation, the Act, resulted in the deaths of eagles. The court made this clear when it concluded that no criminal intent was required because wildlife laws are designed to achieve "social betterment" and because the taking of wildlife has always been regulated by laws not requiring specific intent.[67]

Although the BEPA and MBTA acts are not mirror images of one another, the *Allard* decision makes them more compatible. Actions are still brought under both of them. One such case is *National Wildlife Federation v. Hodel*.[68] In this case the plaintiff brought suit under the Endangered Species Act (ESA), the Bald and Golden Eagle Protection Act (BGEPA), the Migratory Bird Treaty Act (MBTA), and the National Environmental Policy Act (NEPA) to prevent the Department of the Interior from allowing the use of lead shot in hunting migratory waterfowl in the continental United States.[69]

---

65 397 F. Supp. 429 (D. Mont. 1975).
66 Id.at 432.
67 Id.at 433.
68 18 E.L.R. 65894 (1987).
69 About 2400 tons of lead are discharged into waterfowl habitat ever year by hunters. Plaintiff

# WILDLIFE AND HABITAT

The BEPA and MBTA acts also blend together concerning a matter that is not so clear; Indian Treaty Rights. The first time this issue arose was in *United States v. White*.[70] The case involved the prosecution of Jackie White, a member of the Red Lake Band of Chippewas, who was observed shooting and killing a bald eagle. He was charged with the taking of a bald eagle in violation of the Eagle Protection Act. *White* moved for dismissal of the charge on the grounds that the Act was inapplicable to tribal Indians on their reservations exercising traditionally guaranteed tribal hunting rights.[71] *White* based his contention on *United State v. Cutler*[72] in which the district court, basing its decision on the Congressional silence underlying the enactment of the MBTA, held that a treaty Indian was not subject to the MBTA while on an Indian reservation.[73] The district court dismissed the case and the Eighth Circuit Court of Appeals affirmed the dismissal. The Court of Appeals held that although Congress had the right to abrogate an Indian treaty, "the intention to abrogate or modify a treaty (was) not to be lightly imputed to Congress."[74] Citing *United States v. Winas*,[75] the court stated: "The right to hunt and fish was part of the larger right possessed by the Indians in the lands used and occupied by them. Such right, which was not much less necessary to the existence of the Indians than the atmosphere they breathed, remained in them unless granted away."[76]

The Court of Appeals also found that Congress had never expressly abrogated nor modified the Red Lake Band of Chippewa's hunting or fishing rights, and thus could not abrogate nor modify those rights by implication. "The specificity which we require of our criminal statutes is wholly lacking here as applied to an Indian on an Indian reservation."[77]

---

alleged that this lead caused the death of about two million waterfowl annually and had contributed to the death of at least 105 bald eagles over the past twenty years. Plaintiff further alleged that "sub-lethal" lead poisoning caused waterfowl to lose flying ability, become blind, lose weight, and suffer heart damage, thus rendering the birds susceptible to predators and other causes of death. The complaint notes that duck populations have significantly declined over the past few years, and that some species are at their lowest estimated populations in thirty years. Lacing waterfowl wintering habitat with lead just before breeding season, plaintiff argued, put serious stress on already suffering populations. Plaintiff argued that the Secretary of the Interior and the Fish and Wildlife Service (FWS) had the power under the MBTA to ban the use of lead shot, and moreover, have the duty to do so under that Act, the ESA, and the BGEPA. Plaintiff argues for a complete ban since the identification of areas containing the worst lead shot problem was not possible because most birds poisoned by lead are never recovered and sub- lethal lead poisoning often masks the cause of death. It can be said that this case illustrates the compatibility of the two acts. The plaintiffs wanted to force the defendant into banning the use of lead shot because of its effects. This is a clear example of using the MBTA and BEPA to stop the deaths of eagles even though there is no intent to kill any eagles directly.

70  508 F.2d 453 (8th Cir. 1974).
71  Id.at 504.
72  37 F. Supp. 724 (D. Idaho 1941).
73  Id.at 725.
74  *White*, 508 F.2d at 454.
75  198 U.S. 371, 381 (1905).
76  *White*, 508 F.2d at 457 (emphasis added).

# PROTECTION OF WILDLIFE

Despite a very strong dissent by Judge Lay, in which he insisted that the court follow the intent of Congress and save the bald eagle from extinction, this holding is still the law in the Eighth Circuit of Appeals.[78]

Recently in *Lower Brule Sioux Tribe v. State of South Dakota*,[79] the Eighth Circuit Court of Appeals reaffirmed its position, stating:

> The 1944 Flood Control Act, § 4 could also be found to have abrogated treaty hunting and fishing rights, if the White dissent and Fryberg stated the governing rule in this circuit. They do not. Instead the Eighth Circuit requires more specific reference to the tribe and its treaty rights.[80]

The court also pointed to an internal Interior memorandum, predating the 1962 amendments, which stated that Indian treaty rights under the Bald Eagle Act were analogous to those under the Migratory Bird Treaty Act.[81]

The impact of these decisions may be significant. The Eighth Circuit encompasses over 10,000 square miles of Indian reservations, a population of approximately 136,7000 on and off reservation Indians, and a fluctuating population of approximately 2,447 wintering and resident bald eagles.[82]

In contrast to the Eighth Circuit, the area within the jurisdiction of the Ninth Circuit Court of Appeals[83] is guided by the rule set forth in *United States v. Fryberg*.[84]

The facts of this case are that Dean R. Fryberg was an enrolled member of the Tulalip Indian Tribe, and while out hunting deer on his tribe's reservation, approximately 40 miles northwest of Seattle, Fryberg shot and killed an immature bald eagle. He was charged with violating section 668a of the Eagle Protection Act.[85] Fryberg initially claimed that he shot the eagle to obtain its feathers for religious purposes. Conflicting evidence led the district court to find against him on that issue.[86] The court held the Eagle Protection Act, embodying the Congressional intent to save the bald eagle, excluded any hunting of eagles. This ex-

77  Id.at 459.
78  *See* United States v. Winnebago Tribe of Nebraska, 542 F.2d 1002 (8th Cir. 1976).
79  540 F. Supp. 276 (D. S.D. 1982).
80  Id.at 284.
81  Bean, *supra*note 35, at 152.
82  Pitt,*supra*note 13, at 104.
83  An area with 17,320 square miles of Indian Reservations, approximately 350,500 on and off reservation Indians, and some 3,914 wintering and resident bald eagles
84
85  16 U.S.C. § 668(a) (1976).
86  622 F.2d 1010 (9th Cir.), cert. denied, 449 U.S. 1004 (1980).

clusion extended to those Indians enjoying a treaty right to hunt on their reservation.[87]

*Fryberg* appealed to the Ninth Circuit Court of Appeals, and, citing *White*, contended that his treaty rights to hunt on the reservation were neither modified nor abrogated by the Eagle Protection Act.[88]history, despite the

Judge Jameson agreed with Judge Lay's dissent in *White*, noting that the majority's analysis overlooked the broad wording and pervasive purpose which the Act is intended to fulfill; the protection of bald eagles. He stated: "We are persuaded that the surrounding circumstances establish a Congressional determination to modify or abrogate the treaty to the extent of prohibiting the taking, shooting, and killing of bald eagles.[89]

With two differing circuits it would be, needless to say, a very confusing situation. It gets even more complicated when one realizes that the Eighth and Ninth Circuits contain most of the contiguous 48 states' bald eagles along with a very large portion of this country's Indian population. The question is whether Congress, in passing BEPA, has clearly expressed its intention to abrogate existing Indian treaty rights. The question remained unanswered when the Supreme Court denied *Fryberg's* request for certiorari in 1981.[90]

The once muddled picture has recently become clearer. The Supreme Court has recently decided a case which has answered the question of whether or not Congress intended to abrogate Indian treaty rights. The case is *United States v. Dion*.[91] The case involved a member of the Yankton Sioux Tribe who was convicted in the Southern District of South Dakota of shooting four bald eagles on the Yankton Sioux Reservation. The Eighth Circuit Court of Appeals reiterated the *White* holding by stating that under the 1858 treaty, Yankton Sioux were permitted to hunt bald and golden eagles within their reservation for noncommercial purposes.[92] On appeal, the Supreme Court cleared up the picture by reversing the Eighth Circuit. The Court, unanimously, held that the BEPA is to be read as abrogating the rights of Indians to take bald and golden eagles pursuant to treaties with the United States.[93] The Court

---

87  *Fryberg*, 622 F.2d at 1011.
88  Id. The Ninth Circuit Court agreed with *White* in part, holding that Congress did not show an unambiguous express intent to abrogate Indian hunting rights. The Court stated: "[A]bsent explicit statutory language [the court must be] extremely reluctant to find congressional abrogation of treaty rights." However, utilizing the "surrounding circumstances test" expounded in *Rosebud Sioux Tribe v. Kneip*, the court also found that: "[C]ongressional intent may be clear from surrounding circumstanc
89  Id.at 1014.
90  United States v. Fryberg, 449 U.S. 1004 (1981).
91  476 U.S. 734 (1986).
92  752 F.2d 1261 (1985).

stated the following facts were relevant in its decision: (1) the legislative history of the 1962 amendments, in which Congress authorized the Secretary to permit the taking of bald or golden eagles for the religious purposes of Indian tribes upon a determination that such conduct is compatible with the preservation of such eagles, indicates that Congress believed it was abrogating such treaty rights; and (2) Congress considered the special cultural and religious interests of Indians and balanced those needs against the conservation purposes of the statute, providing a specific, narrow exception that delineated the extent to which Indians would be permitted to hunt such eagles.[94]

The Court went further to make the point that Indian treaty rights were abrogated. The Court decided that, even if Congress did not address Indian treaty rights in the Endangered Species Act[95] sufficiently enough to abrogate them, a member of an Indian tribe who is prosecuted under that Act for shooting bald eagles is barred from asserting as a defense that he possesses a treaty right to hunt such eagles, since Congress divested him of this treaty right in passing and amending the Eagle Protection Act which, in relevant part, prohibits exactly the same conduct as does the Endangered Species Act, and for the same policy reasons.[96] The holding of *Dion* illustrates that the taking of eagles is to occur only when such acts are compatible with the preservation of the species. The Court apparently relied on the *Payallap* trilogy[97] to decide that the BEPA is a conservation statute and as such can abrogate Indian treaty rights when:

> (1) The sovereign exercising its police power to conserve a resource has jurisdiction in the area where the activity occurs; (2) the statute applies in a non-discriminatory manner to both treaty and non-treaty persons; and (3) the application of the statute to treaty rights is necessary to achieve its conservation purposes. A total ban of all treaty taking is allowable when necessary to assure the survival of the species.[98]

Although *Dion* makes it clear that the treaties may be abrogated to preserve the species, a question still remains concerning the religious purpose exceptions. In 1962, Congress amended the Act to allow "taking" by special groups for the religious purposes of Indian tribes.[99] Theoretically, non-Indians could be thus permitted by the Secretary to take

93    *Dion,* 476 U.S. 746 (1986).
94    Id.
95    16 U.S.C. § 1531 (E.S.A.).
96    *Dion*, 476 U.S. at 744 (1986).
97    (1) Payallup Tribe v. Department of Game of Washington, 391 U.S. 392 (1968). (2) Payallup Tribe v. Department of Game of Washington, 414 U.S. 44 (1973). (3) Payallup Tribe v. Department of Game of Washington, 433 U.S. 165 (1977).
98    *Pitt, supra*note 13, at 108 (emphasis added).
99    Act of October 24, 1962, 16 U.S.C. § 668(a), 76 Stat. 1246.

the eagles, on or off a reservation, as long as it was for the "religious purposes of Indian tribes." It is difficult to understand, then, how this exception could be interpreted to show an express intent of Congress to abrogate treaty rights of Indians to hunt on their own reservation. This point still remains unlitigated. The Supreme Court has made it clear, in *Dion*, that hunting rights may be abrogated. However, the Constitution does provides for the full exercise of religion in the first amendment. The question is then, what happens when the BEPA collides with the Constitution? The general rule is that a Constitutionally protected right may only be punished if government demonstrates that application of a criminal statute will advance compelling governmental interest and that statute embodies the least restrictive means by which that governmental interest can be vindicated.[100] In *United States v. Abeyta*, a district court held that under the first amendment prosecution of a person taking an eagle for religious purposes upon aboriginal lands was barred.[101]

In *Abeyta* the facts are that Abeyta was a lifelong resident and member of Isleta Pueblo. The pueblo stood within the lands conveyed to the United States under the Treaty of Guadalupe Hidalgo. Abeyta was also a member of the Katsina Society, an independent and sometimes secretive religious society that engages in traditional ceremonial practices deeply rooted in ancient pueblo religion. The tradition and lore of the Katsina Society, like others of its kind, required the ceremonial use of eagle feathers and parts.[102] On or about January 4, 1985, Abeyta killed a golden eagle upon the aboriginal lands and within the exterior boundaries of the Isleta Pueblo, about five miles east of the central Isleta village. Abeyta's sole purpose in killing the eagle was to procure its feathers for the use of them in the religious ceremonies of the Katsina Society. The reason Abeyta did not avail himself of the prescribed procedures, he claims, was because the depository did not effectively fulfill the Pueblos' needs for eagle feathers.[103]

---

100 United States v. Lee, 455 U.S. 252 (1982); Wisconsin v. Yoder, 406 U.S. 205 (1972); Sherbert v. Verner, 374 U.S. 398 (1963).

101 The regulations establish a labyrinthine application procedure by which individual Indians may apply for permits to take or possess eagle parts for ceremonial use. As part of the Secretary's administrative apparatus, the United States Fish and Wildlife Service has established at Pocatello, Idaho a depository for eagle parts and feathers. Applications from Indians for feathers for ceremonial use are, in theory, to be filled from the depository. No eagles are harvested for their parts or feathers. Indeed, no application to kill or otherwise harm a golden eagle has ever been granted. The inventory at the depository is constituted of carcasses of eagles that were killed by accident or that died of natural causes. The 1962 amendments created the "religious purposes" exception and in furtherance of this provision the Secretary has promulgated regulations for the taking of eagles for religious purposes. 632 F. Supp. 1301 (D. N.M. 1986).

102 50 C.F.R. § 22.22 (1984).

103 In its ritual and reverent use of eagles and their feathers in religious ceremony, the Katsina Society is indistinguishable from myriad pueblo religious fellowships. The central tenets of ancient Indian religious faith are shared among New Mexico's pueblos and, of all birds, the eagle holds an exalted position in all pueblo religious societies. The use of their feathers, particularly from the tail and wings, is indispensable to the ceremonies of the Katsina Society and other pueblo rituals. *Abeyta*, 632 F. Supp. at 1302. The ceremonial use of the feathers is especially

There were 527 pending applications in August 1985 with an average two year waiting period. The court also found the request application intrusive on one's privacy to practice religion. *Id.* at 1304.

The court dismissed prosecution for two reasons: the Treaty of Guadalupe Hidalgo and the constitutional concept of the free exercise of religion. The 1848 Treaty of Guadalupe Hidalgo secured the free exercise of the inhabitants' religion without restriction. Because of the combination of the Treaty and the 1962 amendments the court held that the right of free exercise was not abrogated.[104]

The second factor that went into the Court's decision was the Constitutional concept of the free exercise of religion. It is apparent that because Abeyta acted solely for religious purposes his actions were constitutionally protected by the first amendment. Thus the only way he could be prosecuted was if the government could demonstrate a compelling interest. The Court did not find such an interest, stating:

> The government's interest in protection of golden eagles is certainly commendable and important, but the prosecution has not established that it is compelling. The golden eagle is not an endangered species. The uncontradicted testimony at trial established that some eagles could be taken without harmful impact on the remaining population. The government's conservation interests therefore are not compelling and cannot warrant a constriction of Indian religious liberty. Even if the government's interest were compelling, however, it could achieve its ends by means of less burdensome on the free expression of Indian religious faith. The evidence at trial established that the federal administrative apparatus erected to accommodate Indian religious needs is utterly offensive and ultimately ineffectual. The application process is cumbersome, intrusive and demonstrates a palpable insensitivity to Indian religious beliefs. Since some depredating golden eagles are taken by ranchers for non-religious purposes, it is plain that some birds could be made available for religious purposes.[105]

important at the winter solstice. Then, the Katsina, or spirit of life, and the eagle, the embodiment of the overseer of life, are the central forces in pueblo religious belief. The eagle is the primary messenger to the spirit world and the ceremonial use its feathers permits the living to communicate with the spirit world beyond. At the solstice, a fresh set of eagle feathers, including those from the tail, is required to finish costumes used in the Katsina solstice ritual. For the Katsina Society at Isleta Pueblo, it is of religious significance that these feathers be of a bird taken from aboriginal Isleta lands. Without such feathers, the religious purposes of the solstice ceremonies are defeated and a cardinal sacrament of the Isleta people is forfeited. Id.at 1303.

104 Id.at 1306.
105 Id.at 1307.

This decision established that the taking of protected eagles and parts solely for religious purposes is protected, and that it can go hand in hand with the conservation goals of the BEPA.

In addition to activities directed at the eagles themselves are activities which deprecate the habitat. Habitat loss has been one of the most devastating factors in the decline of the eagle. Two recent cases illustrate that the eagles habitat will no longer be casually given away and that it will be protected as much as the eagle itself. In *Texaco, Inc. v. Watt* a district Court's decision is being appealed.[106] The court invalidated surface mining regulations which protect critical habitat for threatened for endangered plant and animals. The regulations were required by the ESA and the BEPA. The appellant claims that federal lands recommended for protecting categories of land management, such as wildlife refuges or national parks, are to be considered unsuitable for surface mining.

In the other case, *Maricopa Audubon Society v. Hodel*, the plaintiffs claim that the discovery of a nesting pair of bald eagles in an area to be flooded for a proposed dam project necessitates a revised environmental impact statement. [107] These cases, although still undecided, show that ground will not be given up without a fight.

As earlier stated, sometimes litigation was avoided because of uncertainty over the constitutionality of the Act. This legal question has never been raised in any reported litigation.[108] Thus, the question still remains open as to whether or not Congress has the inherent power to protect, preserve or maintain places, artifacts, things or animals that are symbolically or historically important to the entire nation, its history or cultural heritage. There are things that just are accepted as symbols of the nation. The U.S.S. Constitution, "Old Ironsides" is federally protected and although incapable of fighting, remains commissioned as the flagship of the United States Navy.[109] Gettysburg, the Vietnam Wall, Pearl Harbor and Bunker Hill are all military parks that pay homage to all fallen soldiers who have died for the country. At least in one case, *Spence v. Washington*, the Supreme Court has held that the nation has a right to adopt a national emblem and the states have a right to protect it.[110] It would seem clear that Congress has the power to adopt, change or protect from desecration a national symbol or article of historical, symbolic importance, and it is beyond doubt that Congress can designate a national bird or an animal as a symbol of America.[111]

---

106  18 E.L.R. 65691 (1987).
107  18 E.L.R. 65894 (1987).
108  Bean, *supra* note 35, at 97.
109  Coggins, *supra* note 54, at 1140.
110  418 U.S. 405 (1974).
111  Coggins, *supra* note 54, at 1141.

# PROTECTION OF WILDLIFE

## The Wild Horse and Burro

The wild horse is unlike any wild animal, in one sense, because it has stirred up so much passion and controversy among the American public. The humanitarian interests and those who perpetuate the mythology of the cowboy and his horse as a symbol of America's rugged Western heritage are opposed by ranchers who are in competition with the horse for parched ground and overgrazed soils of the West.[112]

So sometimes yet, in the realities of silence and solitude, for a few people unhampered a while by things, the mustang walks out with dawn, stands high, then sweeps away, wild with sheet life, and free, free, free--free of all the confines of time and flesh.

The horse (Equus caballus) evolved in North America during prehistoric times and migrated to Asia via the natural land bridge. When the continents separated, the horse became extinct on the North American continent.[113] The horse was reintroduced to the continent by the Spanish explorers Columbus and Cortez in the late 1490s and early 1500s.[114]

As man came west he brought with him his own domesticated horses. Escapees from these wagon trains and pioneer ranches supplemented the herd size to the point that in 1900 there was an estimated two million wild horses.[115] But by that time, the horse faced a predator . . . man. Both were in competition for grazing land and scarce water and vegetation that could be used to support cattle herds.

Part of the problem is the nature of the western ecosystem. Food and water are scarce and this limits the carrying capacity of the range. Carrying capacity is defined as the maximum number of healthy animals that can be maintained by habitat on a given unit of land.[116] This value is determined by the level of resources needed by the population, the

---

112 Horses and humans have shared a long association throughout history. Bones found in caves and cave paintings such as those in Lascaux, France indicate that the early relationship between man and horse was one of predator-prey. J. Berger, Wild Horses of the Great Basin 12 (Univ. of Chicago Press, Chicago, Ill.). Domestic horses have had profound influence on human beings and can be found in art forms and in mythology. Throughout history they played roles in exploration, war, sports, leisure, and agriculture. Some of the best early documentations of horses are found among the Greek and Roman cultures where horses were revered as beasts of beauty, strength, and valor. Some species acquired divine status, becoming symbols of ancient gods. Pegasus, the winged steed and the Centaur, half-man and half-horse were the focus of much lore. Id. Poets such as Shakespeare have immortalized the horse in prose.
113 Johnston, "The Fight to Save a Memory," 50 Texas L. Rev. 1055, 1056-57 (1972).
114 Id. Horses that escaped the Spaniards were either domesticated by the American Indians or ran wild on the plains. The horse flourished in part, because it found an unoccupied ecological niche in a fertile, virgin land and because it faced no natural predator.
115 Pitt, "The Wild, Free-Roaming Horses and Burros Act: A Western Melodrama," 15 Envtl. L. 503, 505 (1985).
116 G. Miller, Living in the Environment 136 (Wadsworth Pub. Co., Belmont, Cal).

existing environmental conditions, and the population's upper and lower limits of tolerance to various environmental factors.[117]

One of these factors, and a crucial one, is the biology of the horse itself. The horse was uniquely fitted for a cursory grass-eating life. It has high crowned permanently growing teeth, necessary for a diet of silica laden grass. Unlike the members of the order Artiodactyla (cattle, sheep, deer, and elk), the horse had two sets of incisors, ideally suited for nipping grass at ground level. Its long legs and high speed were important for traveling between widely scattered concentrations of food and distant water holes, and for escaping from the wolf, its only serious predator.[118]

The horse's digestive system makes it necessary for a horse to constantly graze, and where food is in short supply, this becomes a limiting factor in the overall equation. The digestive system of the horse, however, is considerably less efficient than that of Artiodactyla members. Although both employ microorganism-aided fermentation, the horse's digestion is unregulated and takes place in the large intestine and an enlarged colon, while in a cow, for example, closely regulated digestion takes place in an enlarged and complex stomach. Food takes from 30 to 45 hours to pass through a horse, compared with from 70 to 100 hours to pass through a cow. Because of this inefficient digestive system, the horse needs greater quantities of food per body weight than does the cow.[119] Because of this characteristic, the carry capacity of an ecosystem which includes horses becomes smaller. The horse population is subject to decline due to infertility, disease, starvation and mortality. The horse is in competition with, perhaps, the top predator ever created -- man. Due to man's westward push, facing decreased open range and increasing competition with other ranchers' livestock, wild herds began to diminish in numbers just as did the American Indian and the buffalo.[120]

After World War II, another threat faced the wild herds. Commercial demand for pet food made horse hunting profitable. Commercial hunters systematically rounded up wild horses and burros and sold the animals to slaughterhouses for processing into pet food and fertilizer.[121] The carnage and slaughter became so appalling during the 1950s that wild horse extinction became a frightfully real possibility.[122] In 1959 Congress enacted the "Wild Horse Annie Act."[123] The Act outlawed the

---

117 Id.
118 T. Vaughn, Mammology, 246, 248 (1978).
119 Id.at 243-52.
120 Santini, "Good Intentions Gone Estray, The Wild, Free-Roaming Horse and Burros Act," 16 Land & Water L. Rev. 525 (1981).
121 Pitt, *supra*note 125, at 506.
122 Buckley, "Straying Wild Horses and the Range Landowner: The Search for Peaceful Coexistence," 4 Public Land L. Rev. 29, 30 (1983).
123 In 1950, a Nevada rancher's wife -- named Velma Johnston -- came up behind a cattle truck on

use of aircraft and motorized vehicles for the purpose of hunting or capturing wild horses or burros on lands owned by the federal government.[124]. President Eisenhower signed the Act into law on September 9, 1959. However, despite good intensions by Congress, the law provided only temporary relief to wild horses. It did not protect them from roundups on private lands, from further encroachment upon their habitat, from target shooters, or from non-motorized roundups on public lands. Half-hearted enforcement by local officials made the law totally ineffective, and by 1971 the wild horse population had decreased to an estimated 9500.

Congress again took up the problem in 1971 when Senator Clifford P. Hansen of Wyoming introduced a bill placing wild horses and burros under exclusive jurisdiction of the Secretary of the Interior, but this bill died in committee.[125] The 92nd Congress was then flooded by a nationwide letter writing campaign. The campaign was organized by various horse protection groups and humane societies, and was spearheaded by thousands of school children and readers of every major publication from *Time* to the *Wall Street Journal* and *Christian Science Monitor*.[126]

Many witnesses testified at the House and Senate hearings held in April, 1971, and Senate Bill 1116 emerged from committee virtually unchanged. House Bill 5375 was bitterly contested and sent back to committee for redrafting, emerging as House Bill 9890. The Senate Bill passed without a dissenting vote on June 29, 1971 and House Bill 9890 passed the House unanimously on October 4, 1971.[127] After differences in the two bills were resolved in Conference Committee, the consolidated measure passed both the Senate and the House as the Wild and Free-Roaming Horses and Burros Act. It was signed into law by President Richard Nixon on December 15, 1971.[128]

The bald eagle became the nation's symbol at or near the birth of the country. The horse, who along with man, settled the west was designated a symbol of the nation's heritage by the Wild Horse and Burro Act (WHBA).[129] In the Act's statement of findings and policy, Congress declared:

---

the highway. Blood was streaming down the truck's sides, and the panicked cries of horses could be heard from within. Mrs. Johnston followed the truck to its destination - a slaughterhouse - and began a campaign which would soon earn her the name of "Wild Horse Annie." Mrs. Johnston formed the Wild Horse Organized Assistance, Inc. (WHOA). Soon major publications picked up the story and there was such public outrage at the brutal and inhumane treatment of the wild horse. Id.

124 18 U.S.C. § 47
125 *supra*note 123, at 1060 (1972).
126 Pitt, *supra*note 125, at 526.
127 Pitt, *supra*note 125, at 507.
128 16 U.S.C. §§ 1331-1340 (1982).
129 16 U.S.C. § 1331 (1976).

# WILDLIFE AND HABITAT

Wild free-roaming horses and burros are living symbols of the historic and pioneer spirit of the West; that they contribute to the diversity of life forms within the Nation and enrich the lives of the American people; and that these horses and burros are fast disappearing from the American scene. It is the policy of Congress that wild free-roaming horses and burros shall be protected from capture, branding, harassment, or death; and to accomplish this they are to be considered in the area where presently found, as an integral part of the natural system of the public lands.[130]

The Act seeks to accomplish these goals through a combination of management activities and criminal provisions.[131] Horses or burros protected under this Act which stray from public lands into privately owned lands are protected. However, the owners can call federal marshals or an agent of the Secretary who shall arrange to have the animals removed.[132]

The criminal provisions add teeth to the Act. These provide that any person found guilty of removing or converting a wild horse without authorization from the Secretaries, and anyone causing the death, harassment or sale of horses or their remains to be processed into commercial products, is subject to fine of not more than $2,000, imprisonment for not more than one year, or both.[133] Few cases have dealt with these criminal penalties and there has been a relatively small number of convictions.[134] In 1980, for instance, of the 1860 adopters and 3750 horses inspected for possible violations, there were no prosecuted cases that resulted in convictions.[135] Although the convictions have been about as sparse as the prairie grass, there has been no problem with the validity of the criminal provisions. The Ninth Circuit, in *Johnson*, upheld the constitutionality of the criminal provisions.[136] The court ruled the Act was not unconstitutionally vague, over-broad or arbitrarily enforced.[137]

---

130 Id.
131 The WHBA was created and designed to protect all unbranded and unclaimed horses and burros on public lands of the United States. These animals were to be free from capture, branding, harassment or death. The Act also provides that all such horses and burros on the public lands administered by the Secretary of the Interior through the Bureau of Land Management or by the Secretary of Agriculture, through the Forest Service, are to be committed to the jurisdiction of the respective Secretaries who are directed to protect and manage the animals as components of the public lands. The law further states they are to be managed in a manner that is designed to achieve and maintain a thriving natural ecological balance on the public lands.
132 16 U.S.C. § 1331 (1976).
133 16 U.S.C. § 1338(a) (1976).
134 United States v. Johnson, 685 F.2d 337 (9th Cir. 1982); United States v. Hughes, 626 F.2d 619 (9th Cir. 1980); United States v. Christiansen, 504 F. Supp. 364 (D. Nev. 1980).
135 Bureau of Land Management, "Fiscal Year 1981 Program Accomplishments," Wild Horse & Burro Report 2 (Nov. 1981) (Newsletter).
136 United States v. Johnson, 685 F.2d 337, 338.
137 Id. at 334-40.

# PROTECTION OF WILDLIFE

The overall validity of the Act was established when the Supreme Court rendered its opinion in *Kleppe v. New Mexico*.[138] The *Kleppe* decision is unique in that it is the only interpretation of the WHBA that the Court has issued. The *Kleppe* case began when, at the request of a federal grazing permittee, New Mexico authorities removed certain of the protected burros from federal land and sold them at auction. The federal Bureau of Land Management then demanded that New Mexico recover and return them. Instead, the state sued the Secretary of the Interior to have the federal act declared unconstitutional. The lower court agreed with the state, distinguishing earlier cases on the grounds that in those cases the federal efforts were lawful only because they served to protect the federal lands, whereas here the Act was designed solely to protect the animals.[139]

In the case the Court was squarely confronted with the issue of whether the Congress had the authority to assert jurisdiction over wild horses and burros under the Property Clause.[140] A three-judge district court[141] had ruled the Act unconstitutional reasoning that: (1) the statute was designed to protect wild horses and burros, not federally owned lands; (2) ownership of wild animals was vested in the state as sovereign in trust for the benefit of the people, not the federal government;[142] and (3) the property clause gives Congress the power to regulate wild animals on the public lands only as an incident to its power to protect public lands from damage; therefore, the Act could not be sustained as a valid exercise of power by Congress under the Property Clause.[143] The Supreme Court unanimously reversed, holding that the Property Clause gives Congress the power to protect wildlife on federally owned lands, state law notwithstanding.[144] The Court reserved ruling on whether the Act would be sustained in all its conceivable applications, particularly the permissible reach of the Act under the Property Clause.[145] The Court declared that Congress had the power to regulate and protect any and all wildlife living on federal land.[146] Thus, the validity of the WHBA was established.

Just as Congress did with the BEPA, it found that it was necessary to revise part of the WHBA in 1978. These amendments were contained in the Public Range Lands Improvement Act of 1978 (PRLIA).[147] Congress was confronted with an unusual problem. Unlike 1971, the problem was not the ineffectiveness of the prior legislation in achieving its goals

---

138   426 U.S. 529 (1976).
139   426 U.S. at 539, 541.
140   *supra* note 151.
141   *supra* note 152.
142   *Id.*
143   *Id.*
144   *Id.*
145   *Id.*
146   *Id.*
147   Pub. L. No. 95-514, 92 Stat. 1803 (1978).

of protecting the wild horses and burros from disappearing from the open range. Rather, the issue was whether the 1971 Act had been overly successful to the detriment of the public lands.[148] Additionally, certain abuses were occurring in the Adopt-A-Horse program which required corrections.[149]

The amendments to the Act which were finally adopted reflect the belief that an accurate and scientific inventory of wild horse and burro populations was essential to the effective administration of the public lands in a manner consistent with the "multiple-use" concept. [150] The Act was amended to require that such a current inventory be maintained by the Secretaries in order to determine whether and where an overpopulation existed, whether removal activities of "excess animals"[151] should be undertaken, the appropriate management level of the animals on areas of public domain[152] and how these management levels should be maintained.[153] A research study by private experts on the dynamics of wild horse and burro populations and their interrelationships with wildlife, forage, and water resources was authorized to be completed and submitted to Congress by 1983.[154]

PRLIA did not amend the prescribed amount of management that the 1971 Act called for. Under the 1971 Act, all management activities concerning wild horses "should be at the minimal feasibility level"[155] and are to be "designed to achieve and maintain a thriving natural ecological balance on the public lands."[156]

As has consistently been the case, when Congress has passed an act courts will differ in their interpretations of it. Through case law it appears that there will are three different approaches: (1) The Minimal Feasibility Level, (2) Agency Discretion, and (3) The Thriving Natural Ecological Balance. The difficulty in determining the intensity of wild horse management arises from the tension between the language of sections 1333(a) and 1333(b) of the Act. It is accurate to state that courts ruling in favor of Bureau of Land Management (BLM) horse roundups tend to emphasize broad agency discretion and the "thriving natural ecological balance" phraseology, while opinions rejecting roundups concentrate on the "minimal feasible" language.[157]

---

148  Pitt, *supra* note 125, at 530.
149  *Id.*
150  43 U.S.C. §§ 1901 (1976).
151  16 U.S.C. § 1333(b)(1) (Supp. III 1979).
152  16 U.S.C. § 1333(b)(3) (Supp. III 1979).
153  *Id.*
154  16 U.S.C. § 1333(b)(2) (Supp. III 1979).
155  16 U.S.C. § 1333(a) (1976).
156  16 U.S.C. § 1333(b)(2) (1976).
157  Buckley, "The Appropriate Degree of Management Under the Wild, Free-Roaming Horses and Burros Act," 19 Cal. Western L. Rev. 419, 424 (1983).

The case interpreting the "minimal feasibility approach" is *American Horse Protection v. Kleppe*.[158] The plaintiffs sought a permanent injunction against a proposed horse roundup near Challis, Idaho. The defendant, the BLM, on the basis of a 1975 aerial inventory and reproduction survey, estimated that approximately 509 horses occupied the Challis planning unit. Relying upon its research studies, the BLM concluded that the horse population had been rapidly increasing since 1971. This increase in the number of horses, coupled with the poor condition of the range, exceeded the land's "carrying capacity" twofold, while the number of wildlife and domestic livestock remained relatively constant. As a result the BLM planned to remove 130 to 260 horses from the Challis area. The plaintiffs argued this violated both the Wild Horses Act and the National Environmental Policy Act. The court agreed holding that the proposed roundup breached the Act's mandate requiring all management activities to be at the minimum feasibility level.[159] The court suggested that, under section 1333(a), "careful and detailed consideration must be given to all alternative courses of action" having a "less severe impact on the wild horse population" before any major management plans can be undertaken.[160] The BLM's failure to fully contemplate viable alternatives, such as restricting livestock grazing or pursuing population controls less drastic than removal, was an abuse of discretion violating section 1333(a).[161]

The *Kleppe* court also ruled that the BLM's roundup decision was based on inadequate data and thus was an abuse of discretion.[162] The agency was also found to have abused its discretion by proceeding with a culling proposal before the Challis EIS was completed, and by failing to provide on-site veterinary assistance during the roundup pursuant to section 1333(b).[163]

While the "minimal feasible" issue was the central element in the opinion, it was perhaps the BLM's lack of information which led the court to its holding. The message in *Kleppe* is clear: current and precise data is absolutely required in wild horse management operations. As information concerning horse demography and fertility becomes less accurate, courts will be less willing to permit horse removal at the agency's discretion.[164]

The "agency discretion" approach was defined in *American Horse Protection Association v. Frizzel*.[165] The plaintiffs sought a preliminary injunc-

---

158  6 E.L.R. 20802 (D. D.C. 1976).
159  *Id.*
160  *Id.* at 20804.
161  Id.
162  *Id.* at 20803.
163  *Id.* at 20804.
164  Buckley, *supra* note 170, at 427.
165  403 F. Supp. 1206 (D. Nev. 1975).

tion to prevent the BLM from conducting a proposed roundup of four hundred horses in the Stone Cabin Valley, Nevada rangeland. Nearly seventy-eight percent of the valley's grazing capacity was used by livestock, while roughly ten percent was reserved for wildlife use. The remainder was deemed insufficient to sustain the estimated 900 to 1200 horses in the area. The plaintiffs argued the roundup was an abuse of agency discretion in violation of the Act and NEPA's EIS requirement.[166] The court rejected these contentions on the basis that federal regulations and legislative history gave the BLM broad discretion in determining the necessity of a roundup.[167]

Although *Frizzel* mentions a "high degree of discretionary authority," the opinion does not give the agency permission to ride roughshod. There are limitations beyond those mentioned by *Frizzel*. The court noted the following limitations on discretion: (1) BLM decisions to remove or destroy "excess" horses were required to proceed "under humane conditions and care" and "in the most humane manner possible," and (2) decisions generally were subject to the agency's mandatory duty to protect and manage the horses as components of the public lands.[168] Section 1333(b) also commands the BLM to define management levels, the existence of overpopulation, and the need for removal based upon current horse censuses, upon scientific studies and consultation with public and private experts, and upon court ordered EIS's prepared pursuant to NEPA.[169] These research requirements are mandatory. This means horses will not be removed until there has been an evaluation and accumulation of data. Another restraint on agency discretion is the "minimal possible" language.[170] This court's opinion to allow discretion will aid in adding flexibility to cope with varying environmental conditions and problems.

One additional point to be made is how *Frizzel* and *Kleppe* should be distinguished. The holdings may be attributed to different facts. In *Frizzel*, the plaintiffs' expert witness damaged their position. In *Kleppe*, the BLM debated its own witnesses. However, something more significant distinguishes the decisions. In *Frizzel*, the court expressly limited its holding to the disputed Stone Cabin Valley roundup as an interim measure pending completion of the *NRDC v. Morton* EIS, noting that future roundups must meet NEPA's requirements.[171] The *Kleppe* ruling did not interpret the Challis proposal as temporary.[172]

---

166 *Id*. at 1209, 1215.
167 *Id*. at 1216-17.
168 Frizzel, 403 F. Supp. at 1217 (quoting 16 U.S.C. § 1333(a)-(b) (Supp. IV 1974).
169 16 U.S.C. § 1333(b)(1)(3) (Supp. III 1979).
170 16 U.S.C. § 1333(a) (1976).
171 *Frizzel*, 403 F. Supp. at 1219-20.
172 43 U.S.C. §§ 1701-82 (1976 and Supp. III 1979).

# PROTECTION OF WILDLIFE

The third area, "the thriving Natural Ecological Balance" is probably the most involved and complex. The WHBA is intended to go hand in hand with PRLIA and the Federal Land Policy and Management Act of 1976 (FLPMA) to improve the deteriorating range conditions.[173] The federal government's involvement in improving rangeland conditions began in 1934 with the Taylor Grazing Act.[174] In this Act, Congress sought to reverse the disastrous environmental damage caused by a history of unregulated livestock grazing throughout the West. The Act, along with subsequent amendments, directed the Secretary of the Interior to create livestock grazing districts. Grazing permits and leases were to be issued to regulate use of range resources. The Secretary was also empowered to collect grazing fees and to authorize construction of physical improvements on the land, such as fences, wells, and reservoirs. The Secretary was to protect the range from further injury by modifying numbers of livestock and seasons of use permitted in given areas.[175] After finding that the plethora of land statutes were obsolete, Congress, in 1976 enacted the FLPMA in an attempt to homogenize the federal range policy.[176] The Act prescribes a multiple use of resources on a sustained yield basis to accommodate the different lands under management of the BLM.[177] The FLPMA requires a cataloging of resource conditions as well as public participation as well as scientific input in the planning process. The goal is to fuse these directives into one management scheme.[178] PRLIA, however, was tailored more specifically toward remedying range deterioration. The mandate of FLPMA was reaffirmed by PRLIA when it declared its commitment to:

> manage, maintain and improve the condition of the public rangelands so that they become as productive as feasible for all rangeland values in accordance with management objectives and the land use planning process established (by FLPMA).[179]

Rangeland statutes have had the declared purpose of protecting a fragile ecosystem. To protect and restore a "thriving ecological balance" 16 U.S.C. 1334 provides for removal of a straying wild horse or burro from private land. The Secretary retained the power of removal in order to achieve what he determined to be appropriate management levels.[180] Findings of overpopulation by the Secretary under the amended Act are to be based upon the required current inventories, information contained in land use plans, court ordered environmental impact statements, and additional information such as that contained in the private

---

173  Buckley, *supra* note 170, at 433.
174  43 U.S.C. §§ 315 (1970).
175  Buckley, *supra* note 170, at 433.
176  *Id.*
177  1976 U.S. Code Cong. & Ad. News 6175.
178  Buckley, *supra* note 170, at 434.
179  43 U.S.C. § 1901(b)(2) (Supp. III 1979).
180  16 U.S.C. § 1333(b)(2) (Supp. III 1979).

research study due in 1983; in the absence of such information, the Secretary can make the determination on the basis of all information he has currently available.[181] Once such a determination is made, removal activities are mandatory.[182] Prior to the initiation of removal it is necessary to prepare an environmental impact statement if these activities are deemed to be "major federal action significantly affecting the quality of the human environment.[183] Appropriate management levels of wild horses and burros can be maintained by the Secretary by following a priority list of actions: (1) ordering the destruction, in the most humane manner possible, of old, sick, or lame animals; (2) capturing and removing additional excess animals for which an adoption demanded by qualified individuals exists; and (3) ordering the destruction of additional excess wild horses and burros in the most humane manner possible if a sufficient adoption demand does not exist.[184]

The leading case that defines the parameters of § 1334 is *Roaring Springs Associates v. Andrus*.[185] The plaintiff organization owned unfenced land in eastern Oregon. When wild horses roamed onto its parcels, the association asked federal agents from the Department of the Interior to remove the trespassing animals. After the government refused, the plaintiff petitioned a United States Magistrate to issue a mandamus order.[186] The court ruled that the defendants owed the private landowners a "ministerial duty" under § 1334 to return the wild horses to the public range.[187] The government's defenses of sovereign immunity, of incorporating state estray laws into the Act, and of limiting the scope of § 1334 did not neutralize this mandatory requirement.[188]

The holding makes it clear that agency discretion is inappropriate when dealing with stray removal from private property. The holding was extended in *Fallini v. Hodel*.[189] In this case landowners brought action to compel the Secretary of the Interior to prevent wild horses from straying onto their lands. The district court granted a writ of mandamus and injunction.[190] The circuit court reversed holding that the trial court had no authority to grant mandamus or an injunction compelling the BLM to prevent wild horses from straying onto private lands. The reason advanced by the court was that the WHBA requires removal of wild horses within a reasonable time, and this provides an adequate remedy.[191]

---

181  *Id.*
182  *Id.*
183  42 U.S.C. § 4332(2)(c) (1976).
184  *Id.*
185  471 F. Supp. 522 (D. Or. 1978).
186   *Id.* at 524.
187  *Id.* at 526.
188  *Id.* at 525.
189  783 F.2d 1343 (9th Cir. 1986).
190  Fallini v. Watt, No. Lv. 81-536, R.D.F. (D. Nev. Oct. 3, 1984).
191  Fallini v. Hodel, 783 F.2d at 1347.

# PROTECTION OF WILDLIFE

In *Mountain States Legal Foundation v. Andrus,* a district court in Wyoming extended the removal principle to the public lands contained in the "checkerboard" area.[192] This holding endows the "thriving ecological balance" approach with more regulatory overtones.

Under this holding, the BLM now will have to roundup wild horses whenever they stray onto both public and private tracts. This holding has been criticized as a blatant distortion of § 1334 which was not even cited in the opinion.[193] A district court in Nevada came to a different conclusion.[194]

> [s]ection 1334 makes no distinction between the checkerboard lands and other lands. Certainly, the checkerboard lands are not uncommon in the West . . . . Presumably, Congress was aware of the problems with the checkerboard lands by at least 1978 . . . if not when the Wild Horses Act became law in 1971. Nevertheless, at the time Congress amended the Wild and Free-Roaming Horse Act in October of 1978, it made no amendment of Section 1334 to consider the problems of the checkerboard lands. Therefore, this matter is within the province of Congress and not the district court.[195]

This interpretation makes it inappropriate to apply § 1334 to public property within the checkerboard area absent Congressional action. Again, these two cases, as well as the three approaches, illustrate why management under the WHBA has been difficult.

In another effort to prevent indiscriminate taking of wild horses, the Act permits adoption of those horses. The program started in 1976 and permits a person to pay $125 per horse (up to a maximum of four, unless the Secretary has determined in writing that a qualified person can humanely handle more).[196] After one year, if the horse has been treated humanely, title passes from the government to the individual.[197] Once this title passes, the BLM's guardianship ends. There is also a limited post-adoption inspection and monitoring period to insure protection while title passes.[198] This approach is designed to increase the amount of care which individual applicants should use.

The adoption program has suffered from two main problems. The first concerns horses that eventually end up in the slaughterhouses. Horses

---

192 12 E.L.R. 20105 (D. Wyo. 1981).
193 Pitt, *supra* note 125, at 536.
194 T. Quarter Circle Ranchers, Inc. v. Watt, No. 81-110 (D. Nev. Jan. 29, 1982).
195 *Id.*
196 16 U.S.C. § 1333(b)(2)(B) (Supp. III 1974).
197 16 U.S.C. 1333(c) (Supp. III 1979).
198 *Id.*

have been removed in substantial numbers by BLM range managers, and the commercial exploitation of wild horses and burros has not been prevented. The American Horse Protection Association estimated in 1979 that 50% of the animals adopted through the program were eventually resold to slaughterhouses. The BLM itself admitted to a 10% rate, while other estimates ranged as high as 90%.[199] This practice, though, is not illegal. Once title vests, an owner is basically free to do whatever he wants to do with his own property.

The second problem is funding. The program simply has not kept pace with the accelerated roundups. The BLM estimates that it spends from $300 to $500 per horse that is corralled under the program.[200] To put that in perspective, 17 to 18 million dollars a year is spent to manage and care for wild horses.[201] Because of the high cost and lack of funds post-capture treatment of animals results in overcrowded conditions that border on cruelty. Thus, roundups conducted under the program tragically result in numerous deaths.[202]

When the government, through its actions, causes private property to be destroyed it may be held liable under the fifth amendment. Two holdings coming out of the 10th Circuit Court make it clear that the BLM may be liable for damages caused by wild horses. In *Mountain States Legal Foundation v. Clark* the court of appeals implicitly ruled that foraging by wild horses on privately owned sections within the checkerboard is an unconstitutional taking of property if it results from the government's failure to manage the wild horses. This is the first case in which a court has ruled that the federal government's failure to manage wild animals under its control may be a taking.[203] This holding only compounds the difficulty in management.

A second case refused to grant compensation to landowners for damage caused by protected wild horses and burros.[204] Although the court ruled no "taking" had occurred, their ruling turned on the amount of damage done. The court held that although the animals have diminished value of the property, there will be no taking where owners are not deprived of all "economically viable use" of the land.[205] This holding does two things. Number one is that it unshoulders some of the burden of management it placed on the BLM in *Clark*. The holding seems to recognize the difficulty in administering the Act and lack of

199 Pitt, *supra*note 125, at 537.
200 *Id.*
201 Twenty-nine million dollars is spent on the entire endangered species program that is responsible for 360 species in the U.S. and 960 species worldwide. Hearings on the Dept. of the Interior and Related Agencies Appropriations for Fiscal Year of 1977, 94th Cong., 2d Sess. 1392-93 (1976).
202 Id.at 5, 6, 20-21.
203 740 F.2d 792 (10th Cir. 1984).
204 Mountain States Legal Foundation v. Hodel, 799 F.2d 1423 (10th Cir. 1986).
205 *Id.* at 1434.

funds available to the BLM. The court appears not to want to punish the BLM for these things that lead to the inability to control an impossible situation. Secondly, by imposing an "economically viable" standard, the court has set a very high burden of proof that anyone seeking damages must overcome. Consistent holdings of the *Hodel* variety may aid in salvaging the WHBA.

## COMPARISON OF THE BEPA AND THE WHBA

The WHBA is similar to the BEPA in that both acts were designed to protect two species of animals who have been declared symbols of this nation. Both acts condition the taking of either species on authorization from a Secretary. Through this measure, both acts hope to preserve animals which have become historically symbolic to the nation.

The statutes differ, however, in a variety of important respects: the taking of horses and burros can be done only by an administrator[206] while the eagle law contemplates private action under permit or authorization.[207] Eagles range more widely than horses or burros, they allegedly cause more direct harm to domestic livestock, and they have far less impact upon the flora in an ecosystem. Habitats of horses and burros are to be managed and sanctuaries for them established,[208] while no similar provision was explicitly made for eagles. Civil and administrative penalties attach to violations of the Eagle Act,[209] but only criminal sanctions are available against horse thieves;[210] state-federal cooperation is on a different basis,[211] and some commercial use of the less commercially valuable eagle is permitted while all trade in wild horses and burros is forbidden.[212]

In addition, protection of eagles is not limited to federal lands,[213] and no effort has been made to declare them federal property on or off federal lands.

In terms of constitutionality, the question of legislative power to enact protective statutes is very similar with respect to horses and eagles. The only apparent differences in this regard are that eagles typically travel more widely, the bald eagle is more symbolically significant, and horses and burros have more commercial value.[214]

Questions concerning Congressional power to legislate with respect to domestic wildlife have seldom been raised in the few cases decided by

206 16 U.S.C. § 1338 (Supp. IV 1974).
207 *Id*. § 668(a).
208 *Id*. § 1333(a).
209 *Id*. § 668(b),(c).
210 *Id*. § 1338(a).
211 *Id*. §§ 1333(a), 1336, 668(a).
212 *Id*. § 1338(a)(4),(5).
213 *Id*. § 668(a).
214 *supra* note 54, at 1119.

the Supreme Court. *Kleppe's* limited holding applies only to wildlife on federal land.[215] The other definitive holding is *Missouri v. Holland*.[216] However, that case dealt mainly with esoteric area of treaty implementation. As earlier discussed,[217] Congress has the power to designate and protect items that my be interpreted as symbols of the country. The WHBA clearly states that the purpose of the Act is to protect horses as symbols of America's western heritage.[218] Thus, by analogy the WHBA and BEPA fall well within the Congress' authority to protect and regulate wildlife of symbolic importance to the country.

## CONCLUSION

Because the bald eagle has the status of being our nation's symbol, and more importantly because it is a majestic, noble species, the bald eagle must be protected. Man has taken on the role of protector of wildlife and nature. Thusly, he has assumed the burden of drafting, implementing, and enforcing protective legislation. He has taken steps to discharge his obligation by passing the BEPA.

The statute has claws almost as sharp as the bird it protects. The BEPA imposes heavy fines and jail penalties on offenders. The courts have seen fit to enforce those provisions and to strengthen them with their own interpretations. In a recent case, *United States v. Stenberg*, the Ninth Circuit Court of Appeals held that the defense of outrageous government conduct was inapplicable to one who was actively engaged in violating the law before the government became involved.[219] The case involved an agent posing as a buyer of skins, animals and parts of protected animals including the eagle. The Court found that due to the ongoing violations of wildlife laws, the defense of outrageous government conduct was unavailable to the defendants.[220]

The BEPA has been modified so that there are very few exceptions left, and the procedures to gain these exemptions have be rigidly re-enforced. It appears as if Judge Lay's wish that, "A conservation statute will achieve its purpose as if it applies to everyone," is coming true.[221] Eagles are starting to come back from the DDT tragedy of the 1960s and they still face many problems associated with the constant competition with man. However, through protection and enforcement of the BEPA perhaps our grandchildren will see the eagle in a regal flight just as our forefathers did, and not just as a memory that exists on the back of a quarter.

---

215 *supra* note 151.
216 252 U.S. 416 (1920).
217 See notes 118-121.
218 16 U.S.C. § 1331 (1976).
219 803 F.2d 422 (1985).
220 *Id.* at 437.
221 *White*, 508 F.2d at 461 (Lay, J., dissenting).

The wild horse appears to be in a more inflexible situation. It faces no natural predators and it's habitat has a finite carrying capacity. The problems of over population and competition with man can be, if not solved, at least be dealt with by legislation and efficient administering of the Act. However, there are problems in the administration methodology that must be overcome. The other solution to the problem can come from the sometimes cruel process of natural selection that will result from overgrazing, famine, sickness and starvation.

Congress will debate and fight with ranchers for protection of a noble symbol of the nation's western heritage versus their right to exist as they have for years. Arguments will occur and money will be spent. Meanwhile, the horse continues to roam the plains where answers are as scarce as its resources.

## THE HUNTED OF THE SEA: PROTECTION OF MARINE MAMMALS

### MARINE MAMMALS

Congress was inundated with petitions and lobbying efforts during the early 1970s concerning the preservation and protection of marine mammals. Strong editorial arguments appeared in leading newspapers and on television which began to bring the problems of marine mammal extinction and inhumane hunting methods into the public eye.[222] Scientist and conservationists urged Congress to pass harsher legislation to protect whales, seals, sea otters, dolphins and polar bears.[223]

With a national election approaching in the fall of 1972, some members of Congress began to address these issues.[224] In March, 1971, Congressman Pryor introduced a bill called the Ocean Mammal Protection Act. The proposed law encouraged international cooperation in the fight to preserve depleting stocks of certain marine mammals.[225] Congress held public hearing on the subject in July, 1971, and a Senate Subcommittee held hearings in 1972. Ultimately, a legislative response to the growing marine mammal problem was achieved in 1972 and it was labeled the Marine Mammal Protection Act.[226]

### MAN AND THE MARINE MAMMAL

Oceans over 71 percent of the earth's surface.[227] Exploitation of terrestrial resources has reached the point where an increased use of ocean

---

[222] N.Y. Times (editorial), Feb. 16, 1972, at 38, col. 2.
[223] *Id*. One problem mentioned in particular was the accidental killing of some 200,000 to 400,000 dolphins and porpoises annually who became entangled in the purse seine nets used to catch yellow fin tuna.
[224] N.Y. Times, Mar. 19, Sec. IV, at 15, col. 2.
[225] N.Y. Times, Mar. 25, at 30, col. 4.
[226] 16 U.S.C. § 1361, et seq.

resources has become more and more necessary to meet the needs of an expanding world population. Marine mammals, or cetaceans, provide man with many valuable products such as food and fine lubricants.

Cetacean is the term used to describe a variety of marine mammals which inhabit the oceans. Whales are the largest and most prominent member of the cetacean family. At one time, whales numbered some 4 million and roamed the oceans free. However, by 1972 man's commercial endeavors had threatened the whale population, reducing them to a number of about 1.2 million.[228]

Only several hundred Bowhead and Right Whales remained at the time of the 1972 Senate Hearings.[229]

Equally striking is the fate of the Blue Whale. The Blue Whale, the largest creature in earth's history, diminished to a startlingly low population of some 600 after thriving in the oceans at one time in the hundreds of thousands.[230]

> The Blue Whale is larger than 30 elephants and also larger than the combined size of three of the largest dinosaurs. Its weight of 152 tons is the approximate weight of 2000 humans. Its heart weights 1,2000 pounds, its liver a ton, and its tongue more than one-third ton. For all its massive bulk, the Blue Whale's throat is so small it cannot swallow anything larger than a sardine . . . . It has been estimated, that a large Blue Whale will eat approximately two tons of krill per day.[231]

The enormous size of the Blue Whale is indicative of the size of the threat man's activities have placed on the cetacean population.

Beyond the potential extinction of certain groups of whales due to commercial hunting operations, commercial fishing enterprises accidentally killed hundreds of thousands of porpoises each year.[232] Large schools of tuna congregate beneath groups of porpoises.[233] This phenomenon allows tuna fleets to readily find large schools of tuna. Once spotted, fishermen surround the tuna fish by dragging a purse seine net behind speedy skiffs. However, as a result of this encirclement, the porpoises are trapped in the net along with the tuna. As mammals, the porpoises must surface to breath air in order to live. The purse seine nets drown

---

227  A. Soons, Marine Scientific Research and the Law of the Sea 11 (1982).
228  *Id.*
229  *Id.*
230  *Id.*
231  Levin, Towards More Effective Cetacean Protection, 12 Nat. Resource L. 549, 555 (1979).
232  H.R. Rep. No 707, 92d Cong. 2d Sess. (1972).
233  Nafziger & Armstrong, The Porpoise-Tuna Controversy: Management of Marine Resources After Committee For Human Legislation, Inc. v. Richardson, 7 Envtl. L. 223 (1977).

the porpoises by entangling them in the net below the surface, or by trapping them below the bunching tuna.[234]

This unnecessary killing of dolphins and porpoises, as well as the near extinction of some whales and other cetaceans due to hunting and pollution, prompted the United States Congress to pass legislation meant to curtail these threatening activities.[235] Because of such legislation, the American whaling industry today has drifted into almost complete extinction.[236] Even so, the problems in whaling persist as Japan and the Soviet Union have refused to participate in international bans on whaling.[237] Additionally, new technology has transformed the ancient art and business of whale hunting into a near precision science through the use of sonar and whale-tracking helicopters.[238]

Though America is for all practical purposes out of the whaling industry, it leads the world in commercial tuna fishing.[239] The activity of large fishing fleets has had a dramatic impact on the cetacean population and has been regulated by American legislation and international treaties. The Marine Mammal Protection Act of 1972 has had an impact on American law but the difficulty of achieving meaningful international cooperation in the protection of endangered cetaceans through government regulation and the implementation of more humane hunting techniques is still an existing problem.

## THE MARINE MAMMAL PROTECTION ACT OF 1972

The Act begins by placing a moratorium on the taking of marine mammals and marine mammal products.[240] Congress provided some flexibility in this moratorium. Marine Mammals may be taken without sanction if a permit has been issued to those taking marine mammals for public display or for scientific research.[241] Also, commercial fishermen are excused from taking marine mammals if the protected cetacean is taken incidental to their fishing enterprises.[242] Exemption from the Act's moratorium was further extended to the American Eskimo community and other Alaskan natives.[243] Despite their narrow definition, much controversy has arisen over these exemptions.

---

234 Levin, *supra* note 243, at 564.
235 16 U.S.C. § 1361 et seq.
236 Levin, *supra* note 243, at 561
237 *Id*. at 568, 569 (though Japan agreed to a ban on whaling by 1988 after negotiations with the U.S. in 1968).
238 Note, Legal Aspect of the International Whaling Controversy: Will Jonah Swallow the Whale? 8 N.Y.U. J. Int'l L. & Pol. 211, 214 (1975).
239 Levin, *supra* note 243, at 561 (the U.S. tuna industry directly and indirectly employs nearly 40,000 people who together produce 1.5 billion cans of tuna per year for the American public).
240 16 U.S.C. § 1371.
241 16 U.S.C. §§ 1371, 1374.
242 16 U.S.C. § 1371.
243 16 U.S.C. § 1371.

# WILDLIFE AND HABITAT

## ALASKAN NATIVES

Some states, such as Alaska, Oregon, Washington and California had unique expertise in marine mammal protection well before passage of the MMPA in 1972. For instance, Alaska had state legislation regulating the population of sea lions and seals dating back to 1927. As the federal government assumed more and more jurisdiction over marine mammal conservation, these states rebelled against intrusive and less experienced federal supervision. Yet, despite initial requests for waiver of federal preemption under the MMPA some state conservation managers deferred to federal management to avoid administrative redundancies and to relieve the state of the financial burdens related to marine mammal protection programs.[244] The state of Alaska, however, persisted in its request for waiver of federal preemption and a return to its own state management system. Testifying before a Senate committee, the Commissioner of Alaska's Department of Fish and Game said, "Alaska's self-sufficient marine mammals program, preempted in 1972, was rated by most knowledgeable experts as one of the finest marine mammals management and research programs in the world."[245]

In 1976, the management of the walrus was given back to Alaska, but nothing else.[246] This immediately created a conflict between Alaska and the federal government when, as part of its walrus management program, the state banned hunting in some regions which were the traditional hunting grounds of Togiak people. The Togiak people claimed that the state's regained right to manage the walrus population was limited by their rights to harvest marine mammals under the exemption privileges provided in the MMPA.[247] These exemptions are:

(1) is for susbsistence purposes

(2) is done for purposes of creating and selling authentic native articles of handicrafts and clothing; Provided, That only authentic native articles of handicrafts may be sold in interstate commerce: And provided further,That any edible portion of marine mammals may be sold in native villages and towns in Alaska or for native consumption. For the purposes of this subsection, the term "authentic native articles of handicrafts and clothing" means items composed wholly or in some significant respect of natural materials, and which are produced, decorated, or fashioned in the exercise of traditional native handicrafts without the

---

244  Marine Mammal Protection Act: Hearing on S. 1186 before the Senate Comm. on Com., Sci., and Transp., 97th Cong., lst Sess. 44 (1981) (testimony of Dale Snow, Dep't Fish and Wildlife, Or.).
245  Id. at 47.
246  41 Fed. Reg. 12, 373 (1976) (amended 1979).
247  16 U.S.C. § 1371 reads in pertinent part: (b) *Exemptions for Alaskan natives.*  ...the provisions of this Act shall not apply with respect to the taking of any marine mammal by any Indian, Aleut, or Eskimo who resides in Alaska and who dwells on the coast of the North Pacific Ocean or the Arctic Ocean...

use of pantographs, multiple carvers, or other mass copying devices. Traditional native handicrafts include, but are not limited to weaving, carving, stitching, sewing, lacing, beading, drawing, and painting; and

(3) in each case is not accomplished in a wasteful manner. A federal district court agreed with the claim of the Togiaks and held that the Department of Interior's regulation which lifted MMPA jurisdiction over the Alaskan walrus population did not give the state authority to regulate nonwasteful native use of marine mammals.[248] This ruling effectively nullified Alaska's interest in managing the walrus because the special protections offered in the Act to native groups such as Indians, Aleuts, and Eskimos did not extend to all citizens of the state, and thus violated the equal protection provisions of the Alaska Constitution.[249] Therefore, Alaska revoked its authority to regulate the walrus and renounced the state's interest in regulating other species protected under the MMPA. Thus, the exemption extended Alaskan natives in the MMPA has not only created controversy regarding the Act's total commitment to marine mammal protection but it has also bullied one of the worlds's premier marine mammal management programs out of business.

## SCIENTIFIC RESEARCH AND PUBLIC DISPLAY

The Act authorizes the Secretary of the Commerce to issue permits for the importation of marine mammals for purposes of display or scientific research provided that the permit applicant demonstrates to the Secretary that the use of the permit will be consistent with the purposes and regulations in the Act.[250] The Secretary has delegated the issuance of permits to the National Oceanic and Atmospheric Administration and its subagency, the National Marine Fisheries Service.[251] Both applicants and parties opposed to the permit may seek judicial review of the Secretary's decisions regarding the issuance of permits.[252]

## STANDING

In 1977, the United States Court of Appeals for the District of Columbia held that parties opposed to the issuance of permits, such as animal welfare groups, have standing to sue under the Act.[253] The court found in *Animal Welfare Institute v. Kreps* that the Animal Welfare Institute had standing to sue the Secretary to revoke a permit allowing the importation of seal skins from South Africa, many of which were taken from nursing baby seals in violation of the Act.[254]

---

248 People of Togiak v. United States, 470 F. Supp. 423, 424 (1979).
249 Alaska Const. art. I, § 3.
250 16 U.S.C. §§ 1374(c), (d).
251 16 U.S.C. §§ 1362(11)(a), 134 (a).
252 *Id.*
253 Animal Welfare Inst. v. Kreps, 561 F.2d 1002 (D.C. Cir. 1977).
254 *Id.*

# WILDLIFE AND HABITAT

## STANDARD OF REVIEW

The standard of review courts must use to overturn a decision of the Secretary is the "substantial evidence on the record" test found in the Administrative Procedure Act.[255] Courts typically stay within the boundaries of review, and give deference to the judgments of administrative agencies which support their decisions on highly complex scientific issues using expert advice.[256]

Pursuant to such deference, in *Friends of Animals, Inc. v. Baldridge*, the district court upheld the Secretary's issuance of a permit for the capture and public display of Orca whales.[257] The court's decision in that case was based on a finding by the Secretary that a substantial public benefit would be gained from the display of the whales which outweighed any adverse impact on the Orca whale population.[258] Though there were considerable arguments raised in the case which questioned the actual benefits to the public the court gave deference to the expertise of the Agency, and supported its decision to issue the permit.

In another case, the Ninth Circuit affirmed a lower court ruling that the National Maritime Fisheries Service (NMFS) failed to adequately explain its decision not to prepare an environmental impact statement with respect to its issuing Sea World a permit to capture killer whales.[259] In its application, Sea World requested permission to collect up to 100 killer whales over a five-year period.[260] Up to 10 killer whales would be permanently kept in captivity for research and display and up to 90 would be kept for three weeks or less for research.[261] Pursuant to the Act, public notice of Sea World's permit request was given and a two day public hearing was held after 1200 pro and 1000 con responses had been received regarding the application.[262] Ultimately, the permit was issued but was called to question by several conservation groups which alleged the NMFS violated the National Environmental Policy Act (NEPA) by failing to prepare an environmental impact statement.[263] Sea World intervened in the suit and argued unsuccessfully that the environmental impact statement required by the NEPA is in irreconcilable conflict with the thirty day time limit for processing permit applications set forth in the MMPA.[264] In other words, thirty days is not sufficient time to study and prepare a responsible statement about the environmental impact involved in the taking of a small and specified group of

---

255  16 U.S.C. § 1374(d)(6) (citing 5 U.S.C. § 706(2)(e) (1982).
256  *See Animal Welfare supra*note 265.
257  No. 81 Civ. 1547 (D. D.C. 1982).
258  *Id.*
259  Jones v. Gordon, 792 F.2d 821, 822 (9th Cir. 1986).
260  *Id.* at 823.
261  *Id.*
262  *Id.*
263  42 U.S.C. § 4332(2)(c).
264  *Id.* at 825; 16 U.S.C. § 1374(d).

marine mammals. Though the court agreed that the narrow and restrictive nature of the permit issued to Sea World was commensurate with the concept of due regard for the environment it nevertheless failed to give adequate scientific scrutiny to the matter.It is clear from the foregoing that courts will defer to the expertise of the Secretary when permits are issued. However, if a permit is issued which does not envince signs of that expertise, the court will require the NMFS to be more responsible by demanding each permit be couched in language representative of the complex scientific issues involved thus giving effect to the protective nature of the Act.[265]

## ENFORCEMENT

In light of some recent litigation involving the MMPA it is difficult to determine whether protection of marine mammals continues to be the goal of the Act. Courtroom battles often revolve around enforcement issues which are ancillary to the environmental protection issues addressed by Congress in the MMPA.

For example, in 1988, the Ninth Circuit addressed the issue of whether females employees of the National Oceanic and Atmospheric Administration (NOAA) should be permitted to accompany tuna fishermen on board their vessels in order to monitor compliance with the MMPA.[266]

The Secretary of Commerce developed regulations which required permit holders to allow an employee of NOAA to accompany fishing vessels "for the purpose of conducting research and observing operations, including collecting information which can be used in civil or criminal penalty proceedings, forfeiture actions, or permit or certificate sanctions."[267] The Ninth Circuit supported the constitutionality of this regulation finding it did not exceed the scope of the Secretary's authority to promulgate such a regulation and that the placement of observers on fishing vessels is not an unreasonable warrantless search under the Fourth Amendment.[268]

Prior to 1986, NOAA did not hire women to serve as observers on the tuna boats. In response to this practice, several women complained to the Administration's Civil Rights Division which found that the female applicant's rights were violated under Title VII of the Civil Rights Act of 1964 because they were denied employment as observers solely on the basis of their sex.[269] Pursuant to this finding, by January 1987, four women were assigned to fishing voyages and tuna fleet owners were advised that no special accommodations for the women would be required on their vessels.[270]

---

265 *Id*. at 829.
266 Carribean Marine Services Co. v. Baldridge, 844 F.2d 668, 670 (9th Cir. 1988).
267 50 C.F.R. Part 216.24(f)(1) (1986).
268 Balelo v. Baldridge, 724 F.2d 753, 755 (9th Cir.) (en banc), cert. denied, 467 U.S. 1252 (1984).
269 *Id*. at 670-71.

Fleet owners and their crews responded by filing motions for preliminary injunctions in federal district court. The owners sought and received temporary restraining orders and then the district court granted preliminary injunctions stating that the presence of women on the boats raised a serious question of privacy and interference with fishing operations.[271] The judge found that the hardships involved with female observers tipped the scales sharply in favor of the fleet owners.[272]

The owners and crews supported their motions for preliminary injunctions with declarations concerning the practical working conditions aboard their vessels. First, they stated that there were severe obstacles to privacy on the boats because of the cramped quarters.[273] Common toilets and showers were often used without partitions from the bunk areas where the crew would dress and undress.[274] Also, it was alleged that the crew would dress and undress on deck, shower on deck, and use unenclosed bathroom facilities on deck.[275] The crew complained that female observers on the boat would infringe on their privacy while performing their intimate bodily activities.[276]

Secondly, the declarations claimed that many of the crew members were "crude men with little formal education" which may give rise to their harassment or assault of a female observer.[277] To support this, the owners cited an incident where a Korean officer assaulted an American female observer on his vessel.[278] Ironically, a witness for NOAA said that there were "only" six incidents involving assaults or verbal abuse on foreign fishing vessels over a period of ten years.[279] Fleet owners claimed that the threat of such incidents would cause them to incur liability insurance expenses which would endanger their profits.[280]

Thirdly, vessel owners claimed that the West coast tuna industry was in financial straits and the presence of females on their boats would destroy morale and could distract the crew, making them less productive.[281]

Lastly, the owners contended that the NOAA's own regulations required that the Administration's enforcement activities should be conducted in a manner which would minimize interference with fishing operations.[282]

---

270  *Id.* at 671.
271  *Id.* at 669-71.
272  *Id.*
273  *Id.*
274  *Id.*
275  *Id.*
276  *Id.*
277  *Id.*
278  *Id.* at 672.
279  *Id.*
280  *Id.*
281  *Id.*

# PROTECTION OF WILDLIFE

The Ninth Circuit was unconvinced by the above arguments and lifted the preliminary injunctions, finding that the district court had abused its discretion by overstating the harm likely to ensue as a result of having female observers on tuna boats. The appellate court pointed out that speculative injury did not constitute irreparable injury, and the plaintiff fleet owners did not demonstrate immediate irreparable injury required for injunctive relief.[283] Among its criticisms, the Ninth Circuit said that the district court failed to weigh in the balance the interests of the government and of the public in ensuring the proper enforcement of the MMPA through use of observers on tuna boats.[284] Additionally, the court pointed out that the government and the public had a strong interest in promoting non-discriminatory, gender-neutral hiring.[285] Finally, the court found that the evidence presented by the NOAA which suggested that the inclusion of female observers on boats was well received in other settings.[286]

Thus, as with the jurisdictional battles with the state of Alaska and the determination of various wildlife groups' standing to sue, the goal of the MMPA, to protect marine wildlife, was preserved through another rather circuitous piece of litigation. Obviously, it is not atypical for the courts to contend with intricate legal issues emerging from Congressional enactments which may have nothing to do with the direction and purpose of the legislation. Yet, for proponents of the MMPA, the benefits and protections offered by the Act tend to wither when periferal battles are tied up in the federal courts.

## INTERNATIONAL STUMBLING BLOCKS

Despite the frustrations of many environmentalists, the United States has been much more responsive to the conservation of marine mammals than several other industrial powers (which also happen to have enormous and highly profitable fishing industries). The U.S. whaling industry has diminished to virtual nonexistence, yet, Japan and the Soviet Union continue to harvest whales and other marine mammals at an alarming rate; a rate which is forbidden within the territorial waters of the United States.[287] Both the Soviets and Japan have experimented with "high tech" whaling and sealing vessels as well as cannons which fire harpoon clusters at groups of dolphins.[288] The Japanese diet is dominated by seafood, and has included porpoise for many centuries. It is therefore more difficult to obtain Japanese cooperation in international fleet fishing regulations which protect marine mammals.

---

282  50 C.F.R. Part 216(f)(2) (1986).
283  See *Carribean Marine Services*, *supra* note 278, at 674.
284  *Id.* at 675.
285  *Id.*
286  *Id.* at 672.
287  Levin, *supra* note 243 at 569.
288  1972 Senate Hearings, *supra* note 239, at 366-67.

Additionally, it has been difficult to obtain the cooperation of the United States Supreme Court in following Congress' lead calling for the issuance of sanctions against foreign nations which exceed quotas on marine mammal killing set by the International Convention for the Regulation of Whaling (the Convention).[289]   In 1971, the Pelly Amendment called for economic sanctions against foreign nations issued at the *discretion* of the President provided that the Secretary of Commerce could demonstrate that the  offending nation threatened the effectiveness of an international conservation program.[290]   In 1979, the Packwood Amendment put more teeth into the conservation effort by removing discretion from the President and *mandating* that the President impose sanctions against offending nations.[291]

In 1981, Japan began to exceed quotas set by the Convention.[292]   The Secretary of Commerce recognized the United States could impose sanctions on Japan pursuant to the Pelly and Packwood amendments. However, instead of offering the President proof of the diminished effectiveness of the goals of the Convention, the United States negotiated the issue with Japan.[293]   An agreement emerged from these negotiations whereby Japan promised to limit its harvests and to cease commercial whaling by 1988.[294]   In response to this agreement, several environmental groups filed for a writ of mandamus against the Secretary to follow through with its mandate to inform the President of his non-discretionary duty under the Packwood Amendment to impose economic sanctions against Japan.[295]   Both the district court and the District of Columbia Circuit approved of the writ and ordered the Secretary to act.[296]

However, in a five to four decision, the Supreme Court reversed the appellate decision claiming that legislative history showed the Secretary's actions to be appropriate.[297]

## CONCLUSION

It is clear that the most effective marine mammal protection is going to be achieved through international cooperation and mutuality of enforcement.   The MMPA has been made more effective by its amendments, yet, has not overcome obstacles of enforcement, jurisdiction, and standing to sue under the Act without the heavy involvement of the federal courts.

---

[289]   62 Stat. 1716, TIAS No. 1849.
[290]   22 U.S.C. § 1918.
[291]   16 U.S.C. § 1821(e)(2).
[292]   Japan Whaling Ass'n v. American Cetacean Soc., 478 U.S. 221 (1986).
[293]   *Id.*
[294]   *Id.*
[295]   *Id.*
[296]   American Cetacean Soc. v. Japan Whaling Ass'n., 604 F. Supp. 1398; *see* 768 F. 2d 426.
[297]   478 U.S. at 221.

# PROTECTION OF WILDLIFE

Though it is not unusual to have the courts fine tune discrepancies in the language and meaning of Congressional Acts, it is unfortunate that courtroom litigation often loses touch with the flavor of the original legislation. In the case of the MMPA, Congress articulated its true purpose for passing the law by stating:

> [M]arine mammals have proven themselves to be resources of great international significance, aesthetic and recreational as well as economic, and it is the sense of the Congress that they should be protected and encouraged to develop to the greatest extent feasible commensurate with sound policies of resource management and that the primary objective of their management should be to maintain the health and stability of the marine ecosystem.[298]

Essential to the protection of marine mammals is a court's willingness to weigh this Congressional purpose in the balance when making decisions arising out of the conservation and protection provisions of the MMPA. The aforementioned cases indicate that, by and large, courts have expanded the "rights" of sea mammals by hurdling ancillary issues arising out of MMPA enforcement such as allowing female observers on tuna boats. Also, by granting environmental protection organizations standing to sue under the Act, the courts have given the federal government a longer arm of enforcement through use of information generated by these watchdogs.

However, divided cooperation from other nations in the enforcement of basic marine mammal conservation principles is still a looming problem. Since whales, among other creatures, migrate globally, the only true solution to marine mammal stock depletion is through worldwide enforcement measures.

## MIGRATORY BIRDS

Until 1918 the Lacey Act of 1900 was the only federal statute which attempted to reach the exploitation of wildlife on federal lands. Under the Lacey Act transportation across the state lines of carcasses of animals killed illegally was a federal crime. In 1913 Congress passed a statute which declared that birds were within the custody and protection of the United States and that it was unlawful to shoot them except in accordance with regulations to be promulgated by the Secretary of Agriculture.[299] The statute was declared to be unconstitutional by two federal circuit courts.[300] The United States government appealed these decisions but the Supreme Court never actually decided the constitu-

---

298  16 U.S.C. § 1361(6).
299  37 Stat. 847.
300  United States v. Shauver, 214 F. 154 (1914); United States v. McCullough, 221 F. 288 (1915).

293

tionality of the act.  In 1916 the federal government decided that the best way around contesting this statute was to invoke the treaty power by negotiating a treaty with Great Britain on behalf of Canada for the protection of birds migrating between the two countries.

In 1918 the President signed into law the congressional act known as the Migratory Bird Treaty Act[301] and the Supreme Court upheld the constitutionality of the new act in the landmark decision *Missouri v. Holland*.[302]

The treaty entered into with Canada in 1916 was joined by treaties with Mexico in 1936, Japan in 1972, and Russia in 1976.  The four treaties are incorporated into the act under a section which makes it unlawful to take, kill or possess migratory birds in violation of these specific conventions.[303]

The main purpose of the various conventions involving migratory birds was the protection of the birds by saving them from indiscriminate slaughter and the insuring of the preservation of such migratory birds. The primary means recognized in the conventions was the use of closed seasons to preserve migratory birds, in which no hunting would be lawful except for scientific or propagating purposes and under issued permits.

Each of the conventions added a concept of how migratory birds could be protected.  In addition to the closed season method identified under the Canadian treaty, the protection of migratory birds by families under the Mexican treaty, the protection of migratory birds in danger of extinction under the Japanese treaty, and the protection of nesting colonies of migratory birds and the environment of such birds under the Russian treaty were recognized.

It is interesting to note that all the Conventions entered into between the United States and the other countries and the Migratory Bird Treaty Act recognize that birds constitute a natural resource of great value for not only aesthetic and scientific purposes but also for recreation and economic purposes.  While it is true that the Conventions usually use such words as "taking measures for the management and protection and prevention of extinction of certain birds," nevertheless there is a balancing concept which is focused upon in the United States Treaty Act and its enforcing regulations.  This balancing is the preservation of the bird populations and the preservation of recreation and economic values.

---

[301]  16 U.S.C.A § 703 et seq.
[302]  252 U.S. 416 (1920).
[303]  16 U.S.C.A. § 703.

# PROTECTION OF WILDLIFE

In the later treaties there was a recognition that migratory bird habitat was an important value and efforts should be made by the treaty contracting parties to protect this migratory bird environment.[304]  An explanation for this approach can be found in a reference to American history with respect to wildlife treatment.  The early settlers shot game (including birds) for food staples and to control predators for the safety of themselves and other animals.  In defense of exploitation in American history there was the concept that wildlife resources were infinite. While this concept was eventually put to rest with the disappearance of such species as the bison and game fowl, the answer seemed to lie not in  completely protecting wildlife, including migratory birds, but in regulating the taking and killing of them so as to preserve their value for recreational and economical purposes.

Under the Migratory Bird Treaty Act, Congress has included in its charge to the Department of the Interior an obligation to preserve, distribute, introduce, and restore game birds and other wild birds.[305]

In order to accomplish this purpose the act vests the authority and power for the implementation of the Act in the Department of the Interior.  The Secretary of the Interior is authorized to adopt such measures as may be necessary to carry out the purposes of the act and in addition to purchase such game birds and other wild birds as may be required. In carrying out these duties the Secretary of the Interior is obligated to recognize, as an object of the act, the restoration of birds in those parts of the United States adapted thereto where these birds have become scarce or extinct and to regulate the introduction of American or foreign birds or animals into localities where they have not heretofore existed.[306]

The Secretary of the Interior is authorized to make and publish regulations for carrying out the purposes of the act.[307]

For purposes of propagation, the Secretary of the Interior is authorized to import eggs of game birds, and, is authorized to prescribe any necessary rules and regulations governing the importation of the eggs of such birds for these purposes.[308]

The chief provision of the Act relates to the taking, killing, or possessing of migratory birds.  The act provides that unless and  except as permitted by regulations "it shall be unlawful any time by any means or in any manner to pursue, hunt, take, capture, kill, attempt to take, capture,

---

[304]   See the Japanese and Russian Migratory Bird Treaties.
[305]   16 U.S.C.A. § 701.
[306]   *Id.*
[307]   The Regulations are published in 50 C.F.R. Parts 20 and 21.
[308]   16 U.S.C.A. § 702.

or kill, possess, offer for sale, sell, offer to barter, barter, offer to purchase, purchase, deliver for shipment, ship, export, import, caused to be shipped, exported, or imported, deliver for transportation, transport, or cause to be transported, carry or cause to be carried or receive for shipment, transportation, carriage, export any migratory bird, any part, nest, or egg of any such bird or any product whether or not manufactured which consists, or is composed in whole or part, of any such bird or any part, nest, or egg thereof included in the terms of the Conventions between the United States and Great Britain, the United States and the United Mexican States, and the government of Japan for protection of migratory birds and birds endangered of extinction and their environment."[309]  This section was amended in 1989 to include the convention between the United States and the Union of Soviet Socialists Republic for the conservation of migratory birds and their environment.[310]

The fundamental purpose of the section of the act making it unlawful to hunt or kill except as permitted by regulation, is to protect migratory birds from destruction in an unequal contest between hunter and bird.[311]  This thought may not have been expressed very clearly in any of the conventions entered into between the United States and other countries, but Congress intended to invoke its own powers to accomplish other purposes related to the protection of migratory birds then those required by any of the treaties.[312]

The power vested in the Secretary of the Interior to prohibit the hunting of migratory birds is not confined to those lands to which the federal government has title.[313]

The question of whether or not the Migratory Bird Treaty Act applies to Indian rights to hunt all kinds of birds at any time and in any manner on Indian reservation has arisen in a case in which under a treaty the Shoshone Indians reserved such a right.[314]  Generally Indians enjoy exclusive treaty rights to hunt and fish on lands reserved to them unless such rights are clearly relinquished by a treaty or have been modified by Congress.[315]

The regulations promulgated by the Secretary of the Interior for the implementation of the Migratory Bird Treaty Act provide guidelines for taking, possession, transportation, exportation, importation, and permits.[316]

---

309  16 U.S.C.A. § 703.
310  Pub. L. No. 101-233, 103 Stat. 1977.
311  U.S. v. Olson, 41 F. Supp. 433.
312  Cerritos Gun Club v. Hall, 96 F.2d 620.
313  Bailey v. Holland, 126 F.2d 317.
314  United States v. Cutler, 37 F. Supp 724.
315  United States v. Dion, 476 U.S. 734.
316  50 C.F.R. Part 20.1 et seq.

The regulations apply only to migratory game birds and crows. The regulations preempt any state regulation or statute insofar as they apply to any person who may be acting correctly under state law but in violation of federal law, but they are not intended to preclude states from making and enforcing laws or regulations not inconsistent with the regulations or any convention between the United States and any foreign country.[317]

The regulations define migratory game birds to mean "those migratory birds included in the terms of conventions between the United States and any foreign country for the protection of migratory birds, for which open seasons are prescribed in this part of the regulations and belong to the following families: (1) Anatidae (ducks, geese and swans); (2) Columbidae (doves and pigeons); (3) Gruidae (cranes); (4) Rallidae (rails, coots and gallinules); (5) Scolopacidae (woodcock and snipe).[318]

There had been some confusion as to whether or not the Migratory Bird Treaty Act applied to captive-reared birds. The regulations provide the answer by defining a migratory bird to mean "any bird whatever its origin and whether or not raised in captivity which belongs to a species which is contained in a list of migratory birds in the regulations.[319] In *United States v. Richards*[320] the court held that from a practical standpoint enforcement of the act would be difficult if the defense was available that the bird involved was raised in captivity. The court reasoned that problems relating to captive birds require their inclusion within the definition of migratory birds.

Birds which are migratory only in certain parts of the country are also included. This is true even though some individuals or families do not migrate at all in a particular part of the country. The treaty with Great Britain regulating the hunting and killing of migratory birds provided that it should cover birds including doves and wild pigeons. Therefore these birds which are migratory in some parts of the country are within the scope of the act.[321]

An important part of the regulations relates to hunting methods. The regulations state that migratory birds in which open seasons are prescribed may be taken by any method except those prohibited by the act. The regulations then go on to provide that persons may not take migratory game birds by any of the following methods: (a) trap, snare, net, rifle, pistol, swivel gun, shotgun larger than 10 gauge, machine gun, fish hook, poison, drug, explosive, or stupefying substance; (b) shotgun

---

317  50 C.F.R. Part 20.2.
318  50 C.F.R. Part 20.11.
319  50 C.F.R. Part 10.12.
320  583 F.2d 491.
321  United States v. Lumkin, 276 F. 580.

of any description capable of holding more than three shells; (c) the aid or use of a sink box or other type of low floating device having a depression affording the hunter a means of concealing himself beneath the surface of the water; (d) by aid or use of any motor vehicle, motor driven land conveyance or road craft of any kind; (e) trauma by means of any motor boat or any other craft having a motor attached or any sailboat unless the motor has been completely shut off; (f) by the use or aid of live birds as decoys (this even include the use of tame or captive live ducks or geese as decoys); (g) by the use or aid of recorded or electrically amplified bird calls or sounds or recorded or electrically amplified imitations of bird calls or sounds; (h) by aid of any motor driven land, water or air conveyance or any sailboat used for the purpose of or resulting in the concentrating, driving, rallying or stirring up of any migratory birds; (i) by the aid of baiting on or over any baited area; (j) while possessing shot either in shot shells or as loose shot for muzzle loading other than steel shot or such shot approved as non-toxic by the Director pursuant to the procedure set forth in the regulations (this restriction applies only to the taking of ducks, geese, swans, coots.[322]

The prohibition against baiting involves some interesting situations. Baiting in the regulations is defined to mean "the placing, exposing, depositing, distributing, or scattering of shelled, shucked or unshucked corn, wheat or other grain, salt or other feeds so as to constitute for such birds a lure, attraction or enticement to, on, or over any areas where hunters are attempting to take them. The baited area means any area where shelled, shucked or unshucked corn or other grain, salt or other feed whatsoever capable of luring, attracting, or enticing such birds is directly or indirectly placed, exposed, deposited, distributed or scattered and such areas shall remain a baited area for ten days following the complete removal of all such corn, wheat or other grain, salt or other feed."[323]

In one case involving the concept of baiting, a defendant was convicted under the Act for violating the baiting provision by baiting a particular area before the season had opened to keep the birds there to be shot at after the season opened and by directly placing grain in front of blinds during the season. These acts were determined to be luring which is prohibited under the Act.[324]

In another case a defendant was convicted for violating the Act where he was a landowner and he baited an area on his land some 3700 feet from the area on his property where he was hunting and where it was shown that the baited food was the nearest source of food for the birds resting on his property.[325]

---

322 50 C.F.R. Part 20.21.
323 50 C.F.R. Part 20.21(i).
324 Cerritos Gun Club v. Hall, 96 F.2d 620.

There are some exceptions included under the prohibition against baiting section of the regulations which are important. As an example the regulations provide that the taking of all migratory game birds including waterfowl on or over standing crops, flooded standing crops, (including aquatics), flooded harvested croplands, grain crops, properly shocked on the field where grown or grains found scattered solely as a result of normal agricultural planning or harvesting is not a violation of the Act.[326]

In an interesting case, a fish and wildlife service agent who apparently told a defendant charged with a violation of the Act, that modified livestock feeding operations were exempt from baiting regulations and then proceeded to determine that the corn scattered in the field constituted baiting. As a result of the corn scattered in the field Canadian Geese were killed and wounded. The court held that the defendant in his actions indicated a clear predisposition to violate the baiting regulation, and that the action of the agent was not entrapment.[327]

In one section the regulations provide that it is a violation of the Act and the regulations to take any migratory game during the closed season. Generally "closed season" means at any time unless regulatory schedules are established for seasons with appropriate description of daily bag and possession limits, and shooting hours.[328]

The same prohibition against daily limits and shooting hours are contained in the regulations.[329]

The development of the regulatory schedules, which would permit shooting, involves data gathering programs to determine migratory game bird population status and trends, evaluations of habitat conditions, harvest information and certain other factors having a bearing on the anticipated size of the fall flights of these birds. As a general rule hunting schedules are announced early in the spring and sometime modified based on public comment or on the updating of relevant information. Public hearings are held for the purpose of providing additional opportunities for public participation in the scheduling of regulations.[330]

The regulations provide for different hunting seasons for different kinds of migratory birds and for different parts of the country. As a practical matter the schedules and any limitations on hunting are broken down by areas of the country known as flyways. There are four

---

325  Yandell v. U.S., 712 F.2d 218.
326  50 C.F.R. Part 20.21(i)(1), (2).
327  United States v. Manning, 787 F.2d 431.
328  50 C.F.R. Parts 20.22, 20.100.
329  50 C.F.R. Parts 20.23-.24.
330  50 C.F.R. Part 20.100.

flyways - the Atlantic Flyway, the Mississippi Flyway, the Central Flyway, and the Pacific Flyway. The regulations contain descriptions of the states and areas within the states that are contained in each flyway and the kinds of migratory birds that can be hunted, the seasons in which they can be hunted, and bag limits.[331]

One of the regulations provides not only for a prohibition against the taking of migratory birds in violation of the regulations but also prohibits a person from killing or crippling any migratory bird without making a reasonable effort to retrieve the bird and retain it in actual custody at a place where taken or between that place and either his automobile or principal means of land transportation or his personal abode or temporary or transit place of lodging or a migratory bird preservation facility, post office, or common carrier facility.[332]

One of the prohibitions of the Act is the possession of any migratory game bird or part of a game bird in violation of the Act and regulations. The prohibition against possession applies to any freshly killed migratory game birds during the closed season, any quantity in excess of the possession limit, any quantity in excess of the daily bag limit.[333]

The regulations also provide for the tagging of migratory birds. These apply to the transfer of a migratory bird from one person to another person for the purpose of picking, cleaning, processing, shipping, transportation, or storage or for the purpose of having taxidermy services performed unless the bird has a tag attached by the hunter stating his address, and the total number of species of the birds and the dates such birds were killed. The keeping of birds in a vehicle as the personal baggage of the possessor is not to be considered in storage or temporary storage and does not require a tag.[334]

The regulations also contain prohibitions against the transportation within the United States of any migratory game bird or part of a game bird which is taken in violation of the Act or regulations. This applies not only to game birds taken by the person who is transporting them but also game birds belonging to another person.[335]

There are also prohibitions against the exportation or importation of migratory birds which are taken in violation of the Act or the regulations. However there are permissible importations and exportations provided for under the regulations. Generally the permission to import or export depends upon the appropriate identification of the importer

---

331  50 C.F.R. Parts 20.100-.107.
332  50 C.F.R. Part 20.25.
333  50 C.F.R. Parts 20.31-.35.
334  50 C.F.R. Part 20.36.
335  50 C.F.R. Parts 20.41-.44.

or the exporter on the package or container which contains the bird or parts of the birds.[336]

There is a built-in exception to having in possession migratory game birds or parts of game birds in violation of the Act. This exception allows any person to possess, purchase, sell, barter or transport for the making of fishing flys, bed pillows, and mattresses, or for similar commercial uses, the feathers of migratory waterfowl killed by hunting pursuant to the regulations or seized and condemned by federal or state game authorities. This permission does not extend to a person who sells or offers to purchase feathers and skins for millinery or ornamental use or for the sale or purchase of mounted specimens of migratory game birds taken under the authority of the Act and regulations.[337]

An important provision of the regulation relates to subsistence hunting by Alaska Eskimos and Indians. The regulations provide that Alaskan Eskimos and the Indians may take, possess and transport in any manner and at any time auks, auklets, guillemots, murres, and puffins and their eggs for food and their skins for clothing, but the birds and eggs so taken may not be sold or offered for sale. In Alaska any person may for subsistence purposes take, possess, and transport in any manner and at any time snowy owls and cormorants and their eggs for food and their skins for clothing but the birds and eggs so taken may not be offered for sale.[338]

A special section of the regulations apply to crows. Generally, crows may be taken, possessed, transported, etc. only in accordance with such laws or regulations as may be prescribed by a state provided that this state regulation is in conformity with the regulations in the Migratory Bird Treaty Act. The Act allows the states to provide regulations, however, state regulations may not permit (1) the hunting of crows from aircraft; (2) a hunting season for crows in excess of 124 days during a calendar year, a hunting season during the peak crow nesting period within the state, and the taking of crows by any means other then by firearms, bow and arrow, and falconry.[339]

An extremely important part of the regulations are the sections dealing with non-toxic shot requirements. The Fish and Wildlife Service has determined that it is necessary to protect migratory birds and other wildlife from injury through the use of toxic shots in permitted hunting.

The definition of non-toxic shot is "any shot type that does not cause sickness or death when ingested by migratory birds."[340] The definition of non-toxic shot under current regulations includes only steel shot.

---

336  50 C.F.R. Parts 20.51-.66.
337  50 C.F.R. Part 20.91.
338  50 C.F.R. Part 20.132.
339  50 C.F.R. Part 20.133.

# WILDLIFE AND HABITAT

The regulations establish for the United States during 1977-1978 and subsequent hunting seasons the so called "non-toxic shot zone." The non-toxic shot zones mean all land and water areas within the boundaries of the United States where the use of non-toxic shot is required for waterfowl hunting. This zone can be all or part of a county designated and established for non-toxic shot use.[341]

The regulations make it clear that the prohibition against using toxic shot applies to all persons engaged in waterfowl hunting. Waterfowl is defined under the Act to mean ducks, geese, swans, and coots.[342]

When they first addressed the issue of non-toxic shot, the regulations established a schedule for monitoring and/or converting counties to non-toxic shot zones for hunting waterfowl. The areas in which waterfowl harvest is the greatest were required to implement non-toxic shot zones earlier than those areas in which the harvest was smaller. Beginning with the 1991-92 season non-toxic shot would be required under the regulations in all waterfowl hunting areas in the United States.[343]

The regulations provide that the Director of the U.S. Fish & Wildlife Service is to determine, after a review of supporting data whether there are other kinds of shot which may be acceptable as non-toxic shot in addition to the steel shot. The regulations provide for a detailed procedure for such a determination.[344]

The regulations provide for special procedures for issuance of annual hunting regulations. These regulations cover the establishment of seasons, bag limits, and other requirements for the seasonal hunting of migratory birds. In order to establish these regulations each flyway establishes a council which holds meetings to arrange these regulations. These regulations often vary within flyways and frequently by time periods.[345]

In addition to the flyway councils there is a "Regulation Committee" of the Fish & Wildlife Service which holds meetings to consider regulations for the hunting of migratory birds.[346]

The meeting of the flyway councils and the Regulations Committee are open to the public and notices which state the time, place and general subjects of the meeting are required to be published in the Federal Register.[347]

---

340  50 C.F.R. Part 20.134.
341  50 C.F.R. Part 20.141.
342  *Id.*
343  50 C.F.R. Part 20.143.
344  50 C.F.R. Part 20.134.
345  *Id.*
346  50 C.F.R. Part 20.153.
347  *Id.*

# PROTECTION OF WILDLIFE

The United States Fish & Wildlife Service of the Department of the Interior has published regulations which provide uniform rules and procedures for the application, issuance, renewal, conditions, revocation, and general administration of any permit issuable pursuant to either statutes or regulations involving the hunting of any wildlife.[348]

The service has published additional regulations for the issuance of permits which relate to the hunting of migratory birds, which are supplemental to the general permit requirements published under separate regulations.[349]

These special regulations cover migratory birds, their parts, nest, or eggs.[350]

The regulations provide that anyone who intends to import, export, purchase, sell, barter, or offer for purchase, sale, or barter must have a permit in order to engage in this kind of activity. An exception is contained in the regulations for any lawfully acquired migratory bird or part prior to the federal date of the Migratory Bird Treaty Act.[351]

The regulations establish that no person may take, possess, transport, etc., any migratory bird or part, etc., except as may be permitted under the terms of a valid permit issued pursuant to the regulations established by the United States Fish & Wildlife Service of the Department of the Interior.[352]

The regulations do provide some exceptions which include employees of the Department of the Interior who are authorized to enforce the provisions of the Migratory Bird Treaty Act, state game departments; municipal game farms or parks; public museums, public zoological parks and accredited institutional members of American Association of Zoological Parks and Aquariums; and other public scientific or education institutions who acquire migratory birds or their parts for educational and scientific purposes.[353]

An additional exception is provided for in regulations for captive-reared and properly marked mallard ducks, alive or dead or their eggs.[354] Implied in this exception is the definition of captivity which means that a live raptor is held in a controlled environment and is intentionally manipulated by man for the purpose of producing raptors or selected species and that has boundaries designed to prevent the

---

348  50 C.F.R. Parts 13.1-.51.
349  50 C.F.R. Parts 20.11-.46.
350  50 C.F.R. Part 21.2.
351  50 C.F.R. Part 21.11.
352  50 C.F.R. Part 21.2(a).
353  50 C.F.R. Part 21.12.
354  50 C.F.R. Part 21.13.

raptor's eggs or the gametes of the selected species from entering or leaving the controlled environment.[355]

The permit exception for captive-reared mallard ducks has certain conditions and restrictions connected with the utilization of the exception. Generally speaking the exception in the case of captive-reared mallard ducks requires that the ducks or their eggs may not be taken from the wild, they must be physically marked (removal of the hind toe from the right foot, pinioning of a wing, or banding of one metatarsus with a seamless metal ban or tattooing of a readily discernable number or letter or combination on the web of one foot).[356]

The exception for captive-reared mallard ducks under the regulations permit the killing of the birds (except by shooting) and the transportation and storage of the birds.

This exception is often used by persons who operate game farms or shooting preserves under a state license and this exception is permitted under the regulations provided that the number of the state license or permit or authorization has been legally stamped in ink on the back of each carcass and on the container in which each carcass is maintained.[357]

In addition to captive-reared mallard ducks, the regulations also provide permit exceptions for captive-reared migratory waterfowl other than mallard ducks. The migratory waterfowl covered under these regulations must also be properly marked and in addition such birds alive or dead or their eggs may be lawfully acquired only from holders of a valid waterfowl sale and disposal permit (unless lawfully acquired outside of the United States).[358]

Import and export permits are also required under the regulations. Generally an import permit is required before any migratory birds, their nests, their parts, or eggs may be imported.[359]

An export permit is also required before migratory birds, their parts, nests or eggs may be exported (an exception is provided with respect to mallard ducks that are to be exported to Canada or Mexico).

Applications for permits to import or export migratory birds must be submitted to an appropriate U.S. Fish & Wildlife Service issuing office

---

[355] 50 C.F.R. Part 21.3.
[356] 50 C.F.R. Part 20.13.
[357] *Id.* The migratory bird hunting stamp (duck stamp requirement) does not apply to shooting preserve operations or to modified dog training or field trial operations which also are permitted under the regulations.
[358] 50 C.F.R. Part 20.14.
[359] 50 C.F.R. Parts 20.61-.66.

and must contain identification information as well as data concerning the species and numbers of the migratory birds to be imported or exported and the purpose for the importation or the exportation.[360]

An additional permit condition is that the banding of migratory, bird where required must be done by  official and numbered leg bands issued by the Service.  Any other band, clip, or system of marking is prohibited unless it is specially authorized in the permit.[361]  These banding or marking permits are valid for a period of two years from the date of the issue (unless otherwise stated on the face of the permit).

Before any person may collect migratory birds or their parts for scientific purposes, that person must obtain a scientific collecting permit. The permit can only be obtained by conforming to the application procedure provided for in the regulations and lasts from the date of issue through the 31st day of December of the second full calendar year following the year of issuance (unless a different period of time is prescribed on the permit).[362]

Permits are required before any person may perform taxidermy services on migratory birds or their parts, nests, or eggs.  These taxidermy permits must be applied for from a special agent in charge as provided for in the regulations and are valid from the date of issue through the 31st day of December of the second full calendar year following the year of issue.[363]

Before any person can lawfully sell, trade, donate, or otherwise dispose of any species of captive-reared and properly marked migratory waterfowl or their eggs, that person must have a waterfowl sale and disposal permit.  As in other cases for special permits, this permit must be obtained from a special agent and must be applied for according to specifications provided in the Act.[364]  This permit also is valid from the date of issue through the 31st day of December, the second full calendar year following the year of issue.[365]

The regulations also provide for the issuance of special purpose permits for migratory bird activities outside the scope of the standard form permits provided for in other parts of the regulations.[366]  In order to obtain such a permit the applicant must abide by special procedures contained in the regulations, must submit a detailed statement in these applications describing the project or activity which requires the issuance of such a permit, and a statement specifying the numbers and species of

---

360  50 C.F.R. Part 21.22.
361  50 C.F.R. Part 21.22(c)(1).
362  50 C.F.R. Part 21.23.
363  50 C.F.R. Part 21.24.
364  50 C.F.R. Part 21.25.
365  *Id.*
366  50 C.F.R. Part 21.27.

migratory birds involved and what disposition would be made of the migratory birds.[367]

Regulations provide for federal standards that are applicable to falconry permits. The standards attempt to protect the wild population of raptors and attempts to do so with state cooperation. One of the regulations provides that state laws or regulations must provide certified raptor housing facilities. The test for an adequate facility is one that protects the raptors from environmental predators or undue disturbance. Outdoor facilities must be fenced and covered with a netting or a wire or roof to protect the birds from the disturbance and attack by predators and the area enclosed must be large enough to insure that the birds cannot strike the fence when flying from the perch.[368]

Indoor facilities must also be large enough to allow easy access for the caring of the raptor's housing facility. If more than one raptor is to be kept, the raptor must be tethered or separated by partitions and each area for each bird must be large enough to allow the bird to fully extend its wings.[369]

In addition to the facility itself, state laws or regulations must provide for appropriate equipment. The federal standards require the equipment to include jesses, leashes, and swivels, bath container, outdoor perches, and weighing devices.[370]

The regulations also provide for a marking procedure. Any Peregrine Falcon, Gyrfalcon or Harris Hawk (except a captive-bred raptor lawfully marked by a numbered seamless or seamless band issued by the Service) must be banded with a permanent non-reusable numbered bank issued by the United Stated Fish & Wildlife Service.

The federal regulations also require state laws and/or regulations to provide for certain restrictions on the taking of raptors from the wild. One of the more important federal standards restricts the taking of raptors, over one year old, to American Kestrels and Great Horned Owls (except that any raptor other than endangered or threatened species may be taken under a depredation or special purpose permit).[371]

The federal regulations provide for a system of control of depredating birds. However a permit is required before any person may take, possess or transport migratory birds for depredation and control purposes. The general purpose underlying this section is to provide for the protection from migratory birds of serious damage to agriculture, horticul-

---

367  *Id.*
368  50 C.F.R. Parts 21.21, .28.
369  *Id.*
370  *Id.*
371  *Id.*

ture, and fish culture interests. The permit is issued by the department upon the receipt of evidence clearly showing that migratory game birds have accumulated in such numbers and in particular areas to cause or are about to cause serious damage.[372]

A federal permit is not required to control yellow-headed red-winged, bi-colored red-winged, tri-colored red-winged rustys and brewer's blackbirds, cowbirds, grackles, crows, and magpies, when found committing or about to commit depredation upon ornamental or shade trees, agriculture crops, livestock, or wildlife, or when concentrated in such numbers and manner as to constitute a health hazard or other nuisance.[373]

Another exception to the requirement of a permit in order to control depredation, is a regulation which states that in any county in California in which meadowlarks, horned larks, golden crowned, white crowned, and other crowned sparrows, goldfinches, house finches, acorn woodpeckers, Lewis Woodpeckers, and Flickers are under extraordinary conditions seriously injurious to agriculture and other interests, the Commissioner of Agriculture may without a permit kill or caused to be killed under his general supervision such of these migratory birds as may be necessary to safeguard any agriculture or horticulture crop in the county.[374]

Another specific exception to the requirement of the permit for depredation purposes is a regulation that permits landowners, sharecroppers, tenants, or their employees or agents actually engaged in the production of rice in Louisiana to shot purple gallinules (ionornis martinica) when found committing or about to commit serious depredations to growing rice crops on the premises owned or occupied by these persons.[375]

Landowners, sharecroppers, tenants, or their employees or agents actually engaged in the production of nut crops in Washington and Oregon may also take Scrub Jays without a permit and Stellers Jays when found committing or about to commit serious depredations to nut crops on the premises owned or occupied by these persons.[376]

The Migratory Bird Act contains penalty and forfeiture provisions. The Act provides that whoever in violation of the Act knowingly takes by any manner whatsoever any migratory bird with the intent to sell, offer to sell, barter, or offer to barter such bird or does in fact sell, offer for sale, barter, or offer to barter any migratory bird is guilty of a felony

372  50 C.F.R. Part 21.41.
373  50 C.F.R. Part 21.43.
374  50 C.F.R. Part 21.44.
375  50 C.F.R. Part 21.45.
376  50 C.F.R. Part 21.46.

and can be fined not more than $2,000 or imprisoned for not more than two years or both.[377]

In addition to the penalties the Act also provides for forfeitures. Generally any gun, trap, net or other equipment, vessel, vehicle and any other means of transportation used by any person when engaged in violating the provisions of the Act may be seized and held pending the prosecution of the person arrested for violating the Act and upon conviction for such violation of the act, forfeiture shall be adjudicated as a penalty in addition to any other penalty provided by the Act.[378]

The Migratory Bird Treaty Act was amended in 1960 to add felony penalties for taking a migratory bird with intent to sell or offering to sell or selling a migratory bird. The amendment did not require scienter or that a person knowingly committed this act. In the *United States v. Wulff*[379] the Sixth Circuit Court of Appeals upheld a western district of Michigan decision that the penalty provision of the Migratory Bird Treaty Act was unconstitutional because it did not require knowledge.

In response to this decision Congress in 1986 once again amended the penalty provision of the Migratory Bird Treaty Act to require knowledge on the part of the defendant before he can be held to have violated the penalty provisions of the Act. This amendment requires proof that the defendant knew that his actions constituted a taking, sale, barter, or offer to sell or barter as the case may be and that the item so taken sold or bartered was a bird or portion thereof. It was not intended that proof be required that the defendant knew the taking, sale, barter, or offer was a violation of the Act. Nor that he knew the particular bird was listed in the various international treaties implemented by the Act.[380]

The penalty and violation provisions of the Act also provide for a misdemeanor violation for any person or entity who fails to comply with the regulations made pursuant to the Act. This misdemeanor is a fine of not more than $500, imprisonment for not more than six months or both. This misdemeanor provision of the Act was not amended in 1986 and remains as originally passed. In effect this misdemeanor penalty for violation of the Act constitutes strict liability without proof of any knowledge.[381]

The Act provides that employees of the Department of the Interior authorized by the Secretary of the Interior may enforce the provisions of the Act. Such enforcement includes the power to arrest any person committing a violation of the Act in the presence or view of the author-

---

377  16 U.S.C.A. §§ 707(a)-(b).
378  16 U.S.C.A. § 707 (c).
379  758 F.2d 1121.
380  16 U.S.C.A. § 707(b).
381  16 U.S.C.A. § 707(a).

ized employee and authorize the United States district courts and the United States magistrates to issue warrants in any case justified by the facts indicating a violation of the Act or a potential violation of the Act.[382]

The Act does not prevent states from making or enforcing laws or regulations which are not inconsistent with the provision of the Migratory Bird Treaties or the Migratory Bird Treaty Act.[383]

A sub-chapter of the Migratory Bird Treaty Act is known as the "Migratory Bird Conservation Act." [384]

This sub-chapter establishes the Migratory Bird Conservation Commission which consists of the Secretary of the Interior as Chairman, the administrator of the Environmental Protection Agency, Secretary of Agriculture, two members of the Senate to be selected by the President of the Senate and two members of the House of Representatives to be selected by the speaker. The Commission is created and is authorized to consider and pass upon any area of land, water, or land and water that may be recommended by the Secretary of the Interior for purchase or rental under this sub-chapter and to fix the price or prices at which such area may be purchased or rented.[385] The Secretary of the Interior may purchase or rent areas or interests in the areas which have been approved for purchase or rental by the Commission at the price or the prices fixed by the Commission, and in addition, may acquire by gift or devise any area or interest in these areas.[386]

In order to carry out his responsibilities the Secretary of the Interior is authorized to make all expenditures necessary to secure a safe title to the United States and in acquiring new title or an interest in the lands, may make and grant such easements and reservations which in the opinion of the Secretary will not encumber the areas acquired under the Act.[387] In acquiring any interest in land or water the Secretary of the Interior must obtain the consent of the state in which the area lies.[388]

The area of land, water or interest therein either acquired or reserved under this section of the Act is to be administered by the Secretary of the Interior under rules and regulations prescribed by him to conserve and protect migratory birds in accordance with any treaty obligations and in accordance with sound practices which relate to other species of wildlife found upon these lands or waters. In carrying out such duties the Secretary is authorized to manage timber, range, agriculture crops,

---

382  16 U.S.C.A. § 706.
383  16 U.S.C.A. § 708.
384  16 U.S.C.A. § 715 et seq.
385  16 U.S.C.A. § 715a.
386  16 U.S.C.A. § 715d.
387  16 U.S.C.A. § 715e.
388  16 U.S.C.A. § 715f.

species of animals, and to enter into agreements with public and private agencies to accomplish such purposes.[389]

The Act provides that appropriations will be made by Congress to promote the conservation of migratory waterfowl and to offset or prevent the serious loss of important wetlands and other waterfowl habitat essential to the preservation of such waterfowl. The authorization was for $200 million to be appropriated for the period beginning 1961 and ending when all the amounts authorized have been expended.[390]

The appropriations and the funds accruing from such appropriations are deposited in the Migratory Bird Conservation Fund which was created by another sub-chapter of the Act entitled "A Migratory Bird Hunting Stamp Act."[391]

Another sub-chapter of the Migratory Bird Treaty Act is entitled "The Migratory Bird Conservation Act."[392]

The term migratory waterfowl carries the same definition in this section as it does in other sections of the Migratory Bird Treaty Act.

The "Duck Stamp Act" states that no person over the age of 16 years may take any migratory waterfowl unless at the time of such taking he carries on his person an unexpired federal migratory bird hunting and conservation stamp validated by his signature.[393] The stamp so issued must be exhibited by the person purchasing it and at the request of any officer or employee of the Department of the Interior authorized to enforce the sub-chapter. The stamps are to be issued and sold by the postage service and also by the Department of the Interior. Customarily these stamps are sold at first and second class postal offices and many establishments authorized by the Secretary of the Interior to sell them. The funds received from the sale of these stamps are deposited in the Migratory Bird Conservation Fund. The cost of this stamp was calculated to be $10.00 for the years 1987-88, $12.50 for the hunting years 1989-90, and $15.00 for each hunting year thereafter.[394] The term hunting year means the twelve month period beginning on July lst of any year.

The Migratory Bird Conservation Fund is administered by the Secretary of the Interior but the monies are paid into the United States Treasury and are set aside by that organization as a special fund.[395] The funds on deposit may be used by the Secretary of the Interior to reim-

---

389  16 U.S.C.A. § 715i.
390  16 U.S.C.A. § k-3.
391  16 U.S.C.A. § k-5.
392  16 U.S.C.A. § 718 et seq.  This subsection is popularly known as "The Duck Stamp Act."
393  16 U.S.C.A. § 718a.
394  16 U.S.C.A. § 718b.
395  16 U.S.C.A. § 718d.

burse the postal service for the direct expenditures made by that service for engraving, printing, issuing, selling and accounting for migratory bird hunting stamps. In addition the remainder of the funds are available for the location, ascertainment, and acquisitions of suitable areas for migratory bird refuges under the provisions of this Act.[396]

The Secretary of the Interior is authorized to utilize the funds made available under this sub-chapter to acquire, or defray the expense incident to the acquisition of small wetland and pothole areas. These areas are to be known as "waterfowl production areas."[397]

The Act contains sections which specify to offenses of this particular section of the Migratory Bird Treaty Act. The activities which are prohibited include the transfer of a migratory bird hunting stamp to another person by the person acquiring the stamp; the alteration, mutilation, imitation, or counterfeit of any stamp authorized by the Act; or the knowing use of any stamp which is obtained in violation of the provisions of the Act.[398] A 1988 amendment to this section does permit under regulations by the Secretary of the Interior (and the concurrence of the Secretary of the Treasury) the color reproduction or the black and white reproduction of migratory bird hunting stamps. These reproductions are sold and the proceeds from the sale are deposited in the Migratory Bird Conservation Fund.[399]

The enforcement of this section of the Migratory Bird Treaty Act is vested in the United States district courts and magistrates.[400] The Act provides penalties to be assessed by any person who violates any provisions of the Act and these penalties are the same ones as provided for under the main section of the Migratory Bird Treaty Act (misdemeanor and felony penalties).[401]

## NORTH PACIFIC FUR SEALS

From 1957 through 1980 the United States entered into protocols with Canada, Japan, and the Union of Soviet Socialists Republic concerning the North Pacific Fur Seal (Callorhinus Ursinus). In order to implement its participation under the protocol, the Fur Seal Act in 1966 and amended it in 1983.[402]

The protocol established the North Pacific Fur Seal Commission which was authorized to make recommendations. These recommendations would then be binding on the parties to the protocol upon appropriate

396  *Id.*
397  16 U.S.C.A. § 718d (c).
398  16 U.S.C.A. § 718e.
399  *Id.*
400  16 U.S.C.A. § 718f.
401  16 U.S.C.A. § 718g.
402  16 U.S.C.A. § 1151.

respective national actions. Under the North Pacific Fur Seal Act the Secretary of State, with the concurrence of the Secretary of Commerce, is authorized to accept or reject on behalf of the United States, recommendations made by the Commission.[403]

The act empowers the President of the United States to appoint a Commissioner who serves at the pleasure of the President.[404] The President is also authorized to appoint, as advisors to the commissioner, natives from each of the two inhabited Pribilof Islands and any other interested parties.

The primary objective under the protocol is to formulate and coordinate research programs and to make recommendations based on those research programs, to maximize the sustainable productivity of the fur seal resources so that fur seal populations can be brought to and maintained at the levels which would provide the greatest harvest year after year.

In order to help accomplish this purpose, the North Pacific Fur Seals Act prohibits any person or vessel subject to the jurisdiction of the United States, from egaging in the taking of fur seals in the North Pacific Ocean, or on lands or waters under the jurisdiction of the United States, or using any port or harbor or other place to transport, import, offer for sale, possess fur seals or the parts of fur seals, including seal skins contrary to the provisions of the act.[405]

There are several exceptions to the prohibitions contained in the Act. One of these exceptions accrues to the benefit of Indians, Aleuts and Eskimos who dwell on the coast of the North Pacific Ocean who are permitted to take fur seals and dispose of their skins. A provision of this exception makes it mandatory that the seals taken under this exception are for subsistence use.[406]

One additional provision of the act which relates to Indians, Aleuts and Eskimos, requires that the seals taken for subsistence use can be transported only in canoes propelled entirely by oars, paddles, or sails and maned by not more than five persons each.[407]

Another exception under the act is that the Secretary of Commerce can conduct such scientific research and investigations on the fur seal resources of the North Pacific Ocean as he deems necessary to carry out the obligations of the United States under the Protocol. In doing this scientific research and investigation the Secretary of Commerce is

---

403 16 U.S.C.A. § 1158.
404 16 U.S.C.A. § 1157.
405 16 U.S.C.A. § 1152.
406 16 U.S.C.A. § 1153(a).
407 *Id.*

authorized to permit such activity as taking, transportation, importation, exportation, or possession of fur seals or their parts, provided that such activities are for educational, scientific, or exhibition purposes.[408]

The Secretary of Commerce is authorized under the act to prescribe regulations with respect to the taking of furs seals on the Pribilof Islands and on any land subject to the jurisdiction of the United States. In addition the Secretary of Commerce is authorized to enter into agreements with any public or private agency or person for the purpose of carrying out the provisions of the convention including the taking of fur seals on the Pribilof Islands and the curing and marketing of seal skins and other seal parts.[409]

The Act also mandates that the Secretary of Commerce must give preference to the village corporations of St. Paul and St. George Islands in the taking of fur seals on the village corporation's respective islands and the curing and marketing of seals and skins and other seal parts. In carrying out this responsibility the Secretary is authorized to finance these seal harvests and must deposit any proceeds therefrom in a separate fund in the Treasury.[410]

The Secretary of Commerce or the Secretary of the Department in which the Coast Guard is operating are vested with the enforcement authority to carry out the provisions of the act. This authority includes the activities of seizure, arrest, and seizure of vessels or equipment that may used in any activity which is declared unlawful under the act.[411]

Under a special provision of the act, the Secretary of Commerce is granted authority to administer the fur seal rookeries and other federal real and personal property on the Pribilof Islands to insure that activities on such islands are consistent with the purposes of conserving, managing, and protecting the North Pacific Fur Seal and other wildlife designed to be protected under the act.[412]

It is apparent that major provisions of the act relate to the natives of the Pribilof Islands. Parts of the act provide that the state of Alaska is responsible for meeting the educational needs of the citizens of the Pribilof Islands and that the Secretary of Health and Human Resources must provide medical and dental care to the natives of these Pribilof Islands with or without reimbursement.[413]

---

[408] 16 U.S.C.A. § 1154.
[409] 16 U.S.C.A. § 1155(a).
[410] 16 U.S.C.A. § 1155(c).
[411] 16 U.S.C.A. § 1156.
[412] 16 U.S.C.A. § 1151.
[413] 16 U.S.C.A. §§ 1163, 1164.

## WILDLIFE AND HABITAT

The Act provides for the establishment of a Pribilof Islands Trust in order to promote the development of a stable, self-sufficient, enduring and diversified economy not dependent upon sealing. Provisions of the act dictate how the trusts must be administered, funded, and dispensed.[414]

As is typical with enforcement provisions of other Acts, relating to the protection of fish and wildlife, the North Pacific Fur Seal Act provides that any vessel that is employed in any manner in connection with the violation of the provisions of the act, including its tackle, cargo and store, issubject to forfeiture when taken in violation of a provision of the act. In addition enforcement is enhanced by provisions relating to arrests, searches, and seizures, as well as the issuance of writs and other processes.[415]

The Act also contains a section covering penalties. The penalty provides that any person, who knowingly violates any provision of the Act, is subject to a fine of not more than $20,000 for each violation, or imprisonment for not more than one year, or both. In addition a civil penalty of $10,000 for each violation is also possible under the Act.[416]

Separate sections of the act provides for appropriations to fund the Pribilof Islands Trust, the St. Paul Island Trust, and the St. George Trust.[417]

### REGULATION OF WHALING

There are two acts which express the concern of the United States government with the protection of whales. One of these acts is entitled the Whaling Convention Act[418] and the other act is entitled the Whale Conservation and Protection Act.[419]

The second of these acts, the Whale Conservation and Protection Act expresses the concern of Congress for the protection of whales. In passing the act Congress found that (1) whales are a unique resource of great aesthetic and scientific interest to mankind and are a vital part of the marine ecosystem; (2) whales have been over exploited by man for many years, severely reducing several species and endangering others; (3) the United States has extended its authority and responsibility to conserve and protect all marine mammals including whales out to a 200 nautical mile limit by enactment of the Magnuson Fishery Conservation and Management Act (16 U.S.C.A. 1801 et seq.); (4) the conservation and protection of certain species of whales including California Grey,

---

414  16 U.S.C.A. § 1166.
415  16 U.S.C.A. § 1172.
416  16 U.S.C.A. § 1174.
417  16 U.S.C.A. § 1166.
418  16 U.S.C.A. § 916 et seq.
419  16 U.S.C.A. § 917-917d.

Bowhead, Sperm, and Killer Whale, are of particular interest to the citizens of the United States; (5) increased ocean activity of all types may threaten the whale stocks found within the 200 mile jurisdiction of the United States and added protections since stocks may be necessary; (6) there is an inadequate knowledge of the ecology, habitat, requirements, and population level and dynamics of all whales found in waters subject to the jurisdiction of the United States; (7) further studies of such matters is required in order for the United States to carry out its responsibilities for the conservation and protection of marine mammals.[420]

In order to help solve some of the problems identified in the findings, the act provides that the Secretary of Commerce in consultation with the Marine Mammal Commission and the coastal states shall undertake comprehensive studies of all whales found in waters subject to the jurisdiction of the United States including the Fishery Conservation Zone. These studies are taken so as to consider all relevant factors regarding the conservation and protection of the whales, including the distribution, migration patterns, and population dynamics of the mammals, and the effects on all such whales of habitat destruction, disease, pesticides, and other chemicals, disruption of migration patterns and food shortages for the purpose of developing adequate and effective measures including the passing of appropriate laws and the issuing of appropriate regulations to protect such mammals.[421]

A further provision of the 1976 Act mandated the Secretary of Commerce through the Secretary of State to immediately initiate negotiations for the purpose of developing appropriate bilateral agreements with Mexico and Canada.

The other act, the Whaling Convention Act, was passed in order to permit the United States to participate in its obligations under the International Convention for the Regulation of Whaling signed in Washington on December 2, 1946 by the United States and other governments. Under the Whaling Convention Act the President of the United States is to appoint a United States Commissioner (meaning the member of the International Whaling Commission representing the United States under Article 3 of the Convention).[422]

A further provision of the Act permits the Secretary of State with the concurrence of the Secretary of Commerce to present or withdraw any objections on behalf of the United States government to any regulations or amendments to the schedule to the Convention as adopted by the Commission established by that Convention, and submitted to the

---

420  16 U.S.C.A. § 917.
421  16 U.S.C.A. § 917(a).
422  16 U.S.C.A. § 916a.

United States government in accordance with Article 5 of the Convention.[423]

A major section of the Whaling Convention Act is the declaration that it would be unlawful for any person subject to the jurisdiction of the United States to engage in whaling in violation of any provision of the Convention or any regulation of the Commission or for that matter any regulation of the Secretary of Commerce. In addition it is unlawful under the act for any person to ship, transport, purchase, sell, or offer for sale, import, or export, or have in possession, any whale or whale products taken or processed in violation of the Convention or any other appropriate regulation.[424]

The Act does not prohibit whaling in its entirety. The Act permits the Secretary of Commerce has authority to issue licenses or a scientific permit to engage in whaling. The licenses may be obtained by the payment of a fee and are required for each calendar year or fraction thereof that the licensee intends to engage in whaling.[425]

Before obtaining a license a person who intends to engage in whaling must furnish evidence that the equipment being used is adequate and efficient (in accordance with the provisions of the International Convention) and that any compensation paid gunners and crews on the whaler will not be based on the number of whales taken. In order to keep track of these matters, the Act requires a person to maintain and keep records and reports and to produce them upon request.[426]

The Act provides for fines and penalties for violations of the act. These include a possible fine of not more than $10,000 or an imprisonment for not more than one year, or both.[427]

The enforcement of the Act is vested in duly authorized officers and employees of the Department of Commerce, Coast Guard, or any United States marshall or deputy marshall, a customs officer, and any other person authorized to enforce the provisions of the International Convention as provided by regulation or statute.[428]

In order to avoid duplication in scientific and other types of programs, the Secretary of State has the authority to direct the United States Commissioner to arrange for the cooperation of agencies of the United States government, agencies of state governments, and private institutions and organizations for carrying out the International Convention.[429] An

---

423   16 U.S.C.A. § 916b.
424   16 U.S.C.A. § 916c.
425   16 U.S.C.A. § 916d.
426   16 U.S.C.A. § 916e.
427   16 U.S.C.A. § 916f.
428   16 U.S.C.A. § 916g.
429   16 U.S.C.A. § 916h.

exception to the taking of whales under the Act is for the purpose of conducting biological experiments. The Secretary of Commerce has authority to issue scientific permits and to promulgate regulations covering the taking of whales for scientific or biological purposes.[430]

The regulations concerning compliance with this Act have been promulgated by the Secretary of Commerce.[431]

## THE LACEY ACT

In 1981 Congress amended the Lacey Act.[432] The original Lacey Act, passed in 1900 to outlaw interstate traffic in birds and other animals illegally killed in their state of origin, had been amended several times prior to the 1981 amendments.

Originally, the Lacey Act was aimed at people who killed large amounts of wildlife for sale and was designed as a federal tool to aid the states in enforcing their own laws concerning wildlife.

In 1926 Congress had passed the Black Bass Act, which provided federal sanctions for the illegal interstate transportation for Black Bass taken, purchased, sold, or possessed in violation of any state law. In 1969 the Black Bass Act was amended to cover all species of fish, to encompass foreign commerce and fish taken, bought, sold, or possessed in violation of foreign law.

In 1981, when Congress reviewed the Lacey Act, it was found that some problems had developed which had limited the Act's effectiveness as a wildlife enforcement tool. These problems included penalties which were too low and culpability standards which were too stringent.

To correct these deficiencies, the 1981 amendments generally authorized forfeiture of illegal fish, wildlife, plants, equipment and vehicles, on a strict liability basis. The amendments also changed what previously had been misdemeanor penalties into felony penalties.[433]

The Lacey Act prohibits and makes it unlawful for any person to:

(1) import, export, transport, sell, receive, acquire, or purchase any fish or wildlife or plant taken or possessed in violation of any law, treaty, or regulation of the United States or in violation of any Indian tribal law;

---

430 16 U.S.C.A. § 916i.
431 50 C.F.R. Part 230.1 et seq.
432 16 U.S.C.A. § 3371 et seq.
433 See U.S. Code, Congressional and Administrative News, 1981, p. 1748.

(2) import, export, transport, sell, receive, acquire, or purchase in interstate or foreign commerce any fish or wildlife taken, possessed, transported, or sold in violation of any law or regulation of any state or in violation of any foreign law (this also includes plants falling into the same category);

(3) within the special maritime and territorial jurisdiction of the United States, possess any fish or wildlife taken . . . in violation of any law or regulation of any state, foreign law, or Indian tribal law (included also are plants);

(4) having imported, exported, transported, sold, purchased, or received any fish or wildlife or plant imported from any foreign country or transported in interstate or foreign commerce to make or submit any false record, account, label, or identification thereof;

(5) attempt to commit any of the acts described above.[434]

The Act also made it an offense, and therefore unlawful, for any person to import, export, or transport in interstate commerce any container or package containing any fish or wildlife unless the container or package has previously been plainly marked, labeled, or tagged in accordance with any regulations that pertain to such subject matter by the Secretary of the Treasury.[435]

In 1988 Congress again amended the Lacey Act to make it unlawful for any person, for money or other consideration, to offer or provide guiding, outfitting, or any hunting or fishing license or permit where such services were for the purpose of illegally taking, acquiring, receiving, transporting, or possessing of fish or wildlife.[436]

An additional 1988 amendment made it unlawful for any person to make or submit any false record, account, label, or any false information of any fish, wildlife, or plant which has been or is intended to be imported, exported, transported, sold, purchased, or received from any foreign country or transported in interstate or foreign commerce.[437]

It has become evident that Congress intends the Lacey Act to encompass Indian tribal law. Further, violations of Indian tribal law are to apply to Indians as well as non-Indians. In *United States v Big Eagle*,[438] a

---

[434] 16 U.S.C.A. § 3372(a).
[435] 16 U.S.C.A. § 3372(b).
[436] 16 U.S.C.A. § 3372(c).
[437] 16 U.S.C.A. § 3372(d).
[438] 684 F. Supp. 241.

# PROTECTION OF WILDLIFE

Court found that fishing regulations of the Lower Brule Sioux tribe were applicable to an Indian of another tribe who had violated Indian tribal law regulations.

The prohibition against importing fish or wildlife into the country in violation of any foreign law was tested in a case to determine whether or not the term "foreign law" was void for vagueness. In the case, *United States v. 594,464 Pounds of Salmon, more or less*,[439] the Court held that foreign law included regulations of that foreign country as well as statutes. In this particular case the question involved Taiwanese regulations which were not embodied in any statute.

The Lacey Act provides for civil penalties, criminal penalties, and forfeiture. Civil penalties are assessed against any person who engages in the prohibited conduct and in the exercise of due care should have known that the fish, wildlife, or plants taken were in violation of the Act. The civil penalty is not to exceed $10,000. In cases where the value of the fish, wildlife, or plants have a market value of less than $300 and only the transportation is a violation of the Act, the civil penalty is not to exceed the amount provided by that state or foreign government.

Before a civil penalty may be assessed under the Act, an accused person must be given notice and an opportunity for a hearing with respect to that violation. This hearing is an administrative hearing and the procedure must conform to the Administrative Procedures Act. After exhausting any remedies, any accused person who is found guilty of a violation of the Act may appeal the civil penalty to an appropriate district court of the United States by filing a complaint within thirty days after the final order adjudicating him to be in violation of the Act.[440]

The Secretary of Commerce is given latitude in assessing any civil penalty under the Lacey Act. The Secretary may remit or mitigate the penalty and in doing so must determine the amount of the penalty assessed, taking into account the nature, circumstances, extent and gravity of the prohibited act, and the degree of culpability and the ability of the violator to pay.

It is possible that a person indicted under the Act could use the "innocent owner" defense which, if established, would result in no penalty being assessed. However, the claimant using this defense must prove that he attempted to independently confirm or verify that what was taken in violation of the Act and imported from either a state or foreign country could be lawfully imported or transported in interstate commerce and his reliance upon others, including a shipper, is not sufficient to establish the defense.[441]

---

[439] 687 F. Supp. 525.
[440] 16 U.S.C.A. § 3373.

In addition to civil penalties, the Act provides for criminal penalties. Generally, any person who knowingly violates any provision of the Act is subject to a fine of not more than $20,000 or imprisonment for not more than five years or both.

In addition to the felony aspect of the criminal penalties, there is a misdemeanor section which provides that any person who should know that his conduct would be in violation of the Act may be fined not more than $10,000 or imprisoned not more than one year or both.

There is a special provision that applies to a person who violates the marking provision of the Act. The Act provides a penalty of imprisonment of not more than five years or $10,000 or both for any person who falsely marks a container and the conduct involved also includes the importation or exportation of prohibited fish, wildlife, or plants.

Another part of the criminal penalties that may be imposed against someone who violates the Lacey Act is the suspension, modification, or canceling of any federal fishing or hunting license, permit, or stamp for violations of the Lacey Act.[442]

In additional to civil and criminal penalties, the Secretary of Commerce is authorized under the Act to declare a forfeiture of all fish, wildlife, or plants seized when there has been a final adjudication of a violation of the Act. In addition to the subject matter controlled by the Act, the forfeiture also applies to vessels, vehicles, aircraft, and other equipment used to aid in all of the conduct prohibited under the Act. The property so seized may be disposed of in the same manner that property seized in violation of customs laws may be disposed of.

In addition to having a forfeiture declared for all property seized for a violation of the Lacey Act, a person who has been convicted of that violation may also be assessed for the costs incurred in the storage, care, and maintenance of fish, wildlife, or plants seized in connection with the violation.[443]

The Lacey Act is enforced by the Secretary of Commerce, the Secretary of Transportation, or the Secretary of the Treasury. In enforcing the Act, any of these secretaries may utilize services of any other federal agency or state agency or Indian tribe for purposes of enforcing the Act.[444]

---

[441] *See* United States v. 2507 Live Canary Winged Parakeets, 689 F. Supp 1106.
[442] 16 U.S.C.A. § 3373.
[443] 16 U.S.C.A. § 3374.
[444] 16 U.S.C.A. § 3375(a).

# PROTECTION OF WILDLIFE

The enforcement section of the Act provides that persons authorized by the secretaries may carry out such activities as making arrests, searches, and detaining for inspection and inspection of any vehicle or container which may be used in a violation of the Act.

Jurisdiction for any matters pertaining to the Lacey Act is vested in the United States district courts for the district in which the offense is committed.[445]

The Act also provides for rewards to be offered by the Secretary of Commerce or the Secretary of the Treasury to any person who furnishes information which leads to an arrest, a criminal conviction, civil penalty assessment, or forfeiture of property for violation of the Act.[446]

The administration of the Act is vested in the Secretary of Commerce, after consultation with the Secretary of the Treasury. The Secretary of Commerce is authorized to issue regulations that are necessary to carry in to force and effect the full provisions of the Act.[447]

There are exceptions to the application of the Lacey Act for any activity related to a Fishery Management Plan in effect under the Magnuson Fishery Conservation and Management Act and also to any activity related to the Tuna Conventions Act of 1950 (16 U.S.C. 951-961) or the Atlantic Tunas Conventions Act of 1975 (16 U.S.C. 971-971(h)).

In addition, the Act does not apply to an interstate shipment or transshipment through Indian country or through a state to another state in which the fish, wildlife, or plant may be legally possessed. So, as an example, if illegally possessed fish or wildlife only pass through a state and are transported to a state in which the fish or wildlife is not illegal, the Act does not apply.[448]

This trans-shipment exception does not apply in a case where legally taken wildlife passes through a state in which possession is illegal to a state in which wildlife may be legally possessed.[449]

The Lacey Act specifically repeals the Act commonly known as the Black Bass Act[450] and earlier provisions of the Lacey Act.[451]

---

445  16 U.S.C.A. § 3375(c).
446  16 U.S.C.A. § 3375(d).
447  16 U.S.C.A. § 3376.
448  United States v. Miranda, 835 F.2d 830.
449  United States v. Doyle, 786 F.2d 1440.
450  16 U.S.C. §§ 851-856.
451  16 U.S.C.A. § 3378.

# CHAPTER SEVEN

## INTERNATIONAL COMMITMENTS

Over the years the United States has entered numerous agreements with foreign countries for the purposes of protecting interests of the United States (as well as the interest of other countries) in the area of natural resources. Beginning with the Migratory Bird Treaty entered into with Great Britain on behalf of Canada in 1916, the United States has attempted to join other countries in the world in an attempt to preserve, protect, and develop natural resources common to all countries of the world. The majority of these treaties have been supported by necessary implementing statutes which permit the United States to participate in these treaties to the extent required and to the extent desired.

The reasons underlying the United States entry into these conventions and treaties range from values which reflect purely aesthetic, cultural, and humanitarian interest to intentions that relate primarily to economic values.

For the most part these conventions, treaties and agreements relate to fish and oceans but several concern wildlife and plants.

The coverage of the various conventions, treaties, and agreements, which follows, is not exhaustive, but, is a representation of the major and most far reaching treaties that the United States has entered into in the area of worldwide natural resources.

## THE CONVENTION ON INTERNATIONAL TRADE AND ENDANGERED SPECIES OF WILD FAUNA AND FLORA

The Convention on International Trade and Endangered Species of Wild Fauna and Flora was signed by the United States on March 3, 1973 and ratified by the President of the United States on September 13, 1973.[1]

In addition to the United States, the agreement was signed by over 140 other countries, including all of the major powers of the world.

The contracting states agreed upon entering the Convention that wild fauna and flora in their many beautiful and varied forms are an irreplaceable part of the natural systems of the earth which must be protected for this generation and the generations to come; that wild fauna and flora have aesthetic, scientific, cultural, recreational, and economic values; that peoples and their states should be the best protectors of their own wild fauna and flora; that international cooperation is essential for the protection of certain species of wild fauna and flora against

---

[1]   27 U.S.T., T.I.A.S. 8249.

over-exploitation through international trade, and that it was urgent to take appropriate measures.

The fundamental plan contained in the Convention is the division of species into three classifications labeled as Appendix One, Appendix Two, and Appendix Three.

Included in Appendix One are all species threatened with extinction which may or may not be affected by trade. A fundamental principle provides that trade inspecimens of Appendix One species must be subject to particularly strict regulation in order not to endanger further their survival and that trade must only be authorized in exceptional circumstances.

Species included in Appendix Two are those which, although not necessarily now threatened with extinction, may become so unless trade or specimens of such species are subject to strict regulation in order to avoid utilization incompatible with their survival. Included in this category are other species which must be brought into regulation in order that trade in specimens of certain species needing protection can be effectively controlled.

Appendix Three includes species which any party identifies as being subject to regulation within its jurisdiction for purposes of preventing or restricting exploitation and in need of the cooperation of other parties in the control of trade.

The Convention contains provisions for each Appendix covering trade of those species included in the Appendix. The export of any specimen of a species included in Appendix One under the provisions of the Conventions requires the prior grant and presentation of an export permit. The export permit can only be granted upon the following conditions:

(a) A scientific authority of the state of export has advised that such export will not be detrimental to the survival of that species;

(b) A management authority of the state of export is satisfied that the specimen was not obtained in contravention of the laws of that state relating to protection of fauna and flora;

(c) A management authority of the state of export is satisfied that any living specimen will be so prepared and shipped so as to minimize the risk of injury, damage to health or cruel treatment;

(d) A management authority of the state of export is satisfied that an export permit has been granted for the specimen.[2]

2    Id.at art. III (2).

# INTERNATIONAL COMMITMENTS

The Convention also provides, with respect to species included in Appendix One, that the import of any specimen of a species in this Appendix would require the prior grant and presentation of an import permit and either an export permit or re-export certificate. Import permits can be granted only when the following conditions have been met:

(a) A scientific authority of the state of import has advised that the import will be for purposes which are not detrimental to the survival of the species involved;

(b) A scientific authority of the state of import is satisfied that the proposed recipient of the living specimen is suitably equipped to house and care for it;

(c) A management authority of the state of import is satisfied that the specimen is not to be used for primarily commercial purposes.[3]

The Convention also includes provisions which are applicable to species included in Appendix Two. The export of any specimen of a species included in Appendix Two must be accompanied by the prior grant and presentation of an export permit which can be granted only when a scientific authority of the state of export has advised that; such export will not be detrimental to the survival of the species; that a management authority of the state of export is satisfied that the specimen was not obtained in contravention of the laws of that state for the protection of fauna and flora; and that a management authority of the state of export is satisfied that any living specimen will be so prepared and shipped so as to minimize the risk of injury, damage to health, or cruel treatment.[4]

A scientific authority of each state must monitor both the export permits granted by that state for specimens of species included in Appendix Two and the actual exports of such specimens. If a scientific authority, of the exporting state, determines that the export of these specimens should be limited in order to maintain that species throughout its range at a level consistent with its role in the ecosystems in which it occurs and well above the level at which that species might become eligible for inclusion in Appendix One, the state's scientific authority must advise the appropriate management authority of suitable measures to be taken to limit the grant of export permits for those specimens.[5]

Exports of specimens of species included in Appendix Three also require the prior grant and presentation of an export permit which may

3    *Id*. at art. III (3).
4    Id.at art. IV.
5    Id.at art. V.

be issued on the condition that the management authority of the state of export is satisfied that the specimen was not obtained in contravention the laws of that state for protection of fauna and flora and that the management authority is satisfied that any living specimen will be so prepared and shipped so as to minimize the risk of injury, damage to health or cruel treatment.

The Convention provides details of the information that must be contained in the permit that are applicable to specimens of species listed under Appendices's One, Two and Three and a model form containing those details.[6]

The Convention also contains provisions which relate to the re-export of any specimen of a species included in either Appendix One, Two, or Three. Generally speaking the same restrictions that apply to export apply to re-export.

The Convention contains some exemptions and other special provisions relating to trade. Exemptions apply to a situation where a management authority of the state of export or re-export is satisfied that a specimen was acquired before the provisions of the Convention applied to that specimen, and to specimens of an animal species included in Appendix One which were bred in captivity for commercial purposes or a plant species included in Appendix One artificially propagated for commercial purpose. In situations were the animals species is bred in captivity the management authority of the state of export must issue a certificate so stating.[7]

The Convention provides for several actions that need to be taken by signatories to the Convention. In general the parties to the Convention must take appropriate measures to enforce the provisions of the Convention and to prohibit trade in specimens in violation of the Convention. The measures necessary to accomplish this purpose include penalties for trade in or possession of specimens listed, and the confiscation and return to the state of export of any specimens imported or exported in violation of the Convention.[8]

Each party to the Convention also must take measures to insure that specimens can pass through any formalities required for trade with a minimum of delay. To facilitate such ease of passage, the parties are encouraged to designate ports of exits and entry at which specimens may be presented for clearance.

---

6    Id.at art. VI.
7    Id.at art. VII.
8    *Id*. at art. VIII.

Another action that parties to the Conventions must take is the return of a specimen to the state of export where that export has been in violation of the provisions of the Convention. The specimen must be entrusted to the management authority of the state of confiscation and after consultation with the state of export returned to the state of export at the expense of that state.[9]

In order to fully participate in the provisions of the Convention, each signatory to the Convention must designate one or more management authorities competent to grant permits or certificates on behalf of that state and one or more scientific authorities.[10]

The Convention provides for a Secretariat to administer the requirements of the Convention. Generally the functions of the Secretariat are; to arrange for meetings of the signatories; to perform ministerial duties necessary to accomplish the amendment provisions of the Convention; to undertake scientific and technical studies in accordance with programs authorized by the conference of the parties as will contribute to the implementation of the Convention including studies concerning standards for appropriate preparation for shipment of living specimens and the means of identifying these specimens; to publish periodically and distribute to the signatories to the Convention current additions of the Appendices One, Two and Three, together with any information which will facilitate identification of specimens of species included in the Appendices; to prepare annual reports to the signatories on this work and on this implementation of the Convention and; to make recommendations for the implementation of the aims and provisions of the Convention.[11]

The Secretariat also has watchdog functions under the Convention. The Secretariat is required to communicate, any information received that any species, included in Appendices One and Two, is being affected adversely by trade, to the authorized management authority of the state or states involved.[12]

The Convention provides procedures for the listing of specimens of species in Appendices One, Two and Three. Any party to the Convention may propose an amendment to Appendix One or Two for consideration at the next meeting. After discussion at the Conference, the proposed amendment to Appendices One and Two must be approved by a two-thirds majority of the parties present and voting at the Conference. Any amendment adopted at that Conference is effective ninety days after the ending of the conference.

9   Id.
10  Id.at art. IX.
11  Id.at art. XII.
12  Id.at art. XIII.

Any party may, at any time, submit to the Secretariat a list of species which it identifies as being subject to regulation in accordance with the provisions of the Convention relating to specimens of species listed in Appendix Three. The Secretariat after receiving this list from each party then is required to circulate it to all other parties in the Convention and such list becomes effective ninety days after the circulation. Provisions are also made under the Convention for a withdrawl of a species listed under Appendix Three.[13]

The Convention also provides that the parties to the Convention may adopt stricter domestic measures regarding the conditions for trade, taking possession, of transport of specimens and species included in the Appendices, and the complete prohibition thereof, or domestic measures restricting or prohibiting trade taking, possession, or transport of species not included in any of the Appendices. In addition the Convention has a clause which makes a provision of the Convention not effective when in contravention to the provisions of any domestic measures of a signatory state or of the obligations of the parties derived from any other treaty or convention or international agreement.[14]

The original of the Convention is published in Chinese, English, French, Russian, and Spanish and the copies in each of these languages must be circulated to all parties to the Convention.[15]

## CONVENTION ON NATURE PROTECTION AND WILDLIFE PRESERVATION IN THE WESTERN HEMISPHERE

The United States and other American Republics entered into the Convention on Nature Protection and Wildlife Preservation in the Western Hemisphere in 1940. The Convention was ratified by the United States Senate on April 15, 1941.[16]

The Convention was entered by the parties for the following purposes; "to protect and preserve in their natural habitat, representatives of all species in general of their native flora and fauna, including migratory birds, and in sufficient numbers in areas extensive enough to prevent them from becoming extinct through any agency within man's control; to protect and preserve scenery of extraordinary beauty, unusual and striking geologic formations, regions or natural objects of aesthetic, historic or scientific value in areas characterized by primitive conditions in those cases covered by the Convention and to conclude a Convention on the protection of nature and preservation of flora and fauna . . . ."

---

13  Id.at art. XVI.
14  Id.at art. XIV.
15  Id.at art. XXV.
16  T.S. 981, 56 Stat. 1354.

# INTERNATIONAL COMMITMENTS

The Convention provides that the parties to the Convention will explore at once the possibly of establishing, in their territories, national parks, national reserves, and nature monuments, and strict wilderness preserves as defined in the Convention. In cases where such establishment is feasible the creation of parks, reserves, monuments, and wilderness areas must began as soon as possible.[17]

If a country determines that the establishment of the parks, reserves, monuments and wilderness reserves are impracticable at any particular time, efforts must be taken to select suitable areas as early as possible and the process of transforming them into parks, reserves, monuments and wilderness areas must be undertaken.[18]

Each contracting party is required under the Convention to notify the Pan American Union of the establishment of any park, reserve, monument or wilderness area established as soon as it is so designated and must include in the notification the methods applicable to its administrative control and any legislation that accompanies or is associated with such establishment.[19]

The Convention requires the contracting parties to agree that the resources of the reserves established pursuant to the Convention must not be subject to exploitation for commercial profit. In addition, the parties to the Convention agree to prohibit hunting, killing, and capturing of members of the fauna and destruction or collection of representatives of the flora in national parks except by or under the direction or control of the park authorities or for duly authorized scientific investigations. In addition, the contracting parties agree to provide facilities for public recreation, and education in national parks consistent with nature protection and wildlife preservation.[20]

The Convention requires that parties must maintain the established strict wilderness reserves inviolate as far as practicable except for duly authorized scientific investigations or government inspection or such uses as are consistent with nature protection and wilderness preservation.[21]

In addition to the establishment of national parks, national reserves, national monuments, or strict wilderness areas, the Convention requires governments who have signed the Convention, to agree to adopt or to propose such adoption to the respective appropriate law making bodies, suitable laws and regulations for the protection and preservation of

17  Preamble.
18  Id.
19  Id.at art. II.
20  *Id.*
21  *Id.* at art. IV.

flora and fauna within their national boundaries, but not included in these parks, reserves, monuments and areas. This requirement extends also to laws which will assure the protection and preservation of natural scenery, striking geological formations, and regions of national objects of aesthetic interest or historical or scientific value.[22]

The spirit of the Convention is reflected in an agreement among the contracting parties to cooperate among themselves in promoting the objectives of the Convention and to lend proper assistance to scientists engaged in research and field studies. This cooperation may also extend where appropriate to the entering into of agreements with one another or with scientific institutions of the Americas in order to increase the effectiveness of this collaboration.[23]

The Convention also requires contracting governments to adopt appropriate measures for the protection of migratory birds of economic or aesthetic value and to prevent the threatened extinction of any given species. The Convention does not prohibit a rational utilization of migratory birds for the purposes of sports, food, commerce, and industry, and for scientific study and investigation, provided that adequate measures will be adopted to accomplish the purposes of the Convention.[24]

Each contracting government obligates itself to take necessary measures to control and regulate the importation, exportation, and transport of protected fauna or flora by restricting certificates authorizing the exportation, importation or transportation of protected species and the prohibition of the importation of any species or fauna or flora or any part, protected by the country of origin, unless accompanied by a certificate of lawful exportation.[25]

The Convention contains an appendix which lists species to be of special urgency and importance. The species listed in the appendix are required to be protected as completely as possible and their hunting, killing, capturing, or taking must be allowed only with the permission of the appropriate government authorities of the listing country. The permission given by this appropriate government authority is limited to special circumstances in order to further scientific purposes that are essential for the administration of the area in which the animal or plant is found.[26]

In the original Convention the United States listed in the Appendix the Woodland Caribou, Sea Outer, Manatee, Trumpeter Swan, California

---

22  Id.
23  Id.at art. V.
24  Id.at art. VI.
25  Id.at art. VII.
26  Id.at art. IX.

Condor Swan, Whooping Crane, Eskimo Curlew, Hudson's Godwit, Puerto Rican Parrot and the Ivory Billed Woodpecker.

The Convention provides for the withdrawal of any contracting party from the Convention by a written notice. This so called denunciation would take effect one year after date of receipt of the notification by the Pan American Union.[27]

The original of the Convention is recorded in Spanish, English, Portuguese, and French and deposited with the Pan American Union.

## AGREEMENT ON CONSERVATION OF POLAR BEARS

In 1976 the United States entered into a Convention on the Conservation of Polar Bears with Canada, Denmark, Norway, the Union of Soviet Socialists Republic.[28]

In the Convention, the contracting parties recognize that they are committed to special responsibilities in relation to the protection of the fauna and flora of the Arctic region and that the polar bear is a significant resource of the Arctic region. The parties have determined that the polar bear needs protection and that such protection must be achieved through coordinated national measures taken by the states of the Arctic region.

The crux of the Convention is that the taking of polar bears is prohibited except as provided by certain exceptions under the Convention. For the purpose of the agreement the term taking includes hunting, killing, and capturing.[29]

Under the agreement each contracting party is required to take appropriate action to protect the ecosystems of which the polar bears are a part, with special attention to habitat components such as denning and feeding sites and migration patterns. In addition each party is required to manage polar bear population in accordance with sound conservation practices based on the best available scientific data.[30]

By way of exceptions, the taking of polar bears under the agreement can be permitted when such taking is carried out for bona fide scientific purposes, for conservation purposes, to prevent serious disturbance of the management of other living resources, by local people using traditional methods in the exercise of their traditional rights in accordance with the laws of one of the contracting parties, or wherever polar bears have or might have been subject to taking by traditional means by its nationals. The skins and other items of value resulting from the taking

27  Id.at art. VIII.
28  27 U.S.T., T.I.A.S. 8409.
29  Preamble.
30  Id. at art. II.

which is permitted under the Act cannot be available for commercial purposes.[31]

The use of aircraft or large motorized vehicles for the purposes of the permitted taking of polar bears under the agreement is prohibited.[32]

The contracting parties are under an obligation to prohibit exportation from and importation and delivery into and traffic within its territory, of polar bears or parts thereof taken in violation of the agreement.[33]

Each contracting party must enact and enforce such regulations and other measures as may be necessary to carry into effect the purposes of the agreement. The agreement does not prohibit a state signatory from maintaining or amending existing legislation or other measures or establishing new measures on the taking of polar bears so as to provide more stringent controls than those required under the provisions of the agreement.[34]

The contracting parties are obligated to conduct national research programs on polar bears, particularly research relating to the conservation and management of the species. In conducting research the parties are required to consult with other contracting parties on the management of migrating polar bear populations and, to exchange information on research and management programs, research results and data on bears taken.[35]

The agreement contains a provision which allows the parties to withdraw from the agreement (five years from the date of entry into the agreement) by notifying the Depository Government and the withdrawal becomes effective twelve months after the notice to the Depository Government.

The original agreement has been deposited with the government of Norway and certified copies of it have been transmitted to the Secretary General of the United Nations for Registration and Publication in accordance with Article 102 of the Charter of the United Nations.

## THE INTERIM CONVENTION ON CONSERVATION OF NORTH PACIFIC FUR SEALS

The United States entered a Convention with Canada, Japan, and the Union of Soviet Socialists Republic in 1957.[36] The purpose of the Convention was to take effective measures toward achieving the maximum

---

31   Id.at art. III.
32   Id.at art. IV.
33   Id.at art. V.
34   Id.at art. VI.
35   Id.at art. VII.
36   8 U.S.T., T.I.A.S. 3948.

sustainable productivity of the fur seal resources of the North Pacific Ocean (so that the fur seal populations can be brought to and maintained at the levels which will provide the greatest harvest year after year with due regard to their relation to the productivity of other living resources of the area).

The parties to the Convention felt that in order to determine such measures as were necessary to achieve the purposes of the Convention it was essential that adequate scientific research should be conducted.

An essential provision of the Convention contains an agreement by the parties to coordinate necessary scientific research programs and to cooperate and investigate the fur seal resources of the North Pacific Ocean in order to determine:

(a)What measures may be necessary to make possible the maximum sustainable productivity of the fur seal resources so that fur seal populations can be brought to and maintained at the levels which will provide the greatest harvests year after year;

(b)What the relationship is between fur seals and other living marine resources and whether fur seals have detrimental effects on other living marine resources substantially exploited by any of the contracting parties and if so to what extent.[37]

The research that is to be conducted includes studies of the size of each fur seal herd, its age and sex composition; natural mortality of the different age groups and recruitment of young to each age or size class at present and subsequent population levels; with regard to each of the herds, the effect on the magnitude of variations in the size and the age of sex composition of the annual kill; migration routes of first years and their wintering areas; number of seals from each herd found on the migration routes and in wintering areas and their ages and sexes; extent to which the food habits of fur seals affect commercial fish catches and the damage fur seals inflict on fish gear; and any other objects involved in the achieving of the objectives of the Convention.[38]

In the spirit of cooperation the Convention provided that each contracting party must share information on the number of black pups tagged for each breeding area, the number of fur seals by sex and estimated age taken at sea and in each breeding area the tagged seals recovered on land and at sea. This information was to be furnished to the North Pacific Fur Sale Commission which was established under the Convention.[39]

---

37  Id.at art. II.
38  Id.at art. II (2).
39  Id.

# WILDLIFE AND HABITAT

In Article Three of the Convention the contracting parties agree to prohibit pelagic sealing, except in furtherance of research in the Pacific Ocean North of the 30th parallel of north latitude including the seas of Bering, Okhotsk, and Japan, by any person or vessel subject to its jurisdiction.[40]

To administer the requirements involved, the Convention established the North Pacific Fur Seal Commission which isbe composed of one member from each contracting party. The duties of the Commission are stated to be:

(a) formulate and coordinate research programs designed to achieve the objectives set forth in the Convention;

(b) recommend these coordinated research programs to the respective parties for implementation;

(c) study the data obtained from the implementation of such coordinated research programs;

(d) recommend appropriate measures, to the parties, on the basis of the findings obtained from the implementation of such coordinated research programs, including measures regarding the size, sex and age composition of the seasonal commercial kill from a herd; and

(e) recommend to the parties at the end of the fifth year after entry into force of this Convention or a later year, the method of sealing best suited to achieve the objectives of this Convention. (The later year mentioned above is to be fixed by the parties at a meeting early in the sixth year provided under a later Article in the section).[41]

Each party on the Commission has one vote and decisions and recommendations may be made by unanimous vote.

The Commission must hold an annual meeting at such time and place as it may decide. Additional meetings must be held when requested by two or more members of the Commission. The time and place of the first meeting is to be determined by agreement among the parties.[42]

The expenses of each member of the Commission must be paid by its own government. Joint expenses may be incurred by the Commission and must be defrayed by the party by equal contributions.

---

40   Id.at art. III.
41   Id.at art. V.
42   Id.at art. V (6).

# INTERNATIONAL COMMITMENTS

The Convention provides that the parties agree to implement the Convention's prohibition against pelagic sealing by authorizing officials of these signatory states to board and search a vessel which is believed to be violating the prohibition against pelagic sealing based on reasonable cause. The parties in the Convention also agreed to provide authorization for seizure of the vessel and arrest of any person reasonably believed to be violating the provisions of the Convention.[43]

An article of the Convention provides an extremely important exclusion from the application of the provisions of the Convention. This Article provides that the provisions of the Convention are not to apply to Indians, Ainos, Aleuts or Eskimos dwelling on the coast of the waters of the Bering Sea, the Okhotsk Sea and the Japanese Sea.[44]

The parties to the agreement also agree that each signatory party will implement measures which will not permit any person or vessel to use any of its ports or harbors or any part of its territory for any purpose designed to violate the prohibition against pelagic sealing.[45]

Article IX provides quotas that the parties agree to abide by. This Article provides that of the total number of seal skins taken commercially each season on land there must at the end of the season be delivered a percentage of the number as follows:

> By the Union of Soviet Socialists Republic - to Canada 15 percent, to Japan 15 percent.

> By the United States of America - to Canada 15 percent, to Japan 15 percent.

This Article also provides that the direct and indirect costs of pelagic research in the Western Pacific Ocean are to be divided. Also the parties agree as follows:

(1) Canada and Japan will forego the delivery of the seal skins by the Union of Soviet Socialists Republic (15 percent to each);

(2) The United States of America will increase its delivery to Canada and Japan by a total of 357 seal skins to each of these parties (in addition to the 15 percent required under Paragraph One of Article IX). This equitable division of direct and indirect costs is conditioned upon the commercial killing for both the Commander and Robin Island herds and pelagic research in that area at a level of 2000 or more seals.[46]

---

43 Id.at art. VI.
44 Id.at art. VII.
45 Id.at art. VIII.
46 Id.at art. IX.

The parties to the Convention agree to enact and enforce such legislation as may be necessary to guarantee any observance of the Convention and to make effective provisions with appropriate penalties for violation.[47]

The Convention stipulates that the agreement is to remain in force for six years and thereafter until the entry into force of a new or revised Fur Seal Convention between the parties or to the expiration of one year after such period or six years whichever may be earlier.[48]

The interim Convention signed February 9, 1957 was amended by a protocol signed in Washington, D.C. on October 8, 1963 and once again in October 1969.

## ATLANTIC FISHERIES

The protocol to the International Convention for the Northwest Atlantic Fisheries was signed in Washington, D.C. on July 15, 1963 by the United States of America and eleven other governments. The original protocol was signed February 8, 1949 and amended and extended in 1963.

The Convention covers harp and hood seals. The contracting governments have established a panel with jurisdiction over harp and hood seals in the Convention area. Each signatory to the agreement that has a coast adjacent to the Convention area is to have the right to representation on the panel.

The original Convention covered a broad category of species included under the general term "fisheries." It was made specifically applicable to harp and hood seals by the Amendment signed in 1963.

The original International Convention for Northwest Atlantic Fisheries established panels which had the duty to investigate, protect, and conserve the fisheries of the North Atlantic Ocean in order to make possible the maintenance of a maximum sustained catch from these fisheries.

The 1963 Amendment continued these panels and extended their duties to include harp and hood seals.

## LAW OF THE SEA

The United Nations conducted a United Nations Conference on the Law of the Sea in Geneva, Switzerland from February 24 to April 27, 1958. As part of this Conference there were several Conventions relating to different subject matters concerning the high seas. One of these

---

47 Id.at art. X.
48 *Id*. at art. XIII.

# INTERNATIONAL COMMITMENTS

Conventions entitled "The Convention on the High Seas"[49] served the purpose of codifying the rules of international law relating to the high seas. The term high seas was defined to mean "all parts of the sea that are not included in the territorial sea or in the internal waters of a state."[50]

In addition to the provisions of the Agreements concerning the activity of various states on the high seas, the parties to the Convention agreed, (1) to draw up regulations to prevent pollution of the seas by discharge of oil from ships or pipelines or resulting from the exploitation and exploration of the seabed and its subsoil, (2) to take measures to prevent pollution of the seas from the dumping of radioactive waste, and (3) to take measures to prevent the pollution of the seas or the airspace above resulting from any activities with radioactive materials or other harmful agents.[51]

Another Convention coming out of the Conference of the Law of the Sea was one entitled "Convention on Fishing and Conservation of the Living Resources of the High Seas."[52] This Convention had as its purpose the balancing of the necessity for man to meet the needs of the world's expanding population for food and the danger that some of these resources would be over exploited. The Convention resolved that there was a clear necessity that these problems be solved whenever possible on the basis of international cooperation through the concerted action of all the states concerned.

The signatories to the Convention agreed that all states have a right for their nationals to engage in fishing on the high seas, subject to whatever treaty obligation might be involved, subject to the interest and rights of coastal state parties to this Convention, and, subject to whatever provisions the Convention might produce to conserve the living resources of the high seas.[53]

The fundamental agreement of the parties to the Convention was that states have the duty to adopt or to cooperate with other states in adopting such measures for their respective nationals as may be necessary for the "Conservation of the Living Resources of the High Seas."[54]

The expression "conservation of the living resources of the high seas" was defined to mean "the aggregate of the measures rendering possible the optimum sustainable yield from those resources so as to secure a maximum supply of food and other marine products."[55] These conser-

---

49  13 U.S.T., 5200.
50  Id.at art. I.
51  Id.at art. 24 & 25.
52  17 U.S.T., 5969.
53  Id.at art. I (1).
54  Id.at art. I (2).
55  Id.at art. II.

vation programs are required, under the Convention, to be formulated with a view to securing in the first place a supply of food for human consumption.

The actions to be taken by the signatory states involve both multi-lateral and unilateral measures. Article IV of the Convention provides that if two or more states are engaged in fishing in the same stocks or stocks of fish or other living marine resources in any area or areas of the high seas these states at the request of any of them must enter into negotiations with a view to prescribing by agreement for their nationals the necessary measures for the conservation of the living resources affected.[56] Coastal signatory states are recognized as having a special interest in the maintenance of the productivity of the living resources and any area of the high seas adjacent to that state's territorial sea. A coastal signatory state may, with a view to the maintenance of the productivity of the living resources of the sea, adopt unilateral measures of conservation appropriate to any stock of fish or other marine resources in any area of the high seas adjacent to its territorial sea. States other than the coastal state may engage in fishing in any area of the high seas adjacent to the territorial sea of a coastal state but must enter into negotiations with that coastal state with a view to prescribing by agreement the measures necessary for the conservation of the living resources of the high seas in that area.[57]

In adopting these measures a coastal state must determine that there is a need for urgent application of conservation measures in the light of the existing knowledge of the fishery, that the measures adopted are based on appropriate scientific findings, and that such measures do not discriminate in form or in fact against foreign fishermen.[58]

When any dispute arises between the signatory states relating to covered fisheries, the Convention provides that a Special Commission of five members shall be established for the purposes of settling these disputes.[59] The members of this Special Commission are to be named by agreement between the states in dispute within three months of a request for settlement, and failing any agreement they are to be named by the Secretary General of the United Nations within a further three month period.[60] The Commission however established has the authority under the Convention to determine its own procedure and must render its decision within a period of five months from the time it is appointed (in case of necessity the time limit can be extended for an additional three months).

56   Id.at art. IV.
57   Id.at art. VI.
58   Id.at art. VII.
59   Id.at art. IX (1).
60   Id.at art. IX (2).

# INTERNATIONAL COMMITMENTS

In making its decision the Special Commission must determine that the scientific findings demonstrate the necessity of conservation measures, that the specific measures are based on scientific findings, are practicable, and that the measures do not discriminate in form or fact against the fishermen of other states.[61]

The Convention was signed on behalf of the United States and 36 other states and published in Chinese, English, French, Russian, and Spanish.

Another Convention coming out of the Conference of the Law of the Sea was the "Convention on the Continental Shelf."[62] The purpose of the Convention was to recognize that coastal signatory states exercise sovereign rights over the continental shelf for the purpose of exploring it and exploring its natural resources. The sovereign rights referred to are to be exclusive in the sense that if the coastal state does not explore the continental shelf or explore its natural resources no one can undertake these activities or make a claim to the continental shelf without the express consent of that coastal state. The rights to exclusivity do not depend on occupation or expressed proclamation.[63]

The term continental shelf is defined under the Convention as referring to, "the seabed and subsoil of the submarine areas adjacent to the coast but outside the area of the territorial sea, to a depth of 200 meters or, beyond that limit, to where the depth of the sub-super adjacent waters admits of the exploitation of the natural resources of the said sea; and to the seabed and subsoil of similar submarine areas adjacent to the coast of islands."[64]

The term natural resources referred to in the Convention was defined as to "consist of the mineral and other non-living resources of the seabed and subsoil together with living organisms belonging to sedentary species, that is to say, organisms which, at the harvestable stage, either are immobile on or under the seabed or are unable to move except in constant physical contact with the seabed or the subsoil."[65]

The Convention provides that the exploration of the continental shelf and the exploitation of its natural resources must not result in any unjustifiable interference with navigation, fishing, or the conservation of the living resources of the sea, nor result in any interference with fundamental oceanographic or other scientific research carried out with the intention of open publication,[66] nor may a state impede the laying or maintenance of submarine cable or pipelines on the continental shelf.[67]

---

61   Id.at art. X.
62   15 U.S.T., T.I.A.S. 5578.
63   Id.at art. I & II.
64   *Id* at art. I.
65   Id.at art. II (4).
66   Id.at art. V.

# WILDLIFE AND HABITAT

Where the same continental shelf is adjacent to the territories of two or more states whose coasts are opposite each other, the boundary of the continental shelf must be determined by agreement between the parties. In the absence of such agreement and unless another boundary line is justified by special circumstances, the boundary is the medium line, every point of which is equal distance from the nearest points of the base lines from which the breadth of the territorial sea of each state is measured.[68] If the same continental shelf is adjacent to the territories of two adjacent states the same rules are applicable.

This Convention was signed by the United States and 45 other states, and is printed in English, French, Chinese, Russian and Spanish languages.

## WHALING

Whaling began in the 11th or 12th century and, as early as the 13th century, the world began to notice a depletion of the species. Pelagic whaling began as early as the 15th century. Pelagic whaling refers to the taking and processing of whales on the high seas. By 1975 the whaling industry had reduced the world's estimated number of whales to approximately two million. Further exploitations of the whale populations have decreased that number to approximately one million whales as of today.

Generally speaking whales which are divided into two classifications, Baleen and Tooth Whales, are found in all major oceans of the world. Bowhead and Grey whales are generally found in the Northern Hemisphere. Baleen whales generally migrate from tropical or sub-tropical winter ranges to polar ranges each year.

There had been some awareness of the problem of depleting the whale stocks early in the 20th Century. However, regulations were practically nonexistent and the few regulations that existed were ineffective. The first Convention for the regulation of whaling was signed September 24, 1931.[69]

This Whaling Convention prohibits the commercial hunting of Right Whales and Bowhead Whales and gave some consideration to the prevention of excessive wastage of the other species by requiring whalers to make full use of all carcasses and by banning the killing of calves or suckling whales, immatures and females whales which were occupied by calves or sucklings.[70]

---

67   *Id* at art. IV.
68   *Id* at art VI.
69   49 Stat. 3079, T.I.A.S. 80.
70   Id.at art. V & VI.

# INTERNATIONAL COMMITMENTS

Japan, Germany, Chile, Argentina and the Union of Soviet Socialist Republic were not signatories to the Convention.

The Convention did not establish any administration with powers to issue the regulations. Although two protocols in 1937 and 1938 prohibited the taking of whales below certain minimum lengths, it wasn't until the International Convention for the Regulation of Whaling (The Whaling Convention) was signed in Washington, D.C. on December 2, 1946 that such an administration was created.[71]

The Whaling Convention establishes the International Whaling Commission which meets annually and adopts regulations on catch quotas, protection of species, whaling methods, and other matters.[72]

The International Whaling Commission regulations are contained in a schedule. The schedule is amendable by the International Whaling Commission and in 1982 it adopted the following amendment to the schedule. "Notwithstanding the other provisions of Paragraph 10, catch limits for the killing for commercial purposes of whales from all stocks for the 1986 coastal and the 1985/1986 pelagic seasons and thereafter shall be zero. This provision will be kept under review based on the best scientific advice and by 1990, at least, the Commission will undertake a comprehensive assessment of the effects of this decision on whale stocks and consider modification of this provision in the establishment of other catch limits."[73] This amendment has the potential for the solution of whale depletion. However the Whaling Convention contains an objection procedure which has been used by the three major whaling states Japan, Norway, and the U.S.S.R to relieve themselves of the obligation of this Amendment.

The Whaling Convention when it was originally established had at its inception at least two purposes. One was to achieve the optimum level of whale stocks without causing widespread economic and nutritional distress and the other was to protect whales from over exploitation. However the expressed purpose of making possible the orderly development of the whaling industry makes it clear that the primary purpose of the Convention was to conserve whales stocks for the continued economic functioning of the whaling industry. At the current time all of the major fishing countries of the world are signatories to the Whaling Convention.

In the main, the Whaling Convention attempts to control whaling by controlling the method used to catch whales. Generally the Convention applies to factory ships, land stations, and to ships used for the pur-

---

71  T.I.A.S. 2092.
72  Id.at art. III.
73  Id.at art. I & II.

poses of hunting, taking, towing, holding on to, or scouting for whales. A factory ship is defined as a ship in which or on which whales are treated wholly or in part and a land station means a factory on land to which the whales are taken wholly or in part.[74]

The International Whaling Commission meets annually and has a membership of one voting representative for each signatory party.[75]

The Convention authorizes the International Whaling Commission to engage in studies and investigations relating to whales and whaling, to collect and analyze statistical information concerning the current condition and trend of the whale stocks and the effect of whaling activities thereon, and to study, appraise and disseminate information concerning methods of maintaining and increasing the population of whale stock.[76]

The International Whaling Commission schedules regulate the exploitation of whales by declaring open and closed seasons, open and closed waters, size limits for each species, time methods and intensity of whaling, types and specifications of gear and apparatus and appliances which may be used, methods of measurements, catch returns and other statistically and biological records, and the protected and unprotected species.[77]

The Whaling Convention requires that any amendments to the schedule must be based on scientific findings, and that these amendments can be made only when necessary to carry out the objectives and purposes of the Convention. In addition the Convention requires that the Commission must take into account in any regulations contained in the schedule, the interest of consumer whale products and the whaling industry.[78]

One of the major clauses of the Convention is the objection provision. Objections usually occur when the International Whaling Commission amends the schedule and any signatory to the Convention may object within 90 days of notification of its adoption.[79] Several of the signatories to the Convention including the ones who are major whale hunters (Japan, USA, USSR) have used this provision of the Convention.

The International Whaling Commission's decision to bring commercial whaling to a temporary halt from 1986 prompted the registration of objections by Japan, Norway, and the USSR.

---

74 Id.at art. III.
75 *Id*. at art. II (9).
76 Id.at art. V (1).
77 Id.at art. V (2).
78 Id.at art. V (3).
79 Id.at art. III (4).

# INTERNATIONAL COMMITMENTS

The International Whaling Commission is authorized under the Convention to establish "such committees as it considers desirable to perform such functions as it may authorize."[80] One of the major committees established by the Commission is the Scientific Committee which is responsible for studying information with respect to whale stocks and whaling and for making appropriate recommendations to the Committee.[81]

Another committee, the Technical Committee, advises the International Whaling Commission on non-scientific matters such as aboriginal whaling, humane killing or whaling outside the jurisdiction of the International Whaling Commission.

The International Whaling Commission is authorized to make recommendation to any or all contracting governments on any matters which relate to whales or whaling and to the objectives and purposes of the Convention.[82]

Under this provision the International Whaling Commission has made dozens of recommendations over the years including the suggestion that signatory governments conduct research on the effect of shipping and the offshore mining and drilling activities on whale stocks.

The Whaling Convention does allow party governments to grant special permits authorizing their nationals to kill whales for the purposes of scientific research.[83]

The Convention provides that at least two inspectors are required on each factory ship for the purpose of maintaining 24 hour inspection and that at least one inspector shall be maintained on each catcher functioning as a factory ship. In addition the Convention requires that adequate inspection shall be maintained at each land station. These inspectors are appointed and paid for by the government with jurisdiction over the factory ship or land station in operation and are therefore national enforcement officers responsible to their own governments.

In 1971 the International Whaling Commission set up a scheme whereby international observers are appointed and are responsible to the International Whaling Commission even though their salaries might be paid for by the government which nominates them.

There are no specified number of observers to be placed on the ships and land stations and signatory countries can effectively get around the

---

80  Rules of Procedure of the I.W.C.
81  Id.at art VI.
82  Id.at art. VIII.
83  Id.at art. IX.

requirement by either not paying the cost involved in sending an observer or, as in the case of Japan and the USSR, make mutual arrangements for observers which reduces the effective number of observers.

Each signatory to the Convention is responsible for punishing violations against the provisions of the Whaling Convention which occur when such violations are made by persons or vessels under the jurisdiction of that country.

The Convention requires these signatory parties to take appropriate measures to enforce the terms of the Convention. The United States in response to this requirement has taken appropriate means through the Marine Mammal Protection Act of 1972 and sanctions under the Pelly Amendment to the Fishermen's Protection Act of 1967 and The Packwood-Magnuson Amendment to the Fishery Conservation Management Act of 1976.[84]

The Marine Mammal Protection Act prohibits U.S. citizens or United States registered vessels from engaging in whaling on the high seas. The Pelly Amendment and the Packwood-Magnuson Amendment authorize the United States government to take economic sanctions against any state whose activities diminish the effectiveness of the conservation measures of the International Whaling Convention. The Secretary of Commerce who determines that foreign nationals are conducting fishing operations in a manner or under circumstances which diminish the effectiveness of an International Fishery Conservation Program may under the Pelly Amendment prohibit the importation of fish products from the offending state for such duration as he deems appropriate and to the extent that such prohibition is sanctioned by the general agreement on tariffs and trades. Under the Packwood-Magnuson Amendment, the Secretary of Commerce automatically reduces by 50% the allocation of fish products taken within the United States fishery conservation zone. Under this Packwood-Magnuson Amendment, if the state so involved refuses to change its activity within a year, its entire allocation can be terminated and its nationals will be determined to be unable to fish in all United States coastal waters.

The country which has caused particularly difficult problems for the preservation of whaling stocks is Japan. Under the guise of scientific research, Japan has apparently continued its commercial whaling operations.

---

84  Pelly Amendment to the Fishermen's Proctective Act of 1967, 22 U.S.C.A. § 1978(a)(3) 60;
    Packwood-Magnuson Amendment to the Fishery Conservation and Management Act of 1976, 16
    U.S.C.A. § 1821 (e) (2) and (A) (i).

# INTERNATIONAL COMMITMENTS

In 1988 the Secretary of Commerce recommended to the President the imposition of sanctions against Japan for killing whales under a Japanese research program. The Secretary certified that the Japanese whaling activities diminished the effectiveness of the International Whaling Conventions Conservation program under the Packwood-Magnuson Amendment which resulted in a 50% reduction of fish allocations in the United States 200 miles zone. The sanctions were ineffective because Japan did not have any quotas in the United States 200 mile zone.

Under the Pelly Amendment the President upon receiving certification by the Secretary of Commerce could declare an embargo on the importation of fish products from the offending country. In 1988 President Reagan made a decision to impose sanctions against Japan under the Packwood-Magnuson Amendment but refused to impose trade sanctions against Japan under the Pelly Amendment.[85]

In addition to the International Whaling Convention, whales are also protected by Article 65 of the Law of the Sea Convention which provides that the signatories to the Convention shall cooperate "with a view to the conservation of marine mammals shall work through the appropriate international organizations for conservation and management and study."

The Convention on International Trade and Endangered Species of Wild Fauna and Flora also protects whales to the extent that Sperm, Fin, Sei, Blue, Humpback, Bowhead, Right, Bryde's, Grey, and Bottlenose whales are all currently listed in Appendix One.

The Convention on the Conservation of Antarctic Marine Living Resources[86] indirectly protects whales by regulating the exportation of marine living resources (notably krill) in Antarctica. Since krill is the principal food supply of several species of Baleen Whales the control of this food source could accrue to the benefit of Antarctic whale populations.

## ANTARCTIC PROTECTION

In 1959 the United States and twelve other countries entered the Antarctic Treaty.[87] The basic underlying assumption of the treaty as expressed in 1959 was the recognition by all parties that in the interest of all mankind, Antarctica should continue forever to be used exclusively for peaceful purposes and should not become the seed or object of international discord.

---

85  See The Whale War between Japan and the U.S.: Problems and Perspectives, 17 Denver Journal of International Law and Policy  p. 317.
86  33 U.S.T., T.I.A.S. 10240.
87  12 U.S.T., T.I.A.S. 4780.

# WILDLIFE AND HABITAT

Under Article IX of that 1959 Convention the contracting parties also agreed that the parties should recommend to their governments measures and furtherance of several principles including "preservation and conservation of living resources in Antarctica."

In 1966, at the Fourth Consultative Meeting, the parties agreed and recommended to their governments that certain interim guidelines for the voluntary regulation of Antarctic pelagic sealing be adopted.[88] These guidelines recognized that Antarctic seal stocks were a resource of potential value which at some future date may require a binding international agreement for effective regulation. It is noted that the number of seals taken in specified areas of the Antarctic should not exceed the maximum sustainable yield of that species and that each government signatory to the Convention should provide information as to the number of each species taken and the location from which these species were taken.

In 1964 the signatory parties met again and adopted agreed measures for the conservation of Antarctic fauna and flora.[89] The agreed measures were very broad and included protection for mammals, birds, plants and fish (particularly seals).

The agreement recognized the considerable value of conservation principles developed by the Scientific Committee on Antarctic Research (S.C.A.R) of the International Council of Scientific Unions.

The parties met several times after the 1964 meeting and in 1972 the parties once again met and agreed that it was necessary to provide additional protection for Antarctic seals in conjunction with the purposes established under the Antarctic Treaty signed in 1959.[90]

The 1972 Convention established that there was a general concern about the vulnerability of Antarctic seals to commercial exploitation and the consequent need for effective conservation measures. The parties expressed a desire to promote and achieve the objectives of protection, scientific study and rational use of Antarctic seals and to maintain a satisfactory balance within the ecological system.

The Convention noted that the scientific committee on Antarctic research of the International Council of Scientific Unions had expressed a willingness and a desire to carry out the task requested of it in the 1972 Convention. The Convention identified certain species of seals to be in particular danger and established that the measures undertaken by the Convention were to be applicable to the Southern Elephants Seal, the

---

88 20 U.S.T., T.I.A.S. 6668.
89 17 U.S.T., T.I.A.S. 6058.
90 29 U.S.T., T.I.A.S. 8826.

Leopard Seal, the Weddell Seal, the Craveater Seal, the Ross Seal and the Southern Fur Seal.[91]  Essentially the 1972 agreement requires the contracting parties to adopt for its nationals and for vessels under its flag, laws, regulations and other measures including the permit system to protect Antarctic seals.[92]

These laws, regulations and measures must be adopted based on the best scientific and technical evidence available and must cover the permissible catch, open and closed seasons, open and closed areas, limits relating to sex, size, or age for each species, catch returns, and statistical and biological records.[93]

In addition, the contracting parties may issue permits to kill or capture seals in limited quantities and in conformity with the objectives and principles of the Convention for the purposes of providing indispensable food for men or dogs, to provide for scientific research, or to provide specimens for museums, educational or cultural institutions.[94]

Each contracting party must exchange information and scientific advice with other contracting parties and with S.C.A.R.  The purposes of this exchange of information and scientific advice is to notify all contracting parties and S.C.A.R. what each country is up to and the extent to which the contracting parties are living up to their obligations under the Convention.

S.C.A.R. is invited by the Convention to assess information received pursuant to this Convention, to encourage the exchange of scientific information among the contracting parties and to recommend programs for scientific research, statistical  biological data to be collected, and to suggest amendments to the Convention.[95]

The parties to the Convention have agreed that at any time after commercial sealing has become a problem, a contracting party may propose that a meeting of the contracting parties be convened with a view to developing an effective system of control, including inspection.  The consultation provision of the Convention states that if a two-thirds majority of the contracting parties signatory to the Convention conclude that control is necessary, such control can be implemented.  In addition the parties may establish by a two-thirds majority a scientific advisory committee which may be assigned some or all the functions requested of S.C.A.R. under this Convention, if commercial sealing reaches significant proportions.[96]

---

91  Id.at art. I.
92  Id.at art. II.
93  Id.at art. III.
94  Id.at art. IV.
95  Id.at art. V.
96  Id.at art. VI.

# WILDLIFE AND HABITAT

The Convention provides that the contracting parties must meet within five years after the entry into the Convention and at least every five years thereafter, to review the operations of the Convention.[97]

There is a provision that permits a proposed amendment by one of the contracting parties to become binding on all parties by a vote of approval of two-thirds of the contracting parties.[98]

An Appendix to this agreement (stated to be an integral part thereof) provides direction for the contracting parties in several areas. The permissible catch for any one year restricts the total number of seals of each species killed or captured to 175 for Craveater Seals, 12,000 for Leopard Seals, and 5,000 for Weddell Seals.

In addition the Appendix provides that it is forbidden to kill or capture Ross Seals, Southern Elephant Seals or Fur Seals and it is forbidden to kill or capture any Weddell Seals one year old or older between September 1 and January 31 of any particular year.

The period between March 1 and August 31 inclusive is declared to be a closed season during which the killing or capturing of seals is forbidden. The sealing season is listed as running from September 1 to the last day in February.

The Appendix also lists several areas in which sealing is forbidden or restricted.

The Appendix also requires contracting parties to provide (before October 31 of each year) to all of the contracting parties and to S.C.A.R. a summary of statistical information on all seals killed by their nationals and vessels under their respective flags, in the covered area for the proceeding period, July 1 to June 30.

Also in the Appendix, S.C.A.R., is invited to report on methods of sealing and to make recommendations with a view to insuring that the killing or capturing of seals is quick, painless and efficient. Under this provision contracting parties are required to adopt rules for their nationals and vessels under their respective flags engaged in the killing and capturing of seals giving due consideration to the views of S.C.A.R.

The Appendix also provides that in view of the available scientific and technical data, the contracting parties are prohibited from allowing any of their nationals or vessels under their flag to kill or capture seals in the water, except in limited quantities and only to provide for scientific research.

---

97   *Id.* at art. VII.
98   Id.at art. IX.

348

# INTERNATIONAL COMMITMENTS

## TUNA FISHERIES

In 1966 the United States entered The International Convention For The Conservation of Atlantic Tuna.[99] The purpose of the convention as stated was to consider the interest of the contracting parties in the populations of tuna and tuna-like fishes found in the Atlantic ocean. The convention expressed the desire that the contracting parties cooperate and maintain the populations of these fish at levels which would permit the maximum sustainable catch for food and other purposes.[100]

Under the Convention the contracting parties agree to establish and maintain a Commission to be known as The International Commission for the Conservation of Atlantic Tunas and to appoint not more than three delegates from each contracting party to represent each party on that Commission. All decisions made by the Commission are effective by majority vote with each contracting party having one vote. Two-thirds of the contracting parties are to constitute a quorum.[101]

The responsibility of the Commission under the Convention is to study the populations of tuna and tuna-like fish and such other species of other fishes exploited in tuna fishing in the area covered by the Convention. This study is stipulated to include research on the abundance, biometry and ecology of the fish, the oceanography of their environment, and the effects of natural and human factors upon their abundance.[102]

In carrying out these responsibilities the Commission is charged with the responsibility of utilizing the technical and scientific services of and information from official agencies of the contracting parties and their political subdivisions and any other scientific and technical organizations deemed to be of use and value. In their studies the Commission is charged with the responsibility of collecting and analyzing statistical information relating to the current conditions and trends of tuna fish and resources of the area covered by the Convention.

The Commission studies and appraisals must take into account the bottom line purpose of the convention of insuring the maintenance of the populations of tuna and tuna-like fish to permit the maximum sustainable catch which will insure the effective exploitation of these fishes in the manner consistent with this catch.[103] The Commission after carrying out its responsibilities of study and analysis is required to publish and otherwise disseminate its reports of findings, of statistical, biologi-

---

99 20 U.S.T., T.I.A.S. 6767.
100 Preamble.
101 Id.at art. III.
102 Id.at art. IV(1).
103 *Id*. at art. IV(2).

cal or other scientific information relative to the tuna fisheries of the covered area.

In carrying out its objectives under the Convention the Commission is authorized to establish panels on the basis of species, groups of species, or geographical areas. Each panel so established is responsible for keeping under review the species, group of species or geographic area under its purview and for collecting scientific and other information relating to its responsibilities. Based on the scientific investigation the panel can make recommendations to the Commission.[104]

Any recommendations made by the Commission either upon its own initiative or upon the recommendation of one of the established panels is binding on the party by a majority vote of the members of the commission.[105]

The Convention requires all contracting parties to agree to take actions necessary to establish and insure the enforcement of the Convention and each party must submit to the Commission every two years a statement of the actions taken by it to accomplish the purpose of the Convention.

The Convention requires the contracting parties to agree that there should be a working relationship between the Commission and the Food and Agriculture Organization of the United Nations. To this end the Commission must enter into negotiations with the Food and Agriculture Organization of the United Nations with a view to concluding an agreement which should provide for the director general of the Food and Agriculture Organization of the United Nations to appoint a representative who would participate in all the meetings of the Commission and its subsidiary bodies, (but without a right to vote).[106]

The original document setting up the Convention is deposited with the director general of the Food and Agriculture Organization of the United Nations who is required to send certified copies to the governments who have ratified the Convention.

## CONVENTIONS INVOLVING MIGRATORY BIRDS

Beginning in 1916 the United States has entered, four treaties involving the protection of migratory birds. The first treaty in 1916 was entered into between the United States of America and the United Kingdom of Great Britain and Ireland for the protection of migratory birds in the United States and Canada.[107]

104  Id.at art. VI.
105  Id.at art. VIII.
106  Id.at art. XI.
107  39 Stat. 1702.

# INTERNATIONAL COMMITMENTS

The second convention entered into between the United States and United Mexican States in 1936 protected the migratory birds in their movements across the United States of America and the United Mexican States.[108] The Mexican Treaty was amended in 1972 by making additions to the list of birds listed under Article IV of the 1936 Convention.[109]

The third convention involving migratory birds, entered into between the United States and Japan, was signed at Tokyo on March 4, 1972.[110]

The fourth convention involving migratory birds was entered into between the United States and the Union of Soviet Socialistic Republics in 1976.[111]

The purposes underlying these four treaties are essentially the same. The original treaty with the United Kingdom provided that these migratory birds are of great value as a source of food, or in destroying insects which are injurious to forests and forest plants on the public domain as well as to agriculture crops in both the United States and Canada, but are nevertheless in danger of extermination through lack of adequate protection during the nesting season or while on their way to and from their breeding grounds.[112]

The Mexican Treaty was much in the same vane. It provided that "it is right and proper to protect the said migratory birds whatever may be their origin in the United States of America and the United Mexican States in order that the species may not be exterminated; . . . . it is necessary to employ adequate measures which will permit a rational utilization of migratory birds for the purposes of sport as well as for food, commerce and industry."[113]

The Japanese and the U.S.S.R treaties express substantially the same sentiment except with different wordage. As an example the Japanese Treaty states that "considering that birds constitute a natural resource of great value for recreational, aesthetic, scientific, and economic purposes and that this value can be increased with proper management . . . . considering that island environments are particularly susceptible to disturbance, that many species of birds in the Pacific Islands have been exterminated and that some other species of birds are in danger of extinction . . . "[114]

---

108  50 Stat. 1311.
109  23 U.S.T., T.I.A.S. 7302.
110  25 U.S.T., T.I.A.S. 7990.
111  29 U.S.T., T.I.A.S. 9073.
112  39 Stat. 1702 - Proclamation.
113  50 Stat. 1311 - Proclamation.
114  25 U.S.T., T.I.A.S. 7990.

# WILDLIFE AND HABITAT

This concept as expressed in the convention with the U.S.S.R. is similar.

All of the treaties provide that the contracting parties must agree to establish laws, regulations and provisions to satisfy the protection desired under the various conventions.

The conventions entered into with the United Kingdom for the benefit of Canada and with the United Mexican States are in one sense different than the ones entered into between the United States and Japan and the United States and Russia. Canada and Mexico have common borders with the United States while Japan and Russia do not. In the Japanese and U.S.S.R. conventions each signatory promises to administer its own territory (including the trust territory of the Pacific Islands in the case of Japan) for the purposes intended by the conventions.

Even though the U.S.S.R. and Japan do not have common borders with the United States nevertheless the species of birds named in the various articles or appendices of the convention do migrate between the two countries.

In the Japanese and U.S.S.R. treaties the migratory birds, which are the subject matter of the convention, are identified on the basis of specimens, photographs, or other reliable evidence and when identified are accorded the protection of the convention.

Each of the conventions provides a method of identifying what specific species of birds would be included as migratory birds and therefore within the purview of the conventions. The Canadian Treaty names in considerable detail the specific species of migratory game birds covered by the convention. The Japanese, Mexican, and U.S.S.R. conventions also name particular species of birds covered and in those three conventions a provision is made whereby new migratory birds, to be accorded protection, can be added or deleted from the appendices of these various conventions upon the request of either government.

The conventions also protect not only migratory birds but also their eggs, and prohibit any sale, purchase or exchange of these birds or their eggs taken illegally alive or dead and any sale of the birds or their eggs in violation of the provisions of the convention or the laws and regulations established by signatory parties.

All the conventions also agree that open seasons for hunting migratory birds may be decided by each contracting party respectfully, but that such seasons must be set so as to avoid the principal nesting seasons and to maintain their populations in optimum numbers.

Under all the conventions, the contracting parties agree to exchange data, research, information, publications, and to cooperate with each other in carrying out the purposes of the various conventions.

# INTERNATIONAL COMMITMENTS

As already indicated in an earlier section of this book, the requirements incumbent upon the United States by virtue of entering these various migratory bird conventions with Canada, Japan, Mexico and U.S.S.R. are implemented by an act, the Migratory Bird Treaty Act, and appropriate regulations necessary to allow the United States to discharge its obligation under the treaties.